ADVANCES IN GLOBAL LEADERSHIP

ADVANCES IN GLOBAL LEADERSHIP

Volume Editors: Joyce S. Osland, Betina Szkudlarek, Mark E. Mendenhall
and B. Sebastian Reiche

Recent Volumes:

See more at: http://www.emeraldgrouppublishing.com/products/books/series.htm?id=1535-1203#sthash.q2C5B4kN.dpuf

ADVANCES IN GLOBAL LEADERSHIP
VOLUME 13

ADVANCES IN GLOBAL LEADERSHIP

EDITED BY

JOYCE S. OSLAND
San Jose State University, USA

BETINA SZKUDLAREK
University of Sydney, Australia

MARK E. MENDENHALL
University of Tennessee, USA

B. SEBASTIAN REICHE
IESE Business School, Spain

United Kingdom – North America – Japan
India – Malaysia – China

Emerald Publishing Limited
Howard House, Wagon Lane, Bingley BD16 1WA, UK

First edition 2020

Reprints and permissions service
Contact: permissions@emeraldinsight.com

British Library Cataloguing in Publication Data
A catalogue record for this book is available from the British Library

ISBN: 978-1-83909-593-1 (Print)
ISBN: 978-1-83909-592-4 (Online)
ISBN: 978-1-83909-594-8 (Epub)

ISSN: 1535-1203 (Series)

Printed and bound by CPI Group (UK) Ltd, Croydon, CR0 4YY

ISOQAR certified
Management System,
awarded to Emerald
for adherence to
Environmental
standard
ISO 14001:2004.

ISOQAR
REGISTERED
Certificate Number 1985
ISO 14001

INVESTOR IN PEOPLE

CONTENTS

PART I
EMPIRICAL FINDINGS

PART II
PRACTITIONER'S CORNER

CONCLUSION

LIST OF FIGURES

LIST OF TABLES

LIST OF CONTRIBUTORS

Nancy J. Adler	McGill University, Canada
Myshelle Baeriswyl	Checkpoint, Switzerland
Monwong Bhadharavit	MBSA Company Limited, Thailand
Allan Bird	Pacific University, USA
Richard Bolden	University of the West of England, UK
Nakiye A. Boyacigiller	Sabanci University, Turkey/USA
Adriana Burgstaller	Consultant, Switzerland
Rachel Clark	Continuous Improvement Specialist, Switzerland
Lisa Cohen	Consultant, USA
Dame Polly Courtice	University of Cambridge, UK
Luis Alfonso Dau	Northeastern University, USA
Juergen Deller	Leuphana University of Lüneburg, Germany
Iain L. Densten	University of Melbourne, Australia
Eyrún Eyþórsdóttir	University of Akureyri, Iceland
Sherifa Fayez	AFS Intercultural Programs, Egypt
Natalia Fey	Hanken School of Economics in Helsinki, Finland
Mark Frederick	Global Talent Management Consulting, USA
Norihito Furuya	IGB Network (The Institute of Global Business), Japan
Alessandro Girola	United Nations Alliance of Civilizations, USA
Tina Huesing	New European College, Germany
Monika Imhof	Consultant, Switzerland
Simone Inversini	Work Psychologist, OD Consultant & Executive Coach, Wülser Inversini, Switzerland
Yih-Teen Lee	IESE Business School, Spain
Orly Levy	SOAS University of London, UK
Danielle Lyndgaard	Confederation of Danish Industry, Denmark
Thomas Maak	University of Melbourne, Australia

Fabricia Manoel	AFS Intercultural Programs, Innovation and Programs, Brazil
Martha Maznevski	Western University, Canada
Mark E. Mendenhall	The University of Tennessee, USA
Christof Miska	Vienna University of Economics and Business, Austria
Elizabeth M. Moore	Northeastern University, Massachusetts
Matthias Müller	Consultant, Switzerland
Christian Mulle	Walkout, nature dialogue movement, Germany
Tsedal Neeley	Harvard Business School, USA
Rikke Kristine Nielsen	Aalborg University, Denmark
Tina Nielsen	Municipality of Winterthur, Switzerland
Takahiko Nomura	Kanazawa Institute of Technology and Slow Innovation, Japan
Gary Oddou	The Kozai Group, USA
Joyce S. Osland	San Jose State University, USA
Berta Ottiger-Arnold	University Hospital of Zurich, Switzerland
Simon Papet	Consultant, Ecloo Network, Paris
Nicola M. Pless	University of South Australia, Australia
Sheila M. Puffer	Northeastern University, USA
B. Sebastian Reiche	IESE Business School, Spain
Susanne Reis	Consultant, Susanne Reis & Co., Switzerland
Lisa H. Ruiz	AbbVie Inc, USA
Dominik Scherrer	Ecloo, Switzerland
Heini Shi	New York University, Shanghai
Tim Soutphommasane	University of Sydney, Australia
Günter K. Stahl	Vienna University of Economics and Business, Austria
Betina Szkudlarek	University of Sydney, Australia
Sully Taylor	Executive coach, Portland State University, USA
Robert "Steve" Terrell	Aspire Consulting LLC, USA
Nozipho Tshabalala	Akwande Communications, South Africa
Rorisang Tshabalala	Chapter One Innovation, South Africa
Margarita Vaiman	California Lutheran University, USA
Vlad Vaiman	California Lutheran University, USA

Bert Vercamer	Differencist – Consultant – Strategist, Global Consult Strategy, USA
Davina Vora	State University of New York at New Paltz, USA
David Wesley	Northeastern University, USA
Milda Žilinskaite	Vienna University of Economics and Business, Austria

ABOUT THE AUTHORS

Luis Alfonso Dau is an Associate Professor of International Business & Strategy and the Robert & Denise DiCenso Professor at Northeastern University. He is also a Dunning Visiting Fellow at the University of Reading and a Buckley Visiting Fellow at the University of Leeds. His research focuses on the effects of institutional processes and changes on the strategy and performance of emerging market firms. He examines topics revolving around regulatory reforms, business groups, family firms, global corporate social responsibility, sustainability, formal and informal entrepreneurship, and the implications of culture on international strategy. His research has won numerous awards and has appeared in top journals in the field. He is currently serving as Vice President of Administration and elected member of the Executive Board of the Academy of International Business and is a member of the editorial boards of several leading journals. See luisdau.com for detailed CV.

Jürgen Deller is Professor of Business Psychology at Leuphana University in Lüneburg. His main research interests are in sustainable human resources management, aging workforce issues, as well as in international HRM. Since 2015, he has been a Visiting Professor at the Centre for Diversity Policy Research and Practice at Oxford Brookes University. Dr. Deller's research has won awards and is published in journals, such as the *International Journal of Human Resource Management, Journal of Vocational Behavior*, *Journal of Managerial Psychology*, *International Journal of Selection and Assessment*, and *Work, Aging and Retirement*.

Iain L. Densten, PhD, has held professorships in leadership in the United Kingdom, Australia, and Malaysia. He conducts research and consults worldwide on leadership, burnout, implicit leadership, leadership identities, and eye-tracking. He is a highly qualified and established leadership educator with proven skills to enhance the student experience with strong communication, engaging curricula, and subject-matter expertise. Iain is a dedicated academic with more than 20 years of experience teaching undergraduate and postgraduate students, emerging professionals, and industry leaders in a wide range of environments, including dynamic learning centers and international programs. He is motivated and passionate about inspiring leadership and professional development. Iain is a strong communicator adept at collaborating with colleagues and leading staff to manage classrooms, programs, and departments. He is an Award-winning researcher with versatile academic skill sets leading instruction on Leadership, Positive Psychology, Security, Cross-culture Communication, and Management.

Natalia Fey is a Doctoral Researcher at Hanken School of Economics in Helsinki, Finland. Natalia conducts research on global leadership development in multinational organizations from developed and emerging economies. She is interested in deepening scholarly understanding of how developmental processes of global leaders unfold. In particular, she explores how key global leadership competencies such as cultural intelligence and global mindset of global leaders are enhanced through experiential and immersion learning approaches such as coaching and international experience. Natalia views development of global leaders as a system of complex and nonlinear multilevel processes occurring in cognitive, affective, and behavioral domains. In her research, Natalia draws on more than 15 years of professional experience in intercultural coaching, trainings, and teaching. She is the founder of the company Multicultural Lab where she tests her research ideas. She is an active member of the SIETAR, EIBA, and AOM.

Mark Frederick, PhD, is a Global Coaching and Consulting Professional with over 25 years of experience partnering with Global 500 and Fortune 1000 companies helping them identify, develop, engage, and retain global talent. Mark has coached a wide range of leaders from over 60 different countries, advancing their performance in alignment with business and strategic objectives as well as their organizational and team cultural norms. His extensive experience as a global consulting professional across multiple industries gives him in-depth exposure to a variety of organizational dynamics, particularly in complex and high change environments. Mark is certified to deliver and interpret a variety of assessment instruments useful for developing and coaching global leadership talent. His doctoral degree is in Comparative Literature with an emphasis on Cognitive Psychology and Cultural Studies.

Norihito Furuya, PhD, is Senior Representative of The Kozai Group in Japan. He is also CEO of the IGB Network Company, Ltd (Global Organization and Human Capital Development Institute). IGB Network specializes in global training and coaching for managers, global HR assessment, global HR capital solutions, HRM system and organizational development, and research and development. He has lived and worked in the United States, the Middle East, and the United Kingdom, totaling nine years of overseas working experience as an expatriate manager for Japan Airlines. He has over 30 years' experience working internationally and has extensive experience in conducting training and consultation services in the arena of global human resource management for 35 of the leading firms in Japan. Twelve years ago, he established the International Training Division of JAL Academy, a collaborative venture with JAL, BBC (British Broadcasting Corporation), and Thunderbird (AGISM).

Mark E. Mendenhall holds the J. Burton Frierson Chair of Excellence in Business Leadership at the University of Tennessee, Chattanooga. He is an internationally recognized scholar in the field of global leadership and expatriate studies and is a past president of the International Division of the Academy of Management and a past recipient of the Ludwig Erhard Stiftungsprofessur endowed chair at the

University of Bayreuth. He has coauthored numerous books and journal articles, the most recent book being: "*Responsible Global Leadership: Dilemmas, Paradoxes, and Opportunities*" (2020, Routledge). His research appears in a variety of scholarly publications, including *Academy of Management Review, Journal of International Business Studies, Sloan Management Review, Academy of Management Learning & Education, Human Relations, Journal of World Business,* and *Journal of Business Ethics.* He is also a senior partner in The Kozai Group, a consultancy that specializes in global leadership identification, assessment, and development.

Elizabeth M. Moore, PhD, is a Visiting Assistant Professor in International Business & Strategy at the D'Amore-McKim School of Business, Northeastern University. She recently finished her PhD in Political Science. Her research and teaching interests include formal and informal entrepreneurship, corporate social responsibility, institutional changes, institutional disruptions, transnational institutions, pro-market reforms, firm performance, firm resilience, emerging market firms, and international organizations. Recently, she has added on to her research stream by analyzing the connection between firms and governments in responding to natural and man-made disasters.

Gary Oddou, PhD, emeritus professor of business, has taught, researched, and consulted in the area of international human resource management for over 35 years. His research focuses on expatriate adjustment and training, repatriate reintegration and knowledge transfer, and global leadership. He has published over 50 articles and book chapters and written or coedited several scholarly books and a readings and cases text. He has been invited to speak on these topics at universities and at business conferences in Asia, Europe, Canada, and the United States. He has taught at the National Economics University, Vietnam; Chulalongkorn University, Thailand; Ecole de Management, Lyon, France; and the International Institute for Management Development (IMD) in Lausanne, Switzerland. He is a founding partner in The Kozai Group, a consulting firm that specializes in helping businesses, government agencies, and NGOs assess their human resources for competencies related to international and diverse workforce integration.

Joyce S. Osland, PhD, Senior Editor, earned her PhD at Case Western Reserve University. She was the Lucas Endowed Professor of Global Leadership and Executive Director/Founder of the Global Leadership Advancement Center at San Jose State University's Lucas College and Graduate School of Business until recently retiring. Dr. Osland is an internationally recognized scholar in the field of global leadership and international management and is a past president of the Western Academy of Management. She has received numerous awards for both teaching and scholarship and has published over 150 books, chapters, cases, and articles. She coauthored *Global Leadership: Research, Practice and Development, Managing Across Cultures* and has coedited *Advances in Global Leadership*, Volumes 8–13. Dr. Osland consults with global organizations and is a visiting scholar and lecturer at various universities and is a senior partner with The Kozai Group, which identifies, assesses, and develops global leadership.

Sheila M. Puffer is University Distinguished Professor at Northeastern University, Boston, where she is a professor of international business at the D'Amore-McKim School of Business. She is also an associate at the Davis Center for Russian and Eurasian Studies at Harvard University. Her coauthored book, *Hammer and Silicon: The Soviet Diaspora in the US Innovation Economy*, was published by Cambridge University Press in 2018. Dr. Puffer has been recognized as the #1 scholar internationally in business and management in Russia, the former Soviet Union, and Eastern Europe, according to a 2005 *Journal of International Business Studies*. She has more than 160 publications, including over 80 refereed articles and 14 books. She earned a diploma from the Plekhanov Institute of the National Economy in Moscow and holds BA (Slavic Studies) and MBA degrees from the University of Ottawa, Canada, and a PhD in business administration from the University of California, Berkeley.

B. Sebastian Reiche, PhD, is Professor and Department Chair of people management at IESE Business School, Spain. He received his PhD in management from the University of Melbourne, Australia. His research focuses on the forms, prerequisites, and consequences of global work, international HRM, global leadership, and knowledge transfer. He is Associate Editor of *Human Resource Management Journal*, coeditor of *Advances in Global Leadership*, and regularly blogs about global work (blog.iese.edu/expatriatus).

Betina Szkudlarek is an Associate Professor in Management at the University of Sydney Business School. Betina's core research interests lie at the intersection of cross-cultural management, international HRM, and management of diversity. Her work has been published in top-tier international journals such as *Organization Studies, Human Resource Management*, and *Journal of Business Ethics* and featured in multiple national and international media outlets. Betina has worked with numerous multinational corporations and not-for-profits on developing intercultural competence and fostering global leadership excellence. Beyond her academic commitments, Betina holds the post of a Strategic Sustainability and Growth Consultant with the United National Alliance of Civilizations (UNAOC).

Davina Vora (PhD, University of South Carolina) is an Associate Professor of International Business at the State University of New York at New Paltz (SUNY New Paltz). She enjoys teaching international business and cross-cultural management courses using interactive, experiential methods. Her research interests include multiculturalism, global leadership, psychological attachment, boundary spanning, the influence of culture on individuals and groups, group diversity, and roles of international managers. Her work has appeared in several leading journals such as HBR.org, *International Journal of Human Resource Management, Journal of International Business Studies, Journal of Organizational Behavior, Management International Review*, and *Multinational Business Review*.

She is also active in the Academy of Management, Academy of International Business, and ION.

David Wesley, PhD, is Research Manager at Northeastern University's D'Amore-McKim School of Business. His research encompasses a range of strategic management topics, including international strategy, cultural diversity, intellectual property, and new product development. His award-winning cases have appeared in 30 management textbooks in multiple editions. He is coauthor of a leading book on video game marketing and innovation and teaches global strategy and culture.

ABOUT THE EDITORS

Joyce S. Osland, PhD, Senior Editor, earned her PhD at Case Western Reserve University. She was the Lucas Endowed Professor of Global Leadership and Executive Director/Founder of the Global Leadership Advancement Center at San Jose State University's Lucas College and Graduate School of Business until recently retiring. Dr. Osland is an internationally recognized scholar in the field of global leadership and international management and is a past president of the Western Academy of Management. She has received numerous awards for both teaching and scholarship and has published over 150 books, chapters, cases, and articles. She coauthored *Global Leadership: Research, Practice and Development* and *Managing Across Cultures* and has coedited *Advances in Global Leadership*, Volumes 8–13. Dr. Osland consults with global organizations and is a visiting scholar and lecturer at various universities.

Betina Szkudlarek is Associate Professor in Management at The University of Sydney Business School. Betina's core research interests lie at the intersection of cross-cultural management, international HRM, international business ethics, and management of diversity. Her work has been published in top-tier international journals such as *Organization Studies*, *Human Resource Management*, and *Journal of Business Ethics*. Her work on developing cross-cultural competence has been published in top-tier journals and featured in international media outlets. Betina has worked with numerous corporations on developing Global Leadership excellence. Beyond her academic commitments, Betina holds the post of a Strategic, Sustainability and Growth Consultant with the United National Alliance of Civilizations, where she works with the recipients of the UNAOC and BMW Intercultural Innovation Awards.

Mark E. Mendenhall (PhD, Brigham Young University) holds the J. Burton Frierson Chair of Excellence in Business Leadership at the University of Tennessee, Chattanooga. He is a past holder of the Ludwig Erhard Stiftungsprofessur endowed chair at the University of Bayreuth (Germany) and has been a visiting professor at the Vienna University of Economics and Business (Austria), University of Saarland (Germany), and Reykjavik University (Iceland). Dr. Mendenhall is an internationally recognized scholar in the field of global leadership and international human resource management and is a past president of the International Division of the Academy of Management. Dr. Mendenhall has authored numerous books and scholarly articles in the journals like the *Academy of Management Review, Journal of International Business Studies,* and *Journal of World Business.* His most recent books are *Global Leadership:*

Research, Practice and Development and *Readings and Cases in International Human Resource Management.* He has consulted with and conducted numerous training programs for many leading firms.

B. Sebastian Reiche, PhD, is Professor and Department Chair of people management at IESE Business School, Spain. He received his PhD in management from the University of Melbourne, Australia. His research focuses on the forms, prerequisites, and consequences of global work, international HRM, global leadership, and knowledge transfer. He is Associate Editor of *Human Resource Management Journal*, coeditor of *Advances in Global Leadership*, and regularly blogs about global work (blog.iese.edu/expatriatus).

NEW ADVANCES IN GLOBAL LEADERSHIP: INTRODUCTION TO VOLUME 13

This year was unusual in many respects. Little did we expect that our call for interdisciplinary research on Global Leadership would be of such relevance in the world's continuing attempt to battle the COVID-19 pandemic. As stated in our call for papers, we were:

> ...especially interested in **what other disciplines can contribute to better understand, conceptualize and develop global leadership**. Drawing on other disciplines not only helps a field of research to mature further, but it also helps embed it within the nomological network of related domains.

Beyond theory building and conceptual advancement, we have learnt in the last months that there is a great deal of important knowledge to be drawn and absorbed from multidisciplinary fields, as global leaders address complex, interdependent, and thorny challenges. In this regard, our call for papers could not have been more timely or relevant. As the world situation evolved with respect to COVID-19, so did our thinking as to what this volume should look like. For this reason, the typical papers found in Volume 13 are enhanced by two novel contributions. The first is comprised of contemporary reflections by leading Global Leadership scholars as well as global leaders who had to boldly face the reality of managing unprecedented large-scale problems and by practitioners who help and coach global leaders. In our invitation, we asked them to distill their thinking on the global leadership challenges faced by individuals and communities, as they tackle COVID-19 situations that are novel, complex, and filled with paradox. The resulting brief essays by 25 authors are fascinating snapshots in time, since only history and research will tell which leadership lessons and examples stand the test of time. The essays contain numerous insights that should prove useful for scholars and practitioners alike. The final chapter in this book, written by the editors, is our attempt to categorize and discuss these themes for future research purposes. The second novel contribution in Volume 13 resulted from another targeted invitation, this time to a global collaboration consultant. Demonstrating his preference and talent for collaboration, this evolved into a multidisciplinary, collective writing effort by 21 thinkers and doers from around the world. After describing five success stories focusing on collaboration in crises for this volume of *AGL*, they extracted key lessons on global collaboration that, once again, are useful to both researchers and practitioners.

While the term "global leadership" has been defined in many ways, thereby blurring the conceptual boundaries of the distinct fields of global and comparative leadership, *AGL* adheres to the following narrower definition of global leadership:

> The process and actions through which an individual influences a range of internal and external constituents from multiple national cultures and jurisdictions in a context characterized by significant levels of task and relationship complexity (Reiche, Bird, Mendenhall, & Osland, 2017, p. 556).

As is our practice, Volume 13 combines traditional research papers in Part 1 with practitioner-focused research, insights, and interviews in Part II, and a conclusion that identifies future research directions. The chapters in this volume are briefly introduced below.

PART I: CONCEPTUAL AND EMPIRICAL FINDINGS

Part 1 begins with *Chapter 1*, the invited essays by 25 authors, entitled "Perspectives on Global Leadership and the COVID-19 Crisis." Each essay is listed chronologically to reflect how the pandemic unfolded and influenced their thinking. The authors were given two weeks to write on the role of global leadership in the pandemic. The results range from very practical advice for working virtually, ideas and reflections on how global leaders are handling the crisis to proposed new concepts in global leadership. It is a fascinating and inspiring collection by thought leaders from all sectors.

In *Chapter 2*, "Identifying with Leaders from Another Race: The Impact of Pre-existing Leadership Assumptions and Eye Fixations," Iain Densten explores the role of perceptive cues shaped by implicit leadership ideas and eye fixations in determining how followers identify with a leader from another race. The study draws on a sample of 55 Southeast Asian female participants who viewed a 27-second video of a Caucasian female leader. Specifically, Densten demonstrates that both preexisting leadership prototypes and antiprototypes, as well as eye movements, influenced how the participants answered the Identity Leadership Inventory, which measures prototypicality, advancement, entrepreneurship, and impresarioship. The study provides a compelling example of how global leaders' effectiveness may be shaped by their followers' culturally imprinted preferences. Given the increase in virtual interactions, it also points to the role of global leaders' nonverbal communication behaviors in shaping followers' evaluations of leader identities.

Chapter 3, "The 4 Cs of MNE Strategic Responses to Global Governance," is a conceptual account by Sheila Puffer, David Wesley, Luis Alfonso Dau, and Elizabeth M. Moore. The researchers consider how MNEs address challenges to their ways of conducting business by intergovernmental organizations, international nongovernmental organizations, and nongovernmental organizations, all of which intend to shape global policy agendas. As such, Puffer and colleagues draw on global governance theory from political science, the responsible leadership literature, and the construct of situational strength to propose a typology of how firms can take strategic action. The framework distinguishes between both reactive versus proactive and combative versus collaborative orientations, leading to four distinct strategic responses: Collaborator, Complier, Counteractor, and Combatant. Importantly, the typology highlights how the situational strength of global governance organizations can impact MNEs' choice of strategic responses and the likely implications this choice involves.

In *Chapter 4*, "What Makes for Successful Repatriate Knowledge Transfer? Implications for Repatriate Management and Global Leadership," Joyce Osland, Betina Szkudlarek, Gary Oddou, Norihito Furuya, and Juergen Deller investigate the knowledge transfer experience of 47 repatriates returning from their international assignments to Germany, Japan, and the United States. This exploratory qualitative study portrays knowledge transfer as an iterative, interactive process whose success depends largely on the repatriate's initiative, learning agility, transfer skills, adaptability, and capacity for influencing work unit members. Their findings highlight the role of six transfer skills that repatriates linked to effective transfer. The authors introduce an interactive model of the microprocess of repatriate knowledge transfer. In addition to contributing to theory building about the knowledge transfer process, the study's results are of special relevance to global leaders who are either direct transferors of knowledge across cultural boundaries or who facilitate the process of knowledge transfer by other organizational members.

In *Chapter 5*, "How Global Leaders Learn from International Experience: Reviewing and Advancing Global Leadership Development," Natalia Fey maps and analyzes the extant literature in her dissertation research to explore why an international experience has been linked to global leadership development, dating from the field's initiation. Her database search found 42 articles that focused on international assignments, international corporate training programs, or short-term business travel that related to global leadership development. She analyzed the studies' individual and organizational enablers as well as learning mechanisms. Her integration of the results indicates exactly what and how global leaders learn and lays a clear path for researchers who want to advance this important field of study.

PART II: THE PRACTITIONERS, CORNER

Chapter 6 features "Global Collaboration in Crises," a global collaboration of 25 consultants and managers from around the world who integrate their experience and wisdom on the topic of best practices in collaborative leadership in crisis contexts by first sharing minicase exemplars and then deriving "lessons learned" that global leaders can apply in their own lives. By exploring the collaborative dynamics of global/diverse teams in response to COVID-19, ecological crises, the Tohoku earthquake of 2011, the 2008 financial crisis, and Apartheid in South Africa, this large team of authors delineate practices that likely can be applied across crisis contexts and operate as "rules of thumb" for global leaders who wonder "What should I be primarily focusing on?" when a crisis erupts.

For *Chapter 7*, "An Interview with Hal Gregersen: The Art of Questioning in Global Leadership," Mark Mendenhall interviewed Dr. Hal Gregersen, one of the pioneers in the field of global leadership. He was a coauthor of the seminal work, "Global Explorers: The Next Generation of Leaders" in 1999 that provided the field with one of the early competency frameworks. Since that time, he has studied innovation and the important role that questioning processes play in innovation and leadership. In their interview, they explore the role questioning plays in global leadership and the influence of curiosity in the questioning process. Dr. Gregersen provides insights on how global leaders can build a "questioning culture" in their organizations, why some global leaders are questioning-oriented and some are not, how they can enhance their capability to question more robustly, and the importance of focusing on "keystone questions" to empower one's leadership.

Chapter 8, "How Does an Anthropologist Teach Global Leadership to Engineers? An Interview with Julia Gluesing," features a gifted teacher-scholar who has spent over 30 years working in the automotive industry as a consultant, trainer, researcher, and teacher. Dr. Gluesing was interviewed by Joyce Osland who was particularly curious about the impact of her anthropology background and her career trajectory on her teaching. Dr. Gluesing spoke about her highly successful and unique approach to teaching engineers specifically. In this master class on teaching, she also shared her techniques for teaching culture and global leadership, along with a list of helpful resources.

In *Chapter 9*, "Practitioner Reflections from 25 Years of Developing Global Leadership," Dr. Mark Frederick, a highly experienced consultant, describes how the field has changed and evolved. He helped develop the global leadership services at IOR (International Orientation Resources) in the field's early days and eventually developed his own independent consulting practice. Mark explains the nuts and bolts of global leadership consulting, down to explaining how to choose the best assessment for each situation and structure virtual executive coaching sessions. He also shares best practices from global leadership development programs in leading companies. His knowledge and extensive experience are extremely useful for consultants as well as academics who teach and research global leadership development.

Chapter 10, "Reflections on Developing a Global Leadership Course," authored by Davina Vora, explains all the considerations and details involved in setting up a global leadership course for the first time at a public, regional, US university. Although the number of global leadership courses are growing, creating the first course of its kind on a campus involves pedagogy, logistics, marketing, and sometimes politics. Dr. Vora describes the need for fit with her students and institution. She explains the philosophy behind her course design as well as course assignments. This chapter ends with suggestions, recommendations, and lessons learned. This chapter is a very helpful guide to anyone tasked with developing a new course in global leadership.

Finally, in *Chapter 11*, "At the Heart and Beyond: What Can Global Leadership Researchers Learn from Perspectives on the COVID-19 Pandemic?," the editors discuss common themes and emerging areas for future research that arise from the invited essays on the COVID-19 pandemic. Specifically, this chapter calls for strengthening the link of the global leadership domain with related research fields, expanding the set of necessary global leadership competencies, moving toward a more collective and collaborative understanding of global leadership, further enhancing the growing field of responsible global leadership, examining the various competing tensions that global leaders need to balance, and encouraging global leadership scholars to engage in greater reflexivity.

ACKNOWLEDGEMENTS

We'd like to acknowledge the work and commitment of those who made important behind-the-scenes contributions to this volume. We are indebted to Amber Stone-Galilee, our publisher at Emerald Publishing, Ltd., and to Akilandeswari Lakshmanan and Kavya Ramu and their entire production team for all the support we have received. Anu Sairaj merits special recognition for her role in coordinating and supervising the infinite details involved in manuscript preparation. Anouk Hagen was also extremely helpful in the final preparation of the chapters.

This book would not be possible without the funding Dr. Osland receives from the Lucas Foundation and their generosity to the Global Leadership Advancement Center, housed in the School of Global Innovation & Leadership at San Jose State University. She would also like to thank Dean Dan Moshavi and Belinda Nguyen for their support.

Mark Mendenhall is grateful for the support of the Gary W. Rollins College of Business and the J. Burton Frierson Chair of Excellence in Business Leadership at the University of Tennessee, Chattanooga.

Edited research volumes are often a labor of love, which is certainly true for this book. And while a team of four have formally edited this volume, an army of family members and friends facilitated and inspired the process. This volume is therefore dedicated to all the individuals who continue to support us, but whose names rarely surface through the official publication process.

- Joyce: To Asbjorn, Jessica, Joe, Michael, Anna, Katrina, Scott, and the grands: Zoe, Lucy, Jacob, Gavin, Izzy, and June.
- Betina: To my best friends Kasia and Vera whose support, wisdom, and love is always with me.

- Mark: To my wonderful grandchildren: Will, Amy, Tommy, James, Timothy, Ellie, and Mark.
- Sebastian: To my family, whose strength and support has been remarkable during these taxing times.

REFERENCE

Reiche, B. S., Bird, A., Mendenhall, M. E., & Osland, J. S. (2017). Contextualizing leadership: A typology of global leadership roles. *Journal of International Business Studies, 48*, 552–572.

OBITUARY AND MEMORIAL–BILL MOBLEY

Dr. William Hodges Mobley (November 15, 1941–March 25, 2020)

Dr. William Hodges Mobley, age 78, former President of Texas A&M University (1988–1993) and Former Chancellor of the Texas A&M University System (1993–1994) passed away in Austin, Texas on March 25, 2020 after an 18-month battle with cancer. He dedicated his life to nurturing talents in both the educational and business world.

During his service at Texas A&M, he was a strong proponent for diversity and for integrity in athletics. He promoted minority recruitment and expansion of international educational opportunities for students and faculty. Dr. Mobley was also instrumental in the initial planning of the George H. W. Bush Presidential Library at Texas A&M University.

Dr. Mobley spent the last twenty-five years developing executive talent in the United States and Asia. He founded the Global Research Consortium and the Hong Kong and Shanghai offices of Personnel Decisions International (PDI). As the founder and member of the board of directors of Mobley Group Pacific Ltd, he resided in Hong Kong and Shanghai, China, working with both academic institutions and international corporations to provide support for senior regional and national CEOs and Managing Directors in developing their plans for succession. He advised and coached executives on management and organizational skills. From 2002 to 2009, he served as Professor of Management at China Europe International Business School and became the first Professor Emeritus at CEIBS. A well-respected scholar, he published in leading journals on motivation, leadership and organizational culture. He was the founder and executive editor of the first seven volumes of the *Advances in Global Leadership* series.

He earned his PhD in industrial and organizational psychology from the University of Maryland in 1971. He was a Fellow of the American Psychological Association (APA), Society for Industrial and Organizational Psychology (SIOP), and the Association for Psychological Science (APS), and a member of the Academy of Management (AOM) and the International Association for Applied Psychology (IAAP). He was awarded honorary degrees from several universities. In 2015, he was honored with the *Distinguished Psychologist in Management* award by the Society of Psychologists in Management.

Because Bill played such an important role in developing the field of global leadership and produced seven volumes of *Advances in Global Leadership*, we invited his co-editors to participate in this memorial.

> Bill Mobley was a brilliant and talented man who had a real gift for people. He was able to connect with people and point them toward a shared goal, paving the way for their success. It was his leadership philosophy. He was a visionary who could get others excited about his vision, and then participate willingly in its execution, and always with good humor and encouragement. What I remember most about Bill was shared laughter and shared ideas.
>
> M. Jocelyne Gessner Bay, PhD (*AGL*, vol. 1)
> Director of Organizational Effectiveness
> Bay & Associates

> I had the good fortune to know Bill Mobley for many years starting in graduate school at the University of Maryland. All of the graduate students immediately knew that Bill was going to be a star. He was smart, engaging, and always helpful. Years later I had the pleasure of co-editing one of his Advances in Global Leadership books. His insight into the field of global leadership helped me gain new perspectives and ways of thinking about the influence of societal culture on leadership—an endeavor that has carried me well throughout my career. In short, Bill's career included being a role model for leaders as well as a great leadership scholar.
>
> Peter W. Dorfman (*AGL*, vol. 3)
> Professor Emeritus
> New Mexico State University
> Past President of GLOBE

Bill was my manager, mentor, co-author, and friend. I was extremely fortunate to have met Bill at the start of my career and to be guided and supported by him ever since. He was the person who inspired me, like he did to many others, to step into the fascinating field of organisational psychology. Bill's incredible intellect, generosity and energy has left a deep impact on many scholars, students, and business leaders across the world. He was not only a prominent scholar in global leadership, but also a legendary example of a global leader himself.

Ying (Lena) Wang (*AGL*, vol. 5–8)
Senior Lecturer
RMIT University, Australia

In 2007, I started working with Bill co-editing the Advances in Global Leadership. I was very fortunate to see with my own eyes how Bill was a true global leader who inspired and nurtured the talents of all around him. His legacy will live on.

Ming (Lily) Li (*AGL*, vol. 5–11)
Senior Lecturer in International Human Resource Management
University of Liverpool Management School

I was honored that Bill entrusted Advances in Global Leadership to us. He did a wonderful job of seeking out and publishing authors from all over the world. Thanks to Bill and his co-editors, AGL is the publication outlet that is home to the largest number of articles related to leadership in a global context. He was truly a renaissance man.

Joyce Osland (*AGL*, vol. 8–13)
Senior Editor
Advances in Global Leadership

PART I

EMPIRICAL FINDINGS

PERSPECTIVES ON GLOBAL LEADERSHIP AND THE COVID-19 CRISIS

J. S. Osland, M. E. Mendenhall, B. S. Reiche,

B. Szkudlarek, R. Bolden,

P. Courtice, V. Vaiman, M. Vaiman, D. Lyndgaard,

K. Nielsen, S. Terrell, S. Taylor, Y. Lee, G. Stahl,

N. Boyacigiller, T. Huesing, C. Miska, M. Zilinskaite,

L. Ruiz, H. Shi, A. Bird, T. Soutphommasane,

A. Girola, N. Pless, T. Maak, T. Neeley,

O. Levy, N. Adler and M. Maznevski

ABSTRACT

As the world struggled to come to grips with the Covid-19 pandemic, over twenty scholars, practitioners, and global leaders wrote brief essays for this curated chapter on the role of global leadership in this extreme example of a global crisis. Their thoughts span helpful theoretical breakthroughs to essential, pragmatic adaptations by companies.

Keywords: Covid-19; crisis management; global leadership; complexity; uncertainty; competing tensions

After pondering how we as scholars might help in the COVID-19 pandemic, we issued the following invitation on March 30, 2020.

Advances in Global Leadership, Volume 13, 3–56
Copyright © 2020 Emerald Publishing Limited
All rights of reproduction in any form reserved
ISSN: 1535-1203/doi:10.1108/S1535-120320200000013001

As co-editors of Advances in Global Leadership, we have been pondering the role of global leadership in pandemics, given the current COVID-19 crisis. Because this topic has not been addressed previously, we decided to add to the forthcoming volume 13 a chapter entitled "Perspectives on Global Leadership and the COVID-19 Crisis" that consists of analyses written by global leaders, practitioners, and global leadership scholars. We would be honored if you would join this project and write at least a one or two page perspective by April 14th. We will curate all the submissions into one article that will be co-authored by all of you.

We realize this is a short time period (a necessity given the manuscript deadline), but we thought it would be interesting to put ourselves in the same type of context that global leaders find themselves in – inadequate time and ability to gather enough data to make firm conclusions, quick deadlines wherein a decision must be made, uncertainty, and high risk for having one's ideas and decisions be seen as being woefully in error when looked back upon from the future. In fact, we are giving you two full weeks to write when global leaders have to assess situations, analyze them, and then make decisions often in a day or less.

You are free to analyze and share your perspectives from any lens, perspective, angle, or genre of writing that you would like. The only boundary conditions are that your analysis should focus on how global leaders/global leadership have impacted the human response to the COVID-19 pandemic. AGL generally relies on the following construct definitions of global leadership:

The process of influencing the thinking, attitudes, and behaviors of a global community to work together synergistically toward a common vision and common goals (Adler, 2001; Festing, 2001).

The process and actions through which an individual inspires and influences a range of internal and external constituents from multiple national cultures and jurisdictions in a context characterized by significant levels of task and relationship complexity (adapted from Reiche, Bird, Mendenhall, & Osland, 2017).

We hope that you will participate in this invitation to write under similar conditions that global leaders find themselves in – having to make decisions and take action on multiple issues simultaneously in a VUCA context – and that you will find the challenge to do so both an interesting and exciting one. Please let us know if you are up for the challenge.

To our delight, 22 collaborators accepted our challenge to share their insights and wisdom. We did not edit their work (other than the random comma, etc.). We also excerpted the work of two authors that was already in print. As with our usual submissions, we have divided them into Scholarly Perspectives and Practitioner Perspectives. Their order is chronological according to the date of submission (or publication in the case of the two excerpts). This chronology provides another window onto how rapidly the crisis unfolded and changed, along with our perspectives.

Please note that these perspectives reflect only the authors' opinions on topics of their choice; they do not reflect the opinions of their employers or the *AGL* editors.

SCHOLARLY PERSPECTIVES

Leadership, Complexity, and Change: Learning from the COVID-19 Pandemic

Richard Bolden
March 27, 2020

What a difference a few days make... Perhaps it's the sunny spring days after a long, wet winter; the dog walks spent chatting with teenagers who would normally be off at school; the unexpected free space in my diary with no expectation that I should be in the office; or because so much of what we take for granted has changed so suddenly.

At the time of writing we are in the fourth day of the lockdown called by the UK government to slow the spread of the COVID-19 virus. It's been a tense few weeks as the wave of infections grew ever closer – no longer focused within a far and distant sounding part of China but causing havoc across Italy, France, Spain, the UK and now it seems, pretty much every part of the world. A quarter of the global population – a staggering 2 billion people – are currently in some form of lockdown, confined to their homes in order to slow the spread of the virus and, in so doing, allow time for governments and health services to prepare for the spike in patient numbers and the inevitable rising death toll.

Almost overnight UWE, Bristol – like universities, schools, and colleges around the world – closed its doors and shifted from face-to-face to online delivery. Staff and students have responded with huge adaptability – revising delivery and assessment processes that would have taken months, if not years, through traditional channels. The speed and the scale of changes for organizations in every sector and location are unprecedented. Manufacturers have switched their operations to enable the production of essential items such as ventilators, face masks, hand sanitizer, and paracetamol that are now in such high and urgent demand. Governments have drawn up detailed plans to support individuals and organizations at risk of redundancy/bankruptcy – casting aside the usual economic concerns to focus on social priorities such as protecting the vulnerable, supporting those in financial difficulty and strengthening core public services (particularly health and social care). And communities have rallied together in ways not seen since World War II – providing support and reassurance for the elderly and isolated; sacrificing personal liberties for collective benefit; and finding new ways to connect, communicate, and collaborate.

In the words of the Chinese curse we are indeed living in interesting times (1) – both fraught with risk and opportunity. The turbulence of the last few years has revealed deep divisions within society, as illustrated particularly clearly in the Brexit vote within the UK and Trump presidency in the US. The rise of populism has been associated with skepticism and distrust of experts and evidence, with social media providing the perfect echo chamber for amplifying the polarity of perspectives and questioning the nature of "truth." Differing ideologies and beliefs have been positioned in opposition to one another – them and us, winners and losers, do or die – rather than as an inevitable and desirable characteristic of a diverse and inclusive society, which enables creativity, adaptability, and resilience in times of complexity, uncertainty, and change.

One of the remarkable consequences of the COVID-19 pandemic has been how quickly it has reset the dial on many of these issues – fostering calls for compassion, solidarity, and collective action. At times like this, it is our similarities rather than our differences that define us. This is as true for those in positions of power and privilege as those who are marginalized and/or find themselves living in precarity. We are all susceptible to the virus, all have people we care about who are likely to become very ill or perhaps even die should they catch it, and will all be affected by the economic and social impacts of the outbreak – not just for the months that it lasts but for years to come. The capacity of individuals, families, organizations, communities, and nations to weather the storm is not equal, however, with those with least access to financial, emotional, and other resources most likely to bear the brunt of the suffering.

An unexpected outcome of COVID-19 is the impact on the environment. The reduction in pollution levels around the world during just the relatively short time in which travel, manufacturing, and other environmentally damaging activities have been reduced demonstrates both how directly human activity impacts on the environment and the remarkable ability of the environment, and the animals and plants within it, to recover if given the opportunity. For those who have been calling for a step change for policy, practice, and behavior toward a more sustainable way of life, there is no more compelling evidence of the extent to which this is possible and the environmental benefits it would produce.

For those of us interested in leadership research, education, and practice, there are many important lessons to take from the current situation. I'm sure everyone will have their own take on events but as a starter for ten here are a few of my own takeaways so far.

- **Shared purpose** – After winning a significant majority in the general election of December 2019, Boris Johnson and his government focused on building a sense of urgency and commitment to "getting Brexit done" that largely entrenched rather than unified opinions around this issue. With COVID-19 the focus has completely shifted to a shared purpose that unites rather than divides individuals and communities. It took a little while to get to this point but, for now at least, the nation is far more unified around a common purpose than it has been for many years.
- **Collective leadership** – While there is a tendency to equate "leadership" with the traits and behaviors of individual "leaders," the COVID-19 pandemic demonstrates the need for individuals and groups to work concurrently and collaboratively in order to achieve leadership outcomes. In daily news briefings,

Prime Minister Johnson and members of the cabinet have stood alongside the Chief Medical Officer and other experts to provide clarity and direction to an uncertain population. While this is perhaps the most visible "leadership" at national level, it is abundantly clear that it is dependent on significant acts of leadership elsewhere as well as the active "followership" of those responding to calls for care and consideration.

- **Systems change** – The COVID-19 pandemic is an inherently complex problem that requires expertise and effort from multiple domains to make sense of the issues and to mobilize timely and effective responses. The concept of "systems leadership," increasingly advocated within public services, highlights the need to influence and leverage engagement across organizational, professional, and other boundaries. Frequently this means needing to lead without formal authority – to work with principles of complexity and systems thinking to initiate new patterns of behavior that spread from one context to another. It also involves dismantling and rebuilding systems, structures, and processes – both physical and psychological – that constrain rather than enable transformation and change.
- **Sensemaking** – In times of ambiguity and uncertainty, leadership has a key role to play in helping people to make sense of the situation(s) in which they find themselves. The people who will be recognized as "leaders" are those who are able to frame the context in a way that acknowledges the nature and severity of the issue(s), addresses the concerns of their constituents, and which provides a degree of clarity about the actions/responses that are required. Within the US, Andrew Cuomo, the Governor of New York, has emerged as a key national figure in mobilizing the response to COVID-19 – providing far greater clarity and direction than Trump and now being mooted as the democratic candidate for the next US election despite not even standing as a nominee.
- **Place-based leadership** – While many national figures have struggled to grapple with the scale and implications of the issues posed by COVID-19, local leaders have often responded far quicker and been more effective at mobilizing public, private, voluntary, and community groups and organizations to collaborate and respond. Place-based leadership is responsive to the context that surrounds it – drawing together multiple perspectives and expertise to address issues of concern to citizens within a particular locale – and will be essential not only in dealing with the immediate effects of COVID-19 but in the long period of rebuilding and recovery that will follow the pandemic.

These are just a few initial reflections, and there is far more that could be said. Looking forward I have no doubt that the spring of 2020 will be seen as a defining moment in our understanding of and engagement with leadership, complexity, and change. I only hope that we learn the lessons and make use of them to create a stronger, healthier, kinder, safer world rather than defaulting back to the divisive and destructive policies, practices, and behaviors that preceded the current crisis.

Source: Published with permission of the Bristol Leadership and Change Centre Blog at https://blogs.uwe.ac.uk/leadership-and-change/leadership-complexity-and-change-learning-from-the-covid-19-pandemic/.

Richard Bolden is an experienced Researcher and Educator in the fields of leadership, management, and organizational psychology. He has worked at the Center for Leadership Studies since 2000, conducting a range of applied studies of leadership and leadership development across different contexts and sectors (including small and medium enterprises, Higher Education, leadership competencies, and international development). In addition to his research, Richard teaches and supervises students on a range of programs including the BA in Management and Leadership, MBA, and CPD scheme. Prior to this, Richard was involved in software development in France and as a research psychologist at the Institute of Work Psychology in Sheffield. He has an extensive publication history including numerous journal articles, book chapters, conference papers, and research reports. His international experience includes sub-Saharan Africa, France, Egypt, and the Balkans.

COVID-19 AND CREATING THE FUTURE WE WANT

Dame Polly Courtice
April 2, 2020

Many people will be feeling uncertain, anxious, and even scared. And, of course for others, things have already reached crisis point. But if there is any solace to be had, it is that we are facing this unique moment in history together, 7.8 billion of us, going through the same experience at the same time, creating an unprecedented bond between us.

It is tempting to talk about getting "back to normal," but we will almost certainly not go back to the way things were. In fact, going back to "normal" is also not what many millions of people aspire to or deserve. For many, the current system has failed to deliver health, well-being, and prosperity. Now that the lack of resilience in the "old" system has been revealed, alongside our ability to mobilize vast sums of money and resources when the economy is at risk, expectations will have been raised about what else is now possible in the face of other crises.

Globally, we have to take this moment to reflect on the need to change and transform our society; to explore lessons from the past and reset our expectations for the future. The shocks to the system that we are experiencing now, and anticipate in future, raise so many questions about the things that we have taken for granted, and demonstrate what is possible when we need to respond urgently. Given how many system shocks we see as coming – this is a crucial time to be asking some big questions.

The way nation states govern, coordinate responses, and spend; the relationship between business, government, and civil society; the relationship between globalization and localism; the dominance of competition over cooperation; how and why we work and consume; our attitudes about what we value in society and how we relate to one another; what we need to let go of, and what new possibilities might open up. All these things are being challenged and disrupted. For some, this crisis will harden whatever views they previously held – but for others it will shape new possibilities and understanding. The reality is that our very way of life is likely to be profoundly changed forever. This is an opportunity to shape the future, not just respond to it.

There are some principles that we can trust in and rely upon. For example, the laws of nature, the laws of physics, the interconnectedness of human and natural systems, the emerging clarity about our interdependence and what we value as societies, and the importance of science to inform evidence-led decision-making.

These principles remind us that what we are experiencing now, despite its magnitude, is a mere dress rehearsal for the system shocks that lie ahead, unleashed by climate change and ecosystem collapse, and the inevitable impact on our human systems if left unaddressed. The decade that we earmarked for getting our climate on track for net zero by 2050 and making progress on the UN Sustainable Development Goals will now play out in a new paradigm, where transformational change takes on wholly new possibilities. We can undoubtedly emerge as a stronger global community and more resilient society if we seize the opportunity of this crisis, of this wake-up call, to collectively chart a course toward the future we want.

Source: Published with permission of the Cambridge Institute for Sustainability Leadership at https://www.cisl.cam.ac.uk/news/news-items/creating-the-future-we-want-and-covid-19.

Dame Polly Courtice, DBE, LVO, is Founder Director of the University of Cambridge Institute for Sustainability Leadership (CISL), which since its foundation in 1988 has become an internationally recognized center of excellence in sustainability leadership. She established the Prince of Wales Business and Sustainability Programme in 1994 and serves on the Boards and Advisory Boards for a number of global companies. In 2016, she was appointed Dame Commander of the Order of the British Empire (DBE) for services to Sustainability Leadership.

GLOBAL LEADERSHIP FAILURE: A CASE OF THE COVID-19 PANDEMIC

Vlad Vaiman and Margarita Vaiman
April 3, 2020

Our leaders are failing us once again. Once again, after SARS, Ebola, the 2008–09 worldwide economic recession, and other pivotal events, our governments cannot and will not work together synergistically toward a common goal. That common goal now is to defeat probably the most serious global threat to our civilization that we have seen in generations, the COVID-19 pandemic. This pandemic has brought to the forefront the deep failures of our leaders to work together, and this time the outcome of these failures can be truly devastating. Any global problem of this nature, significance, and scale definitely requires a global approach (Brown, 2020).

So, what prevents our leaders from getting together to find that global approach? After a few decades of speedy globalization, the world has fairly recently started to experience a multitude of opposite trends. Nationalist, and sometimes, openly extremist movements in the US, Austria, Brazil, Denmark, Hungary, the UK, and several other countries have gained some popular support, found their ways to their country's parliaments, and begun influencing – now through the legislative power – both internal and external policies of their respective societies. These policies sowed much division and created deep societal fractures not only within their own countries but also in the international arena, which lead to even more profound divisions even between long-term economic and political allies. And now, when we all need to unite to face the existential threat of COVID-19, our leaders and governments find themselves more isolated, uncooperative, and helpless than ever before. Despite China making a decision to hide the outbreak from public eye in the beginning of 2020, the EU, the US, and the UK apparently knew about an upcoming pandemic already in November–December 2019 but never shared any details with each other and did nothing proactively to get ready.

Another important issue is that there seems to be no single country or leader out there willing and able to take charge in the fight against the pandemic. The traditional world leader, the US, has vacated this "position" at the end of 2016, when "America First!" slogan has become a prominent feature of its official foreign policy. And even if they wanted to, the US could not lead the world in this fight, given the magnitude of trouble the country itself is having while dealing with the pandemic. To start, there is still no nationwide policy that would regulate the government response to the pandemic. Out of 50 states, about a quarter (as of April 2, 2020) has no stay-at-home orders, despite continuous warnings from experts. Also, there seems to be at least two feuding power centers governing the COVID-19 response in the White House – one led officially by the

Vice President, the other one, unofficial, led by the President's son-in-law. In addition, there is a constant confusion emanating from conflicting messages coming out of the White House and the President in particular, who gives one type information one day, and then something completely opposite the next. All in all, this paints a clear picture of the top leadership's failure to deal effectively with a national emergency within one of the largest and certainly the richest country in the world. So, relying on the US and its leadership at this point is not an option.

There is some good news though. Faced with a lack of competence and leadership both locally and on the global scale, other constituents picked up the slack and stepped up to the fore. A considerable number of business and community leaders around the world – entrepreneurs, CEOs, university presidents, clergy, scientists – as well as philanthropists, NGOs, and many others have taken great initiatives to lead and safeguard those they serve (Slaughter, 2020). One excellent example of such initiatives is Open Source Ventilator, a project led by a global virtual team of scientists, journalists, business people, professors, engineers, designers, medical professionals, and other volunteers working together to develop a low-cost, and more importantly, an open-source ventilator to help save lives and facilitate the recovery of COVID-19 patients (OSV, 2020). There are hundreds of similar examples all around the world, which should give those affected by COVID-19 and the rest of us much needed optimism and comfort.

Not all hope is lost for our leaders, however. We strongly believe that a solid collaborative global response is still possible. To accomplish that, each country should follow the following recommendations. First, create a small but nimble intergovernmental agency that would coordinate worldwide medical efforts related to COVID-19 – collecting, processing, and disseminating statistics on the spread of the disease, symptoms, effects of medications, etc. Yes, there is World Health Organization (WHO), but it does not seem to be able to deal with global emergencies the way a smaller agency would. It is therefore important to ensure that each country starts sharing its COVID-19 information with each other and that new agency in order to have access to the up-to-date information and a possible course of action. Second, each country should commit to emergency economic measures, such as temporary elimination to tariffs and other barriers to supply chains, thereby providing an easier flow of health-related products and medications. Third, each country should declare a temporary moratorium on tax collection and guarantee payments to workers who lost their jobs, as well as to everyone forced to stay at home to uphold the quarantine. Those countries that cannot afford to implement these measures should be guaranteed assistance from international financial institutions (e.g., the World Bank). There are quite a few other measures, but the ones described above could be a good start. Only united and with the help of our global leaders, will we able to beat any global emergency, including COVID-19.

REFERENCES

Brown, G. (2020). In the coronavirus crisis, our leaders are failing us. *The Guardian*, March 13.
OSV, Open Source Ventilator. (2020, April 3). About us. Retrieved from https://opensourceventilator.ie/about
Slaughter, A.-M. (2020). Forget the Trump administration. America will save America. *The New York Times*, March 21.

Vlad Vaiman is Professor and the Associate Dean at the School of Management of California Lutheran University and a visiting professor at several premier universities around the globe. Dr. Vaiman has published five very successful books on talent management, and numerous academic and practitioner-oriented articles and book chapters in the fields of talent management and international HRM. His work appeared in *Academy of Management Learning and Education, Human Resource Management, International Journal of Human Resource Management, Human Resource Management Review, Journal of Business Ethics*, and many others. He is also a founder and Chief Editorial Consultant of the *European Journal of International Management* (EJIM), and the editorial board member of several prestigious academic journals. Dr. Vaiman is a highly sought-after consultant and speaker – he is frequently invited to speak on both professional and academic matters to various global corporations and highly acclaimed universities around the world.

Margarita Vaiman is an Adjunct Professor at the School of Management of the California Lutheran University. She received her BSc (honors) in Economics & Econometrics from York University (Canada) and her MBA and MA in Organizational Behavior & Talent Management from Reykjavik University in Iceland. A native of Russia, Prof. Vaiman left her home country at the age of 20 and has since lived, studied, and worked in the US, Canada, Switzerland, Austria, and Iceland, before returning to the United States in 2013. She has extensive experience consulting to a variety of organizations around the world.

THE BAT EFFECT: *GLOBAL* LEADERSHIP IS *NORMAL* LEADERSHIP IN TIMES OF CRISIS

Kristine (Rikke) Nielsen
April 8, 2020

The concept of the butterfly effect known from chaos theory illustrates the idea that small changes such as the movement of the wings of a butterfly can cause large-scale systemic change. In terms of the corona crisis, it was presumably not the metaphorical wings of a butterfly, but the actual wings of a bat that set in motion a train of events that led to the global COVID-19 pandemic. The crisis has swept across the planet demonstrating the global interconnectedness of business, pleasure, and politics.

The Olympics of Everything has been canceled, disrupted, or even closed. At the same time, for a large group of managers, work life goes on under conditions close to business as usual: The global leaders. Now, however, these everyday working conditions of geographical dispersion, VUCA-environment and paradox coping have become common property of managers in general during the crisis. Even managers of small, local businesses are now experiencing and exercising "extreme leadership" – a term that has been used to characterize the job role of global leaders (Osland, Bird, & Oddou, 2012a, 2012b, p. 107). While the interconnectedness of countries, businesses, and people is not new per se, this point has been taken home and to the extreme in a new way and include new groups. This exemplifies that global leadership research and practical knowledge of global leadership is also relevant for nonglobal groups of businesses, managers, and employees – in particular in times of crisis, but also more generally in times of "normal." The COVID-19 pandemic illustrates how "leadership" and "global leadership" – in theory and practice – could benefit from more joint exploration going forward (Osland, Nielsen, Mendenhall, & Bird, 2020; *AGL*'s Volume 13 Call for Papers).

GLOBAL CRISIS – LOCAL RESPONSES

The increasingly blurred boundaries between "home" and "away" in a globalized world may have caused or exacerbated the COVID-19 crisis, and the crisis itself have united businesses and populations in a common global quest to combat corona. The responses to the crisis, however, have been extremely local. Governments and health authorities have pursued highly different paths to deal with COVID-19 depending on the institutional setup and the national cultural values. Borders have been closed, and people have been encouraged to show citizenship by buying local products. This emphasizes the fact that organizations and interactions may be global, but business is local and subjected to the very different local responses of different nations. We are in a situation of decentralized, yet interconnected globality.

This emphasizes the need to continuously pay attention to the "local" as an integral element of global leadership, not is opposite – even for managers operating in a truly global environment. Global leadership has been defined as "the processes and actions through which an individual influences a range of internal and external constituents from multiple national cultures and jurisdictions in a context characterized by significant levels of task and relationship complexity" (Reiche et al., 2017, p. 556). COVID-19 crisis, refugee crisis, financial crisis, and climate crisis are all examples of global crises with local responses. In time of crisis, the aspect of the GL definition that highlights coping with a broad range of jurisdictions and cultures comes to the fore.

RAPIDLY DEVELOPING PANDEMIC VS NATURAL CATASTROPHE IN SLOW MOTION

Unlike the rapidly developing COVID-19 pandemic, the climate crisis develops more slowly and has been referred to as a natural catastrophe in slow motion. COP26 has been postponed due to the COVID-19 crisis, while global warming continues – but we also see a window of opportunity opening. What if governments and business acted with the same agility and resolve in handling the climate crisis as they do in confronting COVID-19? In terms of public/political global leadership, one might hope that Western governments will develop a new understanding for the not-so-active stance on combatting climate change of developing countries, because they have now experienced firsthand/remembered how your worldview can be clouded, when short-term challenges prevent you from seeing the bigger picture. At the same time, citizens across the globe have experienced how for instance air pollution in cities have dropped to historically low levels reminding us that even one month of united abstinence can make a big difference for the common climate good – if we act decisively.

BURNING PLATFORM – LEARNING PLATFORM

Being apart together and leading from a distance through digital communication channels is an integral part of global leaders' collaborative repertoire. Global leaders working under conditions of limited physical contact need to be virtually intelligent – and they need coworkers and employees that possess technological dexterity. During the COVID-19 crisis, the use of virtual collaboration, teaching and meeting has exploded, creating a burning platform for a giant naturally occurring experiment of digital transformation. Both experienced virtual collaborators and newcomers have had to reimagine their work entirely or take their digital interactions to a higher level.

This virtual collaboration system stress test can also be considered a "learning platform" for global leaders going forward. An enormous creativity has been unleashed in terms of new ways of handling present absence, and we should tap into/crowdsource the collective wisdom and creativity in terms of what can be do achieved together even if we are apart. Many employees have experienced a steep learning curve, transforming their work life in ways that seemed unrealistic and unsustainable only months ago. When the dust settles (and the Western world goes back to thinking about the stress and obesity epidemic as their main health concerns...), global leaders and global leadership researchers should be careful to harvest the learnings about virtual connectivity from this period. Among other things, we could reflect on the amount of (inefficient?) time we usually spend on spending time together in vivo, what the exact nature of the "presence premium" actually is, and how being together at the same time is a necessary requirement for efficient virtual collaboration.

REFERENCES

Osland, J., Bird, A., & Oddou, G. (2012a). The context of expert global leadership. In W. Mobley, Y. Wang, M. Li (Eds.), *Advances in global leadership* (Vol. 7, pp. 107–124). Bingley: Emerald Publishing Limited.

Osland, J., Nielsen, R. K., Mendenhall, M. E., & Bird, A. (2020). The birth of a new field from cross-cultural management: Global leadership. In B. Szkudlarek, L. Romani, D. Caprar, J. S. Osland (Eds.), *SAGE handbook of contemporary cross-cultural management*. Thousand Oaks, CA: SAGE Publications.

Reiche, B. S., Bird, A., Mendenhall, M. E., & Osland, J. S. (2017). Contextualizing leadership: A typology of global leadership roles. *Journal of International Business Studies*, *48*(5), 552–572.

Rikke Kristine Nielsen holds a PhD from the Doctoral School of Organization & Management Studies at Copenhagen Business School and is currently Associate Professor of Organizational Communication at the Department of Communication & Psychology at Aalborg University in Copenhagen, Denmark. Nielsen's research interests focus on global leadership development and the paradoxes of border and boundary spanning. Nielsen has published on global leadership in *Advances in Global Leadership*, the *SAGE Handbook of Contemporary Cross-Cultural Management* as well as several Danish research publications. She has been a leading member of the Global Leadership Academy (GLA) – an academia-practitioner research collaboration with Danish MNCs under the auspices of the Danish Confederation of Industry. Research-based management tools from this 7-year project have also been disseminated to the global leadership community in a toolkit, *Grasping Global Leadership – Tools for "Next Practice"* (2018), used in global leadership practice and executive global leadership training.

DYNAMIC BALANCING AS A CORE QUALITY FOR GLOBAL LEADERS IN CRISIS TIME

Yih-Teen Lee
April 13, 2020

With the unexpected spread of COVID-19 across the whole world, human beings have encountered the biggest crisis in modern history. There is an increased urgency to sustain health-care systems to save life. Business organizations, at the same time, are seriously affected and feel uncertain about their survival in the future as a result of extended confinement measures. Millions of workers have lost their jobs and filed for unemployment benefits, if available. If not, they are simply left to survive on their own. Although no one is capable of fully comprehending the impact of COVID-19 at this moment, human beings need to act collectively and quickly to confront such unprecedented challenges. Given global leaders' role in enacting the "process of influencing the thinking, attitudes, and behaviors of a global community to work together synergistically toward a common vision and common goals" (Adler, 2001; Festing, 2001) "in a context characterized by significant levels of task and relationship complexity" (adapted from Reiche, Bird, Mendenhall & Osland, 2017), they are expected to assume crucial responsibilities in leading people and societies to navigate safely through this huge storm and rebuild the future when the crisis passes.

Honored to share some humble reflections on the roles of global leadership in such crisis time, I center my thoughts around the concept of *dynamic balancing*, which refers to the ever-evolving and ongoing process of attending competing demands and formulating one's response to address multiple logics simultaneously. Global leaders need to cultivate a dynamic balancing mindset, and consciously activate it in formulating their vision and behavioral strategies in specific context. I present three specific dimensions of dynamic balancing for global leadership in the current crisis.

The first dimension that requires dynamic balancing in global leadership is *global collaboration and local protection*. Facing a crisis of this scale and scope, well-coordinated collective efforts are necessary for inventing effective medical treatments, for mobilizing resources and materials globally, and for designing adequate economic mechanisms to save businesses and jobs. Yet, what we are seeing so far, at least at the country level, has not been very encouraging. Whereas it is virtuous and fully legitimate for governments and leaders to protect and take care of their own people in difficult times, an overly self-protective attitude, and the actions it engenders, may prevent countries from collaborating to effectively tackle the crisis. Those in global leadership positions are expected to embrace broader visions with longer time horizons and embrace the profound interdependency of human beings in critical global affairs, in formulating their strategic responses. In fact, isolation and self-protection may not be fruitful even in the short run, if the scale and scope of the challenge are larger than the capability of any single company or country. This seems to be the case in the COVID-19 crisis.

A second, and related, dimension is the dynamic balancing of *long-term and short-term perspectives*. Without doubt, global leaders face pressing demands and imperatives of urgency on many fronts during times of crisis. We work against the clock in crisis periods. Whereas global leaders need to ensure short-term needs are met in a fast and efficient way, they also need to exercise their balancing capability to foster long-term thinking and foresee future consequences of their decisions. In fact, in critical moments, the decision we make now will determine how our world and life will become in many years. It is, therefore, the responsibility of global leadership to instill such dynamic balance in their day-to-day decision-making.

The third dimension for dynamic balancing is on *positive and negative emotions*. People experience fear, anxiety, anger, and frustration when their health, family, job, and business are threatened or hit by crisis. Uncertainty and ambiguity usually provoke self-defensiveness. Although negative emotions can be functional in keeping people focused on critical issues and urging people to mobilize resources to address a problem, they can have detrimental effects when they cause people to become narrow-minded and lose the vision to see broader possibilities with longer time horizons. It is the role of global leaders to instill positive emotions, with a sense of hope and love, to enable their people to see possible directions ahead. As a result, people may broaden their perspectives and build creative solutions to solve current challenges with enhanced level of global collaboration.

Global leaders need to mobilize both poles of these dualities and manage these seemingly opposite elements in resolving problems and leading people to collectively create a better future. However, it does not imply that global leaders should always favor the former end of the three pairs of duality (i.e., global collaboration, long-term perspective, and positive emotions). Balancing is the key. This should be a dynamic process with constant monitoring, contingently reinforcing certain poles when the balance is driven to the other ends by situated exogenous and endogenous factors. Under crisis, it is understandable that leaders respond to short-term local protective needs, sharing the gravity of negative emotions with their people. However, it is exactly in such moments that global leaders should mindfully activate dynamic balancing to bring in broader perspective and better equilibrium that allows better quality decision-making. This is not an easy task. To do so, global leaders need courage and wisdom to make tough decisions that, if made in the spirit of dynamic balancing, will pave the way for a brighter future for all of humanity.

REFERENCES

Adler, N. J. (2001). Global leadership: Women leaders. In M. Mendenhall, T Kühlmann & G. Stahl (Eds.), *Developing global business leaders: Policies, processes and innovations* (pp. 73–97). Westport, CT: Quorum Books.

Festing, M. (2001). The effects of international human resource management strategies on global leadership development. In M. Mendenhall, T. Kühlmann, & G. Stahl (Eds.), *Developing global business leaders: policies, processes, and innovations* (pp. 37–56). Westport, CT: Quorum.

Reiche, B. S., Bird, A., Mendenhall, M. E., & Osland, J. S. (2017). Contextualizing leadership: A typology of global leadership roles. *Journal of International Business Studies, 48*, 552–572.

Yih-Teen Lee is Full Professor at IESE Business School. He specializes in leadership, cultural identities, leading multicultural teams and global collaboration in his roles as educator, researcher, and consultant. He is particularly passionate in the concept of balancing and its application in bridging cultural differences. His research in these themes has appeared in leading journals such as *Academy of Management Discoveries, Journal of Management,* and *Journal of Personnel Psychology.* Raised in a Chinese cultural context, Yih-Teen has been living in Europe for over 20 years and is fluent in Chinese, English, French, and Spanish. As a type of multicultural individual, he identifies himself as a rooted global citizen. Currently he splits his life between Barcelona and Paris.

LEADERS' RESPONSES TO THE COVID-19 CRISIS: A FAILURE OF RESPONSIBLE GLOBAL LEADERSHIP

Günter K. Stahl
April 14, 2020

Throughout the COVID-19 crisis we have seen examples of leaders at all levels of government, business, and civil society who rose to the challenge, took personal ownership, and demonstrated authentic human concern. One of the iconic moments of this pandemic was when sailors aboard the aircraft carrier USS *Theodore Roosevelt* applauded their commander, Capt. Brett Crozier, as he disembarked the ship for the last time – an overwhelming show of support for their leader who was relieved of his command by his superiors. Docked in Guam, COVID-19 was racing through the USS *Theodore Roosevelt*. The Navy physicians on the aircraft carrier estimated that at least 50 of his sailors would die if all 5,000 personnel remained onboard in tight quarters. Crozier requested that the vast majority of his crew be evacuated and quarantined while the ship was professionally cleaned. His direct superiors denied this request and searched for other solutions. After four days of waiting while the virus continued to spread throughout the ship, Crozier sent a letter to 20 other Naval officers in the Pacific region sharing his request for evacuation. One of the recipients leaked the letter to the press, and Crozier was sacked for circulating the letter broadly via unsecured email.

While what he did might technically have been a breach of security, Capt. Crozier has been viewed by many as having done the right thing. For US military officers, a foundational leadership principle is that the well-being of the sailors and soldiers always come first, and that they should never be put at unnecessary risk. According to John Kirkby, a retired rear admiral in the US Navy, the removal of a commander who had his crew "at the center of his heart and mind in every decision" right in the middle of a potentially deadly epidemic aboard his ship "was reckless and foolish," sending "a horrible message to other commanding officers" (John Kirkby, CNN, April 3, 2020). In other words, Crozier engaged in responsible leadership that broke rules that minimally impacted Naval security in the face of irresponsible leadership from on high.

There is another important leadership lesson to be learned from this case. In times of crisis, top-level leaders – be it in government, the military, or business – need to empower those who led on the front lines, and not punish mistakes. Missteps can happen, as in the case of the above Navy officer who skipped the chain of command. But failing to act would have been much worse in a situation where the virus would have assuredly raged through the aircraft carrier. Effective crisis management requires qualities such as sound judgment, decisiveness, the ability to take quick action in the face of critical threats, and empathy and genuine care and concern – qualities that Capt. Crozier exhibited in the crisis and that his superiors seemed to be sorely missing.

Among the many glaring failures of leadership and accountability that we witnessed as the crisis unfolded were the actions, or nonactions, of many world leaders. While many democratic governments bungled their response to COVID-19 through their denials, delayed responses, and lack of preparedness for a crisis of this magnitude, many authoritarian leaders endangered the lives of millions with their lies and deceptions, the suppression of information, and with attempts to use the crisis for political gain. Hungary's Viktor Orbán, for example, seized the opportunity of the outbreak to expand his powers to rule by decree, with no end date, and imposed further restrictions on free speech.

Not surprisingly, trust in governmental/political leaders suffered in the crisis. In the 2020 Edelman Trust Barometer's 10-country survey on trust and the coronavirus, politicians and government officials were the least trusted sources of information, along with journalists and the news media (Edelman, 2020 special report). Corporate executives ended up in the middle of the ranking; and scientists and health authorities emerged as the most credible source of information, with 85% of respondents saying they wanted to hear more from scientists and less from politicians; and nearly 60% worrying that the crisis was being used for political gain.

Among the many cases of government leaders who mishandled the crisis are some notable exceptions. For example, led by Tsai Ing-wen, Taiwan's first female president, the Taiwanese government was quick to respond to the crisis and took early decisive measures, including a travel ban, strict punishments for anyone found breaching home quarantine orders, and large-scale testing. Business leaders, too, have gained the trust of their employees and other stakeholders by responding decisively and responsibly to the coronavirus outbreak. Despite some glaring failures of leadership and accountability on the part of corporate executives (e.g., the Uber CEO's refusal to take responsibility for the health and safety of their workers during the COVID-19 crisis), it was encouraging to see that businesses from Alibaba to Amazon were mobilizing to help in the fight against the global pandemic (World Economic Forum, 2020). For example, Jack Ma, through the Alibaba foundation, donated 1.1 million testing kits, 6 million masks, and 60,000 protective suits and face shields to be sent out to African countries.

Despite these notable exceptions, what is clear is that from a responsible leadership perspective (Mendenhall, Zilinskaite, Stahl & Clapp-Smith, 2020), most political and business leaders failed to adequately address the global dimension of the crisis. A global challenge such as the coronavirus outbreak requires a global response; but instead of coordination and collaboration across national borders we saw countries sealing off their borders in an attempt to slow the spread of the pandemic, blaming other countries and competing for scarce resources, and even engaging in absurd conspiracy theories. Responding to a "grand challenge" like a pandemic requires cross-country and cross-sector collaboration (e.g., partnerships with NGOs, public sector entities, and even competitors). Nitin Nohria (2020), in a lucid description of what organizations need to survive a pandemic, stresses the importance of distributed leadership (as opposed to centralized leadership), networked structure (as opposed to hierar-chical structure), and dispersed workforce (as opposed to concentrated work-force), pointing to the need for "a global network of people drawn from throughout the organization that can coordinate and adapt as events unfold, reacting immediately and appropriately to disruptions" (p. 3). He also highlights the importance of global alliances, suggesting that companies should codevelop adequate crisis responses with partners and even competitors.

The bottom line of all this is simple: Local self-isolation and social distancing may be adequate measures to curb the spread of the virus from an epidemiological perspective. In global politics and business, they are a recipe for disaster.

REFERENCES

Edelman. (2020). Edelman trust barometer special report: Trust and the coronavirus. Retrieved from https://www.edelman.com/research/edelman-trust-covid-19-demonstrates-essential-role-of-priv ate-sector#top

Kirkby, J. (2020). Removing the USS Theodore Roosevelt captain was reckless and foolish. *CNN*. Retrieved from https://edition.cnn.com/2020/04/03/opinions/uss-theodore-roosevelt-captain-removal-reckless-kirby/index.html

Mendenhall, M. E., Zilinskaite, M., Stahl, G. K., Clapp-Smith, R. (Eds.). (2020). *Responsible global leadership: Dilemmas, paradoxes, and opportunities*. New York, NY; London: Routledge.

Nohria, N. (2020). What organizations need to survive a pandemic. *Harvard Business Review*, January, 1–5.

World Economic Forum. (2020). How big business is joining the fight against COVID-19. Retrieved from https://www.weforum.org/agenda/2020/03/big-business-joining-fight-against-coronavirus/. Accessed on April 11, 2020.

Günter K. Stahl is Professor of International Management and Director of the Center for Sustainability Transformation and Responsibility (STaR) at the Vienna University of Economics and Business (WU Vienna). He served on the faculty of INSEAD from 2001–2009, is a Senior Academic Fellow of the Centre for International HRM at Judge Business School, University of Cambridge, and has held visiting positions at Duke University's Fuqua School of Business, the D'Amore-McKim School of Business at Northeastern University, the Wharton School of the University of Pennsylvania, and Hitotsu-bashi University, among others. His current research interests include the drivers of corporate responsibility, grand societal challenges and their impli-cations for management and leadership, and the changing nature of global work. He has held responsible positions within various academic associations and is currently a Senior Editor of the *Journal of World Business*.

LOOKING BACK FROM 2030: DREAMING ABOUT GLOBAL LEADERSHIP AFTER THE GREAT CORONA PANDEMIC OF 2020

A "cri de coeur" for Global Leadership Post the Great Pandemic of 2020

Nakiye Boyacigiller
April 14, 2020

Emerita Professor and Former Dean Nakiye Boyacigiller looked down on the faces of the graduating class of 2030 of the Sabanci Business School. She loved commencement exercises and relished the chance to share her experiences with students. She had been particularly happy to accept the invitation this year since she was worried that the younger generation did not know much about the bad old days of parochialism, unfettered capitalism, and the military industrial complex that constantly put profits before people. That is until the Great Corona Pandemic of 2020 (hereafter simply pandemic) changed all that.

The pandemic had ravaged the world and led to a huge number of deaths irrespective of national borders. While the percent of deaths was higher in less developed economies, the shared experience of helplessness changed how people in the industrialized world viewed their poorer brethren. The coronavirus could have killed them too, easily. This realization led to an empathy toward the "other" that heretofore had been lacking when it came to relations between the haves and have-nots. For the first time, "We Are The World" became meaningful beyond being an idealistic song title.

This change in popular sentiment and concern for others led to profound changes in many institutions. During the pandemic, some of the most amazing change was seen in the pharmaceutical industry (Big Pharma). Contrary to its own past history, Big Pharma had pledged that once a vaccine was found they were going to provide it gratis worldwide through an industry-wide fund! Still there was a race to be the first to discover and develop a vaccine against the coronavirus. Competition continued to be the core cultural value underpinning the relations between the firms themselves. Three companies were vying to be the first: BigPharmaA (the US), BigPharmaB (Switzerland), and Big-Pharma (Japan). All were in a race to be first to develop a vaccine that could be tested and then distributed post haste. The world was waiting for them anxiously. Millions of lives were at stake. Their respective teams were working

18–20 hour shifts. The then CEO of BigPharmaA, Ziya Esen, worried how long he could expect his team to keep up this pace. In looking for an answer to this dilemma it occurred to Ziya that perhaps working together with their competitors could help them achieve success quicker. Collaborating rather than competing. He reached out to his counterparts at BigPharmaB and BigPharmaC. Ziya knew they were testing similar compounds. They could use the fact they were across 15 time zones to work on the project 24 hours a day. When one team went to sleep the other would take up the work. This would involve sharing data from and access to their respective laboratories. Opening up the laboratories to their direct competitors obviously needed to be signed off by their respective boards of directors. Here again the reaction was surprising, no obstacle was raised, as long as this was going to help the vaccines get to the world faster!

The whole economic system changed for the better. For years Business School faculty like Nakiye had taught about social responsibility and business ethics. Now, finally stakeholders other than shareholders were influencing corporate decisions. The parochialism that was so evident among political leaders around the world (exemplified by President Trump of the US) was the complete opposite to the corporate response to the COVID-19. Activists around the world fighting the pandemic, and soon climate change, began to look to managers in multinational corporations for global leadership. In time, most leadership positions within the corporate sector as well as the political sector would be held by individuals with a global mindset.

Nakiye sighed. She had lost several good friends to COVID-19 herself. Yet as she ended her talk and began taking questions from the graduates she smiled. During her 30+ years as a business school professor who believed in the inherent goodness of people, she had often been teased as being too naive. But she had never given up hope. All it took was just a worldwide pandemic to change the world for the better, by reminding people of our joint destiny.

Nakiye A. Boyacigiller is Emerita Professor of Management from both Sabanci University (Istanbul, Turkey) where she served 10 years as Dean of Sabanci Businesss School and from San Jose State University (California). Born in the US and educated in Turkey, France, and the US, her research, teaching, and leadership activities all reflect her interests in enhancing the effectiveness of multicultural work groups and cross-border collaboration. A dedicated and award-winning teacher and scholar, Boyacigiller was active in the international community of business school educators, holding advisory board memberships at GIBS (South Africa), WU (Austria), and AACSB, among others. A Fellow of the Academy of International Business (AIB), Boyacigiller has held leadership positions in the top academic associations in her field including most significantly Chair of the International Division of the Academy of Management (1997) and President of AIB (2014–2015).

THE ROLE OF GLOBAL LEADERSHIP IN A PANDEMIC: BEING POSITIVE?

Tina Huesing
April 14, 2020

At a time when "the pulse of the world beats as one" we look for guidance from health experts and we look for leadership, particularly from our heads of states.[1] They influence the thinking and behaviors of people within the borders of their country and beyond. In a global pandemic global leader emerge, and their different approaches to leadership are discussed and compared. While political leaders work with health experts and develop measures that regulate public life, business leaders need to lead their organizations through the economic downturn and out of the economic crisis.

Leaders emerge who operate in one country and are admired and listened to across larger cultural contexts and geographies. Political leaders appeal to everyone within their countries to follow new guidelines (mainly restrictions) and at the same time influence stakeholders outside of their own countries. Global business leaders address their stakeholders around the world and reassure their customers by adjusting business policies. What do leaders with global appeal have in common?

Numerous leadership studies include comments on leaders' personality and especially the need to be positive, e.g., extraversion with positive energy, being inspirational, expressing confidence, being charismatic (Burns, 2010; Judge, Bono, Ilies, & Gerhardt, 2002). And this desire for positivity seems to be universal. "Ideal leaders everywhere in the world are expected to develop a vision, inspire others, and create a successful performance oriented team" (Dorfman, Javidan, Hanges, Dastmalchian, & House, 2012, p. 507). Books like *How To Be a Positive Leader* (Dutton & Spreitzer, 2014) advise us that being positive and optimistic is important, even during tough times. Maybe especially during a crisis, leaders need to encourage and motivate their followers, and to do so, they need to exude positivity and be confidence builders. Positive leaders achieve better results. Business leaders who downsize their operations and lay off employees are expected to do so while putting on a hopeful face and painting a positive picture of the future. This was the advice in previous economic downturns, and this will again be the guidance now.

But do inspirational leaders, those who stay positive even in the face of a global pandemic, provide the best kind of leader to lead us out of this crisis and toward the best possible outcomes?

---

[1]Arne Sorenson, President and CEO, Marriott International on April 10, 2020 in an email to customers.

If a leader needs to always be positive to be effective, does that allow for a realistic picture of the current situation? How honest is the leader when a dire situation is presented as easy to overcome? Recently, ratings of political leaders who paint a more realistic picture of a difficult situation have gone up more than ratings of more optimistic, positive leaders. German Chancellor Angela Merkel painted a dark picture when she warned that up to 70% of the country's population – some 58 million people – could contract COVID-19 (press conference, March 11, 2020). Afterward, she announced far-reaching restrictions to manage the health crisis. The vast majority of Germans approved of the measures that were implemented and wholeheartedly follow the restrictions imposed on them. Even as consumer confidence plummeted, Merkel's approval ratings shot up (ICS, Consumer Consult March 24, 2020). Chancellor Merkel's comments were reported not only in Germany but in Europe and throughout the world. For her somber presentation of the situation she is admired well beyond the confines of her country.

The "rallying around the flag" (Mueller, 1970) might not last, but it does suggest that business leaders who will need to make painful decisions might want to take a more realistic, evidence-based stand rather than an optimistic, positive approach when communicating with their stakeholders around the world. If the global leader communicates a realistic picture of the challenging situation the organization is in, this message will have universal appeal and will allow the followers to embrace the difficult changes that will have to be implemented. Global leaders who understand that honesty and facts are valued more than optimism will enable their followers to draw the right conclusions instead of feeling gaslighted.

This does not mean there is no hope. On the contrary, the crisis can provide an opportunity to question long-held beliefs about the business that might no longer be true (Drucker, 1994). Facing the dire facts can lead to questioning the fundamentals, using this time to explore options, experimenting not just with flextime and flexplace work arrangements but with other aspects of the business as well. Then the doors are open to learning, innovation, and a bright future.

REFERENCES

Burns, J. M. (2010). *Leadership* [originally published 1978]. New York, NY: Harper Perennial Political Classics.

Dorfman, P., Javidan, M., Hanges, P., Dastmalchian, A., & House, R. J. (2012). Globe: A twenty year journey into the intriguing world of culture and leadership. *Journal of World Business*, *47*(4), 504–518.

Drucker, P. F. (1994). The theory of the business. *Harvard Business Review*, *72*(5), 95–104.

Dutton, J. E., Spreitzer, G. M. (Eds.). (2014). *How to be a positive leader: Small actions, big impact.* San Francisco, CA: Berrett-Koehler Publishers.

Judge, T. A., Bono, J. E., Ilies, R., & Gerhardt, M. W. (2002). Personality and leadership: A qualitative and quantitative review. *Journal of Applied Psychology*, *87*(4), 765.

Mueller, J. E. (1970). Presidential popularity from Truman to Johnson. *American Political Science Review*, *64*(1), 18–34.

Tina Huesing, PhD, is a Senior Lecturer at New European College in Munich, Germany. She enjoys teaching international people management, including strategic international human resource management, global leadership, and organizational behavior to students from around the world. She conducts research on global leadership and new workplace practices and consults on organizational structure and culture to help people and organizations be their best. Her article in *Advances in Global Leadership*, vol. 10 was awarded Outstanding Author Contribution in the 2018 Emerald Literati Awards. Her insights are informed by her work in Europe, the US, New Zealand, India, and China.

LEVERAGING THE COVID-19 PANDEMIC TO DEVELOP GLOBAL LEADERS

Christof Miska and Milda Zilinskaite
April 14, 2020

Global leadership in a VUCA – volatile, uncertain, complex, and ambiguous – world has become the norm (Miska, Stahl, & Economou, 2020). Yet, the COVID-19 pandemic redefines VUCA and poses unprecedented challenges for global leaders: national protectionism becoming legitimized, unemployment numbers raising to record-highs, and fundamental personal rights being curbed – all in the name of health protection. These developments make the roles of global leaders appear less relevant, passing the torch to political leaders of local national governments. Even more so, the need for pro-active leadership development seems less relevant and is subject to postponement until after the crisis, perhaps due to anxiety, helplessness, or simply the focus being entirely on the situation at hand. However, we believe that the circumstances of turmoil and disorder associated with the COVID-19 pandemic actually provide a unique developmental opportunity for global leaders. In what follows, we describe a student-initiated component we added to our Leadership Lab at WU Executive Academy, in the hope to support students' learning journey despite – or rather due to – an ongoing global crisis.

WU Executive Academy is the postgraduate business school at WU Vienna University of Economics and Business in Austria. It offers a range of executive business and certification programs, with an annual enrollment of over 2,000 managers and high potentials. The student body is highly diverse, with more than 80 nationalities and a great variety of professional backgrounds represented. In 2018, we launched the Leadership Lab as a compulsory part of the entire first year of the Professional MBA (PMBA) program (typically approximately 100 participants per cohort). This largely virtual course is intended to foster leadership growth, providing reflection opportunities that connect learning points from the various courses to students' personal development. From a didactical point of view, the Leadership Lab fosters cognitive, affective, and behavioral facets in order to generate a learning context characterized by experiential rigor (Black & Mendenhall, 1989; Mendenhall, 2018). Our regular "Online Reflection Intervention" assignments vary in scope and requirements: from artistic work to personalizing sustainable development, to empowering each other as classmates, to discussing PMBA learnings with strangers, and more. Yet they all consistently emphasize the notion of impact via encouraging students to consider the effects that their learning creates not only on themselves but also – through their leadership – on their immediate social networks, organizations, and the broader society.

When in March 2020 the COVID-19 pandemic started hitting Europe, a student approached us suggesting that we may consider this new context as part of the Leadership Lab. Prompted by this request, which we believe sprung at least partially because there was a learning infrastructure in place for it to occur, we designed an optional online intervention on leadership in times of crisis. The assignment comprises a discussion forum with a number of open-ended reflection questions, each dedicated to a specific thematic strand. It encourages students to reflect upon leadership development under the novel circumstances – with the majority of the cohort under lockdown in their homes across the various countries where they reside. We found the nature of the pandemic to align well with the experiential rigor of the Leadership Lab, since crises habitually involve cognitive, affective, and behavioral facets. According to Ellis, Carette, Anseel, and Lievens (2014), systematic reflection requires three components – self-explanation (a process during which leaders analyze their own behaviors to generate explanations about success or failure), data verification (a process during which leaders aim to think of alternate explanations of events before changing their mental models, and to sidestep potential biases), and feedback (both on overall success and failure as well as on the process of reflection). In posing reflection questions, we broadly followed this approach and considered the first two components directly. For example, we asked students: "What have I learned/observed about myself and my reaction to the situation?" or "Has any of my learning in the PMBA program so far contributed to the way I think about the outbreak or to solution seeking?" (self-explanation) as well as "How could we, as a group (PMBA cohort), contribute to solution seeking?" (data verification; due to students' geographical colocation in various countries with diverse crisis-management approaches). For the third component, rather than evaluating and judging student performance, we trusted that the process of virtual interaction would provide an organic and self-reinforcing feedback loop; thus, we ourselves started engaging in the discussion as co-learners rather than instructors.

While at the time of writing, the intervention had only started, we could observe students engaging in reflection on their own behaviors in response to the pandemic. In addition, they exchanged specific expertise relevant to actively managing the crisis; they shared hands-on solutions implemented in their work-places (e.g., an online communication channel for informal virtual socializing within their work teams); and they discussed global organizations' innovative approaches. As follows, with the students' permission, we share excerpts of some of their early contributions:

- A student from Russia described learning with regard to evaluating her control of the situation: "In the beginning, I checked news, socials and tweets ... I was frustrated ... We are all losing control now; the degree of uncertainty is enormous. It hurts us a lot ... it destroys our self-identification. And my solution was ... [to learn to ask myself] – can I control [the situation]? If [the answer is] no – 'go by and forget.' If yes – don't cry and do what you can do." In a follow-up post, the same student described the leadership steps she took to raise the battered morale of her team in the face of significant financial cuts within her company.
- Reflecting on an analytical framework from a past course, a Slovak student asked himself and classmates whether one could employ a similar strategy in analyzing state-level responses to COVID-19: "I see that some of the SCM [Supply Chain Management] principles can be applied to many complex systems in our world, not just organizations. Perhaps, the same frameworks (What, How, How Much and Business/Technical/Leadership dimensions) can be applied to approach the problems we are facing with [COVID-19] ... Would be happy to hear some feedback..."
- Expressing hope in the global leadership potential of his cohort as a whole, a Romanian student wrote: "Within all our fields, if we manage to get beyond the noise, we could identify some emerging trends and synergies that would [create] a greater positive impact for our communities (companies, cities, countries, etc.)"

Overall, while thorough evaluation of this initiative's impact on students' leadership development and competence advancement will only be feasible retrospectively after more time has passed, at this stage we can draw two conclusions. First, taking global leadership development seriously makes it imperative to leverage ongoing rough contexts and situations for learning purposes, even if presently such endeavors might not appear of immediate relevance. Otherwise, we risk developing status-quo leaders capable of dealing with normality or post-factum of a crisis but not as much with the realities of a global leadership context rich in complexity, flow, and presence (Mendenhall, Reiche, Bird, & Osland, 2012). Second, in times where crises seemingly justify national protectionism and de-globalization, it is even more urgent to foster the cross-national and cultural aspects associated with perception, relationships, and self-management competencies (Bird, Mendenhall, Stevens, & Oddou, 2010) of global leadership.

REFERENCES

Bird, A., Mendenhall, M., Stevens, M. J., & Oddou, G. (2010). Defining the content domain of intercultural competence for global leaders. *Journal of Managerial Psychology, 25*(8), 810–828. doi:10.1108/02683941011089107

Black, J. S., & Mendenhall, M. (1989). A practical but theory-based framework for selecting cross-cultural training methods. *Human Resource Management*, *28*(4), 511–539.

Ellis, S., Carette, B., Anseel, F., & Lievens, F. (2014). Systematic reflection: Implications for learning from failures and successes. *Current Directions in Psychological Science*, *23*(1), 67–72. doi: 10.1177/0963721413504106

Mendenhall, M. E. (2018). Can global leadership Be taught online? In *Advances in global leadership* (Vol. 11, pp. 197–214). Bingley: Emerald Publishing Limited. doi:10.1108/S1535-12032018000011007

Mendenhall, M. E., Reiche, B. S., Bird, A., & Osland, J. S. (2012). Defining the "global" in global leadership. *Journal of World Business*, *47*(4), 493–503. doi:10.1016/j.jwb.2012.01.003

Miska, C., Economou, V., & Stahl, G. K. (2020). Responsible leadership in a VUCA world. In M. E. Mendenhall, M. Žilinskaitė, G. K. Stahl, R. Clapp-Smith (Eds.), *Responsible global leadership: Dilemmas, paradoxes, and opportunities*. New York and London: Routledge.

Christof Miska is an Associate Professor at the Institute for International Business at WU Vienna University of Economics and Business in Austria. He is an alumnus of WU Vienna, CEMS (The Global Alliance in Management Education), and the Nordic Research School of International Business (Nord-IB). His research explores the intersection of responsible leadership and cultural/institutional variations, spanning micro, meso, and macro perspectives, and associated areas such as leadership studies and sustainable development.

Milda Žilinskaite is a Senior Scientist and Manager at the Competence Center for Sustainability Transformation and Responsibility (Vienna University of Economics and Business) and a regular guest lecturer at the International Anti-Corruption Academy in Laxenburg, Austria. Milda obtained her PhD in Comparative Literature from the University of California, San Diego. She has worked and/or lived on four different continents. She conducts research and teaches on responsible global leadership, cross-cultural management, sustainable development, and global labor migration

LEADING THROUGH ENVIRONMENTAL JOLTS

Allan Bird
April 15, 2020

A GLOBAL ENVIRONMENTAL JOLT

On December 31, 2019, the Chinese government announced treatment of a novel infectious coronavirus. One month later, on January 30, the WHO announced a global health emergency. Over the next 30 days, as the outbreak of infections extended to all continents save one, national governments began implementing a range of policies, many of them culminating in regional and national quarantines and the closure of nonessential businesses. Unemployment soared even as GNP for many countries declined by 25% or more through the first quarter of 2020. On March 11, the WHO declared the outbreak a global pandemic.

Practitioners and academics have long characterized the global environment as extremely complex, reflecting a dynamic mix of diversity, interdependence, ambiguity, and flux (Osland et al., 2012a, 2012b). The COVID-19 pandemic represents a singular event within that complex environment. It is too early to determine whether it reflects what evolutionary scientists refer to as punctuated equilibrium – a cataclysmic period precipitating a dramatic shift to a new equilibrium. But its impact – like that of a powerful earthquake – is both extraordinary and global. It is a global environmental jolt.

Environmental jolts are defined as "transient perturbations whose occurrences are difficult to foresee and whose impacts on organizations are disruptive and potentially inimical" (Meyer, 1982, p. 515). Environmental jolts are noteworthy because they (1) expose critical linkages, (2) test the integrity and resilience of leaders and their organizations, (3) surface values, and (4) reveal mindsets undergirding adaptive responses. They give rise to unconventional behaviors and afford latitude for experimentation. They also represent unique opportunities to explore the range and contours of global leader capability.

Several features of the pandemic create distinctive challenges for global leaders. First, the jolt exerts impact on multiple fronts – economic, political, social, and medical/health – with the latter imposing particular, uncommon concerns. Second, because of both the health aspects and the size of the economic and social impact, there has been a strong negative affective element. Fear and anxiety are prevalent and have led to overreactions which, in turn, have increased stress, thereby leading to more fear and anxiety. Third, established social support networks, both work/career-related and personal/social, have been curtailed, leading to greater challenges in maintaining psychological health. Coupled with changes in work procedures, many of which decrease or constrain interpersonal interactions, the psychological toll of the jolt is substantial. Fourth, the suddenness and severity of the jolt quickly absorbed slack resources and forced many organizations to substantially curtail major portions of their business operations as well as furlough or cut back work hours for a sizable percentage of their workforce.

IMPLICATIONS FOR GLOBAL LEADERSHIP

Given these considerations, global leaders confront several distinctive challenges. First, it appears the pandemic has shifted global leader roles. Reiche et al. (2017) delineate a typology of global leader roles defined by variations in task complexity and relationship complexity. The pandemic jolt pushed leadership roles in the direction of heightened complexity along both dimensions. It triggered changes in task complexity by increasing the variety and flux of tasks to be performed. Task variety expanded through the introduction of new activities required to maintain existing operations under new conditions as well as through increases in coordination activities both internally with other units and externally with similarly affected buyers and suppliers. Flux intensified as a consequence of rapidly shifting actions on the part of national and local governments. Relationship complexity grew through configurational changes in boundaries in response to increases in virtual work as well as through adjustments in the variety and nature of interdependences.

Paradoxically, even as global leaders experienced sizable resource losses thereby constraining actionable options, they found themselves with more latitude for experimentation. The impact of the jolt shook things up and softened the ground for initiatives that would have been difficult to implement just months earlier. Global leaders with a change orientation are finding myriad opportunities to create new organizational structures, develop new products and services, and revise supplier and buyer relationships.

One of the defining characteristics of global leadership is the volume of boundary spanning required. The pandemic has pushed that further, compelling leaders to communicate in more and varied ways with stakeholders of all varieties. The size and extent of the jolt is also encouraging more collaborative behavior as individual organizations acknowledge that resolving many issues on their own has become more difficult given resource constraints.

Finally, as is often the case with environmental jolts, facades crumble away and the nonessential recedes into the background even as the essential comes to the fore. Global leaders are both coerced and set free to focus on that which is most essential: The process of influencing the thinking, attitudes, and behaviors of a global community to work together synergistically toward a common vision and common goals.

REFERENCES

Meyer, A. D. (1982). Adapting to environmental jolts. *Administrative Science Quarterly*, *27*(4), 515–537.

Osland, J. S., Bird, A., & Oddou, G. (2012b). The context of expert global leadership. *Advances in Global Leadership*, *7*, 107–124.

Reiche, S., Bird, A., Mendenhall, M., & Osland, J. (2017). Contextualizing leadership: A typology of global leadership roles. *Journal of International Business Studies*, *48*(4), 552–572.

Allan Bird (PhD, University of Oregon) is the Associate Vice President of International Affairs and Professor of Business at Pacific University. He has authored, coauthored, or edited nine books, more than 90 refereed journal articles and book chapters. He has published in leading journals, including the *Journal of International Business Studies*, *Academy of Management Journal*, *Strategic Management Journal*, and *Journal of World Business*. His most recent book (with M.E. Mendenhall, J.S. Osland, G.R. Oddou, M.L. Maznevski, M. Stevens, and G. Stahl) *Global Leadership: Research, Practice and Development* (third Edition) was published in 2017. His research interests focus on global leadership and effective management in intercultural contexts, with a particular emphasis on assessment and development.

PERSPECTIVES ON GLOBAL LEADERSHIP AND THE COVID-19 CRISIS

Tim Soutphommasane
April 15, 2020

Interpreting events as they are still unfolding carries the risk of premature pronouncement. Yet we can confidently say that the COVID-19 pandemic has been a global crisis characterized by national responses. It has, at least at the time of writing, not revealed much in the form of global leadership.

Rather, we have seen the opposite: the re-assertion of nationalism and the return of the nation-state. Countries have gone their different ways in responding to COVID-19, with varying success in suppressing the rate of infection. There has been little in the way of global coordination or cooperation, despite ample warning from international authorities for years about the risks of a global pandemic.

Many have almost reverted to type, with policy responses seemingly bearing the imprint of national characteristics, or at least that of their national political cultures. Consider China, the US, the UK, Singapore, or Hungary (to name a few). COVID-19 seems only to have made national differences grow more distinct.

We seem to be returning to a world where national boundaries will again loom large. Countries have pulled up their drawbridges; the free movement of people has been put on hold. It is possible we are seeing a definitive break from the globalized age most of us had come to know as normal.

Indeed, crises create new realities, and it is likely that we will never return to the old normal. Like it or not, we are arguably now in a transition to something else. The nature of the choices we have is, in broad terms, clear. On the one hand, there is the tempting retreat to a narrow safety, founded on fear and sovereignty. Across continents, we have already seen racism and xenophobia emerge as the default popular response. The dangerous trend toward nationalist populism and authoritarianism will only now deepen.

The alternative is not, as some would say, globalization or cosmopolitanism. At least, not anything that resembles a superseding of the nation-state. That ideal was perhaps always illusory. The only other alternative available is nationalism — of a kind apart from jingoism.

Nationalism does come in multiple forms. It need not mean nasty exclusion or aggression. While it is not always expressed in such ways, national sentiment can also be inclusive and generous. It can be an engine for social trust and cooperation. Progressive nation-building – mobilizing national identities, but in ways that are consistent with civil liberties, democratic equality and social justice – may just be the most compelling option available for post-COVID-19 economic and social recovery. Bringing that into reality will, however, demand courageous and imaginative leadership of the kind we have not seen since reconstruction following the World War II.

Tim Soutphommasane, DPhil, is Professor of Practice (Sociology and Political Theory) and Director, Culture Strategy at the University of Sydney. He was Australia's Race Discrimination Commissioner from 2013 to 2018. He is a political theorist and conducts research on patriotism, multiculturalism, identity, and race. He is the author of five books, including *On Hate* (Melbourne University Publishing, 2019), *The Virtuous Citizen: Patriotism in a Multicultural Society* (Cambridge University Press, 2012), and *Reclaiming Patriotism* (Cambridge University Press, 2009).

WHERE ARE THE RESPONSIBLE GLOBAL LEADERS?

COVID-19 Exposes a Huge Leadership Gap in Some of the World's Most Advanced Nations

Thomas Maak and Nicola M. Pless
April 16, 2020

The COVID-19 pandemic has shed light on a significant and fatal lack of responsible global leadership. To begin with, the first thing an observer notes is the fact that despite rather high numbers of infections the number of fatalities in countries like Germany, South Korea, and Switzerland is low. In contrast, in countries with similarly advanced health systems such as the Netherlands, the UK, and the richest nation on earth, the US, is up to 10 times higher.

Looking for an explanation for the differences is a tricky business as testing regimes are different, so are infrastructure and intensive care coverage. Also, the measures taken in these countries are driven by a vastly different sense of urgency. Still, watching the developments in the UK and the US, one cannot help but notice one factor that exacerbates the threat posed by the COVID-19 virus, and that is *bad leadership* (e.g. Kellerman, 2004).

To put it more bluntly, President Trump and Prime Minister Johnson have endangered their countries and own peoples by being, well, themselves double-dealing and self-inflated narcissists (https://www.nytimes.com/2020/04/05/opinion/trump-coronavirus.html), rather than *responsible global leaders in crisis*.

Gladly, the British Prime Minister survived his own infection, but it is telling that his health, and not his failures, blunders, and the fact that people are dying by the hundreds, became the dominant story (https://www.nytimes.com/2020/04/16/opinion/coronavirus-boris-johnson.html).

In contrast, the calm, considerate, and caring approach taken by Mrs Merkel in Germany or the science-based, compassionate but decisive leadership of Jacinta Adern in New Zealand with clear communication and wide-spread testing and treatment has not only helped to save many lives but has worked in congenial ways with well-equipped, professional health systems led by experts working toward a systemic response to the crisis.

Narcissism is not a crime, but it is a psychological disorder that can lead to devastating consequences in times of crisis when the world needs leaders who take charge, build teams of experts around them, consider their responses in light of evidence and scientific advancements, communicate in a calm but compassionate way, with the greater public good in mind. Narcissistic leaders tend to expose

...a grandiose sense of self-importance, are preoccupied with fantasies of unlimited success, power, brilliance, believes that they are 'special', require excessive admiration, have rather unreasonable expectations of favourable treatment or automatic compliance with their expectations, and lack empathy. (American Psychiatric Association, 2013, DSM 5).

In other words, they are rule-book narcissists.

Mr. Johnson was picked for his office as a great tactician and communicator and finally gave the UK its Brexit. But as the virus spread into Europe in February, he went on a holiday with his fiancée somewhere in the British countryside. He only acknowledged that the virus was the country's top priority when the FTSE index went into freefall. But instead of decisive action and coordinating the government's emergency response team, he took the weekend off giving the virus three more days to run its course. He then started to entertain – like the Netherlands – the idea of letting the virus run its course to increase "herd immunity," against the strong advice of experts. His performance since has been contradictory, indecisive, and out of tune, and as a consequence the UK has lost precious time, and Mr. Johnson narrowly escaped his own fatal infection.

As for Mr. Trump, well he has done what a narcissistic leader would do: downplaying the severity of the looming pandemic ("it's going to be just fine"), blaming it on others ("a Chinese virus"), and when he could no longer ignore the developments making an attempt to take the glory as a "war-time president" to fight the "silent enemy." He then confused numbers, made false or misleading claims regarding potential treatment, and Fox News and his allies on the religious right helped spread dangerous messages that COVID-19 was nothing but a "hoax" – much like climate change. Worse still, rather than uniting the country, he encouraged the state governors to compete for limited medical supplies and allowed an incoherent response to the crisis, allowing the virus to spread, which had devastating consequences in New York and especially in the South, where many Americans are uninsured.

Leadership in crisis must be decisive, cautious but compassionate, self-transcendent, and geared toward helping others, with a clear set of priorities and a good sense of the systemic risks involved – based on evidence and science, not on hunches, gut feelings, and self-serving ideologies. The bad leadership of Mr. Johnson and Mr. Trump has cost both countries, whose health systems are ill-prepared, very precious time, and as a consequence, sadly, too many people have died.

When the world recovers from this unprecedented crisis, we as scholars must analyze leadership failure and stress the need for responsible global leaders (Maak & Pless, 2009), reiterating their qualities. We need leaders with a global mindset (Beechler & Javidan, 2007), who feel responsible to all stakeholders, who listen to others and base their actions on a moral compass (Paine, 2006) and a shared concern for the well-being of their constituencies and humanity as a whole (Pless, 2007). Leaders, who are inclusive and compassionate and see the "bigger picture" – connecting past, present, and future as stewards of their countries and organizations. Or, as Anne Tsui (2020) has put it recently, "let us exercise responsible leadership ourselves by studying and advancing responsible leadership, as well as other valuable topics, to contribute to the making of a better world post-COVID-19."

REFERENCES

American Psychiatric Association. (2013) Diagnostic and statistical manual of mental disorders (DSM–5). Retrieved from https://www.psychiatry.org/psychiatrists/practice/dsm

Beechler, S., & Javidan, M. (2007). Leading with a global mindset. *Advances in International Management, 19*, 131–169.

Kellerman, B. (2004). *Bad leadership*. Boston, MA: Harvard Business School Press.

Maak, T., & Pless, N. M. (2009). Business leaders as citizens of the world. Advancing humanism on a global scale. *Journal of Business Ethics, 88*(3), 537–550.

Paine, L. S. (2006). A compass for decision making. Chap. 4. In T.Maak, N.Pless (Eds.), *Responsible leadership*. (pp. 54–67). London: Routledge.

Pless, N. M. (2007). Understanding responsible leadership: Role identity and motivational drivers. *Journal of Business Ethics, 74*, 437–456.

Tsui, A. (2020). Retrieved from https://www.rrbm.network/covid-19-crisis-a-call-for-responsible-leadership-researchanne-s-tsui/

Thomas Maak is Director, Center for Workplace Leadership and the Resident Professor of Leadership at the University of Melbourne. He uses a multilevel lens to research leadership at the individual, group, and organizational level, linking ethical theory, political philosophy, relational thinking, and stakeholder theory. Professor Maak has extensive experience in leadership development and has worked for several years with PricewaterhouseCoopers on their award-winning senior executive program "Ulysses." Beyond leadership research, his research interests include ethical decision-making, political CSR, and organizational neuroscience. His work has been published in journals such as *Academy of Management Learning & Education, Academy of Management Perspectives, Journal of Business Ethics, Journal of Management Studies, Human Resource Management,* and *Organizational Research Methods.*

Nicola M. Pless is the Chair in Positive Business, Professor of Management and Director of the Center of Business Ethics and Responsible Leadership at the

University of South Australia. She has served on the faculties of ESADE, INSEAD and the University of St. Gallen (permanent faculty member). Her international career allowed her to live and work on four continents, in 15 countries and more than 25 cities. She held the 2010 Honorary Jef Van Gerwen Chair (University of Antwerp) and is the winner of the 2013 Aspen Institute's Faculty Pioneer Award for teaching innovation and excellence. She conducts research on responsible leadership and business, global leadership development and responsible management education, mindfulness practices and organizational neuroscience. Her work has received numerous international awards and appeared in *Academy of Management Learning and Education, Academy of Management Perspectives, Human Resource Management, Journal of Business Ethics, Journal of Management Studies, Organizational Research Methods.*

EVERY LEADER NEEDS A GLOBAL LENS

Tsedal Neeley
April 17, 2020

The fact that a microscopic organism first discovered in Wuhan, China, has brought much of the world to a near standstill in a matter of weeks proves beyond a doubt that we are living in an era of global interconnectedness. With its unexpected and unknown appearance and interconnected parts, the coronavirus (hereafter referred to as COVID-19) has spread worldwide at a velocity that has taken billions of people, institutions, and organizations by surprise. More than ever, COVID-19 has demonstrated that every leader must have a global lens whether they operate in a domestic or a global context.

What's more, the nature of the pandemic has rendered the world increasingly volatile, uncertain, complex, and ambiguous (VUCA), a term first used by the US military to describe the environment that military leaders must operate within. VUCA – as a concept as well as a term – has also long applied to the modern business environment faced by global leaders. What we know, through experience and research, about the leadership qualities and aptitudes needed to meet VUCA conditions are now intensely crucial. These aptitudes, which every leader needs to develop, are *global awareness, anticipation, and adaptation.*

Awareness of the essential nature of converging global issues is a first step in gaining global leadership aptitude necessary today. Leaders do not have the luxury of listening solely to news in their part of the world but should strive to maintain a pulse on international events. The regular consumption of international media allows for an understanding of events, geopolitical or otherwise. For example, a mayor of a large city in the US should have been keenly aware of the COVID-19 situation in Wuhan and canceled a gathering of 1.4 million people in

February of 2020. One way of achieving this knowledge is ensuring that senior leadership teams have the requisite international work experiences that equip them with a broader awareness of scenarios that may occur and the corresponding responses to counteract any arising issues. This awareness becomes more applicable as one looks for and finds corresponding challenges and solutions that are similar to that which one has encountered in the past.

Anticipating the impact of events in one part of the world on another is a skill that global leaders must constantly sharpen, especially as it relates to global dynamics interfacing with local dynamics. Anticipating how world events affect local sensitivities is a key capability within global leadership aptitude. For example, as governments, in an attempt to slow the pandemic, mandate stay-at-home orders for millions of people, many of the supply chains delivering regular household goods have become severely impacted as consumer purchasing habits have changed. Teams that include members who stem from diverse geographies can become a competitive advantage through their innate ability to anticipate how global events may impact the business and local or regional economies. Conversely, a leadership team with a narrower lens has a reduced ability to anticipate global macroeconomic trends.

Adapting effectively arises from a diversity of approaches, which itself comes from a talent pool that is broadly representative of nationalities, societies, cultures, religions, racial backgrounds, and so forth. Adaptation is also linked to relevance, as leaders strive to become or maintain participation in different business environments. Diversity inspires the creative thinking necessary to undergo adaptation in ever-changing markets. Nowhere is this more apparent than in the race to come up with a viable vaccine to protect the global population from COVID-19 – virologists and other medical researchers are teaming internationally to discover a solution; many have already mastered the art of adaptation, adjusting to novel working environments, vastly different funding sources, political contexts, or other scenarios. Creativity and innovation arising from diversity improves everyone's ability to adapt to change.

COVID-19 meets every VUCA condition imaginable. Its enormous cost has revealed to the world that the only way to survive VUCA conditions is for leaders to maintain a global lens and develop the global aptitudes necessary to navigate constant changes.

Tsedal Neeley is the Naylor Fitzhugh Professor of Business Administration at the Harvard Business School. With her award-winning book, *The Language of Global Success*, she chronicled the unfettered behind-the-scenes globalization process of a company over the course of 5 years. She has also written extensively about how distributed and global teams succeed. Her work also focuses on how to navigate the global and digital work environment on issues ranging from digital literacy, digital tools, the digital leader, leading agile teams to company-wide digital transformations. Tsedal Neeley received her PhD from Stanford University in Management Science and Engineering, specializing in Work, Technology, and Organizations. She was honored by Thinkers50 "On the Radar list" of emerging thinkers with the potential to make lasting contributions to management.

GLOBAL EPIDEMIC OF BLINDNESS

Orly Levy
April 21, 2020

For more than two decades, we have assumed or rather hoped that world leaders will develop a *global mindset* – the ability to see and understand the world from a global perspective (Levy, Beechler, Taylor, & Boyacigiller, 2007). But as years went by, we have witnessed evermore the emergence of what can be termed a *global blindset* – a profound inability to see and comprehend the world from a global perspective (Levy, 2017). This global shortsightedness is increasingly evident with the coronavirus pandemic – a *global risk* event that has a significant negative impact on multiple countries over an extended period and therefore requires a globally coordinated response (see Beck, 2012 on global risks).

With the human and economic costs of the delayed response now mounting, it is worth asking why has the coronavirus pandemic gone either unforeseen, denied, or downplayed? Why have so many leaders across the world been "blind" to potentially devastating effects of the coronavirus pandemic?

Why did President Xi Jinping of China engage in delaying tactics for six key days (Associated Press, 2020). Why did President Trump downplay the coronavirus threat with a mix of facts and false statements? Why was the British Prime minister Boris Johnson slow to recognize the risks, taking a mid-February holiday at his country home and skipping five Cobra meetings on the virus? (Calvert, Arbuthnott, & Leake, 2020). Why did the Mexican President Andrés Manuel López Obrador encourage his people to eat out at restaurants well into the pandemic? And why did the Brazilian President Jair Bolsonaro nullify the coronavirus risk by labeling it "a little cold"?

Why these leaders appear to be following each other, first walking unconcerned, then with "hesitation, alarm, stumbling, and falling" (Arnheim, 1974, p. 88), as if they were a group of coordinated figures in Bruegel's *The Blind Leading the Blind?* As Britain's foreign minister, Dominic Raab, said

> There's no doubt: We can't have business as usual after this crisis, and we'll have to ask the hard questions about how it came about and about how it could've been stopped earlier. (Reuters, 2020).

The hard question is first and foremost why so many world leaders *did not* develop a global mindset. Why have they failed to recognize the complexity of a world that, for good and for bad, is exceedingly interconnected and interdependent. Why have they gone "blind"? Or maybe have been "…Blind but seeing, Blind people who can see, but do not see" like the afflicted in Saramago's (1999, p. 292) novel *Blindness?*

While we cannot unequivocally associate the lack of global mindset with political ideology or regime type, we can tentatively trace this global epidemic of blindness to three broad factors. The *rise of nationalism* and the *widespread rejection of science* both have had an immediate and detrimental effect on the response to the coronavirus outbreak. A third factor, a *rigged system of wealth,* commonly referred to as crony capitalism or kleptocracy, have had systemic corrosive effect, eroding the duty of care of many world leaders.

Rise of nationalism. Much has been written about the rise of neo-nationalism in response to globalization and to growing social inequality, from Modi's Hindu nationalist party in India to China's and Turkey's mission to restore their former imperial glory, Trump's adoption of immigration and trade policies "with our own interests foremost in mind," the upsurge of far-right politics and ideology in Europe, and the British, Catalan, and Scottish separatist nationalism, to name but a few. What are the implications of nationalism for foreseeing and "seeing" global risks, for recognizing coronavirus as a global health crisis?

As it seems, nationalist mindset promotes the denial of both the *risk* dimension and the *global* dimension of global risks, the coronavirus pandemic included. First, the risk associated with the coronavirus outbreak was concealed and denied as Chinese leaders double down on their efforts to suppress vital information, placing their grip on power, public persona as omnipotent, and national image above free and accurate global flow of information that is essential in confronting pandemics. Further, the risk was also downplayed just because the virus surfaced in another country, as if labeling it "foreign" will make it less risky, Trump's "Chinese virus" is a case in point. Second, nationalist mentality has led to rejecting global coordination, although the coronavirus pandemic is a global health crisis that requires a global solution (see, for example, Albright, 2020). To the extent that the global dimension was recognized, it fueled international competition for resources rather than cooperation, as the recent bidding war among nations for vital medical supplies and ban on exporting essential medical equipment demonstrate. As it seems, foreseeing and "seeing" global risks is exceedingly difficult with a narrow nationalist vision.

Rejection of science. There is already a widespread rejection, politicization, and manipulation of science for political and economic purposes manifested in such debates on climate change and vaccination. The coronavirus pandemic appears to be yet another casualty of an anti-science assault. In China, early warnings about a "strange new virus" issued as early as the end of December were rejected and suppressed. In the US, epidemiological models of the coronavirus threat were met with suspicion and distrust as if they were a hoax meant to bring down Trump (Krugman, 2020). Russia launched yet another campaign of health misinformation, promoting the theory that the coronavirus pandemic was propagated by American scientists. In Brazil, Bolsonaro's rejection of the scientific consensus on the gravity of the coronavirus outbreak has state governors up in arms.

The anti-science discourse, which often goes hand in hand with rightwing nationalism, religious conservatism, and industry interest groups, has already downgraded the status and validity of scientific findings and experts. It provided a vocabulary with which to cast doubt, dismiss, and dispel scientific evidence under the guise of "measured response" supposedly led by capable leaders. Scientists, in contrast, were portrayed as fanning a social panic. Those world leaders who were shortsighted about the coronavirus pandemic typically have a cavalier relation with truth, facts, and evidence; some are actively involved in dismantling scientific institutions and sidelining scientific evidence. Therefore, it should come as no surprise that there were blind to the potentially devastating effects projected by scientists.

Rigged system of wealth. In increasing number of countries, a rigged system of wealth accumulation and distribution has come to dominate life; depending on geography and linguistic preferences, this system has been called *crony capitalism, kleptocracy, plutocracy,* and *corporatocracy,* among others. While scholars have offered various explanations for the mechanisms that "rig" the system, there is a relatively broad consensus on its effects: Economic inefficiency, massive inequality, underfunding of public services, and curbed economic and social opportunities for most citizens (see, for example, Stiglitz, 2016). But above all, such system breeds profound social corruption.

Why might corruption affect the (in)ability of world leaders to "see"? The short answer is that corruption blinds as Moses imparts to his people shortly before his death: "You shall not pervert justice; you shall not show partiality, nor take a bribe, for a bribe blinds the eyes of the wise and twists the words of the righteous" (The Holy Bible Book of Deuteronomy, 1982).[2] A system characterized by widespread social injustice and corruption blinds even the wise because it leads to an endemic indifference and tunnel vision. World leaders fail to "see" the threat either because they are disinterested in "seeing," unconcerned with what they are "seeing," or see the world through a narrow self-interest prism, which is driven by short-term political and economic gains. Further, a rigged system is typically underprepared for handling a major crisis that requires significant public funds and infrastructures. Therefore, denying the crisis becomes the "go-to" response given shortage of resources and capabilities. Many world leaders are heavily invested in a self-congratulating, self-referential status quo that is corrupting and insulating; it makes it impossible for them to adapt or even understand that their vision is obsolete in a world that has changed dramatically.

As it seems, the combination of ramped nationalism, anti-science discourse, and endemic corruption, has bred an epidemic of different kind: Global epidemic of blindness.

REFERENCES

Albright, M. (2020, March 20). Madeleine Albright: Coronavirus should Be a wake-up call for world leaders to work together. *Time*. Retrieved from https://time.com/5807169/madeleine-albright-coronavirus-cooperation/

Arnheim, R. (1974). *Art and visual perception: A psychology of the creative eye*. Berkeley, CA: University of California Press.

---

[2]In Biblical Hebrew, the original language of *the Bible*, the words "bribery" and "corruption" have the same linguistic root. In modern-day Hebrew, these words are often used interchangeably.

Beck, U. (2012). Global risk society. In G. Ritzer (Ed.), *The Wiley-Blackwell encyclopedia of global-ization*. Chichester; Malden, MA: Blackwell Publishing Ltd. doi:10.1002/9780470670590.wbeog242

Calvert, J., Arbuthnott, G., & Leake, J. (2020, April 19). Coronavirus: 38 days when britain sleep-walked into disaster. *Sunday Times* (London). Retrieved from https://www.thetimes.co.uk/article/coronavirus-38-days-when-britain-sleepwalked-into-disaster-hq3b9tlgh

The Holy Bible Book of Deuteronomy. (1982). *New King James version*. Nashville, TN: Thomas Nelson.

Krugman, P. (2020, March 30). This land of denial and death. *New York Times*. Retrieved from https://www.nytimes.com/2020/03/30/opinion/republicans-science-coronavirus.html

Levy, O., Beechler, S., Taylor, S., & Boyacigiller, N. A. (2007). What we talk about when we talk about 'global mindset': Managerial cognition in multinational corporations. *Journal of International Business Studies*, *38*(2), 231–258.

Levy, O. (2017). Global mindset: From the core to the edge and back. Paper presented at the Academy of Management Annual Meeting, Atlanta, August 2017.

Associated Press. (2020, April 15). China didn't warn public of likely pandemic for 6 key days. *New York Times*. Retrieved from https://www.nytimes.com/aponline/2020/04/15/us/ap-as-virus-outbreak-china-delay.html

Reuters. (2020, April 16). China will have to answer hard questions on coronavirus outbreak: UK foreign minister. *Reuters*. Retrieved from https://www.reuters.com/article/us-health-coronavirus-britain-china/china-will-have-to-answer-hard-questions-on-coronavirus-outbreak-uk-foreign-minister-id USKBN21Y2SV

Saramago, J. (1999). *Blindness* Giovanni Pontiero (Trans.). Orlando, FL: Harcourt.

Stiglitz, J. E. (2016). Inequality and economic growth. In M. Jacobs, M. Mazzucato (Eds.), *Rethinking capitalism: Economics and policy for sustainable and inclusive growth* (pp. 134–155). Malden, MA: Blackwell Publishing.

Orly Levy is a Reader in International Management at the School of Finance and Management, SOAS University of London. She received her PhD in sociology from the University of Wisconsin, Madison. She conducts research on global mindset and cosmopolitan disposition, status and power dynamics in global companies, transcultural brokerage, and transnational social and cultural capital. Her work has appeared in leading academic journals such as the *Journal of Management*, *Journal of International Business Studies*, *Human Relations*, *Sloan Management Review*, and *Journal of Organizational Behavior*.

WHEN ARROGANCE KILLS

Nancy J. Adler
April 22, 2020

The pandemic, and its horrible cost in human life, presents us with an extremely complex and dangerous crisis. To act effectively, leaders, including the best of our physicians, politicians, scientists, and businesspeople, need the courage to embrace humility in ways that, sadly, remain all-too-rare in the twenty-first century. Faced with such high levels of ambiguity, leaders need to repeatedly respond by openly admitting that "We don't know" rather than confidently asserting what the public craves to hear. What we so fervently want to hear goes beyond what we know to be true. That lack of truth could easily undermine the health and safety of all of us. Leaders everywhere now recognize that announcements embedded in false certainty (and arrogance), such as those made in the US in early March 2020, diminished the sense of urgency and threat and thereby hindered desperately needed rapid action:

> Excuse our arrogance ... we have the best health care system on the planet...So, ... it's not going to be as bad [here] as it was in other countries.[i]

Sadly, within a month, the US became the world's COVID-19 epicenter, with more deaths than any other country. With this virus, no country is unique. No country is safe.

In times of extreme uncertainty, we trust leaders who reliably exhibit honesty and humility. But humility alone is not enough to successfully fight COVID-19 nor to return society and the global economy to vibrant functioning. Leaders' initial, truthful statement, "We don't know," must always be followed by: "And this is what we are doing to find out." "This is the research we're initiating." "This is the widespread testing we've started." "These are the people from around the world that we've reached out to so we can learn from their successes and not have to repeat their failures."

As citizens, driven by our intense desire for quicker, better outcomes, we remain tempted to invent all-knowing experts when, in fact, there are none. We crave certainty when the reality is that there is none. Our job as citizens is to support our leaders in telling us the truth, including in saying "We don't know yet."

NOTE

i. Goodman, J. David (2020) How Delays and Unheeded Warnings Hindered New York's Virus Fight. *New York Times*, April 8.

Nancy J. Adler, PhD, is the S. Bronfman Professor Emerita in Management at McGill University. She conducts research and consults worldwide on global leadership, cross-cultural management, and arts-inspired leadership practices. She has authored more than 150 articles, produced several films, and published 10 books and edited volumes. She is a Fellow of the Academy of Management, the Academy of International Business, and the Royal Society of Canada and has been recognized as one of the top university teachers in Canada. Adler is also a visual artist known for her paintings, monotype prints, and ceramics. Her artwork is held in private collections worldwide.

TRUST IS A SYSTEMS SKILL, NOT JUST AN INTERPERSONAL SKILL

Martha L. Maznevski
April 26, 2020

In dialogue with senior global leaders navigating through the pandemic, I notice their responses tend to fall into one of two patterns. Those patterns suggest the global leadership should examine building trust as a systems skill, not only as an interpersonal skill. Leaders showing both patterns started the same way early in the crisis. They clarified the same set of priorities: health and safety first, then business continuity. Then they diverged.

Leaders in the first pattern see their office as headquarters of the war room. Everything reports daily in to them, and they send out the orders daily. There are many orders, many reports, and the leader works on overdrive to keep things under control. The message is "trust me and the war room, we know what you should be doing." It works – health and safety records are good, and business continuity is cautiously optimistic. But the local leaders are experiencing very high levels of anxiety and stress. They spend a lot of time in meetings following up on the orders and collecting information. One person I spoke with in a company led like this spends at least 90 additional minutes each day filling out the form to record exactly what she has done during her eight-hour day. Local leaders and employees in these firms feel they are barely hanging on, and they worry about the future.

Leaders in the second pattern see their office as more of a listening hub. They track the global pandemic trends and science and provide the information to the global network. They continuously communicate whether and how the main priorities need to be adjusted. The message is We trust you, you know what you should be doing. Otherwise their main actions are checking in with the local offices to ask "What are you worried about this week? What are you proud of this week? How can I help?" This also works – health and safety records are good, the business continuity is cautiously optimistic. However, the stories inside the local organizations are quite different. Local leaders are exhausted but energized, proud of what they are accomplishing. They feel connected with their local communities, making a difference there. They are innovating and sharing ideas with the global leader about new ways of moving forward post-pandemic. In short, they are acting in ways that reinforce trust throughout the system.

Trust is a belief in the good intentions of another and a willingness to be vulnerable oneself to the actions and decisions of another. Trust is developed over time based on experiences of reliability, and belief in shared values. Both of these pandemic patterns rely on trust in the system, but its nature and role are quite different. In the first pattern, local leaders are asked to trust the global leader. Formal authority and coercive power ensure control, but trust helps. If local leaders trust the global leader and the system of information reporting, they are more likely to put in the effort to report and to implement as directed. In the second pattern, the global leader trusts the local decision makers and the global system of sharing, operating, and decision-making. There is more trust in the system of leadership – the global leader is more willing to be vulnerable to the actions and decisions of the local leaders, and local leaders are more willing to take (cautious) risks in innovating. Both patterns may get their organizations through the pandemic, but the second one is much more likely to have a healthier organization on the other side. One of the leaders in the second pattern explained that

> This is a time to trust. To provide some clear priorities, then to trust and support. *And you needed to build that trust before the crisis. If you didn't have it then, you can't energize it now* [italics added], so you have to control.

This pandemic differentiates global leaders who have built that system of trust before the crisis from those who have not. In this way it highlights the importance of trust as a systems skill, not only a personal skill. Leaders in this second group build trust between themselves and others, and in addition they shape networks and communities of people who trust each other and who act in ways that increase their trustworthiness.

What does "building systemic trust" look like as a skill? Is it an aggregate of interpersonal skills? Is it a subset of what we already call "community building"? How do we recognize it, before a crisis? Do we see it only in its effect on organizational culture, or can we identify the dynamics in process? Systems thinking is the least developed conceptually of the global leadership skills – the pandemic shows us it is time for us to get working on it.

Martha Maznevski is Professor of Organizational Behavior and Faculty Director for Executive Education at Ivey. She is an expert in global teams, global leadership, culture and identity, and empowering individual differences. She has published widely on these topics in academic and management arenas and works closely with leaders and their companies around the world on innovative approaches to leadership at all levels in today's highly complex global environment. Dr. Maznevski completed her PhD at Ivey with research on multicultural teams and has expanded that research stream throughout her career. Her current research unlocks the performance dynamics of lateral teams – teams that coordinate across multiunit organizations such as global key account teams or matrixed product or function groups. She coauthored the popular textbook, *International Management Behavior*, and publishes in leading journals, including *Journal of International Business Studies* and *Strategic Management Journal*.

PRACTITIONER PERSPECTIVES

As mentioned above, we also invited global leaders and coaches/consultants to write about COVID-19. Because their essays are best understood in context, we placed their bios before their reflections.

WHAT NON-GLOBAL LEADERS CAN LEARN FROM GLOBAL LEADERSHIP IN TIMES OF PANDEMICS

Danielle Lyngaard
April 6, 2020

Many domestic leaders are no stranger to some degree of virtual leadership, but there is no doubt that global leaders are some of the best trained in leading from a distance. Of necessity, they are highly experienced in using virtual media to connect with their teams and the individual employee. As a consequence of COVID-19, countries and companies around the world asked many of their employees to work from their homes to minimize the spread of the contagion. Suddenly in spring 2020, leaders across the world have had to adapt to distance leadership overnight. Non-global leaders instantly had to perform distance leadership, virtual leadership, creating and strengthening mutual confidence, and leading conflicts from a distance. Non-global leaders suddenly had to succeed in the context of complexity and uncertainty that results from not being geographically close to all their employees.

In times of a pandemic, such as COVID-19, uncertainty increases complexity, and leaders search for tools and best practices to grasp the new temporary reality in which they must succeed. For decades, global leaders have performed in an environment of high complexity. Applying the tools and best practices from the global leadership field has become not only relevant, but indeed a necessity for many non-global leaders.

The complexity under the COVID-19 circumstances is characterized by a need for flexibility and a displacement in working hours. Many employees working from home have to both work full time and take care of their children who can no longer attend nursery school. Furthermore, some employees must home-school their children and teenagers. They no longer have the advantage of face-to-face meetings when leading employees of different nationalities. And they must make decisions fast and in an environment of great instability and uncertainty, both businesswise and personally. Thus, non-global leadership during a pandemic resembles almost 1:1 the complexity that global leaders face daily.

This insight was helpful when numerous members of the Confederation of Danish Industry called asking for help in shifting to a virtual workplace. We realized that they could learn from global leadership practices and shared one of the global leadership development tools developed by an academic-industry partnership, based on research and best practice.

GUIDELINES FOR VIRTUAL WORK

- **Step 1**: Communicate your ambition for the work of the team in the coming period and the situation in which it is to be done. Be especially clear about the common objectives and hold 1:1 (virtual) sessions with each of the employees and communicate their targets to them clearly and precisely.
- **Step 2**: The team formulates a shared purpose based on the leader's ambition and the team's goals.
  - Why should we do what we are doing together? What purpose does it serve?
  - How does it contribute to the company's overall objectives?
- **Step 3**: Based on the goals, the employees specify the concrete performance targets.
  - What exactly are we aiming to deliver? When do we have to deliver? What qualities are we expected to deliver? How much do we have to deliver?
- **Step 4**: Based on the framework that has been communicated, the team works to formulate shared attitudes/values defining how they intend to work together to achieve the agreed goals.
  - What is important to you in your work together?
  - How can you ensure that you build and maintain trust in each other despite not being together from day to day? How do you want to communicate with each other? How do you resolve disagreements and conflicts within the team? How should your collaboration work from day to day? Do you need to agree on a common language? Response times to e-mails? Anything else?
- **Step 5**: There should be agreements on roles and responsibilities in the team.
  - Regarding the goals we have to achieve, what skills do we need and who in the team has these skills? Do we need any skills that are not present in the team right now? How could we compensate for this?
  - What roles do we need in the team? How do we arrive at the best match between roles and skills? What responsibilities go with the various roles? Who does what in continuation of Step 3?
- **Step 6**: To build a shared commitment, agreements should be made on the obligations of the team members to each other.
  - How do we ensure that we help each other even though we do not all see each other every day? How and when do we ask each other for help? What can we expect from each other from day to day? What do we do if we find that a colleague seems pressured or depressed or does not get back to us as agreed?
  - How do we celebrate our successes in the virtual universe?
- **Step 7**: To ensure that the team fulfills its agreements and mutual commitments, the collaboration should be evaluated as the work progresses. The team should agree on how to do this.
  - How often do we follow-up and evaluate our work together in the team? How do we evaluate?
  - How often do we evaluate our work products and our ability to produce the expected results?
  - How do we ensure that we learn from our failures – and our successes?

The tool has proven to be very helpful to non-global leaders right from the first days of the COVID-19 situation in Denmark. It is a perfect example of how global leaders can help, inspire, and educate their non-global leadership colleagues during a pandemic.

Danielle Bjerre Lyndgaard holds both a Master of Science in Economics and Business Administration and a Master of Management Development from the Copenhagen Business School. She is a Senior Advisor at the Confederation of Danish Industry (DI). In addition to a range of other initiatives related to (global) leadership development, she is responsible for leadership development programs targeting experienced managers as well as foreign managers working in Denmark and globally. Her research interests focus on global leadership development and the paradoxes and complexity in global collaboration. She coauthored six books on (global) leadership and HR. She is a member of the Global Leadership Academy – an academia-practitioner research collaboration with 12 Danish MNCs under the auspices of DI. The research-based management tools developed in this project were published in a practitioner toolkit titled *Grasping GlobalLeadership – Tools for "Next Practice"* (Nielsen & Lyndgaard, 2018). They are used in global leadership practice and executive global leadership training and are available to the public (www.globalledelse.dk/eng). When the COVID-19 crisis began, one of Danielle's primary tasks was to help Danish industry adapt as quickly as possible to the virtual workplace.

PREPARING FOR LIFE AFTER COVID-19 – PART 1

Steve Terrell
April 8, 2020

Today is March 27, 2020. The coronavirus pandemic has yet to peak in the US, and here in Florida we, like the rest of the country, are waiting and wondering. Wondering when it will end, how many more will be infected, who in our circle of family, friends, and colleagues will fall ill before it's all over. Wondering what life will be like after the virus has changed everything. Wondering if we'll even have a "post-COVID-19" life, or if it will stay with us forever, shape-shifting and hovering over us like a malevolent, invisible ghoul.

We can't know what life will be like until it begins taking shape out of the remnants of a burned-out society. We can, however, prepare for an age of increased and unending Volatility, Uncertainty, Complexity, and Ambiguity (VUCA) by enacting a learning mindset and applying the skills required to learn and grow from the experience of living through this challenging time. And, by doing so, we will also be more prepared to influence our future.

A learning mindset is an attitude that predisposes you to be open to new experiences, to believe you can and will learn, and to intentionally grow and develop from your experience. According to research conducted at the University of Virginia, "Managers with a 'learning mindset' are characterized by a continuous sense of ongoing learning and transformation and received the highest job performance ratings of all those studied."[i] And, in an article published by *Harvard Business Review* online, Gottfredson and Reina pointed out that

> A learning mindset involves being motivated toward increasing one's competence and mastering something new.... Leaders with a learning mindset, compared to those with a performance mindset, are more mentally primed to increase their competence, engage in deep-level learning strategies, seek out feedback, and exert more of an effort. They are also persistent, adaptable, willing to cooperate, and tend to perform at a higher level.[ii]

It is especially important to have a learning mindset during challenging or difficult situations, because those are the very experiences that offer significant risks of failure as well as opportunities for personal development. People with a learning mindset who encounter difficult challenges have a strong tendency to create something of value from the crucible of negative experiences. As a result, they create their own virtuous cycle of learning and performance, enabling them to learn more from their experiences, which in turn results in their being more resilient and performing better in VUCA conditions. This leads to achievement of better results and reinforces the importance and value of the learning mindset.

Developing a learning mindset is not a panacea. There is no silver bullet or cure-all. The virus is on its own timeline, and we must only deal with its reality, not fantasize that we can bend reality to suit our needs. However, applying the learning mindset concept to "Life After COVID-19" is a way of being fully present in our world, intentionally taking responsibility for our life and way forward, and purposefully transforming ourselves through experience.

NOTE

i. Isabella, L. A., & Forbes, T. (April, 1994). Managerial Mindsets Research Project: Executive Summary. Darden Graduate School of Business Administration, University of Virginia, Charlottesville; and personal interview with the authors, June 13, 1994.

ii. Gottfredson, R., & Reina, C. (January 17, 2020). To Be a Great Leader, You Need the Right Mindset. *Harvard Business Review online*. Retrieved 6/3/2020 at https://hbr.org/2020/01/to-be-a-great-leader-you-need-the-right-mindset.

Robert "Steve" Terrell, EdD, is founder and President of Aspire Consulting, LLC, an Executive Leadership Development coaching and consulting firm. He conducts research and consults on global leadership, global leadership development, and experience-based leader development. He is the author of *Learning Mindset for Leaders: Leveraging Experience to Accelerate Development*, a practical handbook that serves as a workbook companion to a virtual leadership development program. He has written case studies, book chapters, and articles for leading professional publishers. His consulting clients are typically Fortune 500 companies in financial services, pharmaceuticals, biotechnology, health care, insurance, federal government, and assorted others.

POST COVID-19, HOW WILL I COACH GLOBAL LEADERS DIFFERENTLY?

Sully Taylor
April 9, 2020

As I look at the landscape of global leaders influencing the trajectory of this pandemic of COVID-19, I ask myself: where are the successful responses? Where are the failures? Who is responding well, and what does that look like? I think we can safely say that managing our way through crises such as COVID-19 with the least amount of damage to people and economies is going to be one of the crucial challenges for global leaders in the future. It is going to take close, quick, and coordinated cooperation among global leaders of all stripes – business, political, nonprofit – from many nations. The conditions that give rise to pandemic diseases are likely to grow, not diminish, as the world population continues to increase and the crowding into urban areas continues even as the destruction of what sustains a healthy global living environment (clean air, clean water, etc.) marches on.

So if the world will need global leaders to be even better prepared to deal with pandemics such as these, what do I believe have been the underlying dimensions that have characterized failure, and those that have characterized success? And how do I as someone involved in the development of global leaders *want my beliefs about these dimensions to instill how I coach and what I coach to?*

Let me start by speaking to what I keenly feel that I need to be coaching to, in particular the theory or beliefs I hold of what constitutes human development. Robert Kegan argues that there are three major plateaus of adult mental development, which he calls the socialized mind, the self-authoring mind, and the self-transforming mind (Kegan & Lahey, 2009). All are tied to the level of mental complexity that person has developed. The key aspect of the highest plateau, which only about 7% of all leaders exhibit, is the ability to have a viewpoint or vision, but to be able to step back and see it objectively, and to seek out learning that tests or modifies it. With a self-transforming mind

we can step back from and reflect on the limits of our own ideology or personal authority; see that any one system or self-organization is in some way partial or incomplete; be friendlier toward contradiction and opposites; seek to hold on to multiple systems rather than projecting all but one onto the other. Our self coheres through its ability not to confuse internal consistency with wholeness or completeness, and through its alignment with the dialectic, rather than either pole. (Kegan & Lahey, 2009, p. 17).

Leaders at this third level are guided by purpose and intention but are always open to acknowledging the limits of their own beliefs and understanding and are willing to hold contradictions but make decisions while being aware of them. They acknowledge their interdependence with others and exhibit the humility needed to continuously learn.

> These leaders are able to meet the adaptive challenges that are required by global pandemics and make adaptive changes that ... can only be met by transforming your mindset, by advancing to a more sophisticated stage of mental development. (Kegan & Lahey, 2009, p. 29).

My commitment: I am committed to constantly asking myself what plateau my client is inhabiting and helping her move to as high a point on the adult mental development curve as possible.

A second part of what I want to be coaching to concerns the leader's purpose. Throughout our engagement, we explore how adopting a particular business strategy, or learning a certain skill, or making a particular decision or holding certain conversations helps them achieve their purpose(s) – or not. I have usually remained fairly agnostic about what clients create for their purpose(s), although I do urge them to think how their purpose(s) serves the world. Yet this can become an abdication of the responsibility to support their development of a wider and higher vision of their leadership and its impact.

There must be a moral vision that guides me as I support them in defining their purpose(s), a moral vision of what constitutes a thriving and healthy person, business, community, and world. It must be a "loose" moral vision. Why is this needed? Because when faced with a challenge as important and far-reaching as the COVID pandemic, leaders who automatically prioritize their responsibility for creating thriving, healthy communities will be guided to make choices that may be "against" their short-term bottom lines or political futures, knowing that the bigger, long-term outcomes matter more than they do.

For me, a fairly "loose" moral vision that can guide me is the Noble Eightfold Path from Buddhism, which constitutes "a practical, direct experience method for finding meaning and peace in your life...each of the eight path factors defines one aspect of behavioral development (e.g., right view, right intention, right speech) needed for you to move from suffering to joy" (Moffit, 2008, p. 227) – and by extension and implication, helping others move from suffering to joy as well. It would constantly probe whether a client's intended actions were likely to be beneficial or harmful to others. It would constantly ask: "in service of what," with the "what" being a consideration of something or someone beyond the client himself.

My commitment: I am committed to deepening my own understanding and practice of the Noble Eightfold Path, such that it informs the way in which I pursue my own life and coaching purposes(s), and to more consciously imbue my coaching explorations with my clients with moral wisdom.

Neither of these two commitments is possible without the third: having the capability of expressing what needs to be said to a client. This is about having the skill AND the courage to use all of the "voices" of a "mindful coach" (Silsbee, 2010). In particular, the three "sharpener" voices of reflector, teacher, and guide are required to support the development of greater mental complexity and greater adherence to the principles of the Eightfold Path. The reflector voice especially supports the growth of the client's self-awareness, of how his actions or thoughts support his purpose(s) (or don't). This is the voice that provides direct and honest feedback, that helps him see himself as others do, that recognizes that as a coach we do not serve when we accept that the client knows himself best. Of course, when using this "voice" we must be careful to never make the client feel inadequate, and we must be cautious of any agenda or judgment that arises in us as a coach.

My commitment: I am committed to cultivating deeper understanding of the role of sharpener voices in the development of leaders and especially deeper courage to deploy these voices when necessary and developing ever keener understanding of how to use such sharpener voices in culturally appropriate ways.

This is how I will be different as a coach of global leaders when this is over.

REFERENCES

Kegan, R., & Lahey, L. (2009). *Immunity to change: How to overcome it and unlock the potential in yourself and your organization.* Boston, MA: Harvard University Press.

Moffitt, P. (2008). *Dancing with life: Buddhist insights for finding meaning and joy in the face of suffering.* New York, NY: Macmillan.

Silsbee, D. (2010). *The mindful coach: Seven roles for facilitating leader development.* San Francisco, CA: Jossey-Bass.

Sully Taylor (PhD, University of Washington) is Professor Emeritus of International Management and Human Resource Management at Portland State University, School of Business Administration, where she served as Associate Dean for Graduate Programs and is past Chair of the International Management Division of AOM. In addition, she is the recipient of two Fulbright awards, and for over two decades taught regularly at the IE Business in Madrid. Her research focused on global leadership and developing global mindset both at the individual and organizational levels, and the results were published in journals such as *Academy of Management Review* and *Journal of International Business Studies.* In 2013, she received her Coaching Certification from New Ventures West and since retirement from PSU in 2015 has been coaching leaders in academia and business.

WORK IN THE TIME OF COVID-19

Lisa Ruiz
April 14, 2020

The pandemic of COVID-19 has changed the world and the way we work and live in a matter of weeks. As global leaders, we have had to adapt and respond to the urgent widespread health emergency. We are still in the middle of the crisis, and so our level of success in managing through is still to be decided. I am frequently reminded of the concept of expert cognition as real-time problem-solving (Osland et al., 2012a, 2012b; Osland, Oddou, Bird, & Osland, 2013) that I first encountered in a doctoral class on global leadership.

Teams across the company began assessing which roles and functions needed to be on site and which could work remotely. For those needing to be on site, a strategy for health surveillance of staff was coupled with a plan to maintain enough separation between employees. The operations group needed to ensure that there was plan for more frequent and cleaning and rotating shifts. With offices around the world, the timing of these transitions has been occurring in waves.

For those working from home, it was important to ensure that everyone had what they needed to be effective, including keyboards, printers, and monitors. IT staff needed to ensure that the servers and bandwidth were in place to support the increased usage of virtual meeting platforms. As issues arise, we work together to strategize and come up with a creative solution.

Communication has been a key component of the COVID-19 strategy. Leadership throughout the organization is making a concerted effort to communicate so that all employees are informed and connected across the globe. All communications share the information but also focus on the human element. Employees have been encouraged to share their stories and post pictures from the home-work environment. To date we have met all our commitments and are also supporting the communities in which we work. I think we are rising to the challenge.

REFERENCES

Osland, J., Bird, A., & Oddou, G. (2012c). The context of expert global leadership. In W. H. Mobley Y. Wang, M. Li (Eds.), *Advances in global leadership* (Vol. 7, pp. 107–124). Oxford: Elsevier.

Osland, J., Oddou, G., Bird, A., & Osland, A. (2013). Exceptional global leadership as cognitive expertise in the domain of global change. *European Journal of International Management, 7*(5), 517–534.

Lisa H. Ruiz, PhD, is Senior Director, Regulatory Portfolio Management at AbbVie Inc. She has over 29 years of experience in the pharmaceutical industry leading global teams in the development and execution of regulatory strategies supporting registration of AbbVie's portfolio of products. She is also an adjunct professor of global leadership, innovation, and design thinking at Lake Forest Graduate School of Management and consultant in creative leadership practice in their Center for Leadership. AbbVie Inc. is heavily involved in COVID-19 research and philanthropy, and Dr. Ruiz's perspective focuses on the early internal adjustments and logistics large global companies faced while at the same time not losing sight of the human element.

CREATE A NEW WORLD

Heini Shi
April 14, 2020

Tens of millions of people have lost their jobs since the COVID-19 outbreak, while the World Trade Organization predicts that in 2020 international trade of goods may plunge by up to 32% or more as a result of the pandemic. The world will be a different place after the pandemic, so will be the businesses and the consumerist society we have known. There will not be a "normal" to which we can return.

While scientists research potential cures and politicians debate the misconduct of others, business leaders must re-assess risks associated with the liability of supply chains, assets, and operations, and most importantly, employees' lives. It becomes apparent that production of key components concentrated in certain geographic areas is risky – from large automobile parts to tiny raw materials in antibiotics (known as active pharmaceutical ingredients) – any unexpected event can interrupt supply chains causing devastating ripple effects.

What will the business landscape look like after this seismic event? The global production will inevitably reorganize, starting with those of high value-added and "strategic" importance whose definition may be flexible in "wartime" with a virus as the enemy. Initial steps are already being taken when Japan announced to financially support firms to pull out from China, the "World Factory," and to relocate in other countries. While it is unrealistic to predict patterns of the future global companies, I believe there may be three possible directions. First, even though the initial investments will be substantial, companies may use robotics, 3D technologies, and the Internet of Things to efficiently manufacture certain products in their home countries at a comparable cost with that of some emerging economies where the labor costs, among others, have consistently increased. Second, reducing overhead, shortening supply chains, and seeking synergy may be initial steps to take, but they could imply further concentration of resources and possibly conflict with the local firms, especially the vulnerable small and medium ones. Third, societies have now become highly divided with respect to values and ideologies. It is plausible that global production will reorganize at a geographic level through greater regional integration, and among nations sharing similar value systems and administrative rules.

This historic event is affecting more than 200 countries and may last longer than we anticipate. Under this scenario, what should business leaders do in the new reality? The other side of the coin for a crisis can be opportunity. The world situation calls for a new type of leadership from the private sector. I would advocate this following new approach with the acronym of **CREATE**:

CREATIVITY (FOR PROBLEM-SOLVING)

Uncertainty is the new normal. More companies should place creativity as a core value of their business practices, focusing on solving problems. In the midst of crises, business communities around the world are creatively and promptly solving problems. GM, Ford, and GE Healthcare are collaborating to produce ventilators, while Tesla and Virgin Galactic have developed similar devices. Another example is in Taiwan, where new facial mask production plants were opened within a month and have now surged to be the world's number two producer of this essential medical gear by producing 13 million masks every day.

RESILIENCE

During the outbreak, this unshakable leadership attribute is constantly evoked around the world as people are coping with significant distress in their personal and professional lives. Under a pandemic, the positions of all the players – people, organizations, and governments – in society can alter quickly. Acceptance of the possibility of change is the first step toward preparing for it. Defining a sense of purpose, along with sound business expertise and trust, could be beneficial in a time of hardship.

EMPATHY (FOR PARTNERSHIP)

Empathy in today's context of an escalating crisis is particularly pivotal in establishing and consolidating partnerships and global cooperation. Only united organizations can survive and thrive.

ACTION (FOR SUSTAINABILITY)

Massive loss of human lives and resources in this pandemic has showcased the transience and impermanence of life. The outbreak is often seen as a consequence of our consistent ignoring of sustainability, including the environment, workforce health, and other human rights. I am not alone in hoping that the pandemic serves as a wake-up call. It is time to lean forward and act now and search for remedies and new solutions to people's needs.

TECHNOLOGICAL SAVVY

How can we lead teams remotely? In a time of mass confinement, this question has greater urgency and need for exploration. Technological savvy is now a key competence for leaders as it provides a foundation for effective leadership. Technology offers opportunities to leaders and their teams to create appropriate tools to collaborate innovatively and productively.

EMBRACE

Leading in the digital era requires a new skill set and mindfulness of time frame. Optimizing efforts to stay healthy (mentally and physically) and maintain a positive attitude is essential. I subscribe to Mike Tyson's saying, "Everybody has a plan until they get punched in the mouth." The world under pandemic is a world in combat. Leaders surely need to strategize and design different scenarios, but they must swiftly adjust when confronted with problems. Embrace the new challenges and CREATE a new world!

Heini Shi is a Professor of Practice in Management at New York University Shanghai (NYU Shanghai). Dr. Shi has global policy and business experience in over 40 countries where she directed complex project implementation, created public–private partnerships, and advised on market expansion strategies. Shi has developed leadership programs and taught at leading business schools in Europe, China, and the US. Shi worked as Program Manager at the World Bank, United Nations Conference of Trade and Development (UNCTAD), and United Nations Development Programme (UNDP), where she designed and managed economic policy and social development projects. She was also an advisor to the multinational law firm Allen & Overy, consulting with European firms on their Chinese investments.

THE ROLE OF CIVIL SOCIETY AND GRASSROOTS ORGANIZATIONS IN PANDEMICS: IN SUPPORT OF SOCIAL COHESION

Alessandro Girola
April 16, 2020

The outbreak of COVID-19, which has now infected over two million people, has resulted in the death of thousands of people worldwide.[3] Well over 100 countries

---

[3] As of early June, 2020, there are almost 6.5 million cases reported in 188 countries).

across the globe have instituted either a partial or full lockdown, affecting billions, and many others have restricted the freedom of movement for some or all of their citizens.

The rapid spread has also made clear how interconnected the world we live in has become, and, at the same time, how interdependent we are. As the virus affects everybody and does not know borders or walls, this crisis is reminding us all of our common humanity, and how our lives are so reliant on reciprocal support. Despite this, COVID-19 is risking undermining the social cohesion within countries, as its impact reaches deep into our society. Increased instances of hate speech and stigmatization of certain groups unjustly perceived to be associated with the spread of the virus have been reported.

This crisis should be a wake-up call to remind global leaders that cooperation and collaboration is crucial and a whole-of-society approach is needed. Ellen Johnson Sirleaf, Nobel Laureate and the President of Liberia during the Ebola outbreak in West Africa in 2014, wrote in a recent open letter to BBC reflecting on the current situation and the lesson learned from the past outbreak: "Fear drove people to run, to hide, to hoard to protect their own when the only solution is and remains based in the community." As we are adjusting to this new normal in the era of the COVID-19, global leaders should recognize that civil society plays a critical role in supporting communities. The work of civil society and grassroots organizations (CSOs), faith-based organizations (FBOs) and youth-led organizations is essential in keeping large marginalized populations connected and informed, particularly at the local level. In many parts of the world, such organizations are among the few that are assisting vulnerable populations and adapting, often in creative ways, responses to the local community context. Since they often serve as one of the main communication channels, they have the potential to support social cohesion, particularly in moments of crisis. During this period, CSOs, FBOs, and youth-led organizations around the globe are supporting volunteerism, running awareness campaigns, contributing to the dissemination of a message of solidarity, and staying at the forefront of keeping communities connected and informed. Now more than ever, their work is essential and must be supported as part of an all-of-society approach needed to beat this pandemic.

Alessandro Girola is a programming coordinator at the United Nations Alliance of Civilizations (UNAOC) in New York City. In his work, he coordinates projects and initiatives focused on preventing intercultural tensions and crises, combatting stereotypes, discrimination and xenophobia, as well supporting innovative grassroots initiatives contributing to intercultural dialogue. After receiving degrees in Economics from Bocconi University and in International Affairs from Columbia University, he gained extensive experience working in the financial sector, academia, and various international organizations, including the African Development Bank and UN Women.

Disclaimer: The views expressed in this piece are my own and do not necessarily represent those of the United Nations.

CONCLUSION

We hope you enjoyed this buffet of thoughtful ideas from world-class thinkers and doers as much as we did. We are extremely grateful to the contributors to this chapter for pushing other commitments to the back burner in order to share their perspectives and wisdom. For health-care workers and those personally affected by COVID-19, this is an incredibly busy and stressful time. We send our heartfelt thanks to the former, our condolences to those who have lost loved ones, and our deep sympathy to those who have lost jobs and income and struggle with basic survival in an economic collapse. Many of us have been quarantined in recent months and given an opportunity to reflect on a great number of issues, including our own lives and purpose. It is our hope that we take advantage of this stillness to consider how we as individuals, leaders, and societies can chart a course of globally cooperative, shared leadership that benefits everyone.

IDENTIFYING WITH LEADERS FROM ANOTHER RACE: THE IMPACT OF PRE-EXISTING LEADERSHIP ASSUMPTIONS AND EYE FIXATIONS

Iain L. Densten

ABSTRACT

This chapter investigated how pre-existing ideas (i.e., prototypes and anti-prototypes) and what the eyes fixate on (i.e., eye fixations) influence followers' identification with leaders from another race. A sample of 55 Southeast Asian female participants assessed their ideal leader in terms of prototypes and antiprototype and then viewed a 27-second video of an engaging Caucasian female leader as their eye fixations were tracked. Participants evaluated the videoed leader using the Identity Leadership Inventory, in terms of four leader identities (i.e., prototypicality, advancement, entrepreneurship, and impresarioship). A series of multiregression models identified participants' age as a negative predictor for all the leader identities. At the same time, the antiprototype of masculinity, the prototypes of sensitivity and dynamism, and the duration of fixations on the right eye predicted at least one leader identity. Such findings build on aspects of intercultural communication relating to the evaluation of global leaders.

Keywords: Global leader behavior; implicit leadership theory; leader identity; eye tracking; nonverbal behavior; Southeast Asia; intercultural communication, Caucasian females

The global leadership literature is evolving from a predominant focus on competencies (Mendenhall et al., 2017; Osland, 2013) to one that examines the

Advances in Global Leadership, Volume 13, 57–83
Copyright © 2020 Emerald Publishing Limited
All rights of reproduction in any form reserved
ISSN: 1535-1203/doi:10.1108/S1535-120320200000013002

influences of cognition and culture (Herman & Zaccaro, 2014). This approach produces a more comprehensive understanding of global leaders in terms of assumptions, beliefs, and expectations (Cotter & Reichard, 2019; Lord & Emrich, 2001). However, individuals typically recall previous judgments of their leadership observations, rather than just actual behaviors (Hastie & Park, 1986). While observed behaviors "are crucial in explaining leadership perceptions" (Lord & Emrich, 2001, p. 32), subsequent reliance on the perceptions of leadership introduces a degree of distortion into any evaluation (Behrendt, Matz, & Göritz, 2017). Preferences introduced by pre-existing leadership ideas and eye movements cause such distortion that influences perception. This chapter investigates how these preferences among female Asian followers influence their evaluation of a Caucasian female leader.

Preferences embedded within visual and cognitive mechanisms act as shortcuts (Chong, Djurdjevic, & Johnson, 2017; Hayward & Ristic, 2017) and enable global leaders and their followers to perceive events by assessing specific cues quickly (Frischen, Bayliss, & Tipper, 2007). These preferences evolved to improve survival (Antonakis & Eubanks, 2017). In terms of leadership, such preferences enable followers to pay particular attention to cues displayed by leaders who successfully coordinated and facilitated group responses to survival challenges (Grabo, Spisak, & van Vugt, 2017). Global leaders need to understand this "cue-process" link within the contextualization of cultural systems to lead effectively in global settings (Curran, 2019). We aim to investigate how such links operate within an interracial and intercultural context to advance global leadership. Specifically, we study how leaders' communication behaviors help to negotiate identities embedded in another race. As a result, we aim to build on a significant global leadership research stream suggested by Chen and Starosta (1998), namely intercultural communication.

We investigate intercultural communication in terms of how selective observations and pre-existing leadership ideas influence the evaluations of individuals who are attempting to lead a group. More specifically, we aim to study how the selective nature of eye fixations and the presence of pre-existing leadership assumptions influence the rating of leaders who lead another race. Our proposed relationship asserts that individuals use visual and cognitive "shortcuts" when they evaluate their leaders. We contend that both eye fixations and pre-existing leadership ideas are a type of "shortcuts" and operate as mechanisms or processes that enable sense-making of the environment to occur. Neither mechanism can provide a complete and objective assessment of everything in the environment (Chong et al., 2017; Rúas Araújo, Puentes-Rivera, & Direito-Rebollal, 2017), but instead seeks to identify the most salient data for individuals to assess. We assert that by investigating the focus of these mechanisms, and how they interrelate critical insights about the assessment of displayed leadership behaviors should emerge.

We recognize that the literature would theoretically support the notion that eye fixations and pre-existing leadership assumptions can independently influence the evaluations of others. For example, eye fixations (a) are the most preeminent source of sensory information (Fernald, 1997), (b) operate primarily as a temporal mechanism that collects specific salient visual information (Rayner, 1998), and (c) enable us to evaluate the interests and intentions of others (Pfeiffer et al., 2012). Pre-existing leadership assumptions provide cognitive structures known as implicit leadership theories (Eden & Leviatan, 1975). Individuals categorize behaviors into leadership types that then inform evaluations and help them determine how much they identify with the leader (Lord & Maher, 1993). We contend that information generated from eye fixations and categorized during cognitive processing influence evaluations. However, previous research has never empirically investigated how both mechanisms together influence the assessment of leaders.

Why should considering the actual behaviors, sensory information, and cognitive structures of observers advance our understanding of leader evaluation? We argue that understanding how and why we select particular events or issues allows for a more comprehensive understanding of leadership in several ways. Firstly, leadership occurs through the presence of traits and behaviors that take the form of verbal and nonverbal communication cues. Observing them in detail facilitates the salient physical or explicit mechanics of leadership to be identified and investigated. Secondly, eye fixations are unobtrusive and accurate measures of cues (Alfandari, Belopolsky, & Olivers, 2019). Thirdly, cognitive structures of observers provide the means to classify patterns of communication cues (Lord, Epitropaki, Foti, & Hansbrough, 2020). They represent the perceptions of leadership (or pre-existing leadership ideas), and thus, the means to separate actual behaviors from perceived behaviors. Therefore, this chapter aims to investigate the prediction of leadership by evaluating observations, through eye fixations and the impact of pre-existing leadership ideas.

We address shortcomings in the literature on eye fixations and leadership in several ways. Firstly, we have narrowed the focus of this chapter to the evaluation of Asian female adult followers and their assessment of a single Caucasian female leader. Such an investigation should help further build our understanding of the female leadership of females from another race. The uniqueness of our sample enables us to begin to (a) address the underrepresentation of female followers and leaders in the leadership literature, (b) investigate followers' evaluations of leaders expected to project more communal traits (Johnson, Murphy, Zewdie, & Reichard, 2008), (c) take into account the pre-existing ideas held by females followers, in terms of their prototypes and antiprototypes (Scott & Brown, 2006), and (d) focus on females who have superior gaze cueing abilities compared to males (Bayliss, Pellegrino, & Tipper, 2005). Further, while previous leadership research has focused on facial expressions of emotions and leadership perceptions (for review, see Trichas, Schyns, Lord, & Hall, 2017), such research has not taken advantage of the highly accurate eye-tracking technology.

Secondly, the integration of eye-tracking and video technology, and subsequent incorporation into the study, enables (a) new, unprecedented access to a dynamic social scene, which is closer to real-life settings (Klin, Jones, Schultz, Volkmar, & Cohen, 2002), (b) the control of the leader and environmental stimuli and thus, ensuring the followers evaluated the same experience (Shondrick, Dinh, & Lord, 2010), and (c) the utilization of a multimethod approach that integrates objective and subjective variables (van Knippenberg & Sitkin, 2013). Thirdly, the study focuses on how observation traits and behaviors can predict leadership, which, according to Lim and Ployhart (2004), has a surprisingly spare body of empirical research. Previous research on face cues (i.e., face-ism) has called for further investigation of moderating conditions and mediating mechanisms (Antonakis & Eubanks, 2017).

LITERATURE REVIEW

Observational leadership research is rare (Cook & Meyer, 2017). Mainstream leadership research still heavily relies on questionnaires to capture leadership behaviors (van Knippenberg & Sitkin, 2013). Such reliance is remarkable since nonverbal communication fuels between 65% and 93% of all human interactions (Birdwhistell, 1970). Only a thin slice or a few seconds of seeing another's nonverbal behaviors is enough for instant and effortless judgments (Tskhay, Xu, & Rule, 2014).

Fundamental to our understanding and application of leadership is the idea that by displaying particular traits and behaviors, individuals can lead others. The observations of leaders and their followers are central and even critical to theoretical development, and the provision of evidence-based leadership advice and guidance. While observations of leaders and followers comprise of both verbal and nonverbal behaviors, individuals have great difficulty in remembering them accurately. As a result, researchers have sought to identify patterns of observations rather than individual traits and behaviors when they develop concepts of leadership (Foti & Hauenstein, 2007). These concepts represent cognitive symbols that have meaning (Podsakoff, MacKenzie, & Podsakoff, 2016) and form the basis for understanding the perception of leadership and the evaluation of leaders (Lord & Maher, 1993).

Leadership concepts are abstract (e.g., charisma) and represent underlying latent variables that have approximate measures of specific salient observable traits and behaviors. Such abstract concepts attempt to mirror how leadership resides in the minds of followers and leaders. A critical challenge within leadership literature is to identify (a) the most salient cues among an almost endless array of appearing and disappearing stimuli and (b) how these cues are cognitively categorized. The use of abstract concepts, rather than directly observed traits and behaviors, enables the introduction of relevant, exciting, and dynamic conceptual ideas into the study of leadership phenomena. For example, transformational leadership, charisma, and social identity leadership are abstract concepts and represent judgments about leaders.

Individuals typically recall previous judgments of their leadership observations, rather than just actual behaviors (Hastie & Park, 1986). Lord and Maher (1991, p. 32) suggest that observed behaviors "are crucial in explaining leadership perceptions." Unfortunately, reliance on the perceptions of leadership introduces a degree of distortion into any evaluation since the perceptions of leadership differ from actual leadership behaviors or cues (Behrendt et al., 2017). Shondrick et al. (2010) suggest that observed leadership behaviors are assimilated immediately into pre-existing leadership ideas during perception. Individuals are more likely to recall and use pre-existing leadership assumptions or implicit leadership theories rather than remembering the actual behaviors.

Leadership Observation

Leaders and followers are not passive observers of verbal and nonverbal cues. They actively process them using "shortcuts" via visual and cognitive mechanisms (Lord, Day, Zaccaro, Avolio, & Eagly, 2017). Reactions to these cues indicate how these visual and cognitive mechanisms are preferentially processing them (Frischen et al., 2007). The link between these cues and mechanisms has evolved to respond to the need for social interactions to survive (Antonakis & Eubanks, 2017).

Grabo et al. (2017) argue that from an evolutionary psychology perspective, our ancestral environment required group responses to increase the likelihood of survival. Thus, the preference for a leader would be for individuals able to successfully coordinate group responses to survival challenges. Therefore, paying attention to individuals whose cues facilitated group responses was essential for followers or group members' survival (van Vugt & Ronay, 2014). We support the idea that successful leadership is perceptible from nonverbal cues in the context of groups. Leaders and followers must continually and dynamically interact with each other to produce successful outcomes (Tskhay et al., 2014). It is implausible to suggest that the survival of followers may be contingent on their ability to identify cues among verbal and nonverbal signals that indicate the leadership potential of others.

Individuals perceive the world within social categories (Turner, 2010), which is the mechanism for determining group membership (Giessner, van Knippenberg, & Sleebos, 2009). Leaders influence this mechanism by how they represent their group and define group membership. After all, several researchers have long suggested that leadership is a group process (for a review see Thomas, Martin, & Riggio, 2013). Leadership effectiveness is contingent on the extent leaders embody attributes, beliefs, and values that make a particular group stand out from other groups (Turner & Haslam, 2001). A shared group identity among followers is a powerful influence on their perceptions, evaluations, and behaviors (Turner, 2010).

Social Identity Theory of Leadership

Social identity explains how people respond to events and people, and thus provides a useful framework to understand diversity in the global workforce. In practical terms, social identity informs leaders how to lead and how others react to them. Social influence is structured by individuals' membership in social groups (Hogg, 2004). The Social Identity Theory of Leadership is emerging as a leading theory that explains the social influence evident in the leader–follower relationship (van Dick et al., 2018).

The social identity process builds and clarifies this premise within the social identity theory of leadership (Haslam, Reicher, & Platow, 2011). This theory attempts to understand the leadership phenomena by examining how leaders create a collective self and identity among their followers (Oc & Bashshur, 2013). Several questions underpin this examination regarding how leaders define "Who are we?" "What do we stand for?" and "How will we progress?" These questions are fundamental to understanding the capacity of leaders to mobilize and shape the energies of potential followers (Steffens, Haslam, Reicher, et al., 2014). A leader who creates a collective self and identity among their followers (Oc & Bashshur, 2013) can galvanize their coordinated efforts and overcome otherwise self-serving motivation. Followers' are more susceptible to the influence of others when they internalize a sense of shared group identity. This type of collective approach places the group process at the cornerstone of the analysis of leadership (Turner & Haslam, 2001).

An essential premise of the social identity theory of leadership is that the subjective "sense of self" among followers operates at varying levels of abstraction (Turner, 2010). Identities range from being a unique individual to a group member (Turner, 2010). In simple terms, people can not only think of themselves as "me" and "you" (i.e., personal identity) but also as members of a group, "we" and "us" (i.e., "social identity," Reicher, Spears, & Haslam, 2010). The adoption of these prosocial behaviors enables individuals to gain positive feelings of worth or to protect or defend the group against threats (Hopkins et al., 2007). Leaders achieve this type of influence by encouraging their followers to adopt prosocial behaviors and categorize themselves as a group member. Followers are more likely to endorse the vision of their leader as "right" and "proper" when they recognize the leader as prototypical of the group (Haslam et al., 2011).

According to Steffens, Haslam, Reicher, et al. (2014, p. 1002), the social identity theory of leadership "is a recursive, multidimensional process that centers on leaders' capacities to represent, advance, create, and embed a shared sense of social identity for group members." This theory builds on substantive research that has investigated how effective leaders create (a) shared understanding (Steffens, Haslam, Kerschreiter, Schuh, & van Dick, 2014), (b) sense-making and giving (Morgeson, DeRue, & Karam, 2010), and (c) collegiality (Druskat & Wheeler, 2003). These leadership approaches build on the social identity theory (Tajfel & Turner, 1979) and self-categorization theory (Turner, 2010), which place group processes at the cornerstone of the analysis.

Recognition creates a sense of social bond, affiliation, or identification between the leader and their follower(s). This bond bestows an ability on these leaders to act and make decisions for the group, and also allows follower members to feel good about those leaders' decisions (Thomas, Amiot, Louis, & Goddard, 2017). When followers identify with their group, they can develop a personal bond with the in-group leader and even attribute charisma to that leader (Steffens, Haslam, & Reicher, 2014). According to Turner (2010), creating a shared identity through self-categorization is the basis for the processes of social influence. Identification occurs when shared group interests are embedded in the characteristics of a particular in-group, which are distinct from other groups. The power of this type of collective orientation is a central premise of social identity analysis of leadership (Grace & Platow, 2015). This orientation entails "deeply meaningful shared experiences, beliefs, values, or goals" that motivate group members, "beyond self-interest to focus on the well-being of a group" (Hickman & Sorenson, 2014, p. 4).

The Identity Leadership Inventory (ILI, Steffens, Haslam, Reicher, et al., 2014) is the predominant instrument that investigates identity within the leadership process. Van Dick et al. (2018) conducted a validity study across 20 countries. They confirmed a four-construct structure, namely, prototypicality (i.e., being one of us), advancement (i.e., doing it for us), entrepreneurship (i.e., crafting a sense of us), and impresarioship (i.e., making us matter). Followers evaluate these ILI leader identities using one of two cognitive processes (Lord & Maher, 1991), namely inference-based processing (Haslam & Platow, 2001) and recognition-based processing (Lord, De Vader, & Alliger, 1986). The latter is related to pre-existing and inherent leadership characteristics (Epitropaki & Martin, 2005).

Implicit Leadership Theories

Recognition-based processes are well established in the implicit leadership theories literature (Lord & Brown, 2004). They represent an essential process in the evaluations of leaders and followers throughout the globe (Lord et al., 2020). Foti, Hansbrough, Epitropaki, and Coyle (2017) review of Implicit Leadership Theory Questionnaire (ILTQ) findings support this recognition-based mechanism existing within either a relational influence process (Riggs & Porter, 2017; Tsai et al., 2017) or a connectionist representation of the ILTQ (Alipour, Mohammed, & Martinez, 2017; Trichas et al., 2017). Further, according to Nichols and Erakovich (2016), recognition-based perceptual processes involve the fit between observed leader behavior and the ILTQ leadership prototypes and antiprototypes held by the observer. Such results provide a stable reference point or benchmark which followers use to evaluate their actual or observed leaders.

The ILTQ assessment is recognition-based and records the personal schemas of followers within the categories of prototypes and antiprototypes (Epitropaki & Martin, 2004). These personal schemas are pre-existing ideas about leadership that are profoundly influential in leadership evaluation, despite being potentially unrelated to what the follower or leader has experienced. ILTQ is the most often used instrument, which consisted of both core prototypic and antiprototypic trait factors. Epitropaki and Martin (2004) tested the generalizability and further developed this ILTQ and produced a shortened version of 21 items and a six-factor structure, which were confirmed in several organizational settings. The leader prototypes are intelligence, sensitivity, dedication, and dynamism, and the antiprototypical are masculinity and tyranny.

A study by Trichas et al. (2017) explored a link between the ILTQ and specific emotions and overall leadership impressions of two leaders using static and dynamic video observations. They found that cognitive processes mediated patterns of traits inferences during brief exposure to the face of leaders. These findings build on a previous study demonstrating that dimensions central to the ILTQ could be inferred from the facial expression of others (Trichas & Schyns, 2012). Facial cues alone are enough to accurately infer the domain (i.e., businessperson, military officer) of a leader. Such an inference is called "face-ism" (Olivola, Eubanks, & Lovelace, 2014).

The Current Study

As previously established, followers throughout the globe evaluate their leaders on their ability to promote specific ILI leader identities, such as prototypicality, advancement, entrepreneurship, and impresarioship. According to the social identity theory of leadership, this is achieved by leaders creating a collective self and identity among their followers (van Knippenberg, van Knippenberg, De Cremer, & Hogg, 2004). The ILI measures four specific identities (Steffens, Haslam, Reicher, et al., 2014). We argue that pre-existing leadership assumptions consisting of prototypes and antiprototypes (Epitropaki & Martin, 2004; Steffens, Haslam, & Reicher, 2014) influence follower inferences or evaluations about these leader identities.

The leader identity of prototypicality represents the unique qualities and attributes that define and differentiate the group and are associated with the leader (Steffens, Haslam, & Reicher, 2014; Steffens, Haslam, Reicher, et al., 2014). Leaders who appear as an ideal member of the group gain influence over the group (Barreto & Hogg, 2017). The implicit leadership prototypes of sensitivity, dedication, intelligence, and dynamism represent highly prized attributes and characteristics in groups throughout the globe (Foti, Hansbrough, Epitropaki, & Coyle, 2014). Leaders perceived as being open and accessible by their followers (e.g., being thoughtful, committed, bright, and enthusiastic) are likely to operationalize the schemas associated with these implicit leadership prototypes. In contrast, leaders who are perceived as being aloof (e.g., being distant and dominant) are more likely to operationalize the schemas associated with the implicit leadership antiprototypes (De Cremer, van Knippenberg, van Dijke, & Bos, 2006). We anticipate that prototypes of sensitivity, dedication, intelligence, and dynamism will increase the leader identities of prototypicality. In contrast, the antiprototypes of masculinity and tyranny should decrease the leader identities of prototypicality. Hence,

H_1: The implicit leadership prototypes of sensitivity, dedication, intelligence, and dynamism for the Asian female followers will positively predict the videoed Caucasian female leader identity of prototypicality.

H_2: The implicit leadership antiprototypes of masculinity and tyranny for the Asian female followers will negatively predict the videoed Caucasian female leader identity of prototypicality.

The leader identity of advancement represents the promotion of core interests, concerns, and ambitions of the group associated with the leader (Steffens, Haslam, Kerschreiter, et al., 2014; Steffens, Haslam, Reicher, et al., 2014). Leaders who champion and promote collective group interests are more likely to be regarded as "true" and "authentic" (Steffens, Mols, Haslam, & Okimoto, 2016). They promote an important collective dimension that influences followers (Gill & Caza, 2018). Leaders who show concern and respect, express support, and look out for the welfare of followers (i.e., consideration, see Tremblay, Gaudet, & Parent-Rocheleau, 2018) are more likely to operationalize the schemas associated with the implicit leadership prototypes. In contrast, perceived disinterested leaders are more likely to operationalize schemas related to implicit leadership anti-prototypes. We anticipate that prototypes of sensitivity, dedication, intelligence, and dynamism will increase the leader identity of advancement, while the antiprototypes of masculinity and tyranny should decrease the leader identity of advancement. Hence,

H_3: The implicit leadership prototypes of sensitivity, dedication, intelligence, and dynamism for the Asian female followers will positively predict the videoed Caucasian female leader identity of advancement.

H_4: The implicit leadership antiprototypes of masculinity and tyranny for the Asian female followers will negatively predict the videoed Caucasian female leader identity of advancement.

The leader identity of entrepreneurship represents the promotion of cohesion and inclusiveness of the group associated with the leader (Steffens, Haslam, Kerschreiter, et al., 2014; Steffens, Haslam, Reicher, et al., 2014). Leaders who emphasize qualities, attributes, and behaviors that feature commonalities are more likely to convince followers they are one of them (Haslam et al., 2011). Thus, leaders who encourage or craft a sense of collective identity among followers (Steffens & Haslam, 2013) are likely to operationalize the schemas associated with the implicit leadership prototype. Alternatively, leaders promoting disagreement and resentment among followers are more likely to operationalize the schemas related to the implicit leadership antiprototype (Schyns & Schilling, 2011). We anticipate that prototypes of sensitivity, dedication, intelligence, and dynamism will increase the leader identity of entrepreneurship. At the same time, the antiprototypes of masculinity and tyranny should decrease the leader identity of entrepreneurship. Hence,

H_5: The implicit leadership prototypes of sensitivity, dedication, intelligence, and dynamism for the Asian female followers will positively predict the videoed Caucasian female leader identity of entrepreneurship.

H_6: The implicit leadership antiprototypes of masculinity and tyranny for the Asian female followers will negatively predict the videoed Caucasian female leader identity of entrepreneurship.

The leader identity of impresarioship represents developing structures, implementing practices, formalizing rituals, and organizing events within the group associated with the leader (Steffens, Haslam, & Reicher, 2014; Steffens, Haslam, Reicher, et al., 2014). Leaders who initiate structure, embed a sense of us among followers, and encourage feelings of worth (Haslam et al., 2011) are likely to operationalize the schemas associated with the implicit leadership prototype. Alternatively, leaders who erode, disable, and destroy structures are more likely to operationalize the schemas related to the implicit leadership antiprototype

(Haslam et al., 2011). We anticipate that prototypes of sensitivity, dedication, intelligence, and dynamism will increase the leader identities of impresarioship. At the same time, the antiprototypes of masculinity and tyranny should decrease the leader identities of impresarioship. Hence,

H_7: The implicit leadership prototypes of sensitivity, dedication, intelligence, and dynamism for the Asian female followers will positively predict the videoed Caucasian female leader identity of impresarioship.

H_8: The implicit leadership antiprototypes of masculinity and tyranny for the Asian female followers will negatively predict the videoed Caucasian female leader identity of impresarioship.

As previously established, observing the face is the most critical class of visual stimuli in our environment (Xiao et al., 2014). The face is a powerful influence on the perceptions of individuals (Olivola et al., 2014). Face to face exchange is central to dyadic and small group leadership because leadership perceptions rely heavily on the face to face processing of social interactions (Lord & Maher, 1991). A one-second exposure to the face of a political leader can produce accurate judgments about competence, intelligence, and leadership (Todorov, Mandisodza, Goren, & Hall, 2005). The duration of eye fixations is related to attention and cognitive processing (Todorov, Olivola, Dotsch, & Mende-Siedlecki, 2015). Thus, we argue that follower inferences or evaluations about these leader identities are influenced by how long their gaze fixates on specific aspects of the leader's face. We anticipate that the duration of fixations on individual facial features will increase the four leader identity scores. Hence,

H_9: The Asian female followers' fixations on the videoed Caucasian female leader's face (i.e., the area of interest (AoI) of the left eye, right eye, nasion, upper nose, lower nose, and upper lip) will positively predict their leader identities of prototypicality, advancement, entrepreneurship, and impresarioship.

METHOD

Participants

This chapter used a convenience sample of 55 female Asian followers from an Australian University located in the Southeast Asian region. Most participants were Chinese (60%) with Indian, Malaysian, and Indonesian, making up the remaining 40%. Overall, the sample is described as local undergraduate students (41.4), postgraduate students (20.7%), academic staff (22.4%), and university professional staff (15.5%). The average age was 26.3 years.

Ethics

Human Research Ethics Committee approved this study, and we followed all principles and guidelines. Signed and dated consent was provided by each participant who, upon completion of the experiment, was paid 15 Malaysian Ringgits/dollars for their involvement.

Materials

We tracked the eye fixations of participants using the Tobii 1750 eye tracker (0.5-degree precision, 17 inches, 50 Hz sample rate, and 1,280 × 1,024 pixels resolution) during a viewing of the 27-second video of a suggested leader. This video and subsequent questionnaires were administered using the Tobii Studio Program. A YouTube video was selected (https://www.youtube.com/watch?v=R1LvH0SXo80) and modified to show 27 seconds out of 4.29 minutes. The video presented a seated Caucasian female leader, whose head, upper body, and arms/hands were visible. She looked directly at the camera and used an engaging style of communication to discuss the importance of reducing procrastination. Her talk attempted to encourage the viewer to stop procrastinating and adopt proactive behaviors. Such a presentation demonstrates a fundamental aspect of leadership, namely consideration, which, according to Judge, Piccolo, and Ilies (2004), is strongly related to leader effectiveness.

The ILTQ (Epitropaki & Martin, 2004) has 21 items. Participants rated the characteristics of their ideal leader on a seven-point Likert scale (1 = "not at all characteristic," 4 = "neutral," 7 = "extremely characteristics," and NR = "not relevant"). This instrument reportedly measures six factors of leader prototypes and leadership antiprototypes. The leader prototypes were (a) sensitivity – (3 items: sincere, helpful, understanding), which had a Cronbach Alpha of 0.71; (b) intelligence – (4 items: intelligent, educated, clever, and knowledgeable) which had a Cronbach Alpha of 0.73; (c) dedication – (3 items: dedicated, motivated, and hardworking), which had a Cronbach Alpha of 0.49; and (d) dynamism – (3 items: energetic, strong, and dynamic), which had a Cronbach Alpha of 0.59. The leadership antiprototypes were (a) tyranny – (6 items: domineering, pushy, manipulative, loud, conceited, and selfish), which had a Cronbach Alpha of 0.77; and masculinity – (2 items: male and masculine), which had a Cronbach Alpha of 0.75.

Participants evaluated the Caucasian female leader on the content and delivery of video using the ILI (Steffens, Haslam, Reicher, et al., 2014), which has four leader identities, namely, prototypicality: being one of us – four items, which had a Cronbach Alpha of 0.82, advancement: doing it for us – four items, Cronbach Alpha of 0.83; entrepreneurship: crafting a sense of us – four items, Cronbach Alpha of 0.85, and impresarioship: making us matter, Cronbach Alpha of 0.87. Participants indicated how representative this leader in the video is of their group. A seven-point Likert scale (1 = "not at all representative" to 7 = "completely representative," and NR = "not relevant") was used to record their responses.

Several demographic control variables were used to examine the sample (i.e., age, education, income, and full/part work experience), and participant types (i.e., undergraduate, postgraduate, academic, and professional staff). However, age was selected as the most prominent demographic variable because age is a crucial influence on the other demographic variable. For example, younger participants would most likely be among the undergraduate students, have the lowest education qualifications, and have worked less than academics. The other variables do not significantly change the findings.

Procedure

Each experiment occurred in a quiet room with consistent illumination. Participants were first surveyed to ensure their eyes were capable of adequately seeing the screen (Pernice & Nielsen, 2016) and then comfortably seated at a desk, approximately 70 cm from the eye tracker screen, which had a mouse connected to the computer that was running the Tobii Study Program. Each participant was then asked to complete the ILTQ (Epitropaki & Martin, 2004), via 21 questions that individually appeared on the screen, and were answered using a mouse. After completing these items, the eye movements were calibrated for each participant to ensure no error vectors. Then, the participant viewed the 27-second video of the Caucasian female leader. The experiment ended when the participants completed the ILI (Steffens, Haslam, Reicher, et al., 2014) and a short demographic questionnaire. The Tobii Studio Program tracked the eye movements and identified fixations that occurred on five facial regions (i.e., left and right eyes, nasion, upper and lower nose, and upper lip) or AoI. The AoI on each frame of the video was altered to ensure they consistently covered the five facial regions, which resulted in a dynamic AoI, rather than a static AOI.

Planned Statistical Analysis

SPSS 26 was used to analyze the means, standard deviation, reliabilities, and correlations relationships of variables within the study. A series of hierarchical multiple linear regressions then tested the hypotheses whose effect size was examined using f^2 (see Selya, Rose, Dierker, Hedeker, & Mermelstein, 2012). We decided $f^2 = 0.30$ suggests a medium-large effect (Cohen, 1988).

RESULTS

Descriptive Statistics

Table 1 identified a range of means for the ILI leader identities and ILTQ prototypes and antiprototypes, which are consistent with previous studies (Steffens, Haslam, Reicher, et al., 2014). The magnitudes of the duration of the fixations on the AoI (i.e., five facial features) are also consistent with the expected cultural background of the followers of East Asian culture. For example, fixations on the eyes had the lowest means among all the facial features, which suggest a degree of direct eye contact avoidance by the followers. The avoidance of looking directly in the eye of others and the belief that excessive eye contact is impolite is characteristic of individuals from an East Asian culture (Sue & Sue, 1990).

Hierarchical Multiple Linear Regression

Table 2 shows four hierarchical multiple regression models. These models predict ILI leader identities based on ILTQ leadership prototypes and antiprototypes, and eye-tracking fixation durations on AoI among 55 Asian female followers. The selected background variable of age was a unique predictor of the four ILI leader identities: prototypicality ($\beta = -48, p < 0.001$), advancement ($\beta = -0.28, p < 0.05$),

Table 1 Means, Standard Deviation, and Correlations for Asian Participants (n=58)

Factors	M	SD	1	2	3	4	5	6	7	8	9	10	11	12	13	14	15	16
1. Age	26.30																	
Leader Identities																		
2. Prototypicality	4.51	1.09	−.35**															
3. Advancement	4.67	1.17	−.20	.66**														
4. Entrepreneurship	4.91	1.01	−.28*	.59**	.70**													
5. Impresarioship	4.49	1.30	−.27**	.73**	.77**	.55**												
Implicit Leadership Traits																		
6. Sensitivity	6.18	.84	−.08	.48**	.25	.14	.31*											
7. Dedication	6.45	.57	.08	.23	.17	.02	.21	.60**										
8. Intelligence	6.01	.67	.13	.19	.12	.14	.13	.31*	.38**									
9. Dynamism	3.43	1.15	.19	.17	.33*	.29*	.32*	.36**	.41**	.63**								
10. Masculinity	2.71	1.48	.22	−.16	−.33**	−.28**	−.19	−.24	−.17	.04	.02							
11. Tyranny	6.03	.80	.07	−.07	−.14	−.01	.05	−.35**	−.16	.21	.27*	.30*						
Fixation Durations on Area of Interest																		
12. Eye Left	.97	.86	−.13	.11	.08	.05	.05	.23	.18	.27*	.19	−.18	−.14					
13. Eye Right	1.19	1.27	.03	.05	.30*	.21	.41**	−.20	−.30	−.13	.06	.17	.18	−.02				
14. Nasion	1.74	1.81	−.02	.03	−.01	−.04	.06	.09	.07	.11	.02	.17	.02	.11	−.02			
15. Upper Nose	2.46	2.51	.09	.18	.05	.04	.07	.28*	.06	.02	.16	.05	−.08	.03	−.14	.05		
16. Lower Nose	3.15	3.50	.37**	.11	−.04	.04	.07	−.02	.05	−.01	.10	.26	−.01	−.02	−.05	−.01	.15	
17. Upper Lip	3.80	3.58	.29*	−.12	−.14	−.11	−.07	−.19	−.10	−.04	−.06	.06	.28*	.05	−.11	−.14	−.15	.11

Note: *. <.05; **. <.01; ***<.001, Leader identity prototypicality = being one of us, Leader identity advancement = doing it for us, Leader identity entrepreneurship = crafting a sense of us, and Leader identity impresarioship = making us matter

Table 2 Multiple regressions for Age, Leader Identities, Implicit Leadership Traits, and Fixations Duration on AoI (n=58)

	Prototypicality			Advancement			Entrepreneurship			Impresarioship		
	Model 1	Model 2	Model 3	Model 1	Model 2	Model 3	Model 1	Model 2	Model 3	Model 1	Model 2	Model 3
Demographic												
Age	−.35**	−.32**	−.48***	−.20	−.19	−.28*	−.28*	−.30*	−.44**	−.27*	−.29*	−.49***
Implicit Leadership Traits												
Sensitivity		.50***	.45**		−.19	.03		−.03	−.05		.21	.16
Dedication		−.06	.03		.06	.10		−.19	−.10		.02	.21
Intelligence		.08	.23		−.13	.02		−.02	.113		−.15	.08
Dynamism		−.01	−.11		.46**	.33		.48***	.39*		.36*	.19
Masculinity		−.01	−.13		−.29*	−.39**		−.23	−.34*		−.11	−.26*
Tyranny		.11	.07		−.02	−.08		−.09	−.15		.11	−.02
Fixation Durations on AoI												
Left eye			−.12			−.14			−.17			−.21
Right eye			.25*			.44**			.29*			.62***
Nasion			.03			.08			.05			.14
Upper nose			.13			.09			.07			.12
Lower nose			.32***			.12			.24			.27**
Upper lip			.12			.09			.11			.24*
R^2 Adjusted	.10	.25	.32	.02	.18	.27	.06	.18	.21	.06	.17	.49
d.f.	57	57	57	57	57	57	57	57	57	57	57	57
F	7.66**	3.72**	3.06**	2.22	2.82*	2.61**	4.74*	2.77**	2.17**	4.45*	2.62*	5.26***
Dublin			2.50			2.43			2.34			2.52
f^2			.47			.73			.57			.96

Note: * <.05, ** <.01, *** <.001; AoI = Area of interest; Leader identity prototypicality = being one of us, Leader identity advancement = doing it for us, Leader identity entrepreneurship = crafting a sense of us, and Leader identity impresarioship = making us matter entrepreneurship ($\beta = -44$, $p < 0.01$), and impresarioship ($\beta = -0.49$, $p < 0.001$). In other words, the older the participants, the less likely they were to consider the videoed leader to be representative of them.

The leadership prototype of sensitivity was a unique predictor of a single ILI leader identity: prototypicality ($\beta = 0.50$, $p < 0.001$). In other words, the more participants recognized the leadership prototype of sensitivity as being characteristic of their ideal leader, the more they would infer the videoed leader was being one of us. The leadership prototype of dynamism was a unique predictor of a single ILI leader identity: entrepreneurship ($\beta = 0.39$, $p < 0.05$). In other words, the more participants recognized the leadership prototype of dynamism as being characteristic of their ideal leader, the more they would infer the videoed leader was crafting a sense of us. The leadership antiprototype of masculinity was a negative predictor of advancement ($\beta = -0.39$, $p < 0.01$), entrepreneurship ($\beta = -34$, $p < 0.05$), and impresarioship ($\beta = -0.26$, $p < 0.05$). In other words, the more participants recognized the leadership antiprototype of masculinity as being characteristic of their ideal leader, the less they would infer the videoed leader was doing it for us, crafting a sense of us, and making us matter. The leadership prototypes of dedication, intelligence, and tyranny were not unique predictors of any ILI factor.

The right eye (AoI) was a unique predictor of all four ILI leader identities: prototypicality ($\beta = 0.25$, $p < 0.05$), advancement ($\beta = 0.44$, $p < 0.01$), entrepreneurship ($\beta = 0.29$, $p < 0.05$), and impresarioship ($\beta = 0.62$, $p < 0.01$). In other words, the more participants fixated on the right eye of the videoed leader, the more they would infer this leader was being one of us, doing it for us, crafting a sense of us, and making us matter. The lower nose (AoI) was a unique predictor of two ILI leader identities: prototypicality ($\beta = 0.32$, $p < 0.001$) and impresarioship ($\beta = 0.27$, $p < 0.01$). In other words, the more participants fixated on the lower nose of the videoed leader, the more they would infer this leader was being one of us and making us matter. The upper lip (AoI) was a unique predictor of a single ILI leader identity: impresarioship ($\beta = 0.24$, $p < 0.01$). In other words, the more participants fixated on the upper lip of the videoed leader, the more they would infer this leader was making us matter.

DISCUSSION

This chapter supports the findings of Tavares, Sobral, Goldszmidt, and Araújo (2018) that all prototypes are not of equal importance or receive the same distinct weighing in the formation of recognition-based leadership perceptions. Such a heterogeneous relationship is an intercultural communication challenge for global leaders.

Prototypes

In detail, sensitivity was the highest predictor for all the implicit leadership prototypes, but only positively predicted one of the four leader identity, i.e., prototypicality (H_1).

Such a prediction is not surprising. Sensitivity involves the leader being sympathetic, sensitive, compassionate, understanding, sincere, warm, forgiving, and helpful (see Johnson et al., 2008). These characteristics promote identity by encouraging the formation of relationships, emphasize harmony, seek affiliation, and thus, enable leaders to be recognized as representing their group (Steffens, Haslam, Reicher, et al., 2014). We suggest that the leader's display of "helping others" cues within the video is most likely the stimulus recognized and classified by the followers. Previous research has established that "helping others," functions as a significant identity-affirming process, i.e., "this is who we are," (Harth, Leach, & Kessler, 2013), and builds a socially defined shared sense of "us" (Reicher, Haslam, & Hopkins, 2005). Such identity-defining cues may explain the underlying behavioral links or triggers between events in the video and the subsequent leader evaluations.

Showing sensitivity toward followers is a people-oriented leadership approach in a variety of global settings, where leaders demonstrate concerns for the feelings of followers and treat them with respect. Previous leadership research would classify these behaviors as consideration, which has been a widely accepted pillar of leadership for some time (Judge et al., 2004). Being sensitive to situational and interpersonal cues indicates a high self-monitoring individual (Foti & Hauenstein, 2007) who can emerge as a leader (Zaccaro, Foti, & Kenny, 1991). In conclusion, the prototype of sensitivity appears to be implementing a principle of social identity leadership, which is the need to be perceived as an in-group prototype. In other words, being sensitive to others may enable a "person-centered" approach and self-sacrificial persona to be perceived (De Cremer et al., 2006).

The behaviors displayed by the Caucasian female leader appear to tap into the importance followers implicitly place on leaders acting sensitively. Such behaviors may represent the prototypicality of how a leader promotes group survival among southeast Asian followers. Such a unique finding raises a fundamental question as to why the leader prototype of sensitivity does not predict any of the other ILI leader identities. Previously, Johnson et al. (2008) classified sensitivity as a communal prototype. Thus, leaders who provide group-specific cues should be more likely recognized as doing it for us, crafting a sense of us, and making us matter.

The leadership prototype of dynamism was a positive predictor of the leader identity, entrepreneurship. This finding suggests that leaders who match their follower's prototype of being "dynamic" are associated more with the leader identity of entrepreneurship (H_5). Leaders who are perceived as dynamic can utilize emotional contagion processes that encourage others to idealize them (Bono & Ilies, 2006), and express emotions to influence their followers (Sy, Choi, & Johnson, 2013). The use of behaviors that elicit emotions is an essential skill for leaders to manage receptivity, mobilization, and learning aspects of teams and organizations (Huy, 1999). In conclusion, the leadership prototype of dynamism appears to be implementing a principle of social identity leadership, which is the need to behave in ways that advance the interests of the group (Haslam et al., 2011).

Antiprototypes

This chapter partially supported H_4, H_6, and H_8, which suggested that the implicit leadership antiprototypes would negatively predict the ILI leader identities. Specifically, the implicit leadership antiprototype of masculinity was a negative predictor of three leader identities. In contrast, the implicit leadership antiprototype of tyranny did not predict any leader identities. Interestingly, behaviors associated with these antiprototypes, such as threats, intimidation, punishment, hostility, obstructiveness, maleness, and assertiveness (Schyns & Schilling, 2011), did not explicitly appear in the video. Both antiprototypes are assessing agentic expectations (Johnson et al., 2008) about the motivation for power and control over others, assertiveness, efficacy, and mastery of leaders (De Cremer et al., 2006). Only masculinity predicted the three leader identities (i.e., advancement, entrepreneurship, and impresarioship), which is intriguing. These findings challenge the status of masculinity as being of low importance (Epitropaki & Martin, 2004) or lacking significance (Riggs & Porter, 2017) within a global context.

The implicit leadership antiprototype of masculinity taps into behaviors associated with defending one's own beliefs, being independent, and acting assertively (e.g., Bem, 1981). Previous studies have linked masculinity with events such as leader emergence (Kent & Moss, 1994) and managerial advancement (Marongiu & Ekehammar, 1999). A metaanalysis by Koenig, Eagly, Mitchell, and Ristikari (2011) supports a relationship between masculinity and leadership. However, such findings do not explain why masculinity is acting as a negative predictor of these leader identities. Perhaps the answers lay in how the leader identities operate at the group level (see Turner, 1991). Fears about masculinity are detrimental to shared interests or group survival. They are foremost in the minds of followers. Such findings raise an interesting question. Specifically, what happens when female Caucasian leaders display masculine behaviors and tap into these pre-existing implicit fears among East Asian female followers?

Eye Tracking

This chapter partially supported H_9. That is, the duration of eye fixations on the leader's face would predict several ILI leader identities. Specifically, followers' fixation durations on the videoed leader's right eye (AoI) was a predictor of the four leader identities (i.e., prototypicality, advancement, entrepreneurship, and impresarioship). Such a finding suggests that the tone or style (i.e., caring) of the videoed leader is matching the attention preference of their followers (Glaholt & Reingold, 2012), and thus influencing the cognitive processing of the message (Mele, Federici, & Dennis, 2014). The dominance of the followers' fixation on the leader's right eye over the left eye in this chapter confirms a left perceptual bias among followers (Williams, Grealy, Kelly, Henderson, & Butler, 2016). This bias occurs as a reflex response when viewing faces (Leonards & Scott-Samuel, 2005).

Interestingly, the predictive power of the right eye (AoI) fixation did vary across the four leader identities. This finding suggests that followers are linking different attributes to each leader identity based upon seconds of exposure to the videoed leader. Such links can have important ramifications or associations with critical group outcomes. For example, the followers' fixation duration on the videoed leader's right eye was the highest predictor for the leader identity of impresarioship. Thus, fixations associated with followers inferring their leader is making us matter may recognize leaders developing a shared identity, in terms of creating social building blocks (Putnam, Roman, Zimmerman, & Gothard, 2016) that produce a team identity (Steffens, Haslam, & Reicher, 2014).

The followers' fixation durations on the videoed leader's right eye (AoI) were the second-highest predictor for the leader identity of advancement. Hence, fixations associated with followers inferring their leader is doing it for us may recognize leaders as acting reasonably and appropriately (De Cremer et al., 2006), which enables the maintenance of social groups (Ikanga, Hill, & MacDonald, 2017). The followers' fixation durations on the videoed leader's right eye (AoI) were the third-highest predictor for the leader identity of entrepreneurship. Accordingly, fixations associated with followers inferring their leader is crafting a sense of us may recognize leaders as actively shaping social identities (Haslam et al., 2011) that emphasizes how changes will be viable, successful, and beneficial for them (Ullrich, Wieseke, & Dick, 2005). The followers' fixation durations on the videoed leader's right eye (AoI) were the fourth-highest predictor for the leader identity of proto-typicality. Consequently, fixations associated with followers inferring leaders as being one of us may recognize leaders role modeling activities (van Dick & Kerschreiter, 2016) and their identification as a leader (Schuh et al., 2012).

The fixation durations of the videoed leader's lower nose and upper lip (AoIs) predicted specific leader identities, namely prototypicality and impresarioship. The lower nose uniquely indicates where a leader is looking and the focus of their attention (Driver et al., 1999). Such attention or eye time may demonstrate to the follower their leader's priorities and preparedness to sacrifice their resources (e.g., time and responsiveness). Consequently, the leader's identities of being one of us and making us matter appeared linked to the priorities and sacrifices of leaders.

The fixation duration on the videoed leader's upper lip (AoI) was a unique predictor of the leader identity of impresarioship. Such fixations help followers identify the emotional state of the leader may be experiencing, e.g., joy, disgust, fear, anger, sadness, and shame (Schurgin et al., 2014). How well leaders and followers govern their emotions influence the motivation to affiliate with each other. Leaders who demonstrate a desire to affiliate with their followers are more likely to gain an identity of making us matter.

Finally, this chapter identified the importance of follower's age in the prediction of videoed leader's identity among all the ILI leader identities of prototypicality, advancement, entrepreneurship, and impresarioship. Such a finding supports previous studies that have highlighted the role of age in (a) spontaneous categorizing (Cañadas, Lupiáñez, Kawakami, Niedenthal, & Rodriguez-Bailon, 2016), stereotyping, and leader prototyping (Koenig et al., 2011), (b) acting as social influence, similar to how leaders socially display self-confidence, credibility, competence, bearing, and demeanor (van Dick et al., 2018), and (c) determining the strength of social influence (Podsakoff & Schriescheim, 1985). Previous global leadership research appears to have ignored the impact that age differences between a leader and follower have for intercultural leadership communication competencies (Tucker, Bonial, Vanhove, & Kedharnath, 2014).

Global Leadership Implications

This chapter answers the call for more novel forms of empirical global leadership research (Reiche, Mendenhall, Szkudlarek, & Osland, 2019). Eye tracking enables the nature of eye movements and subsequent performance to be objectively understood (Panchuk, Vine, & Vickers, 2015). Such methods uniquely allow the impact of very short exposures to global leaders to be investigated in detail, and the investigation of moderating and mediating variables. These types of exposure were powerful enough to enable inferences about leader identity to be recorded by participants. Such evaluations were found to be influenced by implicit leadership theories; however, such relationships were found to be heterogeneous, which may explain why intercultural communication can be a disorienting experience for global leaders (see Ensign, 2019).

Cotter and Reichard (2019) established the link between crucial psychological resources and successful cross-cultural interactions. Such a connection may explain why the prototype of sensitivity is a strong predictor for the leader identity of prototypicality. Perhaps, sensitivity is an attribute or prototype of a successful global leader with psychological resources. Luthans and Youssef-Morgan (2017) suggest that these psychological resources include cross-cultural hope, efficacy, resilience, and optimism. Consequently, leader identity may act as an underlying pathway or social mechanism linking psychological resources to successful cultural interactions. The same logic may explain why masculinity had the opposite relationship. That is, masculinity acts as a negative stimulus, which Cameron (2008) suggests involves threat and deficiency needing to be urgently addressed and resolved.

The context of this chapter is central to understanding the implications of the findings, and thus appreciating the cultural background of the followers and the leader is critical. The leader depicted in the video comes from a Western culture. Individuals from such cultures are generally quite comfortable in establishing mutual gaze and using direct eye contact. Both methods are essential signaling tools for a variety of social information (Kleinke, 1986). As a Westerner, the leader expresses the uniqueness of her identity in how she conveys her thinking and signaling how she is feeling (Kim & Sherman, 2007). These cultural characteristics are readily apparent from the video and provide underlying or contextual information about the leader from which the followers' draw inferences about how much she identifies with their group. Thus, the cultural background of the leader could influence the inference-based cognitive processes of the followers.

The alternative cognitive process is a recognition-based process, which is likely to be influenced by the cultural background of the followers, who in this chapter come from an East Asian culture. Followers of such a culture are socialized "not to stick out," control the expression of their thoughts, and suppress the signaling of their feelings to preserve harmonious relationships with others (Kim & Markus, 1999). "Culture is an effective agent that influences" (Vogeley & Roepstorff, 2009, p. 513) these individuals, resulting in an interplay between Western and East Asian cultures within this type of interpersonal communication. The pivotal contextual role that culture plays (see Gobel, Chen, & Richardson, 2017) may be evident in the video. The leaders from a Western culture use direct eye contact to signal interest, attentiveness, and respect (Kleinke, 1986). By contrast, the followers from East Asian culture respectfully respond by avoiding or reducing direct eye contact (Sue & Sue, 1990). Such an observation could explain why the duration of both eye fixations is relatively small compared to the other facial fixation duration.

Limitations

This chapter has several limitations. Firstly, while the 27-second video was realistic, the video did depict an artificial social context to examine the leader evaluation. However, the video is viewed via a computer screen, which is very similar to how individuals experience virtual meetings and calls, which are the norm in most workplaces and homes. We believe that the benefit of being able to provide a replicable leadership experience outweighs the limitations of video usage. Secondly, the followers were unable to influence the natural reactions or experience reciprocal results with the depicted leader in the video (Mohan & Lee, 2019). Technology that enables videos to respond to the viewers is not yet available. However, the video allowed us to overcome the limitations of retrospection, unspecified time frames, and person-whole approach. According to Hunter, Bedell-Avers, and Mumford (2007), these limitations severely inhibit temporal inferences and, thereby, causality.

Thirdly, a larger sample size than 55 participants from different cultures, regions, and with different demographics (e.g., males) would have provided greater generalizability of these results. However, the sample size achieved was almost twice as large as many leading studies (see Loos & Bergstrom, 2014). A key strength of this research is its focus on a specific and underrepresented segment of the population. It is also worth highlighting again that the followers are rating the same leader and their behavior, rather than different leaders. Fourthly, the study did specify only a general group (i.e., undergraduate, postgraduate, academic, and professional staff) for each follower to belong. However, further refinement of each group would produce greater complexity and requires more retrospective analysis (e.g., group relevance, previous experience, and role with the assigned group).

Future Research

The future for eye-tracking leadership research is very bright, with a few studies published (Densten & Borrowman, 2017). Thus, the field is pristine and ready for exploration. We suggest that future studies should integrate other research methods (e.g., biological responses), and use multimethod research approaches that measure different facets, manifestations, and functions of the brain (Christopoulos, Uy, & Yap, 2016). The use of eye-tracking technology and video enables the collection of significantly more data than traditional methods, which presents a significant challenge for future researchers. Eye tracking allows us to access the "language of the eyes" (Frischen et al., 2007, p. 694). Future research needs to build a robust dictionary to help others interpret and advance our understanding of the leadership perceptions in the global environment.

CONCLUSION

This chapter scratches the surface of how pre-existing leadership assumptions and eye fixations influence follower identification with their leaders. The findings of this study demonstrate some of the difficulties involved in intercultural communication and the accurate evaluation of global leaders. The study also builds on the appreciation that individuals have mechanisms that enable them to recognize leadership suitability quickly, and the face serves as a highly diagnostic tool to identify leadership. The study demonstrates that during social interactions, the eyes convey a wealth of information about their direction of attention, emotional, and mental states, which mirror perceptional processes. Finally, this study demonstrates the capacity of eye-tracking technology to provide new and exceptionally accurate insights into the global leadership phenomena. Furthermore, the study builds our understanding of the gap between perceptions and reality in cross-cultural contexts. We hope this study encourages others to incorporate this new technology into global leadership research.

REFERENCES

Alfandari, D., Belopolsky, A. V., & Olivers, C. N. L. (2019). Eye movements reveal learning and information-seeking in attentional template acquisition. *Visual Cognition, 27*(5–8), 467–486. doi:10.1080/13506285.2019.1636918

Alipour, K. K., Mohammed, S., & Martinez, P. N. (2017). Incorporating temporality into implicit leadership and followership theories: Exploring inconsistencies between time-based expectations and actual behaviors. *The Leadership Quarterly, 28*(2), 300–316. doi:10.1016/j.leaqua.2016.11.006

Antonakis, J., & Eubanks, D. L. (2017). Looking leadership in the face. *Current Directions in Psychological Science, 26*(3), 270–275. doi:10.1177/0963721417705888

Barreto, N. B., & Hogg, M. A. (2017). Evaluation of and support for group prototypical leaders: A meta-analysis of twenty years of empirical research. *Social Influence, 12*(1), 41–55. doi:10.1080/15534510.2017.1316771

Bayliss, A. P., Pellegrino, G. D., & Tipper, S. P. (2005). Sex differences in eye gaze and symbolic cueing of attention. *Quarterly Journal of Experimental Psychology, 58A*(4), 631–650. doi:10.1080/02724980443000124

Behrendt, P., Matz, S., & Göritz, A. S. (2017). An integrative model of leadership behavior. *The Leadership Quarterly, 28*(1), 229–244. doi:10.1016/j.leaqua.2016.08.002

Bem, S. L. (1981). Gender schema theory: A cognitive account of sex typing. *Psychological Review, 88*(4), 354–364. doi:10.1037/0033-295X.88.4.354

Birdwhistell, R. L. (1970). Masculinity and femininity as display. In *Kinesics and context: Essays on body motion*. Philadelphia, PA: Pennsylvania University Press.

Bono, J. E., & Ilies, R. (2006). Charisma, positive emotions and mood contagion. *The Leadership Quarterly, 17*, 317–334.

Cameron, K. S. (2008). Paradox in positive organizational change. *The Journal of Applied Behavioral Science, 44*(1), 7–24. doi:10.1177/0021886308314703

Cañadas, E., Lupiáñez, J., Kawakami, K., Niedenthal, P. M., & Rodriguez-Bailon, R. (2016). Perceiving emotions: Cueing social categorization processes and attentional control through facial expressions. *Cognition & Emotion, 30*(6), 1149–1163. doi:10.1080/02699931.2015.1052781

Chen, G. M., & Starosta, W. J. (1998). *Foundations of intercultural communication*. Boston, MA: Allyn & Bacon.

Chong, S., Djurdjevic, E., & Johnson, R. E. (2017). Implicit measures for leadership research. In B. Schyns, R. J. Hall, & P. Neves (Eds.), *Handbook of methods in leadership research* (pp. 13–47). Cheltenham: Edward Elgar Publishing.

Christopoulos, G. I., Uy, M. A., & Yap, W. J. (2016). The body and the brain: Measuring skin conductance responses to understand the emotional experience. *Organizational Research Methods, 16*, 1–27. doi:10.1177/1094428116681073

Cohen, J. (1988). *Statistical power analysis for the behavioral sciences* (2nd ed.). Hillsdale, NJ: Lawerance Erlbaum Association.

Cook, A., & Meyer, B. (2017). Assessing leadership behavior with observational and sensor-based methods: A brief overview. In B. Schyns, R. J. Hall, & P. Neves (Eds.), *Handbook of methods in leadership research* (pp. 73–102). Cheltenham: Edward Elgar Publishing.

Cotter, K. C., & Reichard, R. J. (2019). Developing cultural competence through engagement in cross-cultural Interactions. In J. S. Osland, S. Reiche, B. Szkudlrek, & M. E. Mendenhall (Eds.), *Advances in global leadership*, (Vol. 12, pp. 49–78). Bingley: Emerald Publishing Limited.

Curran, K. A. (2019). Global identity tensions for global leaders. In J. S. Osland, S. Reiche, B. Szkudlrek, & M. E. Mendenhall (Eds.), *Advances in global leadership* (Vol. 12, pp. 109–123). Bingley: Emerald Publishing Limited.

De Cremer, D., van Knippenberg, D., van Dijke, M., & Bos, A. E. R. (2006). Self-sacrificial leadership and follower self-esteem: When collective identification matters. *Group Dynamics: Theory, Research, and Practice, 10*(3), 233–245. doi:10.1037/1089-2699.10.3.233

Densten, I. L., & Borrowman, L. (2017). Does the implicit models of leadership influence the scanning of other-race faces in adults? *PLoS One, 12*(7), 1–15. doi:10.1371/journal.pone.0179058

Driver, J., Davis, G., Ricciardelli, P., Kidd, P., Maxwell, E., & Baron-Cohen, S. (1999). Gaze perception triggers reflexive visuospatial orienting. *Visual Cognition, 6*(5), 509–540. doi: 10.1080/135062899394920

Druskat, V. U., & Wheeler, J. V. (2003). Managing from the boundary: The effective leadership of self-managing work teams. *Academy of Management Journal, 46*(4), 435–457. doi:10.2307/30040637

Eden, D., & Leviatan, U. (1975). Implicit leadership theory as a determinant of the factor structure underlying supervisory behavior scales. *Journal of Applied Psychology, 60*(6), 736–741. doi: 10.1037/0021-9010.60.6.736

Ensign, T. G. (2019). Triggers of transformative learning in global leadership development: The disorientation index. In J. S. Osland, S. Reiche, B. Szkudlrek, & M. E. Mendenhall (Eds.), *Advances in global leadership*, (Vol. 12, pp. 125–150). Bingley: Emerald Publishing Limited.

Epitropaki, O., & Martin, R. (2004). Implicit leadership theories in applied settings: Factor structure, generalizability, and stability over time. *Journal of Applied Psychology, 89*(2), 293–310. doi: 10.1037/0021-9010.89.2.293

Epitropaki, O., & Martin, R. (2005). From ideal to real: A longitudinal study of the role of implicit leadership theories on leader-member exchanges and employee outcomes. *Journal of Applied Psychology, 90*(4), 659–676.

Fernald, R. D. (1997). The evolution of eyes. *Brain, Behavior and Evolution, 50*(4), 253–259. doi: 10.1159/000113339

Foti, R. J., & Hauenstein, N. M. A. (2007). Pattern and variable approaches in leadership emergence and effectiveness. *Journal of Applied Psychology, 92*(2), 347–355. doi:10.1037/0021-9010.92.2.347

Foti, R. J., Hansbrough, T. K., Epitropaki, O., & Coyle, P. (2014). Special issue: Dynamic viewpoints on implicit leadership and followership theories. *The Leadership Quarterly, 25*(2), 411–412. doi: 10.1016/j.leaqua.2014.02.004

Foti, R. J., Hansbrough, T. K., Epitropaki, O., & Coyle, P. T. (2017). Dynamic viewpoints on implicit leadership and followership theories: Approaches, findings, and future directions. *The Leadership Quarterly, 28*(2), 261–267. doi:10.1016/j.leaqua.2017.02.004

Frischen, A., Bayliss, A. P., & Tipper, S. P. (2007). Gaze cueing of attention: Visual attention, social cognition, and individual differences. *Psychological Bulletin, 133*(4), 694–724. doi:10.1037/0033-2909.133.4.694

Giessner, S. R., van Knippenberg, D., & Sleebos, E. (2009). License to fail? How leader group pro-totypicality moderates the effects of leader performance on perceptions of leadership effec-tiveness. *The Leadership Quarterly, 20*(3), 434–451. doi:10.1016/j.leaqua.2009.03.012

Gill, C., & Caza, A. (2018). An investigation of authentic leadership's individual and group influences on follower responses. *Journal of Management, 44*(2), 530–554. doi:10.1177/0149206314566461

Glaholt, M. G., & Reingold, E. M. (2012). Direct control of fixation times in scene viewing: Evidence from analysis of the distribution of first fixation duration. *Visual Cognition, 20*(6), 605–626. doi: 10.1080/13506285.2012.666295

Gobel, M. S., Chen, A., & Richardson, D. C. (2017). How different cultures look at faces depends on the interpersonal context. *Canadian Journal of Experimental Psychology, 71*(3), 258–265. doi: 10.1037/cep0000119

Grabo, A., Spisak, B. R., & van Vugt, M. (2017). Charisma as signal: An evolutionary perspective on charismatic leadership. *The Leadership Quarterly, 28*(4), 473–485. doi:10.1016/j.leaqua.2017.05.001

Grace, D. M., & Platow, M. J. (2015). Showing leadership by not showing your face: An anonymous leadership effect. *SAGE Open, 5*(1), 1–10. doi:10.1177/2158244014567476

Harth, N. S., Leach, C. W., & Kessler, T. (2013). Guilt, anger, and pride about in-group environmental behavior: Different emotions predict distinct intentions. *Journal of Environmental Psychology, 34*, 18–26. doi:10.1016/j.jenvp.2012.12.005

Haslam, A. S., & Platow, M. J. (2001). The link between leadership and followership: How affirming social identity translates vision into action. *Personality and Social Psychology Bulletin, 27*(11), 1469–1479. doi:10.1177/01461672012711008

Haslam, A. S., Reicher, S. D., & Platow, M. J. (2011). *The new psychology of leadership: Identity, influence and power.* East Sussex: Psychology Press.

Hastie, R., & Park, B. (1986). The relationship between memory and judgment depends on whether the judgment task is memory-based or on-line. *Psychological Review, 93*(3), 258–268. doi:10.1037/0033-295X.93.3.258

Hayward, D. A., & Ristic, J. (2017). Feature and motion-based gaze cueing is linked with reduced social competence. *Scientific Reports, 7*, 44221. doi:10.1038/srep44221

Herman, J. L., & Zaccaro, S. J. (2014). The complex self-concept of the global leader. In J. S. Osland & M. Li (Eds.), *Advances in global leadership* (Vol. 8, pp. 93–111). Bingley: Emerald Publishing Limited.

Hickman, G. R., & Sorenson, G. J. (2014). *The power of invisible leadership: How a compelling common purpose inspires exceptional leadership.* Los Angeles, CA: SAGE.

Hogg, M. A. (2004). Social identity and leadership. In D. M. Messick & R. M. Kramer (Eds.), *The psychology of leadership: New perspectives and research* (pp. 53–80). Mahwah, NJ: Lawrence Erlbaum Associates.

Hopkins, N., Reicher, S., Harrison, K., Cassidy, C., Bull, R., & Levine, M. (2007). Helping to improve the group stereotype: On the strategic dimension of prosocial behavior. *Personality and Social Psychology Bulletin, 33*(6), 776–788. doi:10.1177/0146167207301023

Hunter, S. T., Bedell-Avers, K. E., & Mumford, M. D. (2007). The typical leadership study: Assumptions, implications, and potential remedies. *The Leadership Quarterly, 18*(5), 435–446. doi:10.1016/j.leaqua.2007.07.001

Huy, Q. N. (1999). Emotional capability, emotional intelligence, and radical change. *Academy of Management Review, 24*(2), 325–345. doi:10.5465/amr.1999.1893939

Ikanga, J., Hill, E. M., & MacDonald, D. A. (2017). The conceptualization and measurement of cognitive reserve using common proxy indicators: Testing some tenable reflective and formative models. *Journal of Clinical and Experimental Neuropsychology, 39*(1), 72–83. doi:10.1080/13803395.2016.1201462

Johnson, S. K., Murphy, S. E., Zewdie, S., & Reichard, R. J. (2008). The strong, sensitive type: Effects of gender stereotypes and leadership prototypes on the evaluation of male and female leaders. *Organizational Behavior and Human Decision Processes, 106*(1), 39–60. doi:10.1016/j.obhdp.2007.12.002

Judge, T. A., Piccolo, R. F., & Ilies, R. (2004). The forgotten ones? The validity of consideration and initiating structure in leadership research. *Journal of Applied Psychology, 89*(1), 36–51. doi: 10.1037/0021-9010.89.1.36.

Kent, R. L., & Moss, S. E. (1994). Self-monitoring as a predictor of leader emergence. *Psychological Reports, 66*(3), 875–881. doi:10.2466/pr0.1990.66.3.875

Kim, H. S., & Markus, H. R. (1999). Deviance or uniqueness, harmony or conformity? A cultural analysis. *Journal of Personality and Social Psychology, 77*(4), 785–800. doi:10.1037/0022-3514.77.4.785

Kim, H. S., & Sherman, D. K. (2007). "Express Yourself": Culture and the effect of self-expression on choice. *Journal of Personality and Social Psychology, 92*(1), 1–11. doi:10.1037/0022-3514.92.1.1

Kleinke, C. L. (1986). Gaze and eye contact: A research review. *Psychological Bulletin, 100*(1), 78–100. doi:10.1037/0033-2909.100.1.78

Klin, A., Jones, W., Schultz, R., Volkmar, F., & Cohen, D. (2002). Visual fixation patterns during viewing of naturalistic social situations as predictors of social competence in individuals with autism. *Archives of General Psychiatry, 59*(9), 809–816. doi:10.1001/archpsyc.59.9.809

Koenig, A. M., Eagly, A. H., Mitchell, A. A., & Ristikari, T. (2011). Are leader stereotypes masculine? A meta-analysis of three research paradigms. *Psychological Bulletin, 137*(4), 616–642. doi: 10.1037/a0023557

Leonards, U., & Scott-Samuel, N. E. (2005). Idiosyncratic initiation of saccadic face exploration in humans. *Vision Research, 45*(20), 2677–2684. doi:10.1016/j.visres.2005.03.009

Lim, B. C., & Ployhart, R. E. (2004). Transformational leadership: Relations to the five-factor model and team performance in typical and maximum contexts. *Journal of Applied Psychology, 89*(4), 610–621. doi:10.1037/0021-9010.89.4.610

Loos, E., & Bergstrom, J. R. (2014). Older adults. In J. R. Bergstrom & J. A. Schall (Eds.), *Eye tracking in user experience design* (pp. 313–329). Boston, MA: Morgan Kaufmann.

Lord, R. G., & Brown, D. J. (2004). *Leadership processes and follower self-identity*. London: Lawrence Erlbaum Associates.

Lord, R. G., & Emrich, C. G. (2001). Thinking outside the box by looking inside the box. *The Leadership Quarterly, 11*(4), 551–579. doi:10.1016/S1048-9843(00)00060-6

Lord, R. G., & Maher, K. J. (1991). *Executive leadership and information processing: Linking perceptions and organizational performance*. New York, NY: Routledge, Chapman & Hall.

Lord, R. G., & Maher, K. J. (1993). *Leadership and information processing: Linking perceptions and performance*. London: Routledge.

Lord, R. G., De Vader, C. L., & Alliger, G. M. (1986). A meta-analysis between personality traits and leadership perceptions: An application of validity generalization procedures. *Journal of Applied Psychology, 71*(3), 402–410. doi:10.1037/0021-9010.71.3.402

Lord, R. G., Day, D. V., Zaccaro, S. J., Avolio, B. J., & Eagly, A. H. (2017). Leadership in applied psychology: Three waves of theory and research. *Journal of Applied Psychology, 102*(3), 434–451. doi:10.1037/apl0000089

Lord, R. G., Epitropaki, O., Foti, R. J., & Hansbrough, T. K. (2020). Implicit leadership theories, implicit followership theories, and dynamic processing of leadership information. *Annual Review of Organizational Psychology and Organizational Behavior, 7*(15), 15–26. doi:10.1146/annurev-orgpsych-012119-045434

Luthans, F., & Youssef-Morgan, C. M. (2017). Psychological capital: An evidence-based positive approach. *Annual Review of Organizational Psychology and Organizational Behavior, 4*(1), 339–366. doi:10.1146/annurev-orgpsych-032516-113324

Marongiu, S., & Ekehammar, B. (1999). Internal and external influences on women's and men's entry into management. *Journal of Managerial Psychology, 14*(5), 421–433. doi:10.1108/02683949910277175

Mele, M. L., Federici, S., & Dennis, J. L. (2014). Believing is seeing: Fixation duration predicts implicit negative attitudes. *PLoS One, 9*(8), e105106. doi:10.1371/journal.pone.0105106

Mendenhall, M. E., Osland, J., Bird, A., Oddou, G. R., Stevens, M. J., Maznevski, M. L., & Stahl, G. K. (2017). *Global leadership: Research, practice, and development*. New York, NY: Taylor & Francis.

Mohan, G., & Lee, Y. (2019). Temporal dynamics of collective global leadership and team psychological safety in multinational teams: An empirical investigation. In Y. Lee (Ed.), *Advances in global leadership* (Vol. 12, pp. 29–47). Bingley: Emerald Publishing Limited.

Morgeson, F. P., DeRue, D. S., & Karam, E. P. (2010). Leadership in teams: A functional approach to understanding leadership structures and processes. *Journal of Management, 36*(1), 5–39. doi:10.1177/0149206309347376

Nichols, T. W., & Erakovich, R. (2016). Authentic leadership and implicit theory: A normative form of leadership? *The Leadership & Organization Development Journal, 34*(2), 182–195. doi:10.1108/01437731311321931

Oc, B., & Bashshur, M. R. (2013). Followership, leadership and social influence. *The Leadership Quarterly, 24*(6), 919–934. doi:10.1016/j.leaqua.2013.10.006

Olivola, C. Y., Eubanks, D. L., & Lovelace, J. B. (2014). The many (distinctive) faces of leadership: Inferring leadership domain from facial appearance. *The Leadership Quarterly, 25*(5), 817–834. doi:10.1016/j.leaqua.2014.06.002

Osland, J. S. (2013). An overview of the global leadership literature. In M. E. Mendenhall, J. S. Osland, A. Bird, G. R. Oddou, M. L. Maznevski, M. J. Stevens, & G. K. Stahl (Eds.), *Global leadership: Research, practice, and development* (pp. 40–79). New York, NY: Routledge.

Panchuk, D., Vine, S., & Vickers, J. N. (2015). Eye tracking methods in sport expertise. In J. Baker & D. Farrow (Eds.), *Handbook of sport expertise* (pp. 176–187). New York, NY: Routledge.

Pernice, K., & Nielsen, J. (2016). *Eye tracking methodology: How to conduct and evaluate usability studies using eye tracking.* Fremont, CA: Nielsen Norman Group.

Pfeiffer, U. J., Schilback, L., Jording, M., Timmemans, B., Bente, G., & Vogeley, K. (2012). Eyes on the mind: Investigating the influence of gaze dynamics on the perception of others in real-time social interaction. *Frontiers in Psychology, 3*, 1–11. doi:10.3389/fpsyg.2012.00537

Podsakoff, P. M., & Schriescheim, C. A. (1985). Field studies of French and Raven's bases of power: Critique, reanalysis, and suggestions for future research. *Psychological Bulletin, 97*(3), 387–411. doi:10.1037/0033-2909.97.3.387

Podsakoff, P. M., MacKenzie, S. B., & Podsakoff, N. P. (2016). Recommendations for creating better concept definitions in the organizational, behavioral, and social sciences. *Organizational Research Methods, 19*(2), 159–203. doi:10.1177/1094428115624965

Putnam, P. T., Roman, J. M., Zimmerman, P. E., & Gothard, K. M. (2016). Oxytocin enhances gaze-following responses to videos of natural social behavior in adult male rhesus monkeys. *Psychoneuroendocrinology, 72*, 47–53. doi:10.1016/j.psyneuen.2016.05.016

Rayner, K. (1998). Eye movements in reading and information processing: 20 years of research. *Psychological Bulletin, 124*(3), 372–422. doi:10.1037/0033-2909.124.3.372

Reiche, B. S., Mendenhall, M., Szkudlarek, B., & Osland, J. (2019). Global leadership research: Where do we go from here? In J. S. Osland, B. S. Reiche, B. Szkudlarek, & E. Mendenhall Mark (Eds.), *Advances in global leadership* (Vol. 12, pp. 211–234). Bingley: Emerald Publishing Limited.

Reicher, S., Haslam, A. S., & Hopkins, N. (2005). Social identity and the dynamics of leadership: Leaders and followers as collaborative agents in the transformation of social reality. *The Leadership Quarterly, 16*(4), 547–568. doi:10.1016/j.leaqua.2005.06.007

Reicher, S., Spears, R., & Haslam, A. S. (2010). The social identity approach in social psychology. In M. Wetherell & C. T. Mohanty (Eds.), *Sage identities handbook* (pp. 45–62). London: Sage.

Riggs, B. S., & Porter, C. O. L. H. (2017). Are there advantages to seeing leadership the same? A test of the mediating effects of LMX on the relationship between ILT congruence and employees' development. *The Leadership Quarterly, 28*(2), 285–299. doi:10.1016/j.leaqua.2016.10.009

Rúas Araújo, X., Puentes-Rivera, I., & Direito-Rebollal, S. (2017). Eye tracking: Methodological and theoretical review. In F. Freire, X. Rúas Araújo, F. V. Martínez, & X. García (Eds.), *Media and metamedia management. Advances in intelligent systems and computing* (Vol. 503, pp. 317–322). Cham: Springers International Publishing.

Schuh, S. C., Zhang, X.-A., Egold, N. W., Graf, M. M., Pandey, D., & van Dick, R. (2012). Leader and follower organizational identification: The mediating role of leader behavior and implications for follower OCB. *Journal of Occupational and Organizational Psychology, 85*(2), 421–432. doi:10.1111/j.2044-8325.2011.02044.x

Schurgin, M. W., Nelson, J., Iida, S., Ohira, H., Chiao, J. Y., & Franconeri, S. L. (2014). Eye movements during emotion recognition in faces. *Journal of Vision, 14*(13), 1–16. doi:10.1167/14.13

Schyns, B., & Schilling, J. (2011). Implicit leadership theories: Think leader, think effective? *Journal of Management Inquiry, 20*(2), 141–150. doi:10.1177/1056492610375989

Scott, K. A., & Brown, D. J. (2006). Female first, leader second? Gender bias in the encoding of leadership behavior. *Organizational Behavior and Human Decision Processes, 101*(2), 230–242. doi:10.1016/j.obhdp.2006.06.002

Selya, A. S., Rose, J. S., Dierker, L. C., Hedeker, D., & Mermelstein, R. J. (2012). A practical guide to calculating Cohen's f2, a measure of local effect size, from PROC MIXED. *Frontiers in Psychology, 3*(APR), 1–6. doi:10.3389/fpsyg.2012.00111

Shondrick, S. J., Dinh, J. E., & Lord, R. G. (2010). Developments in implicit leadership theory and cognitive science: Applications to improving measurement and understanding alternatives to hierarchical leadership. *The Leadership Quarterly, 21*(6), 959–978. doi:10.1016/j.leaqua.2010.10.004

Steffens, N. K., & Haslam, S. A. (2013). Power through 'us': Leaders' use of we-referencing language predicts election victory. *PLoS One, 8*(10), e77952. doi:10.1371/journal.pone.0077952

Steffens, N. K., Haslam, A. S., Kerschreiter, R., Schuh, S. C., & van Dick, R. (2014). Leaders enhance group members' work engagement and reduce their burnout by crafting social identity. *Zeitschrift für Personalforschung, 28*(1/2), 173–194. doi:10.1688/ZfP-2014-01-Steffens

Steffens, N. K., Haslam, A. S., & Reicher, S. D. (2014). Up close and personal: Evidence that shared social identity is a basis for the 'special' relationship that binds followers to leaders. *The Leadership Quarterly, 25*(2), 296–313. doi:10.1016/j.leaqua.2013.08.008

Steffens, N. K., Haslam, A. S., Reicher, S. D., Platow, M. J., Fransen, K., Yang, J., ... Boen, F. (2014). Leadership as social identity management: Introducing the Identity Leadership Inventory (ILI) to assess and validate a four-dimensional model. *The Leadership Quarterly, 25*(5), 1001–1024. doi:10.1016/j.leaqua.2014.05.002

Steffens, N. K., Mols, F., Haslam, S. A., & Okimoto, T. G. (2016). True to what we stand for: Championing collective interests as a path to authentic leadership. *The Leadership Quarterly, 27*(5), 726–744. doi:10.1016/j.leaqua.2016.04.004

Sue, D. W., & Sue, D. (1990). *Counseling the culturally different: Theory and practice* (2nd ed.). New York, NY: John Wiley & Sons.

Sy, T., Choi, J. N., & Johnson, S. K. (2013). Reciprocal interactions between group perceptions of leader charisma and group mood through mood contagion. *The Leadership Quarterly, 24*(4), 463–476. doi:10.1016/j.leaqua.2013.02.002

Tajfel, H., & Turner, J. C. (1979). An integrative theory of intergroup conflict. In W. G. Austin & S. Worchel (Eds.), *The social psychology of intergroup relations* (pp. 33–47). Monterey, CA: Brooks/Cole.

Tavares, G. M., Sobral, F., Goldszmidt, R., & Araújo, F. (2018). Opening the implicit leadership theories' black box: An experimental approach with conjoint analysis. *Frontiers in Psychology, 9*(100), 1–11. doi:10.3389/fpsyg.2018.00100

Thomas, G., Martin, R., & Riggio, R. E. (2013). Leading groups: Leadership as a group process. *Group Processes & Intergroup Relations, 16*(1), 3–16. doi:10.1177/1368430212462497

Thomas, E. F., Amiot, C. E., Louis, W. R., & Goddard, A. (2017). Collective self-determination: How the agent of help promotes pride, well-being, and support for intergroup helping. *Personality and Social Psychology Bulletin, 43*(5), 662–677. doi:10.1177/0146167217695553

Todorov, A., Mandisodza, A. N., Goren, A., & Hall, C. C. (2005). Inferences of competence from faces predict election outcomes. *Science, 308*(5728), 1623–1626. doi:10.1126/science.1110589

Todorov, A., Olivola, C. Y., Dotsch, R., & Mende-Siedlecki, P. (2015). Social attributions from faces: Determinants, consequences, accuracy, and functional significance. *Annual Review of Psychology, 66*(1), 519–545. doi:10.1146/annurev-psych-113011-143831

Tremblay, M., Gaudet, M.-C., & Parent-Rocheleau, X. (2018). Good things are not eternal: How consideration leadership and initiating structure influence the dynamic nature of organizational justice and extra-role behaviors at the collective level. *Journal of Leadership & Organizational Studies, 25*(2), 211–232. doi:10.1177/1548051817738941

Trichas, S., & Schyns, B. (2012). The face of leadership: Perceiving leaders from facial expression. *The Leadership Quarterly, 23*(3), 545–566. doi:10.1016/j.leaqua.2011.12.007

Trichas, S., Schyns, B., Lord, R. G., & Hall, R. J. (2017). "Facing" leaders: Facial expression and leadership perception. *The Leadership Quarterly, 28*(2), 317–333. doi:10.1016/j.leaqua.2016.10.013

Tsai, C.-Y., Dionne, S. D., Wang, A.-C., Spain, S. M., Yammarino, F. J., & Cheng, B.-S. (2017). Effects of relational schema congruence on leader-member exchange. *The Leadership Quarterly, 28*(2), 268–284. doi:10.1016/j.leaqua.2016.11.005

Tskhay, K. O., Xu, H., & Rule, N. O. (2014). Perceptions of leadership success from nonverbal cues communicated by orchestra conductors. *The Leadership Quarterly, 25*(5), 901–911. doi:10.1016/j.leaqua.2014.07.001

Tucker, M. F., Bonial, R., Vanhove, A., & Kedharnath, U. (2014). Leading across cultures in the human age: An empirical investigation of intercultural competency among global leaders. *SpringerPlus, 3*(1), 127. doi:10.1186/2193-1801-3-127

Turner, J. C., & Haslam, A. S. (2001). Social identity, organizations, and leadership. In M. Turner (Ed.), *Groups at work: Theory and research* (pp. 25–65). London: Routledge.

Turner, J. C. (1991). *Social influence*. Milton Keynes: Open University Press.

Turner, J. C. (2010). Social categorization and the self-concept: A social cognitive theory of group behavior. In T. Postmes & N. R. Branscombe (Eds.), *Key readings in social psychology: Rediscovering social identity* (pp. 243–272). New York, NY: Psychological Press.

Ullrich, J., Wieseke, J., & Dick, R. V. (2005). Continuity and change in mergers and acquisitions: A social identity case study of a German industrial merger. *Journal of Management Studies, 42*(8), 1549–1569. doi:10.1111/j.1467-6486.2005.00556.x

van Dick, R., & Kerschreiter, R. (2016). The social identity approach to effective leadership: An overview and some ideas on cross-cultural generalizability. *Frontiers of Business Research in China, 10*(3), 363–384. doi:10.3868/s070-005-016-0013-3

van Dick, R., Lemoine, J. E., Steffens, N. K., Kerschreiter, R., Akfirat, S. A., Avanzi, L., … Sekiguchi, T. (2018). Identity leadership going global: Validation of the identity leadership inventory across 20 countries. *Journal of Occupational and Organizational Psychology, 91*(4), 697–728. doi:10.1111/joop.12223

van Knippenberg, D., & Sitkin, S. B. (2013). A critical assessment of charismatic—transformational leadership research: Back to the drawing board? *The Academy of Management Annals, 7*(1), 1–60. doi:10.1080/19416520.2013.759433

van Knippenberg, D., van Knippenberg, B., De Cremer, D., & Hogg, M. A. (2004). Leadership, self, and identity: A review and research agenda. *The Leadership Quarterly, 15*(6), 825–856. doi:10.1016/j.leaqua.2004.09.002

van Vugt, M., & Ronay, R. (2014). The evolutionary psychology of leadership. *Organizational Psychology Review, 4*(1), 74–95. doi:10.1177/2041386613493635

Vogeley, K., & Roepstorff, A. (2009). Contextualising culture and social cognition. *Trends in Cognitive Sciences, 13*(12), 511–516. doi:10.1016/j.tics.2009.09.006

Williams, L. R., Grealy, M. A., Kelly, S. W., Henderson, I., & Butler, S. H. (2016). Perceptual bias, more than age, impacts on eye movements during face processing. *Acta Psychologica, 164*, 127–135. doi:10.1016/j.actpsy.2015.12.012

Xiao, N. G., Perrotta, S., Quinn, P. C., Wang, Z., Sun, Y. P., & Lee, K. (2014). On the facilitative effects of face motion on face recognition and its development. *Frontiers in Psychology, 5*, 1–16. doi:10.3389/fpsyg.2014.00633

Zaccaro, S. J., Foti, R. J., & Kenny, D. A. (1991). Self-monitoring and trait-based variance in leadership: An investigation of leader flexibility across multiple group situations. *Journal of Applied Psychology, 76*(2), 308–315. doi:10.1037/0021-9010.76.2.308

THE 4 CS OF MNE STRATEGIC RESPONSES TO GLOBAL GOVERNANCE

Sheila M. Puffer, David Wesley, Luis Alfonso Dau and Elizabeth M. Moore

ABSTRACT

This chapter centers on the global leadership of enterprises and their strategic business decisions as they interact with intergovernmental organizations (IGOs) and nongovernmental organizations (NGOs) in constructing a supranational global governance regime to address complex global issues. As the world faces myriad issues that transcend state borders, negative externalities of globalization, such as climate change and pandemics, are straining the current system and threatening vulnerable populations. To better understand how firms address these challenges, we present a stakeholder framework involving multinational enterprises (MNEs) in a supranational context and examine their relationships with IGOs, international nongovernmental organizations, and NGOs. A typology of firm behavior is introduced to describe four strategic responses to increased pressure for corporate social responsibility that represent the extent to which firms take leadership roles. Case studies illustrate each of the four archetypes, namely the collaborator, the complier, the counteractor, and the combatant. The situational strength of global governance organizations can have an influence on which strategic response MNEs choose, and ultimately on how MNEs decide to engage in socially responsible behaviors. The interrelatedness of MNEs and global governance organizations will continue to grow as humankind grapples with complex global issues that threaten our way of life. The 4 Cs of MNE strategic responses inform how firms may choose to respond to these challenges.

Advances in Global Leadership, Volume 13, 85–104
ISSN: 1535-1203/doi:10.1108/S1535-120320200000013003

Keywords: Global governance; strategic responses; multinational enterprises (MNEs); nongovernmental organizations (NGOs); intergovernmental organizations (IGOs); supranational context

THE 4 CS OF MNE STRATEGIC RESPONSES TO GLOBAL GOVERNANCE

Global problems continue to arise that individual states, or actors, alone cannot combat. These problems include, but are not limited to, environmental issues (e.g., hurricanes, seawater level risings, pollution), terrorism and security issues (e.g., data privacy, international terrorist attacks), economic crises (e.g., the 2008 global financial crisis, the 2020 coronavirus–induced global economic shock), political turmoil (e.g., Hong Kong and China, Russia, and Ukraine), and social issues (e.g., gender equality, democratization efforts, pandemics). As these problems abound, states globally attempt to coalesce power and converge their agendas to use collective action measures to create global standards and global regimes. Political science, particularly international relations, has discussed the possibility of global governance for quite some time. That discipline recognizes the state as the primary actor responsible for participating in, and legitimizing, global regulatory regimes. While states are indeed essential actors, so too are multinational enterprises (MNEs) given their centrality in cross-border trans-actions. MNEs may be best positioned to construct and legitimize global stan-dards through their strategic actions.

In keeping with the definition adopted throughout this book, we construe global leadership to be "the process and actions through which an individual influences a range of internal and external constituents from multiple national cultures and jurisdictions in a context characterized by significant levels of tasks and relationship complexity" (Reiche, Bird, Mendenhall, & Osland, 2017, p. 556). Although this definition focuses on the individual level, the overarching literature examines both the individual and organizational level. In this chapter, we focus on the organizational level, the MNE, while recognizing that executives are key decision makers for those organizations.

In the context of the rapidly changing global environment, we address the following question: How do MNEs address challenges to their ways of con-ducting business posed by intergovernmental organizations (IGOs), international nongovernmental organizations (INGOs), and nongovernmental organizations (NGOs), all of which are attempting to create global policy agendas? Addition-ally, how does the situational and institutional strength of these global and domestic organizations impact (1) whether firms act proactively or reactively and (2) whether firms behave in socially responsible or irresponsible ways? Relatedly, our research evokes questions about the potential role that firms can play in shaping and supporting the global agenda or the possible outcomes that may come if firms actively combat this agenda.

To help answer these questions, we provide a framework that outlines four ways that firms can take strategic action: reactively or proactively, in combination

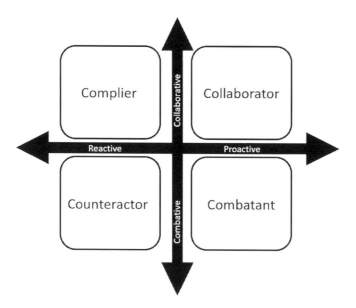

Fig. 1.   The 4 Cs of MNE Strategic Responses to Global Governance
Entities.

with a combative or collaborative orientation. We label the four quadrants, presented in Fig. 1, as *Collaborator, Complier, Counteractor*, and *Combatant*. We will describe each quadrant and illustrate them with brief case studies of companies and their interactions with IGOs, INGOs, and NGOs on the topics of the environment, human rights, and technology. We draw upon and extend the responsible leadership framework developed by Stahl and Sully de Luque (2014) as well as global governance theory from political science (Dominguez & Flores, 2018). Specifically, we focus on the supranational context that Stahl and Sully de Luque (2014) identify as a distal context antecedent to behavioral intention and ultimately responsible leader behavior, which can consist of doing good or avoiding harm. We draw on this work, which includes Mischel's (1973) construct of situational strength as a moderator between the supranational context and behavioral intention. We build on extant literature by highlighting the role that firms can play in legitimizing or challenging global governance regimes. We also discuss how our four quadrants relate to choices of doing good and avoiding harm as outlined by Stahl and Sully de Luque.

This chapter is structured as follows. We begin with a theoretical justification for the relationship between global governance and global leadership by MNEs. We then introduce our typology of MNE global leadership strategic responses to global crises and pressure from IGOs, INGOs, and NGOs in the process of constructing global policy agendas. We identify, describe, and offer illustrative examples of each type. This chapter concludes with implications for theory and practice.

GLOBAL GOVERNANCE THEORY FROM THE POLITICAL SCIENCE PERSPECTIVE

Global governance theory, a prominent theory in political science, has been recognized in the international business literature but has not been applied to its full potential in that context. The theory traces its origins in international relations and political science to the 1970s and gained increasing momentum during the Cold War in the late 1980s as a way to establish a collective political world order through global policies created by the interdependence of actors. The established world political order was upended with the fall of communism when dozens of independent countries were created, and their economies attempted the transition to more market-based ones. Globalization of markets and production took hold, with multinationals spanning the world to take advantage of new business opportunities. The construct of global governance was created in recognition of an increasingly interconnected world in which the distinction is blurred "between public authority and private initiative, and steadily transforms the role of state and nonstate actors operating at different levels of analysis" (Dominguez & Flores, 2018). International relations experts and other political scientists saw the growing prominence and influence of business enterprises and NGOs rising to challenge the traditional role and power of governmental institutions. A notably extreme scenario was presented in a 1990s series of essays entitled, Governance Without Government (Rosenau & Czempiel, 1992).

Of the many definitions of global governance, we utilize the following to guide our discussion. Global governance is "the complex of formal and informal institutions, mechanisms, relationships, and processes between and among states, markets, citizens, and organizations – both intergovernmental and nongovernmental – through which collective interests are articulated, rights and obligations are established, and differences are mediated" (Thakur & Van Langenhov, 2006, p. 233). This literature has largely viewed the state as the primary actor. Yet, as MNEs continue to engage in cross-border interactions, we believe that their responsible leadership behavior and strategic choices are central to the construction of global policies. Thus, we draw upon the rich literature on global governance from political science to better understand, conceptualize, and develop the construct of global leadership.

The contribution of this chapter is the development of a stakeholder framework involving MNEs in a supranational context and their relationships with IGOs, INGOs, and NGOs. IGOs include the United Nations, the World Bank, the International Monetary Fund, and the Global Reporting Initiative. The role of the United Nations in global governance has been extensively studied (Rittberger, 2002; Weiss & Thakur, 2010). INGOs and NGOs include environmental activist organizations such as Greenpeace, climate change groups such as Citizens Climate Lobby, 350.org, human rights groups such as those focusing on labor exploitation, and social movements such as the #metoo movement exposing sexual harassment.

Global problems continue to exert pressure on states and international organizations (e.g., IGOs, INGOs, and NGOs) to construct global governance regimes that can help resolve complex global problems through collective action. Some companies donate to NGOs and INGOs to demonstrate good corporate citizenship. Often, however, corporate philanthropy has been about improving the bottom line. Lev, Petrovits, and Radhakrishnan (2010) demonstrated that corporate charitable contributions can offer firms "competitive advantage (e.g., spurring innovation, improving the labor force, influencing legislators and regulators)," but when it comes to achieving a "desired social impact," the connection is less clear.

Limited Success of IGOs at Addressing Global Issues

Pogge (2002, p. 47) argues that international recognition and support for corrupt regimes in developing countries are to blame for many of the injustices against the world's poor. It is this "international resource privilege" that causes the resource curse and hinders "progress toward democratic government, economic growth, and the eradication of poverty." Although, in some cases, IGOs like the World Bank have unintentionally facilitated the plunder of poor nations by providing funding for mining projects and encouraging the privatization of state industries, international organizations have generally condemned the abuses of mining and oil companies. Many IGOs, INGOs, and NGOs are currently working to improve social and environmental conditions in less developed parts of the world.

Several scholars have proposed schemes that would help reduce the exploitation of the poor. They include imposing a global resources dividend (Pogge, 2001), creating international industry associations that exclude violators (Singer, 2010), and imposing sanctions on countries that export natural resources without adequately compensating citizens (Wenar, 2008). Although there are signs that some world leaders have begun to implement some of the proposed principles, in most cases corrupt governments find ways to circumvent international norms. For them, the risk of prosecution is outweighed by the enormous financial benefits of the current system.

Wenar (2008) has called for a restructuring of global trade to prevent illegally obtained resources from being transferred to developed country buyers. Specifically, he proposes a Clean Trade Act and a Clean Hands Trust. If adopted internationally, the Clean Trade Act would prohibit the trade in illegitimately acquired natural resources from the "worst of the worst" countries. They include places like Equatorial Guinea and the Democratic Republic of the Congo where, despite great natural resource wealth, most people live in deplorable conditions. The Clean Hands Trust would impose tariffs on countries that attempt to circumvent the Clean Trade Act by purchasing goods from banned countries. For example, if China were to purchase $3 billion in oil from Equatorial Guinea, the United States could impose equivalent sanctions on imported Chinese goods and then hold that money in trust for the people of Equatorial Guinea once a legitimate government is installed.

In practice, however, sanctions often prove ineffective. Moreover, as relations become antagonistic, the ability to influence the behavior of violators is diminished (Stone, 1988). In some cases, isolation may even help tyrants remain in power by creating what Stone (1988, p. 282) calls "a martyr identity." For example, Fidel Castro effectively "used threatening rhetoric to consolidate support" and used "the US embargo to excuse Cuba's economic problems" (Weinmann, 2004, p. 22). Not surprisingly, in the 60 years since the Cuban embargo began, little progress has been made toward securing freedom and democracy.

A More Effective Approach: IGOs and Extraterritorial Enforcement of MNE Activities

A more effective approach involves shifting the burden from government officials to corporate executives and firms. The US Foreign Corrupt Practices Act (FCPA), which punishes companies and executives for bribing foreign officials, has proven effective in reducing corruption globally by using market mechanisms to encourage compliance (Foley & Haynes, 2009). To date, the US Department of Justice has levied billions of dollars in fines on US and foreign companies listed on US stock exchanges and has sent high-ranking executives to prison. The FCPA is arguably the first serious effort by a global economic power to reshape the world order in a positive way. Other wealthy countries can add needed momentum by enacting and enforcing similar laws. In Europe, for example, anticorruption laws have been in place for many years, but European governments have been less aggressive in prosecuting violators.

At present, corporations are generally not held accountable for violations of international law in areas such as the environment and human rights, leaving "large protection gaps for victims" (Ruggie, 2007, p. 24). The British government has taken the first step toward holding governments and mining companies accountable through its Extractive Industries Transparency Initiative (EITI). The initiative, which began in 2002, "aims to strengthen governance by improving transparency and accountability in the extractives sector" (EITI, 2009). Currently, EITI compliance is voluntary and there are no formal penalties for EITI violations by member states or mining companies. Moreover, the initiative focuses primarily on financial transparency and does not directly address issues such as human rights and environmental destruction. As such, the EITI has a limited ability to influence corporate behavior in less developed countries.

Stone (1988) argues that intangible incentives, such as membership in an organization, are less likely to change behavior than "quantifiable, material inducements" like fines and prison sentences. Nevertheless, impartial monitoring of mining companies could help to eventually pave the way for an expanded enforcement mechanism by providing normative behavioral expectations (Ruggie, 2007). For example, the Dodd-Frank Act of 2010 sought to create greater transparency through new reporting requirements for extraction companies, although some provisions were repealed in 2019. In addition, voluntary associations such as the EITI and the UN Global Compact have encouraged many large multinational firms to codify human rights policies for the first time (Ruggie, 2007).

The Alien Tort Claims Act (ATCA) provides another avenue to combat the harms of mining by allowing NGOs and foreign individuals to sue companies in

US federal court. The ATCA has resulted in major settlements against companies like Unocal, Royal Dutch Shell, and Chevron (Branson, 2011). Unfortunately, legal cases often fail for lack of funding. Until recently, executives from multinational corporations realized that if they continued to prolong or appeal ATCA cases, litigants would eventually run short of funds.

Although litigation investment has finally given impoverished indigenous communities the financial means to mount serious legal challenges, it is not without limitations. Even when plaintiffs have access to fiscal resources, they may face years of appeals and countersuits before they receive any form of compensation. Moreover, litigation compensates only for existing harms and does nothing to address the immediate threat posed by new mining and oil concessions.

Given the increasing interaction between firms and these diverse types of organizations, we believe it is critical to understand MNEs' responses to regulations and the challenges they pose.

GLOBAL GOVERNANCE AND RESPONSIBLE GLOBAL LEADERSHIP

The management literature has begun to address the role of business in global governance. Notably, a special issue of the *Journal of Business Ethics* was published in 2014 on "Global Governance: CSR and the Role of the UN Global Compact." The United Nations Global Compact was seen as a platform for corporations, NGOs, and other stakeholders to debate and agree upon a set of global ethical norms and practices since no global state existed to provide such principles. It was argued that adhering to such a code would be in the best interests of corporations since it would reduce uncertainty in the business environment. Another noteworthy contribution to bringing business into the global governance arena was provided by Maak, Pless, and Voegtlin (2016) who focused on the individual level of analysis and the relationship between CEOs and political corporate social responsibility. Specifically, they asserted: "A CEO's responsible leadership style (determined by their value orientation) influences a firm's engagement in political CSR and its effectiveness in dealing with political CSR challenges in a global world" (p. 465).

We draw upon a model of the antecedents of responsible leader behavior developed by Stahl and Sully de Luque (2014) as a useful launching pad for our discussion from the management literature. Among the antecedents included in their model is the supranational context, which the authors note includes NGO activism, global governance, and the UN Global Compact. These bodies are seen as having the potential to affect leaders' behavioral intentions and behaviors, depending on situational strength. As conceived by Mischel (1973), strong situations tend to suppress the behavioral expression of personality traits. Strong behavioral norms, strong incentives, and clear expectations help create strong situations. When strong supranational structures are in place, such as strict enforcement of regulations by international bodies and protection of stakeholder rights through the UN Global Compact, managers tend to comply and there is less room for them to act according to their personal dispositions. Stahl and Sully de Luque point out that, somewhat paradoxically, strong situations reduce managers' discretion to do both harm and good. Those authors distinguish between two types of socially responsible behavior. Avoiding harm involves refraining "from activities that have harmful consequences for others," whereas doing good involves "engaging in activities aimed at enhancing societal welfare." Similarly, they identify two types of socially irresponsible behavior – doing harm, i.e., engaging "in activities that have harmful consequences for others," and not doing good, i.e., refraining "from engaging in activities that are aimed at enhancing societal welfare." Our global governance framework will elaborate upon these constructs through an examination of responsible global leadership at the organizational level.

THE 4 CS OF MNES AND GLOBAL GOVERNANCE: COLLABORATOR, COMPLIER, COUNTERACTOR, AND COMBATANT

We now present the four main archetypes we have developed to classify firm strategic responses to the increase in IGOs, INGOs, and NGOs globally (see Fig. 1). For each we will outline, describe, and offer brief case studies as illustrations. The archetypes represent four combinations of two variables depicting potential actions by MNEs in relation to other global governance entities: a relationship dimension – collaborative or combative – in combination with a temporal dimension – proactive versus reactive. The relationship dimension involves an MNE's decision about whether to engage in a positive way with other stakeholders to work toward an outcome that positively addresses a complex global issue, or to resist collaboration and pursue objectives of primary benefit to the MNE. The temporal dimension involves an MNE's decision of whether to take the lead in addressing an issue of common concern or whether to wait and see how other actors behave before developing a strategic response. We begin with a description of the two collaborative positions, collaborator and complier, followed by the two combative positions, counteractor and combatant.

The Collaborator

The collaborator represents the archetype in the top right quadrant of the typology. These firms are both willing to collaborate with IGOs and take a proactive stance when doing so. They respond to social movements and current events and take positions before pressure is exerted from any global governance organization. Collaborators exhibit a desire to establish a connection between firms and the establishment of global rules. These firms recognize that there are problems that extend beyond domestic borders and thus pose global challenges. To respond to these challenges effectively, collaborators work with IGOs, INGOs, and NGOs to set standards and lead by example.

In this scenario, firms not only collaborate with current social movements and international organizations, but they also take the initiative before these organizations exert pressure on them. This demonstrates a firm's desire for long-term gains and setting global agendas. In doing so, they are norm-setters and global leaders in creating global standards and regulations, positioning themselves to play an active role in global governance initiatives. This helps to augment the legitimacy and authority of global organizations and global governance by signaling the participatory role of a key global actor that has received relatively less attention in the global governance literature – the firm.

Collaborators anticipate changes in government policy and are at the forefront of global policy shifts. Toyota, for instance, anticipated the shift toward cleaner energy when it introduced the Prius hybrid vehicle in the late 1990s. The Prius used Toyota's most popular gas engine on a platform that enabled the company to react relatively rapidly to changes in demand forecasts. By manufacturing the hybrid gas-electric model on production lines that manufactured other models, production slots could be allocated to different models depending on current demand. As such, the risks of failure were greatly reduced. When demand exceeded forecasts, Toyota's competitors were left scrambling to enter the hybrid market, often with limited success (Wesley & Spital, 2010).

As the shift to clean energy intensifies, the automotive industry is spawning new collaborators in related industries that offer complementary products and services. For instance, electric cars require recharging, usually at night when electricity demand is well below peak. This creates opportunities for companies in the electricity generation and distribution industry to invest in smart grids that combine solar and wind energy with local battery storage. Volkswagen is one company that is working with regulators and energy companies to install new electric car infrastructure in various countries, partially not only to rehabilitate the company's image following the dieselgate scandal but also to remain relevant in a changing political environment that is moving away from fossil fuels such as diesel.

The climate crisis has spawned other areas of collaboration between corporations, INGOs, and policymakers. Oxfam worked with insurance provider SwissRe to develop products for African farmers impacted by climate change. Previously, crop insurance was typically only available in developed countries. In 2010, SwissRe opened a pilot project in Ethiopia. By reducing the risk to local farmers, the project encouraged investment in the agricultural sector, thereby enhancing global food security. The success of that project allowed SwissRe to expand its offerings across Ethiopia and eventually develop similar products for other countries (Doh, London, & Kilibarda, 2012).

SwissRe was also a lead company in The We Mean Business INGO focused on committing large corporations to move to 100% renewable energy. Other members of the coalition included the World Business Council for Sustainable Development (WBCSD), "a global, CEO-led organization of over 200 leading businesses working to accelerate the transition to a sustainable world" (What We Do, 2020). By 2020, We Mean Business had signed up more than 200 companies to commit to 100% renewable energy, including tech giants (Google, HP), food companies (Nestlé, Mars), automotive manufacturers (BMW), banks (Citi, Wells Fargo), and many others (Energy Commit to Action Campaign, 2020).

Investment firms are also working with IGOs and INGOs to lessen their impact on the environment, particularly within the framework of the Paris Climate Agreement. In 2019, the Government Pension Fund of Norway, the world's largest sovereign wealth fund with more than $1 trillion in assets under management, announced its divestment of fossil fuels. Much of those funds would be shifted to renewable energy projects (Ambrose, 2019). Following that announcement, in 2020, global investment firm Blackrock, with more than $7 trillion in assets under management, announced that it too would be divesting of fossil fuels. In a public letter, CEO Larry Fink cited Blackrock's work with IGOs, namely the UN-sponsored Task Force on Climate-related Financial Disclosures (TCFD), the UN's Principles for Responsible Investment, and the Vatican's carbon pricing regime as providing a framework for its actions (Fink, 2020).

In applying Stahl and Sully de Luque's (2014) framework of four options that firms can choose of doing good, doing harm, or avoiding the two, collaborators can be seen as engaging in socially responsible behavior by taking the initiative to do good in addressing complex global problems. They also avoid doing harm. They take advantage of the opportunity to do so as a result of the weak situational strength in the supranational context. Other global institutions have yet to enact regulations or provide incentives for positive actions, leaving it to the discretion of proactive MNEs to take the lead and serve as catalysts for positive change in the global arena. They could do so as a result of other factors noted in Stahl and Sully de Luque's model – leader characteristics and/or characteristics of the MNE itself, among others.

The Complier

The complier is depicted in the top left quadrant of the typology. Like the collaborator, these firms are willing to work, or at the very least actively comply with standards set by IGOs, INGOs, and NGOs. Unlike the collaborator, the complier does not act preemptively or proactively. These firms do not take initiative based on social movements or in response to global problems. This is not to say that these firms do not care about these issues, but they fail to take a leadership role to act in conjunction with global organizations aiming to alleviate these problems. The complier will not be the first to act, but rather responds to changes in global governance. At the same time, the complier does adhere to the regulations and global governance standards once they have begun to change. When the complier faces increasing pressure from IGOs, INGOs, and NGOs, it actively makes the strategic choice to align with the changes in global regulations. This aligns the complier with the collaborator when it comes to adherence to working toward global governance. This signals to other actors that the complier believes in the authority and legitimacy of global governance but does not take a participatory role in the process.

Smith (2003) notes that an increase in activism by NGOs in less developed countries is beginning to force companies to reassess their corporate social responsibility practices. In Peru, some multinational corporations have entered into "social contracts" by committing themselves to "competitive business practices consistent with respect for human rights in all aspects of their operations" (Cragg, 2000, p. 212). One such company is BHP Billiton, which entered into a partnership with Oxfam and other NGOs to improve mine safety and provide compensation to indigenous communities for past wrongs (Mego, 2005). In 2001, BHP Billiton's Tintaya Copper Mine in Peru was the focus of numerous confrontations between residents and mine officials. The community eventually turned to Oxfam, which in turn presented the company with a list of grievances including forced evictions, loss of livelihoods, harassment of residents by mine staff, and environmental destruction (Barton, 2005).

Although BHP Billiton initially refuted these grievances, Oxfam "created a linkage directly back to the transnational's (BHP) headquarters in Australia. This linkage had a direct impact on the company's willingness to establish an ultimately successful dialogue process" (Slack, 2009, p. 130). The following year, Oxfam and BHP Billiton established the Oxfam Community Aid Abroad's Corporate Community Leadership Program (CCLP) in Orissa, India, which introduced mining managers "to best practice examples of community development, effective community dialogue methodologies and the negative impact that poorly managed minerals operations can have on impoverished communities" (BHP Billiton, 2004). Peruvian mine managers who participated in the joint program returned with a different view of NGOs and residents. They were no longer viewed as adversaries, but rather as partners (Rangan, Barton, & Reffico, 2006).

In 2004, "after nearly three years of talks, the communities and the company signed an agreement in which the company committed to give the communities land equivalent to the amount of territory that was expropriated by the state and acquired by BHP Billiton, as well as an additional 25 to 50 percent more land, depending on the quality" (Mego, 2005). Many rural Peruvians regard their government with deep mistrust (Vizcarra, 2010). Therefore, the decision to exclude the Peruvian government from the Tintaya Dialogue Table was critical to a successful outcome. In addition, Oxfam used its international presence to create dialogue through a third country, Australia, where the relationship between the NGO and the mining company had not been polluted by political ideology. Future confrontations between residents and BHP Billiton were resolved more quickly because of the trust and lines of communication that had been created between the mining company and NGO advocates. Peruvian media coverage was also more favorable to both the mine and the indigenous community because of the credibility created through the dialogue process (Rangan et al., 2006).

Like collaborators, compliers can be viewed as being socially responsible in that they avoid harm and do good. But they are followers rather than pathbreakers and hold back from doing good that is not in their direct business interests until global governance bodies enact regulations requiring compliance. The passage of laws and imposition of regulations by bodies in the supranational context creates high situational strength. Compliers respect that strength perhaps despite leader or organizational characteristics that might not be in alignment with supranational regulations.

The Counteractor

The counteractor is found in the bottom left quadrant of the typology. Counteractors exhibit behavior that is both reactive and noncompliant. In other words, the counteractor exhibits a form of passive resistance. Like the complier, strategic behavior is reactive, rather than proactive. However, when these firms experience pressure or opportunities to work with IGOs, INGOs, and NGOs, they opt to take a role in counteracting the global governance agenda. These firms' first strategic priority is the success of the firm, which they believe is extant to the global organizations. Such firms show a preference for adhering to home and host country regulations, while signaling that global regulations need not be followed or strengthened. These companies not only fail to act in socially responsible ways but they also actively counter policies that may impose restrictions on their harmful behaviors. Ruggie (2007, p. 23) points out that "determined laggards find ways to avoid scrutiny." This position, whether purposeful or not, threatens the legitimacy and authority of global organizations and global governance.

The counteractor makes the strategic decision not to align with global regulations in order to promote the success of the firm in its home and host markets. In this way, the counteractor shares the combative position of the combatant. In this quadrant, many natural resource companies can be found. In a conflict in the Russian arctic, Villo, Halme, and Ritvala (2020) describe "powerful resistance maneuvers" by the Russian energy giant Gazprom against the INGO Greenpeace, which, in 2013, boarded a Russian oil rig to protest arctic drilling. Gazprom's position as a state-owned MNE gave it leverage to bring Russian governmental action against Greenpeace in the form of vessel seizure and severe criminal charges against protesters. When Greenpeace successfully appealed the seizure to the International Tribunal for the Law of the Sea, the Russian government initially disregarded the ruling, but eventually acquiesced. Nevertheless, Villo et al. (2020) argue that the ability of IGOs and INGOs to influence counteractors is often overstated in state capitalist contexts that are often prevalent in less developed countries, noting that Greenpeace's actions appear to have had no impact on Gazprom's business practices.

According to Alderman and Daynard (2006), companies can employ a "scorched earth" strategy when facing potentially wide-reaching litigation. This counteractor move involves appealing verdicts and creating procedural delays to force plaintiffs to continue spending money to pursue cases. Eventually, plaintiffs will not have the funds to continue pursuing their claims. The first industry to employ this tactic was the asbestos industry. Later, the tobacco industry followed a similar practice. More recently, food corporations are using a scorched earth strategy to avoid potentially damaging obesity claims. In both the tobacco and fast food industries, consumers have sought redress for what they perceive as deceptive advertising. For example, the tobacco industry advertised "light" cigarettes in such a way that some consumers believed that they were less harmful to health than regular cigarettes. Similarly, the food industry advertises "low sugar" and "low fat" products which give the impression of healthier choices, when in fact the sugar and fat substitutes are also unhealthy. The scorched earth strategy has also been effective in preventing regulatory action against natural resource companies for widespread environmental harms.

Counteractors clearly engage in socially irresponsible behavior in two ways. They conduct business as usual that serves their own interests and that continues to do harm to other stakeholders in the global arena. At the same time, they fail to do good by ignoring, blatantly or through passive resistance, calls to action by global governance organizations. The situational strength of the supranational context is weak and is no match for powerful MNEs that acquire their power from such sources as high demand or scarcity of their products, collusion with government officials, and the like. This weak situational strength provides opportunities for MNEs to be guided by leader, organizational, or other characteristics that put the firm's interests first at the expense of other stakeholders.

The Combatant

The combatant occupies the bottom right quadrant of the typology. Combatants share the proactive qualities with the collaborator, along with the combative qualities of the counteractor. These firms make strategic choices that come before, or at the same time as, global social movements and global regulatory changes, and those choices distance the combatant firms from IGOs, INGOs, and NGOs. The combatant may believe the criticisms of global organizations' abilities to create and enforce global regulations. While these firms may act in accordance with home and host country regulations, they might not believe that the global agenda will solidify. Whether knowingly or not, these firms signal a disbelief in global governance and, in doing so, allow the opportunity for other firms to follow suit. Thus, these firms do not take a participatory role in setting a global agenda or creating global standards. In fact, by proactively fighting against global regulatory standards, combatants challenge the legitimacy and authority of global organizations and governance movements.

Perhaps more than any other type of organization, a number of those involved in the sharing economy exemplify the combatant archetype. As tech startups, they are industry disruptors that created new business models for which few regulations existed at the time of their founding that pertained to their novel operations. Examples include Uber, Lyft, Airbnb, and Flytenow. Flytenow, for instance, was dubbed the "Uber of the Skies," by facilitating flight sharing between airline passengers and small aircraft operators. Flytenow failed to win approval from the US Federal Aviation Administration, which determined that Flytenow's customers, namely private pilots, would be violating "holding out" regulations if they used the service. Yet in Europe other companies followed Flytenow's example, where regulators adopted new rules to allow flight sharing (Wesley & Montgomery, 2019). In the United States, policymakers in Washington are considering adopting similar rules.

Combatants operate in contexts of weak situational strength since few regulations existed at the time of their founding that applied to their new business models. Regulatory bodies need time to evaluate these startups and develop laws and regulations to ensure they operate responsibly with other stakeholders in mind. Combatants are proactive and, because of their newness, have an opportunity to engage in socially responsible and/or socially irresponsible behavior until regulatory bodies and NGOs catch up with them. They may do good for consumers by reducing prices and increasing competition, utilizing underused resources such as personal vehicles and accommodations, and adding variety to product and service offerings. Yet, simultaneously they can do harm to competitors, workers, society, and the environment, thus the need for regulation. It can be challenging for supranational organizations to put pressure on such disruptors because national and local governments often have different views of how to regulate such organizations. Thus, it can be difficult to reach consensus at the supranational level as to the appropriateness of regulations.

IMPLICATIONS FOR THEORY AND FUTURE RESEARCH

In this chapter, we have taken an interdisciplinary approach to global issues by drawing upon the global governance literature in political science and combining it with the global leadership literature in international business. We discussed how the global governance perspective has come to recognize that governmental and other supranational bodies cannot resolve complex global issues alone and that MNEs play a crucial role in addressing these challenges. We also drew upon the international business literature that typically has the MNE as its focus. We found the model developed by Stahl and Sully de Luque (2014) to be a useful framework since they included global governance organizations operating in the supranational context as a set of important antecedents of responsible leader behavior. Our major contribution is identifying four types of strategic responses available to MNEs in their relationships with global governance organizations. Utilizing combinations of collaborative versus combative in combination with proactive versus reactive orientations, we described how MNEs can be collaborators, compliers, counteractors, and combatants. We showed how the situational strength of global governance organizations can have an influence on which strategic response MNEs choose, and ultimately on how MNEs decide to engage in socially responsible and/or socially irresponsible behaviors by doing good or harm and/or refraining from doing good or harm.

Further research can explore potential antecedents of what prompts MNE leaders to choose among the four strategic decisions developed in this chapter in their relationships with other global governance organizations. Other antecedents can be drawn from Stahl and Sully de Luque's (2014) model of responsible leader behavior and include leader characteristics, the organizational and situational proximal contexts as well as the institutional distal context. Our typology has added to understanding of their supranational box and its relation to the four MNE strategic responses we developed.

The situational strength (Mischel, 1973) of the relationship between MNEs and other global governance organizations can also be explored further. Research could determine how to modify the situational strength from those interactions with the aim of fostering responsible leader behavior of doing good rather than simply avoiding harm. Even further, specific measures are needed to increase global governance organizations' situational strength to discourage irresponsible leader behavior of doing no good (beyond making profits), and to eradicate practices that do actual harm (polluting, violating human rights).

Another fruitful area of research can draw upon the construct of institutional relatedness from the international business literature. Recognizing the role of businesses as institutions, institutional relatedness has been defined as "an organization's informal linkage with dominant institutions that confer resources and legitimacy" (Peng, Lee, & Wang, 2005, p. 622). As we have discussed, in a supranational context, three major institutions with which MNEs have institutional relatedness are IGOs, INGOs, and NGOs. The extent of informal linkages, as well as formal ones, that MNEs forge with these types of institutions can have an impact on firms' financial performance and reputation. Moreover, the linkages and participation that MNEs have with these institutions can help shape the global policy agenda. The key is to determine effective ways to strengthen institutional relatedness to find common ground among MNEs and global governance institutions to foster collaboration rather than confrontation. For instance, perhaps industry associations could serve as boundary spanners between MNEs and global governance organizations to buffer the relationship and focus on mutually agreed upon goals.

IMPLICATIONS FOR PRACTICE

Impact on MNE Performance and Reputation

A crucial question at the heart of MNE strategic responses in the global governance arena is what impact do these different responses have on firm performance and reputation? While combatants and counteractors in our typology may enjoy higher financial returns in the short run, their reputations as responsible global players may suffer in the process. And when the situational strength of global governance organization increases, such firms may end up paying a heavy price through fines and an even more tarnished reputation in the eyes of their customers, suppliers, and other stakeholders. In contrast, collaborators and compliers may have lower financial returns in the short run but with a stronger reputation as well as avoiding penalties that could be imposed in the future. Collaborators especially may enjoy additional reputational benefits for taking the lead in addressing global issues beyond what global governance bodies have accomplished.

MNEs involved in mining in Peru illustrate various choices that companies have made in their business practices and government relationships. The Peruvian government monitors some 250 social conflicts per month, of which nearly half are environment related and 60% involve some form of violent confrontation. According to Amezaga et al. (2010, p. 24), "about a third of all current social conflicts in Peru are associated with mining." Such confrontations have proven costly to mining companies. For example, protests against Newmont Mining Corporation in 2004 forced the company to abandon expansion plans. In addition, cleanup costs for spills associated with poor safety practices have cost the company tens of millions of dollars (Bergman & Knappenberger, 2005), and lawsuits filed in US courts have cost Newmont millions more in settlement claims. Mining companies may choose a path of collaboration, as BHP Billiton has done, or confrontation, as Newmont Mining Corporation has done. Since both approaches involve costs, determining which one offers the best financial return may prove impossible.

Increasing Situational Strength of Global Governance Bodies

Increased situational strength of global governance organizations can have a significant impact on MNEs and their strategic responses. An example of increased situational strength can be found among NGO environmental groups. Some have found new ways to redress the financial imbalance when facing defendants with deep pockets. The advent of investment funds specializing in corporate litigation has helped balance the power of plaintiffs and defendants. These funds agree to pay plaintiffs' legal expenses in exchange for a percentage of any awards. As such, the scorched earth strategy is becoming less viable for corporate defendants. Arguably the best-known example of corporate litigation was the Lago Agrio case in Ecuador, which resulted in an $18 billion award against Chevron for polluting the Amazon rainforest and causing death and illness in several indigenous communities (Aguinda et al. vs. Texaco, Inc., 93-CV-07527 JSR.) In that case, the plaintiffs were backed by a UK-based investment firm and other institutional investors who agreed to cover the cost of appeals.

MNEs Can Be in Multiple Quadrants Simultaneously

It is important to note that MNEs can operate in multiple quadrants simultaneously. Google, for instance, deals with both the harms and the benefits of the Internet. Technology and the Internet have created opportunities to both exploit and protect the environment, minorities, and communities. Conventional wisdom holds that computer networks facilitate "the self-organization of human communities" (Feenberg, 1991). On the other hand, direct personal relations have a higher social value than secondary relations that are mediated by "mechanical connections" (Cerulo & Ruane, 1998). Although the communicative dimension of computing may be transforming social relationships by forcing activist organizations to rethink the way they approach specific issues, traditional key success factors such as trust and leadership may still be important. If so, building trust and leadership may require direct personal contact between activists and the organizations they support.

In the Internet space, Google can be seen as being in several quadrants. It could be viewed as a counteractor in that it was found to have spread conspiracy and hate videos to millions of viewers, including children. At the same time Google has been a collaborator with global governance organizations in promoting human rights around the world including in China, where the company is banned because it will not allow censorship on its platforms. Google offers advanced protection to safeguard vulnerable people, such as journalists, human rights workers, and targeted politicians. And it develops cybersecurity tools to protect against cyberattacks, which it shares freely, even with its competitors. Through its Advanced Protection Program (APP) and Project Shield, Google actively resists what it deems to be "oppressive regimes" by protecting journalists and human rights workers from state sponsored cyberattacks, spying, and other technology-based threats (Whitacker, 2017). Google works directly with INGOs like the International Consortium of Investigative Journalists (ICIJ), which recommends the APP to its members. One proponent of Google's APP is Spencer Woodman, an ICIJ journalist who notes that "[l]ast year alone, a record number of journalists were killed in Mexico, reporters were imprisoned in Myanmar and journalists in Turkey faced criminal charges en masse" (Woodman, 2018). Project Shield similarly uses Google's vast security apparatus to protect vulnerable organizations from cyberattacks at no cost. These include human rights organizations, news outlets, and election monitors.

Leadership Characteristics and the 4 Cs

A number of leadership characteristics may either drive or buffer MNE choices of the four strategic responses in our framework. As summarized by Stahl and Sully de Luque (2014), these include personality traits, cognitive moral development, and moral philosophies. For instance, individuals with personality traits such as neuroticism focus on advancing their own interests and are less likely to engage in activities to improve broader societal conditions. They may advocate for combatant or counteractor strategic responses. Those having higher stages of cognitive moral development consider societal benefit in their decision-making and are less likely to engage in unethical behavior (Trevino, 1992). Therefore, they may opt for the collaborator response, or at least the complier response. And Maak et al. (2016) distinction between instrumental and integrative responsible leadership styles may affect the choice of strategic organizational responses. Instrumental responsible business leaders place most of their emphasis on business performance and interact with a limited number of business stakeholders, such as governments and investors, and devote limited attention to broader societal issues. Such individuals may be inclined toward compliant, combative, or counteractive stances to protect the interests of the MNE. Those with an integrative responsible leadership style go beyond simply representing their firms' interests to external stakeholders. Rather, they take a balanced approach to achieving business and societal objectives. Thus, they would be more likely to adopt a collaborative strategic response for the MNE to bring stakeholders together through communication, collaboration, and alignment around issues of mutual concern.

CONCLUSION

Nearly a century ago, public opinion began to shift toward a view that the business corporation as an economic institution has a social service function in addition to a profit-making objective (Dodd, 1932). In the early part of the twentieth century, corporate citizenship came to be seen both as a duty to society and a way to preserve the corporate system from the "successive cataclysms" that were sweeping Asia and Eastern Europe at the time (Berle, 1932, p. 1372). Responsible global leadership is needed more than ever in the twenty-first century. A provocative new book on global governance from a political science perspective suggests that the institutional structure of the global political arena is dominated by hierarchies and power inequalities that by their very nature create contestation, resistance, and distributional struggles (Zurn, 2018). Our typology of four strategic responses available to MNEs, informed by the literature on responsible global leadership, offers a more nuanced approach and a range of responses that involve doing or avoiding harm, or doing good or avoiding doing so. The interrelatedness of MNEs and global governance organizations will only continue to grow as humankind grapples with complex global issues that threaten our way of life.

REFERENCES

Alderman, J., & Daynard, R. A. (2006). Applying lessons from tobacco litigation to obesity lawsuits. *American Journal of Preventive Medicine, 30*, 82–88.

Ambrose, J. (2019, June 12). World's biggest sovereign wealth fund to ditch fossil fuels. *The Guardian.* Retrieved January 15, 2020, from https://www.theguardian.com/business/2019/jun/12/worlds-biggest-sovereign-wealth-fund-to-ditch-fossil-fuels

Amezaga, J. M., Rotting, T. S., Younger, P. L., Nairn, R. W., Noles, A. J., Oyarzu N, R. & Quintanilla, J. (2010). A rich vein? Mining and the pursuit of sustainability. *Environmental Science & Technology, 45*, 21–26.

Barton, B. (2005). *A global/local approach to conflict resolution in the mining sector: The case of the Tintaya dialogue table* (Master's thesis in law and diplomacy). Somerville, MA: Tufts University.

Bergman, L., & Knappenberger, B. (2005). *Frontline/World: Stories from a small planet.* Alexandria, Va.: PBS Video.

Berle, A. A., Jr. (1932). For whom corporate managers are trustees: A note. *Harvard Law Review, 45*, 1365–1372.

BHP Billiton. (2004, September 16). Annual health, safety, environment and community report. Retrieved from https://www.bhp.com/community/community-and-sustainability-reports/2004/09/2004-annual-health-safety-environment-and-community-report/

Branson, D. M. (2011). Holding multinational corporations accountable Achille's heels in alien tort claims act litigation. *Santa Clara Journal of International Law, 9*(1), 227–250.

Cerulo, K. A., & Ruane, J. M. (1998). Coming together: New taxonomies for the analysis of social relations. *Sociological Inquiry, 68*, 398–425.

Cragg, W. (2000). Human rights and business ethics: Fashioning a new social contract. *Journal of Business Ethics, 27*, 205–214.

Dodd, E. M., Jr. (1932). For whom are corporate managers trustees? *Harvard Law Review, 45*, 1145–1163.

Doh, J. P., London, T., & Kilibarda, V. (2012). *Building and scaling a cross-sector partnership: Oxfam America and Swiss Re empower farmers in Ethiopia.* Ann Arbor, MI: William Davidson Institute Global Lens Case 1-429-185.

Dominguez, R., & Flores, R. V. (2018, July). *Global governance*. Oxford: Oxford Research Encyclopedia, International Studies Association and Oxford University Press (Published online). Retrieved from https://oxfordre.com/internationalstudies/internationalstudies/view/10.1093/acrefore/9780190846626.001.0001/acrefore-9780190846626-e-508

EITI. (2009, September 14) Addressing the roots of Liberia's conflicts through EITI. Retrieved from https://eiti.org/blog/addressing-roots-of-liberias-conflicts-through-eiti

Energy Commit to Action Campaign. (2020). Retrieved January 13, 2020, from https://www.cdp.net/en/campaigns/commit-to-action/energy

Feenberg, A. (1991). *Critical theory of technology*. New York, NY: Oxford University Press.

Fink, L. (2020, January 14). *Larry Fink's letter to CEOs*. Retrieved from https://www.blackrock.com/corporate/investor-relations/larry-fink-ceo-letter

Foley, V., & Haynes, C. (2009). The FCPA and its impact in Latin America. *Currents: International Trade Law Journal*, *17*(2), 27–42.

Global Governance: CSR and the Role of the UN Global Compact (2014). *Special Issue of the Journal of Business Ethics*.

Lev, B., Petrovits, C., & Radhakrishnan, S. (2010). Is doing good good for you? How corporate charitable contributions enhance revenue growth. *Strategic Management Journal*, *31*, 182–200. doi:10.1002/smj.810

Maak, T., Pless, N. M., & Voegtlin, C. (2016). Business statesman or shareholder advocate?: CEO responsible leadership styles and the micro-foundations of political CSR. *Journal of Management Studies*, *53*(3), 463–493. doi:10.1111/joms.12195

Mego, A. (2005). Experiences with dialogue. *Latinamerica Press*, *37*(2), 16.

Mischel, W. (1973). Toward a cognitive social learning reconceptualization of personality. *Psychological Review*, *80*(4), 252–283.

Peng, M. W., Lee, S.-H., & Wang, D. Y. L. (2005). What determines the scope of a firm over time? A focus on institutional relatedness. *Academy of Management Review*, *30*(3), 622–633.

Pogge, T. W. (2001). Eradicating systemic poverty: Brief for a global resources dividend. *Journal of Human Development*, *2*, 59–77.

Pogge, T. W. (2002). Moral universalism and global economic justice. *Politics, Philosophy & Economics*, *1*, 29–58.

Rangan, V., Barton, B., & Reffico, E. (2006). *Corporate responsibility and community engagement at the Tintaya copper mine*. Harvard Business School Case Study.

Reiche, B. S., Bird, A., Mendenhall, M. E., & Osland, J. S. (2017). Contextualizing leadership: A typology of global leadership roles. *Journal of International Business Studies*, *48*, 552–572.

Rittberger, V. (2002). *Global governance and the United Nations system*. New York, NY: United Nations University.

Rosenau, J. N., & Czempiel, E.-O. (1992). *Governance without government: Order and change in world politics*. Cambridge: Cambridge University Press.

Ruggie, J. (2007). Report of the special representative of the secretary-general on the issue of human rights and transnational corporations and other business enterprises. In J. Ruggie (Ed.), *Business and human rights: Mapping international standards of responsibility and accountability for corporate acts* (pp. 1–25). United Nations General Assembly Distribution A/HRC/4/35.

Singer, P. (2010, November 17). The diamond industry's search for clarity. *The Guardian*. Retrieved from https://www.theguardian.com/commentisfree/libertycentral/2010/nov/17/diamond-industry-search-clarity

Slack, K. (2009). Digging out from neoliberalism: Responses to environmental (mis) governance of the mining sector in Latin America. In J. Burdick, P. Oxhorn, & K. Roberts (Eds.), *Beyond neoliberalism in Latin America? Societies and politics at the crossroads* (1st ed., Studies of the Americas, pp. 117–134). New York, NY: Palgrave Macmillan.

Smith, N. C. (2003). Corporate social responsibility: Whether or how? *California Management Review*, *45*, 52–76.

Stahl, G. K., & Sully de Luque, M. (2014). Antecedents of responsible leader behavior: A research synthesis, conceptual framework, and agenda for future research. *Academy of Management Perspectives*, *28*(3), 235–254.

Stone, D. A. (1988). *Policy paradox and political reason*. Glenview, IL: Scott Foresman.

Thakur, R., & Van Langenhove, L. (2006). Enhancing global governance through regional integration. *Global Governance: A Review of Multilateralism and International Organizations, 12*(3), 233–240.

Trevino, L. K. (1992). The social effects of punishment in organizations: A justice perspective. *Academy of Management Review, 17*(4), 647–676.

Villo, S., Halme, M., & Ritvala, T. (2020). Theorizing MNE-NGO conflicts in state-capitalist contexts: Insights from the Greenpeace, Gazprom and the Russian state dispute in the Arctic. *Journal of World Business, 55*(3), 101068. doi:10.1016/j.jwb.2019.101068

Vizcarra, C. (2010). Book review: Corrupt circles: A history of unbound graft in Peru. *Journal of Economic History, 70*, 1008–1009.

Weinmann, L. (2004). Washington's irrational Cuba policy. *World Policy Journal, 21*, 22–31.

Weiss, T. G., & Thakur, R. (2010). *Global governance and the UN: An unfinished journey*. Bloomington, IN: Indiana University Press.

Wenar, L. (2008). Property rights and the resource curse. *Philosophy & Public Affairs, 36*(1), 2–32.

Wesley, D., & Montgomery, S. (2019, February 15). Flytenow, Inc.: Regulatory challenges in the sharing economy. Retrieved January 10, 2020, from https://www.iveycases.com/ProductView.aspx?id=100751

Wesley, D., & Spital, F. (2010, March 6). Launch of the Ford Fiesta diesel: The world's most efficient car. Retrieved January 10, 2020, from https://store.hbr.org/product/launch-of-the-ford-fiesta-diesel-the-world-s-most-efficient-car/910M40

What We Do. (2020). Retrieved January 13, 2020, from https://www.wemeanbusinesscoalition.org/about/

Whitaker, N. (2017, November 14). Our efforts to help protect journalists online. Retrieved January 10, 2020, from https://blog.google/outreach-initiatives/google-news-initiative/our-efforts-help-protect-journalists-online/

Woodman, S. (2018, January 29). *5 digital security tools to keep you, your work, and your sources safe*. Retrieved January 10, 2020, from https://www.icij.org/blog/2018/01/five-digital-security-tools-to-protect-your-work-and-sources/

Zurn, M. (2018). *A theory of global governance: Authority, legitimacy, and contestation*. Oxford: Oxford University Press.

WHAT MAKES FOR SUCCESSFUL REPATRIATE KNOWLEDGE TRANSFER? IMPLICATIONS FOR REPATRIATION AND GLOBAL LEADERSHIP

Joyce S. Osland, Betina Szkudlarek, Gary R. Oddou, Norihito Furuya and Juergen Deller

ABSTRACT

Knowledge transfer is an important global leader (GL) competency, given their role as knowledge brokers and capacity builders. However, knowledge transfer skills and the transfer process itself have received scant attention from both global mobility and leadership scholars. Similarly, multinationals have seldom systematically collected and utilized repatriate knowledge, despite the competitive advantage it represents in a global knowledge economy. To fill this gap, an exploratory qualitative study employing critical incidents and interviews with a multi-country sample of 47 German, Japanese, and US repatriates identified variables that facilitate knowledge transfer attempts to the work unit. Our findings corroborate the proposed variables in a conceptual model of the transfer process and articulate the transfer skills that help explain their ability to transfer. Most importantly, our findings introduce an interactive transfer model that explicates the microprocess of transfer in the repatriate–work unit relationship. We conclude with implications for global leadership research and HRM practice.

Advances in Global Leadership, Volume 13, 105–128
ISSN: 1535-1203/doi:10.1108/S1535-120320200000013004

Keywords: Global leadership; knowledge transfer; repatriate knowledge transfer; knowledge transfer skills; HRM practices; global leadership development

Given the challenges of today's global economy, the transfer of knowledge across global boundaries is a crucial resource for multinational enterprise survival and sustained competitive advantage (Grant, 1996; Gupta & Govindarajan, 2000). It is therefore a key priority for global leaders (GLs) (Bird & Oddou, 2013). Hinds (2020) found information power (Raven, 1965) to be the first type of power that GLs resorted to when influencing both global and domestic followers. The automotive leaders in his study used the following kinds of information when making a change request of followers: (1) additional facts and figures related to the change; (2) new perspectives; (3) new connections; and (4) new opportunities. The qualitative portion of Hinds' (2020) study revealed the microprocess between the transferor and the recipient of knowledge. Before using information power, GLs determined the quality and quantity of information that would be most effective with individual followers before the initial transfer and, if the change request proved unsuccessful, again prior to a subsequent request. According to Pauleen, Rooney, and Holden (2010), poor-quality knowledge transfer processes on the part of GLs can have detrimental effects on the firm's functioning. Although research on the intersection between global leadership and knowledge transfer is limited, the findings seem to indicate that expertise in transferring global knowledge is of critical importance to effective global leadership.

Expatriation has long been considered a key element of global leadership development (e.g., Black, Morrison & Gregersen, 1999; McCall & Hollenbeck, 2002; Osland, 2001). As part of their career development process, some GLs have the opportunity for an international assignment (IA) (Oddou & Mendenhall, 2018). Thus, a useful resource for understanding key aspects of global leadership knowledge transfer is the increased quantity of research on expatriate and repatriate knowledge transfer, our particular focus in this study.

Personnel rotation, and particularly expatriation, is a key method for acquiring and transferring knowledge (Argote, 1999; Harzing, Pudelko, & Reiche, 2016). Caligiuri and Bonache's (2016) review of global mobility framed the field's increasing emphasis on knowledge transfer in terms of the changing function of expatriation from control to organizational development or capacity building. Most firms, however, fail to systematically gather and compile the knowledge repatriates brought back from IAs (Oddou, Szkudlarek, Osland, Deller & Blakeney, 2013). Thus, the primary onus for transfer continues to rest on the initiative of individual repatriates, sometimes aided by empowering managers (Bucher, Burmeister, Osland & Deller, 2020). As mentioned above, expatriation is also a well-accepted method for developing GLs (e.g., Aycan, 2001; Mendenhall, 2006) and, as Bird (2001) argues, expatriation is the primary mechanism of creating and acquiring relevant global leadership knowledge. The nexus among IAs, knowledge transfer, and global leadership is therefore evident.

The strategic role of repatriates as GLs and carriers of global competency is an important source of competitive advantage (Caligiuri, 2006; Caligiuri & Lazarova, 2001; Furuya, Stevens, Bird, Oddou, & Mendenhall, 2009), not only as valuable, inimitable, and often incalculable resources (Fink, Meierewert, & Rohr, 2005) but also as quantifiable outcomes. For example, repatriate knowledge transfer (RKT) correlates with organizational innovativeness (Wang & Li, 2016), and intercultural experience acquired during IAs is directly tied to the firm's financial performance (Carpenter, Sanders, & Gregersen, 2001). Nonetheless, repatriate "know-how" is still better recognized by the external market than by the organizations that assigned and paid for their IAs (Mäkelä, Suutari, Brewster, Dickmann, & Tornikoski, 2016). Kamoche's (1997) warning about "dysfunctional labor turnover and the spillage of knowledge" (p. 218) did not result in greater efforts to retain repatriates (see Lazarova & Cerdin, 2007; Stahl, Chua, Caliguiri, Cerdin, & Taniguchi, 2009; Ye, Li, & Tan, 2017 on repatriate turnover). Although a greater understanding of knowledge transfer can be a competitive advantage (c.f., Argote & Ingram, 2000), RKT remains one of the weakest links in international management (Appafram & Sheikh, 2016; Szkudlarek, 2010; Szkudlarek & Sumpter, 2015). Given the lack of organizational effort to capture global knowledge, understanding the individual's role in the transfer assumes even greater importance. Their role in this process is indisputable in studies that stress the importance of the employee's proactivity in RKT (e.g., Berthoin Antal, 2001). Few studies, however, empirically investigated the specific factors that facilitate this process in various contexts or identify the relative influence of these factors.

We begin with a review of relevant literature and follow with a detailed report of empirical findings. In this exploratory study, we interviewed 47 repatriates from three countries and focused on their perception of variables facilitating or hindering RKT. Our purpose was to discover whether there were additional variables to those proposed in the conceptual model developed by Oddou, Osland, and Blakency (2009). After corroborating extant variables from that model, we identify their relative importance for the RKT process. We also introduce a new subset of RKT skills that facilitate knowledge flow and an interactive model of repatriate knowledge transfer with the work unit from the perspective of the individual. These skills likely to be are critical for the effectiveness of GLs in their effort to facilitate knowledge flows within and between organizational units. We conclude with implications for researchers working in the domains of RKT and global leadership and offer practical recommendations for successful knowledge transfer.

LITERATURE REVIEW

The Importance of Repatriate Knowledge in Global Leadership

Employee transformational work experiences, such as those elicited during IAs, constitute both global leadership learning and development opportunities for individuals as well as know-how necessary for achieving organizational objectives and growth (Bird & Oddou, 2013). Bird and Oddou (2013, p. 306) refer to IAs as "spirals of knowledge creation." International assignees acquire both intangible, tacit know-how, often subconsciously internalized and integrated by the individuals, and explicit and tangible information, often acquired independent of the context and the individual experiences of the learner (Nonaka, 1994). Yet, even if sojourning individuals do acquire invaluable knowledge of strategic relevance to their organizations, this knowledge is lost if not disseminated successfully throughout the organization upon repatriation. Below we discuss the key factors affecting the RKT process.

Repatriate Knowledge Transfer

Two conceptual RKT models guided the RKT domain's development thus far. Lazarova and Tarique's (2005) prescriptive model is rooted in HRM and organizational behavior concepts. They argue that RKT requires a fit between individual readiness to transfer knowledge and organizational receptivity and between repatriate career objectives and appropriate career development opportunities. Oddou et al.'s (2009) multidisciplinary model describes the RKT phenomenon in terms of three primary components: the repatriate's characteristics (transferors); the work unit's characteristics (recipients); and the transfer process, which is affected positively or negatively by the shared field (the socialization period, communication frequency, and development of mutual trust, which culminates in the perception of repatriates as outsiders or insiders) impacting the relationship between transferors and recipients. Both models stress the critical role played by repatriating individuals, but neither model has been tested empirically. Individual characteristics of repatriates' disseminative capacity have proved to be key elements in successful RKT (Arzensek, Kosmrlj, & Sirca, 2014; Oddou et al., 2013; Sanchez-Vidal, Sanz-Valle, & Barba-Aragon, 2016). Scholars identified numerous factors framed as facilitators of RKT (Crowne, 2009; Zulkifly, Ismail, & Hamzah, 2019; Lazarova & Tarique, 2005, Oddou et al., 2009; Sanchez-Vidal et al., 2016). The six main categories (personality traits, motivation, behavioral stance, abilities/skills, individual's work role, and relationships) that play a role in RKT are described below.

First, research suggests that personality traits are important enablers of RKT (c.f., Furuya et al., 2009). Yet, some scholars argue that personality characteristics can be difficult to measure and can vary in their outward manifestation depending on the context (Roberts & Pomerantz, 2004). As behaviors and attitudes are more readily trained and modified than personality, it may be more useful to understand the actual behaviors and attitudes leading to successful RKT, which personality traits might influence.

Second, motivation to transfer has been shown empirically to facilitate RKT (Berthoin Antal, 2001; Huang, Chiu, & Lu, 2013; Oddou et al., 2013; Sanchez-Vidal et al., 2016). This has been conceptualized as repatriate career considerations (Breitenmoser, Bader & Berg, 2018; Lazarova & Tarique, 2005; Oddou et al., 2009) or personal commitment (Berthoin Antal, 2001;

Oddou et al., 2009). Lazarova and Tarique (2005) argued conceptually that motivation to transfer is externally encouraged through various MNCs support practices. Similarly, Furuya et al. (2009) showed that organizational support before and after repatriation resulted in greater knowledge transfer, readjustment, and performance. However, other empirical studies found that organizational support during expatriation and reentry had limited, if any, impact on RKT (Burmeister & Deller, 2016; Sanchez-Vidal et al., 2016). With respect to intrinsic motivation, empirical research indicates that repatriates' natural inclination and internal sense of responsibility to share the newly acquired expertise is of relevance to RKT (Berthoin Antal, 2001; Oddou et al., 2013). Oddou et al. (2009) argue that both intrinsic and extrinsic motivators affect RKT. Huang et al. (2013) found that motivation and opportunity mediated the relationship between knowledge governance mechanisms (particularly formal and informal mechanisms) and repatriate knowledge sharing. More empirical research is needed to provide definitive answers to questions about the role played by extrinsic and intrinsic motivators in RKT.

Third, researchers have suggested and found across a variety of types of repatriates that proactivity to transfer knowledge is key (Berthoin Antal, 2001; Carr, Inkson & Thorne, 2005; Hall, 1996; Lazarova & Tarique, 2005; O'Sullivan, 2002; Oddou et al., 2013). For example, Roberts (2012) and James (2019) found that proactivity can be seen in the type of language and mental frameworks repatriates use to bridge any communication gap with others. Furthermore, such proactivity has also been used to build trust and legitimacy with repatriates' superiors and peers (Roberts, 2012), another element related to RKT that will be discussed later.

Fourth, several conceptual models refer to the ability to transfer knowledge as important predictors of RKT success (Crowne, 2009; Lazarova & Tarique, 2005; Oddou et al., 2009). Lazarova and Tarique's (2005) proposed model simply mentions repatriate ability as a category but fails to specify its contents. The Oddou et al. model (2009) specifies ability as expertise and social networks. Crowne (2009) focuses on repatriates' ability to enact feedback seeking behaviors as proposed facilitators of RKT. Yet, no empirical research has studied transfer abilities in the context of repatriation.

Fifth, other enablers of RKT include the individual's work role (Oddou et al., 2009), such as their reentry position, and both the amount of influence it carries over subordinates (e.g., an expert role, managerial role, etc.) and the coherence it reflects with the lessons learned in their IA position (i.e., the similarity between the IA position and the reentry position). Oddou et al. (2009) postulate this influences how relevant the repatriate's knowledge is and therefore its acceptance by other workgroup members. A recent empirical study of 129 repatriates and their supervisors (Froese, Stoermer, Reiche, & Klar, forthcoming) shows that repatriate embeddedness fit, defined as the degree of perceived compatibility between a repatriate's knowledge and skills and the requirements of their work unit, has a positive effect on RKT.

Finally, the relationship between transferors and recipients impacts the transfer process. Oddou et al. (2009) maintain that repatriates have to be trusted and accepted by the work unit for transfer to occur. Burmeister et al. (2015) confirmed that trust between repatriates and their work unit (as perceived and reported by the knowledge sender) was important to sharing. She and her colleagues focused explicitly on the microprocesses that took place during the RKT process, which includes a mutual assessment of the trustworthiness of repatriates and recipients (Burmeister et al., 2015). Similarly, social networks (Crowne, 2009) and social capital (c.f., Ismail et al., 2019; Kostova & Roth, 2003; Reiche, 2012) have been shown to facilitate transfer. For example, the richness of ties between the expatriate and host-country nationals can potentially provide a broader base for continuous knowledge sharing upon reentry. These strong relationships, as opposed to weaker arms-length interactions, have more potential to be effective when transferring tacit knowledge (Mäkelä, 2007). Finally, Appafram and Sheikh (2016) point toward mentoring, a relational activity, as a form of social interaction in RKT (see also Chen & Vogel, 2016). In sum, these findings highlight partial support for the importance of repatriate and work unit relationships in the RKT process.

To summarize, there is general conceptual agreement, but limited empirical proof, that numerous repatriate characteristics, as well as the repatriate–work unit relationship, affect RKT. Both conceptual and empirical researches treat these variables as equally important, thereby limiting our understanding of the dynamics of the RKT process. Therefore, our study was undertaken (1) to gain a deeper understanding of the previously proposed but largely unexplored individual-related aspects of RKT using a multi-country, qualitative repatriate sample; (2) to better understand the relative importance of those aspects; and (3) to obtain a richer, more detailed comprehension of the microprocesses involved in RKT to advance research and practice at the intersection of RKT and global leadership.

METHODOLOGY

Data Collection

The sample consists of 47 repatriates—15 each from Germany and the United States and 17 from Japan. The sample was drawn from the IT, automotive, retail, and manufacturing industries and included four German, two Japanese, and five US global companies with numerous expatriates and two common characteristics. All companies are large and successful, evidenced by their listing on the German DAX, Japanese Nikkei, or the US Fortune 500. Because this was an exploratory study, the two sampling criteria were (1) adequate time in an expatriate assignment to allow for adaption and the acquisition of global knowledge and (2) enough time after repatriation to transfer knowledge. Thus, subjects had been abroad for at least 12 months and returned between 6 months and 5 years to ensure sufficient support and opportunities for RKT and enough recency for accurate retrospective accounts. We interviewed 40 repatriates in person; the remaining seven interviews took place by phone due to repatriate schedules. Interviews lasted from 60 to 90 minutes.

About 36 interviewees were male (77%); 11 were female (23%). The average age was 37.8 years; average assignment length was 25.3 months. Over one-third (37%) had multiple IAs; one repatriate had three international posts, the others had two.

A semi-structured interview protocol addressed five areas: types of knowledge acquired during the IA, the reentry experience, variables influencing the transfer, critical incidents of both successful and unsuccessful knowledge transfer attempts to the work unit, and recommendations for other repatriates/HRM/company about RKT. Interviews included questions such as: "Was the assignment you were given upon reentry a natural follow-up in terms of capitalizing on what you experienced and learned in the international assignment?" "Can you think of a specific decision or situation in your work unit where you have made an important impact that was primarily a result of a capability/perspective you gained during your international experience?" Interviewees were also asked to describe a critical incident (Flanagan, 1954) of both a successful and an unsuccessful attempt to transfer repatriate knowledge to their work unit.

Data Analysis

Both the German data and the US data were coded and conclusions were agreed upon by pairs of native speakers. A native speaker collected and coded the Japanese data; two other team members, in consultation with the native speaker, coded the English-translated summaries of the Japanese data. Content analysis was done using the conventional content analysis approach, at times supported with directed coding (Hsieh & Shannon, 2005). Conventional content analysis is employed to describe a phenomenon in the most comprehensive way (Hsieh & Shannon, 2005, p. 1279). This inductive bottom-up theorizing, where new themes are extracted directly from the empirical data (Shepherd & Sutcliffe, 2011), was the primary focus of our data analysis process.

Directed content analysis is used to validate or extend an existing theory or model (Hsieh & Shannon, 2005, p. 1281) and could be seen as having theoretical links to both analytic induction and inductive bottom-up theorizing. Analytic induction allows moving back and forth between the existing theory, the data collection, and the theory development. This approach, originally proposed by Znaniecki (1934), is used to readjust and redefine concepts, theories, and models (Manning, 1982). In our case, existing RKT models served as an initial knowledge claim to be redefined through collected empirical data. Both approaches rely on similar inductive assumptions, with the latter achieving rigor by focusing on thorough scrutiny of evidence that refutes the initial knowledge claim and the former by achieving robustness and utility of codes (Silverman, 2010).

Besides applying content analysis, we also tabulated frequencies of our findings, as the number of the interviews is too small for a full and representative quantitative analysis. In a developing field like RKT, however, frequencies can give a first estimate of the quantitative importance of categories, with the caveat that such results must be treated with caution and require validation in subsequent research with large samples. The relative influence of the RKT variables was determined by the frequency of their mention in answers to open-ended questions (Duriau, Reger, & Pfarrer, 2007). The authors grouped the frequency counts into quartiles to more easily represent relative importance to RKT: 0%–25% of the repatriates who mentioned a given variable (first quartile—"unimportant"), 26%–50% (second quartile—"somewhat important"), 51%–75% (third quartile—"important"), and 76%–100% (fourth quartile—"very important").

Results

The results section presents the findings in the following sequence. First, we report the repatriate characteristics found in the data that corroborate previously proposed relationships in models of RKT or prior research. To provide a baseline for their relative weight, the frequencies of all these variables also appear in Table 1. The narrative includes representative quotations to reveal the feeling or intensity of the frequency response. Finally, we present new emergent themes— transfer skills and a new interactive model of RKT that conveys the overarching story of the RKT process.

Table 1. Repatriate Knowledge Transfer (RKT) Variables in Ascending Order of Relative Importance.

RKT Variables	Number of Interviewees Who Mentioned these Variables as Facilitators of RKT	Percentage of Interviewees and Quartile	Relative Level of Importance
Position influence	16	34% Second quartile	Somewhat important
Career considerations	17	36% Second quartile	Somewhat important
Relevant role responsibilities	18	38% Second quartile	Somewhat important
Social network	22	47% Second quartile	Somewhat important
Relevant repatriate knowledge	25	53% Third quartile	Important
Work unit acceptance	25	53% Third quartile	Important
Personal commitment	31	66% Third quartile	Important
Perceived trust	42	89% Fourth quartile	Very important

Note(s): N = 47.
0%–25% (First quartile) = not important.
25%–50% (Second quartile) = somewhat important.
50%–75% (Third quartile) = moderately important.
75%–100% (Fourth quartile) = important.

REPATRIATE CHARACTERISTICS THAT FACILITATE REPATRIATE KNOWLEDGE TRANSFER

Variables categorized as contextual conditions and repatriate motivation were frequently mentioned as either somewhat important or important facilitators, corroborating previous findings that repatriates perceive the primary initiative and responsibility for knowledge transfer as theirs.

CONTEXTUAL CONDITIONS THAT FACILITATE REPATRIATE KNOWLEDGE TRANSFER

Contextual conditions comprise individual-level variables—relevant repatriate knowledge, position influence, relevant role responsibilities, and social capital—that are rooted in the repatriate's context. Some of these variables are fully or partially outside the repatriate's control. For example, the IA knowledge that repatriates acquire is determined in part by the location and job responsibilities of their assignment; and its relevance depends upon the assigned repatriate role and perceptions of the work unit.

Perceived Relevance of Repatriate Knowledge

Although all interviewees were able to readily identify their acquired knowledge, for actual transfer to occur, it must be perceived as relevant. We define relevant knowledge as *the knowledge repatriates acquired during the international assignment that has some application to their reentry work environment.* Thus, repatriate knowledge is categorized here as a contextual condition because it is valued differently depending on the work unit in question. Based on a frequency count of repatriates mentioning this as important to the transfer, it is thus located in the third quartile and therefore an "important" RKT facilitator.

The following quote from a US returnee underscores what happens when repatriate knowledge is perceived as irrelevant by a work unit manager.

> The boss that I had had me doing a bunch of stuff that didn't have anything to do with experience that I could pass on. ...it was about a year where I was not able to use any knowledge I'd acquired... Or even when I tried [to transfer my knowledge] it wasn't appreciated... a couple of times he [the boss] would actually say "shut up."

Position Influence

Only 16 repatriates identified position influence as a factor in successfully transferring knowledge, placing this variable into the "somewhat important" quartile. However, not having asked repatriates if they returned to a managerial role limits the ability to generalize from these results. Some participants did observe the benefits of position influence in other repatriates. One said the following:

> A lot of them [company repatriates] came back in some sort of team lead/leadership role where they were able to freely direct people or share their knowledge. "Hey, this is what we did" and it worked well.

Moreover, many participants acknowledged the importance of the work unit manager's role in facilitating their own RKT. Thus, position influence clearly plays a role in RKT.

Relevant Role Responsibilities

When asked about critical factors in successful RKT, 18 repatriates identified similar or related job responsibilities between the expatriate position and the repatriate job. Thus, this response falls into the second quartile and appears to be "somewhat important." A German repatriate acknowledged the importance of the right reentry position:

> I do think that my knowledge is more actively used because I have been specially given this position... I think knowledge transfer has really a lot to do with the position.

In theory, such similarity of job responsibilities inherently makes repatriates' knowledge more relevant and contributes to the real and perceived criticality of that knowledge by the work unit. However, with few exceptions, the firms studied made few attempts to tie reentry jobs to the knowledge acquired as an expatriate. Reflecting the frustration of failed knowledge transfer attempts, a Japanese repatriate expressed that "repatriates are assigned to work that has nothing to do with their [former IA] job responsibilities."

Social Networks

Twenty-two respondents mentioned that social networks facilitate RKT, placing this variable into the "somewhat important" quartile as well.

Further analysis of the interviews, however, clarifies the potential value of this variable in RKT beyond the frequency categorization. We found that interviewees personally rely on their networks for a variety of purposes: information acquisition, problem resolution, consultation on potential promotions, and job placements based on their exposure and knowledge about employees in other countries.

Importantly, however, repatriates use their networks not only to transfer knowledge themselves but also to benefit the organization by serving as boundary spanners and brokers of knowledge transfer. For instance, as a result of his expatriate experience and the network he developed, a Japanese repatriate stated, "I am sometimes asked to help others communicate with foreign clients and partners [that I associated with in my IA]." They connect members of their network with one another and confer the trust needed between those members to transfer knowledge. An American repatriate aided coworkers to access help and build their own networks during both his IA and reentry.

> I not only make sure the knowledge transfer occurs, but it also helps them to build a network... One of the most important things about going out on assignment was being expected to bring my network and leave them [foreign company employees] with continuous access to it. Of course, there is an opportunity to do that when I come back too—to put the people here in touch with networks and other places that can help them.

Thus, repatriates serve not only as direct sources of knowledge to the work unit but also as knowledge brokers who put people in their domestic and global networks into contact with one another to share knowledge.

Social networks also contributed to building credibility and trust, both internationally and at the home office. Some repatriates benefited as "friends of friends." A US repatriate recounted, "Because I already knew some team members from various venues, their acceptance made it easier to be trusted and accepted by the ones I did not [know]." This particular aspect of trust will be explored further in the section titled "Relational Space between the Repatriate and the Work Unit."

MOTIVATION TO TRANSFER KNOWLEDGE

Given the onus on repatriates to initiate transfer, a willingness to transfer knowledge or an interest in doing so seems a necessary condition for RKT. Repatriates had to *want* to transfer what they have learned, especially given the obstacles this can entail. Although the interviewees' motives for transferring knowledge varied widely, they centered primarily on personal commitment and integrity, while career considerations were less frequently mentioned in the interviews.

Career Considerations

Seventeen repatriates mentioned some type of career consideration, such as reputational gains, as a motive for transferring knowledge; as such, this variable falls into the "somewhat important" quartile. However, the interviewees seldom referred to their own career goals or mentioned any official company-sponsored career development plans that facilitated knowledge transfer. One of the few comments categorized as personal career considerations related to reputational capital, mentioned by an American:

> The reward for me was to have great results in my job, have a great reputation based on that, or build my reputation based on that.

Others mentioned indirect career impacts as a motivator that will hopefully pay off over time. For example, a Japanese manager reflected that RKT has an indirect impact on career progress in his organization.

> There is no formal mechanism for giving any special reward. However, if repatriates utilize their own acquired skills and knowledge and make a considerable contribution to the company, they are normally given a high evaluation.

Personal Commitment

Thirty-one repatriates mentioned their commitment was a major reason behind their attempts to transfer knowledge. This reflects an "important" relationship between personal commitment and RKT. Their commitment took two different

forms, one related to the work unit and/or the organization and the other associated with the personal conviction that knowledge transfer is the right thing to
do, a form of personal integrity. Contrastingly, only *one* repatriate noted that
there were financial incentives to encourage repatriates to transfer knowledge.

Work Unit/Organizational Commitment

The first type of commitment related to a desire to help the work unit and/or the
organization be more successful. An American repatriate described his commitment to the company in these terms:

> Well, [I transferred knowledge] just because it's there. I care about the company, I care about
> the success, I care about the quality of every decision that's made. And if I have an opportunity
> to positively impact the decision or make the decision a much more quality event, then I'm
> just—for me as a person—I'm going to do that.

Personal Integrity

The second type of personal commitment repatriates mentioned concerned
intrinsic moral schemas, explaining that sharing their knowledge was "the right
thing to do." A German repatriate explained his motive for sharing knowledge as
a variant on "paying it forward":

> I have become rich abroad and I try somehow to pass it on, and this happens every day—even
> without encouragement.

RELATIONAL SPACE BETWEEN THE REPATRIATE AND THE WORK UNIT

In addition to the personal contextual conditions and motivations of the repatriate,
other factors that facilitate RKT pertain to the relational space between the
repatriate and the work unit. This space can be described in part by whether
repatriates are viewed as outsiders or insiders by the work unit. Viewed as an in-
group member, there is a greater likelihood of work unit acceptance and trust
between that repatriate and other work unit members. The variables in this category were found to be either "important" or "very important" in facilitating RKT.

Perceived Trust

Forty-two repatriates acknowledged the importance of trust in successful RKT,
making it the most frequently mentioned variable. Both the repatriate and the
work unit must perceive one another as trustworthy. Some repatriates transfer
knowledge only after assessing the work unit member(s)' trustworthiness. For
instance, a German repatriate shared only technical knowledge rather than things
related to social capital ("personal things or how I can change someone's
behavior") when there was no trust between him and his coworkers.

The interviewees frequently acknowledged that the work unit has to first trust the repatriate, as another German repatriate explained.

> The trust [on the part of the work unit] must be there to say: "He [the repatriate] has built this knowledge that I take now. And I trust that the colleague knows, because he has had this [IA] experience."

Acceptance

Acceptance is sometimes an outcome of the socialization process that takes place in the shared field between the repatriate and the work unit. Twenty-five respondents stated that work unit acceptance is a key element in RKT, putting it into the "important" quartile. As with trust, gaining acceptance can take both time and effort, particularly when personnel changes occur during their time abroad.

The realization that one often becomes an out-group member during the IA is sobering and anxiety-producing for some repatriates. An American documented both feeling like an outsider and the length of time needed to gain acceptance:

> No one cared about what I thought or could bring to the table; decision making was centralized with the manager. He didn't elicit my views, just the in-group's views. The work unit had been ordered to find a place for me, so the acceptance level was not high, and it took me about a year to find my place.

For a summary of the relative value of the aforementioned repatriate characteristics that facilitate RKT, arranged from the least important to the most important, see Table 1. Overall, our results corroborate the conceptual propositions and limited empirical research findings in the field. Importantly, the results also extend our understanding of the relative importance of previously identified research variables.

EMERGENT THEMES

In addition to the RKT facilitators in Table 1, two novel concepts emerged in the data—transfer skills on the part of repatriates and an interactive model of RKT.

Repatriate Knowledge Transfer Skills

A specific set of transfer behaviors surfaced in descriptions of critical incidents and in response to an open-ended question regarding "factors that facilitated or impeded your attempt to share your overseas knowledge." Content analysis revealed six skills, described below in three categories: self-related, process, and interpersonal skills. See Table 2 for representative quotations for each skill component.

Table 2. Components of Repatriate Transfer Skills and Representative Quotations.

Transfer Skills	Representative Quotations
Self-related	
Self-monitoring	"You cannot talk too much about your experience; they were not there and so, in a sense, don't care and cannot understand. So, you have to be careful about going and talking too much about it, even though you want to." (USA)
	"I could manage to share knowledge and skills with my colleagues. However, when I was speaking only about my overseas experiences to my friends, some of them seemed uninterested and maybe upset with me. [...] They felt that I was showing off with my overseas experiences." (Japan)
Persisting	"I think you have to be committed. I think it's commitment and it's also persistence. So, if I got easily discouraged because I tried to transfer the knowledge and I didn't penetrate in my first couple of conversations, and then if I just said, 'Well, forget it. If they don't want to know, I don't care,' then that's a problem – you won't be successful." (USA)
	"It is important to have a strong will to try to pass my own message to explain my experiences and knowledge to the current office colleagues and department." (Japan)
Process-oriented	
Assessing	"Before the transfer can take place it is very important to know how much knowledge and skills the overseas assignees actually acquired. And whether it is relevant." (Japan)
	"If I feel like I've got an idea or an experience, which in a specific situation can be helpful, then of course I try to offer a person my knowledge by saying: this is the way I have done this or that before." (Germany)
Contextualizing	"One has to be aware of differences in work styles between Japan and overseas in order to be able to utilize the skills and knowledge after repatriation." (Japan)
	"The re-entry process is simply focused on getting into your new job and doing it. It's not about bridging the old [international assignment] experience to the new [re-entry] experience. [...] I think sometimes the experiences are so different that people don't know how to connect what you learned to where they are." (USA)
Timing	"I had to listen first to understand what is important to [my colleague]. Weeks before [the knowledge transfer took place] I noticed that he was unhappy, and I just listened and let him talk. [...] I was able to fall back on it and then respond personally to him. Not mechanically, but based on what I've learned over time, about him personally regarding how he feels and what interests him." (Germany)
	"I did not always attempt to transfer knowledge, because although I have a will to convey my idea and information to others, I have to be careful in selecting the right timing and the right people." (Japan)
Interpersonal	
Empathizing	"Empathy for these people you work with now. [...] If you don't have empathy, then you will not be able to transfer knowledge." (Germany)
	"Suddenly my perspective was changed. You begin to listen to the things that you didn't listen to before; you read between the lines, you hear between the lines differently. [...] I was put in a circumstance where there was no way I could have been successful had I not learned to listen differently." (USA)

Self-related Skills

(1) *Self-monitoring the content and amount of knowledge shared, guided by situational cues to social appropriateness*: Interviewees frequently criticized other repatriates who fail at knowledge transfer because they lacked the ability to monitor their conversation. Talking too much about international stories, knowledge, and comparisons and failing to pick up on the work unit's negative reaction resulted in perceptions of some repatriates as arrogant "know-it-alls" and tuning them out. Therefore, the work unit was not motivated to listen when such repatriates tried to transfer knowledge, and lack of self-monitoring seemed to cement their status as an out-group member. In contrast, successful transferors were more adept at reading social cues and reactions to their IA stories and information. They quickly realized that they had to limit how much they talked about the IA and curbed any tendency to assume or convey that their international knowledge and experience equated to superiority. Thus, successful RKT seems to require high self-monitoring, which Snyder (1986) describes as self-observation and self-control guided by situational cues to social appropriateness.

(2) *Persisting in attempts to transfer knowledge*: The benefit of framing transfer as an ongoing influence process requiring persistence was a recurring theme in the interviews. This validates Cross and Prusak's (2003) portrayal of general knowledge transfer as an influence process. In the RKT context, the interviewees described the transfer process as a difficult one requiring patience, persistence, and the ability to influence others and adapt one's approach until they were successful. One-time attempts, especially in the beginning of reentry, were unlikely to succeed, but unsuccessful transferors often gave up after a failed attempt.

Process Skills

(1) *Assessing the relevance of their knowledge to the work unit*: Part of successful transfer means recognizing what specific IA knowledge, out of the entire store of a repatriate's global knowledge, is really critical to the work unit and being able to assess and understanding how that piece of knowledge relates to the work unit. This required listening carefully to work unit discussions about problems so that repatriates could demonstrate that their expertise is relevant and contributes to solutions. Assessing also involved determining how much knowledge to transfer so that the work unit is not overwhelmed.

(2) *Contextualizing the knowledge to the local context so that recipients can understand it*: Two RKT barriers surfaced in this study that highlight a need for contextualization. First, some work unit members who lack global exposure and IA experience had no context to help them understand the nature or importance of repatriate knowledge. Second, xenophobic responses to "foreign" IA knowledge sometimes prevented a fair hearing of repatriate knowledge and served as a barrier to RKT. Consequently, successful

transferors learned to find ways to contextualize their knowledge by relating it to the circumstances of the work unit and the organization. This involved explaining information in terms that the work unit could understand and tying the knowledge to local conditions in resistant or cautious work units. In extreme cases, this process involved stripping the acquired knowledge of any reference to a foreign source or IA and simply presenting it to the work unit as "objective" information untethered to geography.

(3) *Timing when their transfer has the greatest chance of acceptance*: Choosing the right time to transfer knowledge played an important role in RKT. Successful repatriates waited for a teachable moment when the work unit members were ready to receive knowledge—for example, when they were grappling with an issue related to the repatriate's expertise, had exhausted all other avenues of problem solving, or realized that the repatriate's prior knowledge transfer was extremely useful. More generally, RKT had a greater chance of success if repatriates waited until they were accepted by the work unit and had earned a sufficient level of both trust and credibility in their eyes.

Interpersonal Skills

(1) *Empathizing and reading the socioemotional contextual cues regarding the RKT process*: Successful RKT also required empathy, which allowed the repatriates to understand and interpret the socioemotional contextual clues in the RKT process. For example, empathy allowed them to perceive the trust level and attitudes of receivers toward both the foreign knowledge and its source. It also enabled them to overcome work unit reluctance or fear toward new knowledge. The ability to emotionally relate to the work unit and its members helped repatriates better utilize the previously mentioned transfer skills.

INTERACTIVE MODEL OF REPATRIATE KNOWLEDGE TRANSFER

Repeated examination of the variables facilitating RKT and the transfer skills that became evident brought into focus how the various parts function as a whole. The picture is clearly one of an interactive and iterative nature. Below we present a "live" model of repatriate-work unit RKT, illustrated in Fig. 1. The dotted lines in the model represent potential actions in the RKT process.

(1) The impetus for RKT comes from either the repatriate or, less frequently, the work unit, as shown in the upper left of the model.
(2) In the simplest case, when the repatriate initiates the transfer or the work unit asks repatriates for IA knowledge, the repatriate knowledge is consequently accepted and used, resulting in Success. If the work unit demonstrates a high demand for repatriate knowledge and there are no transfer obstacles, RKT facilitators (Contextual Conditions, Repatriate Motivation and Transfer

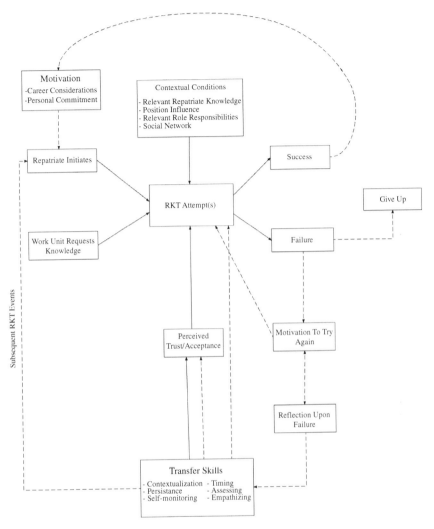

Note. Dotted lines represent potential actions.

Fig. 1.   Interactive Model of Repatriate Knowledge Transfer.

Skills, and Perceived Trust and Acceptance) may play a less significant role in the transfer process.

(3) Successful RKT might result in more work unit requests for different knowledge or more repatriate-initiated transfer attempts, as shown by the dotted line running from the Success box to the Repatriate Initiates and Work Unit Requests Knowledge boxes.

(4) When the RKT situation is more complex, more facilitators (Contextual Conditions, Perceived Trust and Acceptance on the part of the work unit, Motivation, and Transfer Skills) influence the RKT process.

(5) When the initial RKT attempt results in failure, there are three options.

• First, repatriates who fail and are not motivated to try again end the RKT process at the Give Up option in the model.

• Second, repatriates who fail may choose to make another attempt utilizing the same transfer method, taking the model's path from Failure to the Motivation To Try Again option, and on through RKT Attempt(s). If another component of the model has changed in the meantime (e.g., Perceived Trust/Acceptance), the same RKT method may be successful; otherwise, another failure is likely.

• Third, repatriates who fail but are motivated to try again and figure out what went wrong undergo a reflection period. This focus on learning from experience often leads to the realization that a simplistic attempt at knowledge transfer is not sufficient. Instead, they acquire a more accurate understanding of the RKT process. Their path leads from Failure, through Reflection Upon Failure to Transfer Skills to Motivation to Try Again. Their subsequent success or failure may depend upon the accuracy of their reflection or the presence of other barriers.

(6) Some repatriates already possess and enact transfer skills at the beginning of their repatriation period. Presumably, these skills may help them develop work unit trust and acceptance, which is reflected in the solid line from Transfer Skills to Perceived Trust/Acceptance. Other repatriates only acquire these skills after reflecting upon failed RKT or being open to external interventions like feedback, coaching, or training. Transfer skills can mediate successful knowledge transfer; the situation, however, can determine whether all skills are required in similar degrees. These skills can be deployed to retry transferring the original knowledge, as evidenced by the dotted line up to RKT Attempt(s), or they can be utilized in subsequent RKT events, as shown by the dotted line to the left and upwards to the Repatriate Initiates box.

(7) If perceived trust and acceptance were lacking in previous attempt(s) to transfer knowledge, more trust building or perhaps time and effort are necessary to gain acceptance before another attempt at knowledge transfer will be successful. This is indicated by the dotted line from the Skills box to the Perceived Trust and Acceptance box and then upwards to RKT Attempt(s).

DISCUSSION

From a conceptual perspective, this qualitative study makes several significant contributions. First, it provides evidence of the importance of RKT variables related to individual characteristics and the work unit relationship from countries in three different world regions. Second, our data support the primarily conceptual nature of RKT models and provide guidance for future empirical research. This study is the first to rank the relative importance of RKT variables, highlighting the prominence of perceived trust. Third, this study unpacks broad conceptual constructs, such as repatriate ability and motivation, into more relevant and fine-grained micro-level variables. These are especially important to GL development and effectiveness given the criticality of GL skills in gaining sustainable competitive advantage in a global context (Petrick, Scherer, Brodzinski, Quinn, & Ainina, 1999). Fourth, we identify the novel concept of RKT transfer skills, which appear to mediate RKT success. Finally, we introduce a dynamic, interactive model of RKT, taking a microprocess approach. The model's primary lesson is that the context of RKT is not identical, simple, or static. Instead, RKT is an iterative, interactive process whose success depends largely on the repatriate's initiative, learning agility, transfer skills, adaptability, and capacity for influencing work unit members.

Although empirical research confirms the role of the ability to transfer knowledge in RKT (Burmeister et al., 2015), scant attention has been paid to the specific behaviors used in successful transfer. Our findings describe transfer skills that assess knowledge criticality and work unit receptivity, timing and contextualization of the knowledge to enhance absorption based upon empathy and perspective taking, and persistence in the face of failed attempts. Successful transferors quickly recognize the constraints in RKT, acknowledge their mistakes, and adapt their behavior accordingly. Throughout the process, successful transferors self-monitor their own behavior. These findings are consistent with Crowne's (2009) hypothesis that feedback seeking behaviors from repatriates (and work units) can contribute to RKT. By contrast, unsuccessful transferors were described as arrogant know-it-alls and abandoned transfer efforts after meeting initial resistance.

STUDY LIMITATIONS

The limitations of a qualitative study of this nature pertain primarily to restrictions on generalizability and the tentative nature of our findings. The multi-country sample reflects our effort to avoid the limitations of a single culture sample. However, small numbers prevent cross-cultural comparisons and generalizations among the German, Japanese, and US subsamples. More quantitative studies are needed to determine if cultural differences impact specific RKT variables.

Because we did not interview the work unit or supervisors, we do not know how they perceived the repatriates' transfer efforts or whether they utilized their knowledge. Their perspectives would be extremely valuable in future research, as would the measurement of organizational policies that influence and facilitate RKT.

In sample selection, we targeted countries with developed economies that send out high numbers of expatriates. It is possible, however, that there is less receptivity in such countries to knowledge emanating from lesser developed countries or from subsidiaries that are perceived as marginal (Gupta & Govindarajan, 2000; Taylor & Osland, 2011). Furthermore, our sample includes highly ranked MNCs. Business success can breed a sense of superiority and indifference to external sources of knowledge, which might cause IA knowledge to have less perceived currency. By contrast, there is evidence of more receptivity to repatriate knowledge in India (Kulkarni, Lengnick, & Valk, 2010; Valk, Van der Velde, Van Engen, & Szkudlarek, 2015) and to returnee knowledge in South Korea (Roberts, 2012). This has been attributed to a greater hunger to learn from more developed economies. Thus, our findings may not be generalizable to countries at all stages of globalization or to businesses of varying size with different trajectories in global business and rankings.

A few US firms in this sample seemed "more global," as evidenced by greater global mindset and receptivity to repatriate knowledge and an organizational culture in which knowledge sharing was directly linked to global strategy. Their interviewees voiced fewer complaints about RKT, repatriation, and HR support, and their IA knowledge was requested both within and beyond their work unit. It is possible these firms also had a closer alignment among talent mobility, HRM, and business goals and have integrated reentry jobs into the career management process in order to attract and retain high potentials sent on IAs (Brookfield, 2016).

In summary, future RKT sample selection and theory building should take into consideration these contingencies: the degree of economic development, perceived currency of repatriate knowledge and its source, and the alignment between organizational culture and learning orientation and between global strategy and HRM. We confirmed Wang's (2015) finding that knowledge transfer is influenced by xenophobia. Its impact on the perceived currency of global knowledge in RKT in this study should not be overlooked in future research and sample selection.

FUTURE RESEARCH DIRECTIONS

Empirical studies of the RKT variables in Table 1 could further test their relative importance and interactions. The contingencies reflected in the interactive model provide a promising new avenue for RKT theory building and research, with the hope of moving beyond the field's reliance to date on the MOA framework (motivation, opportunity, ability) (Blumberg & Pringle, 1982). For example, do optimal work unit or organizational situations for RKT imply a lesser need for RKT facilitators and transfer skills? Is a threshold level among several variables required for successful RKT? Does length of time since reentry interact with perceived trust and acceptance to influence repatriate ability and motivation to transfer knowledge or work unit receptivity? Transfer skills also represent a ripe field for study. Is the list in Table 2 complete? What are the best ways to measure and develop these skills? If companies were to select expatriates on the basis of existing transfer skills, would they demonstrate significantly higher levels of knowledge during both IAs and repatriation?

Although we did not focus broadly on work unit characteristics in this study, other research has identified RKT facilitators among work unit recipients as strong global strategic goals, high absorptive capacity, supportive work unit managers, and the presence of other repatriates (Bucher et al., 2020; Burmeister, Lazarova, & Deller, 2018; Oddou et al., 2013). Perhaps a high degree of these variables might necessitate fewer repatriate RKT facilitators and less transfer skills in particular. Until more work units and their managers develop this capacity, however, the greater burden for RKT will continue to fall on repatriates.

These findings also have implications for global leadership research. First, the interactive model could inform Hinds' (2020) exploratory findings on the process GLs use to convey information power. Second, how relevant are these or other knowledge transfer skills for all contexts in which GLs transfer knowledge? Third, does success in RKT correlate with subsequent GL effectiveness?

Practical Implications

This study's key practical implications include paying close attention to reentry jobs that allow repatriates to employ their IA knowledge and retain their global networks; developing transfer skills in repatriates; providing training to repatriates and their managers on the RKT process; and creating a global learning-oriented organizational culture that links RKT to global strategy and provides opportunities and reinforcement for RKT. All of these steps will enrich the GL capacity within organizations and improve the likelihood that organizations can utilize the strategically important expertise repatriates gain from IAs. Unless organizations and work units understand the enormous value of repatriate knowledge and make a concerted effort to facilitate RKT, they risk losing one of their most valuable investments to the competition.

The complex nature of global knowledge and its transfer is of strategic importance to global leadership. Bird's (2001) perspective on careers as repositories of knowledge argues for both IAs and repatriation as invaluable developmental opportunities for GLs (Bird & Oddou, 2013). Enhancing the skills required to transfer relevant knowledge and improving the microprocess of its flow are increasingly important in today's knowledge-dependent global economy.

ACKNOWLEDGEMENTS

The authors wish to acknowledge the contributions of Roger Blakeney to this program of research.

REFERENCES

Appafram, N., & Sheikh, A. Z. (2016). The utilisation of repatriate knowledge by multinational companies: An interview study. *International Journal of Employment Studies, 24*(1), 42–61.

Argote, L. (1999). *Organizational learning: Creating, retaining and transferring knowledge.* Norwell, MA: Kluwer Academic Publishers.

Argote, L., & Ingram, P. (2000). Knowledge transfer: A basis for competitive advantage in firms. *Organizational Behavior and Human Decision Processes, 82*(1), 150–169.

Arzensek, A., Kosmrlj, K., & Sirca, N. T. (2014). Slovenian young researchers' motivation for knowledge transfer. *Higher Education, 68*(2), 185–206.

Aycan, Z. (2001). Expatriation: A critical step toward developing global leaders. In M. E. Mendenhall, T. Kuhlman, & G. Stahl (Eds.), *Developing global business leaders: Policies, processes and innovations* (pp. 119–136). Westport, CN: Quorum Books.

Berthoin Antal, A. (2001). Expatriates' contributions to organizational learning. *Journal of General Management, 26,* 62–84.

Bird, A. (2001). International assignments and careers as repositories of knowledge. In M. E. Mendenhall, T. Kühlman, & G. K. Stahl (Eds.), *Developing global business leaders: Policies, processes, and innovations* (pp. 19–36). Westport, CN: Quorum.

Bird, A., & Oddou, G. R. (2013). Global leadership knowledge creation and transfer. In M. E. Mendenhall, J. S. Osland, A. Bird, G. Oddou, M. Maznevski, G. Stahl, & M. Stevens (Eds.), *Global leadership: Research, practice and development* (2nd ed., pp. 80–96). New York, NY: Routledge.

Black, J. S., Morrison, A. J., & Gregersen, H. B. (1999). *Global explorers: The next generation of leaders.* Hove: Psychology Press.

Blumberg, M., & Pringle, C. D. (1982). The missing opportunity in organizational research: Some implications for a theory of work performance. *Academy of Management Review, 7*(4), 560–569.

Breitenmoser, A., Bader, B., & Berg, N. (2018). Why does repatriate career success vary? An empirical investigation from both traditional and protean career perspectives. *Human Resource Management, 57*(5), 1049–1063.

Brookfield Global Mobility Trends. (2016). Brookfield global relocation services. Retrieved May 27, 2020, from http://globalmobilitytrends.bgrs.com/

Bucher, J., Burmeister, A., Osland, J. S., & Deller, J. (2020). The influence of empowering leadership on repatriate knowledge transfer: Understanding mechanisms and boundary conditions. *International Journal of Human Resource Management.* doi:10.1080/09585192.2020.1771400

Burmeister, A., & Deller, J. (2016). A practical perspective on repatriate knowledge transfer: The influence of organizational support practices. *Journal of Global Mobility, 4*(1), 68–87.

Burmeister, A., Deller, J., Osland, J. S., Szkudlarek, B., Oddou, G., & Blakeney, R. (2015). The micro-processes during repatriate knowledge transfer: The repatriates' perspective. *Journal of Knowledge Management, 19,* 735–755.

Burmeister, A., Lazarova, M. B., & Deller, J. (2018). Repatriate knowledge transfer: Antecedents and boundary conditions of a dyadic process. *Journal of World Business, 53*(6), 806–816.

Caligiuri, P. (2006). Developing global leaders. *Human Resource Management Review, 16*(2), 219–228.

Caligiuri, P., & Bonache, J. (2016). Evolving and enduring challenges in global mobility. *Journal of World Business, 51,* 127–141.

Caligiuri, P., & Lazarova, M. B. (2001). Strategic repatriation policies to enhance global leadership development. In M. E. Mendenhall, T. M. Kuhlman, & G. K. Stahl (Eds.), *Developing global business leaders: Policies, processes, and innovations* (pp. 243–256). Westport, CT: Quorum Books.

Carpenter, M., Sanders, W., & Gregersen, H. (2001). Bundling human capital with organizational context: The impact of international assignment experience on multinational firm performance and CEO pay. *Academy of Management Journal, 44*(3), 493–511.

Carr, S. C., Inkson, K., & Thorn, K. (2005). From global careers to talent flow: Reinterpreting 'brain drain.' *Journal of World Business, 40*(4), 386–398.

Chen, Z., & Vogel, D. (2016). How mentorship improves reverse transfer of tacit knowledge in Chinese Multinational Companies (MNCs). In D. Vogel, X. Guo, H. Linger, C. Barry, M. Lang, & C. Schneider (Eds.) *Transforming healthcare through information systems* (pp. 125–134). Cham: Springer.

Cross, R., & Prusak, L. (2003). The political economy of knowledge markets in organizations. In M. Easterby- Smith, & M. Lyles (Eds.), *The Blackwell handbook of organizational learning and knowledge management* (pp. 454–472). Malden, MA: Blackwell Publishing.

Crowne, K. A. (2009). Enhancing knowledge transfer during and after international assignments. *Journal of Knowledge Management, 13,* 134–147.

Duriau, V. J., Reger, R. K., & Pfarrer, M. D. (2007). A content analysis of the content analysis literature in organization studies: Research themes, data sources, and methodological refinements. *Organizational Research Methods, 10*(1), 5–34.

Fink, G., Meierewert, S., & Rohr, U. (2005). The use of repatriate knowledge in organizations. *Human Resource Planning, 28*(4), 30–36.

Flanagan, J. C. (1954). The critical incident technique. *The Psychological Bulletin, 51*(4), 327–358.

Froese, F. J., Stoermer, S., Reiche, B. S., & Klar, S. (forthcoming). Best of both worlds: How embeddedness fit in the host unit and the headquarters improve repatriate knowledge transfer. *Journal of International Business Studies.*

Furuya, N., Stevens, M., Bird, A., Oddou, G., & Mendenhall, M. (2009). Managing the learning and transfer of global management competence: Antecedents and outcomes of Japanese repatriation effectiveness. *Journal of International Business Studies, 40*, 200–215.

Grant, R. M. (1996). Prospering in dynamically-competitive environments: Organizational capability as knowledge integration. *Organization Science, 7*(4), 375–387.

Gupta, A., & Govindarajan, V. (2000). Knowledge flows within multinational corporations. *Strategic Management Journal, 21*, 473–496.

Hall, D. T. (1996). Protean careers of the 21st century. *Academy of Management Executive, 10*(4), 8–16.

Harzing, A. W., Pudelko, M., & Reiche, B. S. (2016). The bridging role of expatriates and inpatriates in knowledge transfer in multinational corporations. *Human Resource Management, 55*(4), 679–695.

Hinds, B. (2020). The nature of global leaders' power (Unpublished doctoral dissertation). Lisle, IL: Benedictine University.

Hsieh, H. F., & Shannon, S. E. (2005). Three approaches to qualitative content analysis. *Qualitative Health Research, 15*(9), 1277–1288.

Huang, M. C., Chiu, Y. P., & Lu, T. C. (2013). Knowledge governance mechanisms and repatriate's knowledge sharing: The mediating roles of motivation and opportunity. *Journal of Knowledge Management, 17*(5), 677–694.

James, R. (2019). Repatriates' work engagement: Proactive behavior, perceived support, and adjustment. *Journal of Career Development*, 0894845319886104.

Kamoche, K. (1997). Knowledge creation and learning in international HRM. *International Journal of Human Resources, 8*, 213–225.

Kostova, T., & Roth, K. (2003). Social capital in multinational corporations and a micro-macro model of its formation. *Academy of Management Review, 28*(2), 297–317.

Kulkarni, M., Lengnick-Hall, M. L., & Valk, R. (2010). Employee perception of repatriation in an emerging economy: The Indian experience. *Human Resource Management, 49*(3), 531–548.

Lazarova, M. B., & Cerdin, J. L. (2007). Revisiting repatriation concerns: Organizational support versus career and contextual influences. *Journal of International Business Studies, 38*(3), 404–429.

Lazarova, M., & Tarique, I. (2005). Knowledge transfer upon repatriation. *Journal of World Business, 40*(4), 361–373.

Mäkelä, K. (2007). Knowledge sharing through expatriate relationships: A social capital perspective. *International Studies of Management & Organization, 37*, 108–125.

Mäkelä, L., Suutari, V., Brewster, C., Dickmann, M., & Tornikoski, C. (2016). The impact of career capital on expatriates' perceived marketability. *Thunderbird International Business Review, 58*(1), 29–40.

Manning, P. K. (1982). Analytic induction. In P. K. Manning, & R. B. Smith (Eds.), *A handbook of social science methods* (pp. 273–302). Cambridge, MA: Ballinger.

McCall, M. W., & Hollenbeck, G. P. (2002). *Developing global executives: The lessons of international experience.* Boston, MA: Harvard Business Press.

Mendenhall, M. E. (2006). The elusive, yet critical challenge of developing global leaders. *European Management Journal, 24*(6), 422–429.

Nonaka, I. (1994). A dynamic theory of organizational knowledge creation. *Organization science, 5*(1), 14–37.

Oddou, G., Osland, J. S., & Blakeney, R. (2009). Repatriating knowledge: Variables influencing the "transfer" process. *Journal of International Business Studies, 40*, 181–199.

Oddou, G., Szkudlarek, B., Osland, J. S., Deller, J., & Blakeney, R. (2013). Repatriates as a source of competitive advantage: How to manage knowledge transfer. *Organizational Dynamics, 42*(4), 257–266.

Osland, J. S. (2001). The quest for transformation: The process of global leadership development. *Developing global business leaders: Policies, processes, and innovations*, 137–156.

O'Sullivan, S. L. (2002). The protean approach to managing repatriation transitions. *International Journal of Manpower, 23*(7), 597–616.

Pauleen, D. J., Rooney, D., & Holden, N. J. (2010). Practical wisdom and the development of cross-cultural knowledge management: a global leadership perspective. *European Journal of International Management*, *4*(4), 382–395.

Petrick, J. A., Scherer, R. F., Brodzinski, J. D., Quinn, J. F., & Ainina, M. F. (1999). Global leadership skills and reputational capital: Intangible resources for sustainable competitive advantage. *Academy of Management Perspectives*, *13*(1), 58–69.

Raven, B. H. (1965). Social influence and power. In I. D. Steiner, & M. Fishbein (Eds.), *Current studies in social psychology* (pp. 371–382). New York, NY: Holt Rinehart & Winston.

Reiche, B. S. (2012). Knowledge benefits of social capital upon repatriation: A longitudinal study of international assignees. *Journal of Management Studies*, *49*(6), 1052–1077.

Roberts, M. J. D. (2012). International returnees and the capturing of foreign knowledge by emerging market firms (Doctoral dissertation). Canada: University of Western Ontario.

Roberts, B. W., & Pomerantz, E. (2004). On traits, situations, and their integration: A developmental perspective. *Personality and Social Psychology Review*, *8*(4), 401–416.

Sanchez-Vidal, M. E., Sanz-Valle, R., & Barba-Aragon, M. I. (2016). Repatriates and reverse knowledge transfer in MNCs. *International Journal of Human Resource Management*, 1–19.

Shepherd, D. A., & Sutcliffe, K. M. (2011). Inductive top-down theorizing: A source of new theories of organization. *Academy of Management Review*, *36*(2), 361–380.

Silverman, D. (2010). *Doing qualitative research: A practical handbook* (3rd ed.). London: Sage Publications.

Snyder, M. (1986). *Public appearances, private realities: The psychology of self-monitoring*. New York, NY: Freeman.

Stahl, G., Chua, C. H., Caligiuri, P., Cerdin, J. L., & Taniguchi, M. (2009). Predictors of turnover intentions in learning-driven and demand-driven international assignments: The role of repatriation concerns, satisfaction with company support, and perceived career advancement opportunities. *Human Resource Management*, *48*(1), 89–109.

Szkudlarek, B. (2010). Reentry—a review of the literature. *International Journal of Intercultural Relations*, *34*(1), 1–21.

Szkudlarek, B., & Sumpter, D. M. (2015). What, when, and with whom? Investigating expatriate reentry training with a proximal approach. *Human Resource Management*, *54*(6), 1037–1057.

Taylor, S., & Osland, J. S. (2011). The impact of intercultural communication on organizational learning. In M. Easterby-Smith, & M. A. Lyles (Eds.), *Handbook of organizational learning and knowledge management* (2nd ed., pp. 581–604). Chichester: John Wiley & Sons.

Valk, R., Velde, M. V. D., Engen, M. V., & Szkudlarek, B. (2015). Warm welcome or rude awakening? Repatriation experiences of Indian and Dutch international assignees and intention to leave the organisation. *Journal of Indian Business Research*, *7*(3), 243–270.

Wang, D. (2015). Activating cross-border brokerage: Interorganizational knowledge transfer through skilled return migration. *Administrative Science Quarterly*, *60*, 133–176.

Wang, J., & Li, B. (2016). Impact of repatriate's knowledge transfer on enterprise performance: The mediating effect of ambidexterity innovation. *Journal of Systems Science & Information*, *4*(1), 56–67.

Ye, X., Li, L., & Tan, X. (2017). Organizational support: mechanisms to affect perceived over-qualification on turnover intentions a study of Chinese repatriates in multinational enterprises. *Employee Relations: The International Journal*, *39*(7), 918–934.

Znaniecki, F. (1934). *The method of sociology*. New York, NY: Farrar & Rinehart.

Zulkifly, N. A., Ismail, M., & Hamzah, S. R. A. (2019). Predictors of knowledge transfer between expatriates and host country nationals. *European Journal of Management and Business Economics*.

HOW GLOBAL LEADERS LEARN FROM INTERNATIONAL EXPERIENCE: REVIEWING AND ADVANCING GLOBAL LEADERSHIP DEVELOPMENT

Natalia Fey

ABSTRACT

International experience (IE) has been acknowledged to be the most useful method for developing global leaders. However, not everyone benefits equally from IE. During the last two decades, our understanding of why this is the case and how global leaders learn from IE has rapidly increased. Several individual and organizational enablers facilitating global leader learning from IE have been identified in the literature, as have learning mechanisms that make such learning possible. However, the literature remains fragmented, and there is a great need to integrate the findings in the field. Therefore, the present paper systematically examines peer-reviewed studies on global leaders' learning from IE published between 1998 and 2019. The study contributes to the extant literature by identifying and integrating individual enablers, organizational enablers, and key learning mechanisms from global leaders' IE and by suggesting topics for future research.

Keywords: Global leader; global leadership development; developmental method; international experience; learning process; learning mechanism

Advances in Global Leadership, Volume 13, 129–172
ISSN: 1535-1203/doi:10.1108/S1535-120320200000013005

THE NATURE OF THE PROBLEM AND THE PURPOSE OF THE STUDY

Developing global leader competencies requires fundamental human transformation; it does not involve adding incrementally new techniques to one's managerial skill portfolio. (Mendenhall, 2006, p. 425)

Interest in global leadership development (GLD) is strong today among scholars and practitioners alike, and global training and development constitutes one of the key research areas in the field of global leadership (GL) (Osland, Li & Wang, 2014; Vijaiakumar, Morley, Heraty, Mendenhall, & Osland, 2018). This is not surprising because evidence suggests that a multinational corporation's (MNC's) ability to develop global leaders positively affects its financial performance (Adler & Bartholomew, 1992; Stroh & Caligiuri, 1998), and the shortage of effective global leaders has been recognized to be a major obstacle facing globally operating companies (Bird & Mendenhall, 2016; PwC, 2017). International experience (IE) has long been recognized as a leading tool for fostering global leaders (Mendenhall, 2008). It is defined in this study as experience gained from living and working outside of a person's home country. IE, however, does not automatically result in increased GL ability unless learning from the experience takes place (Li, Mobley, Kelly, 2013; Ng, Van Dyne, & Ang, 2009a, 2009b; Terrell & Rosenbusch, 2013; Walker, 2018). Furthermore, such learning does not always happen, or it happens in varying degrees.

Scholars have identified a variety of individual and organizational factors that facilitate global leader learning from IE. For example, individual factors include extroversion (Caligiuri & Tarique, 2009), global competencies (Furuya, Stevens, Bird, Oddou, & Mendenhall, 2009), divergent learning style (a learning style emphasizing concrete experience and reflective observation) (Li, 2009; Li et al., 2013), positive attitude toward learning, engaging in self-reflection (Terrell & Rosenbusch, 2013), self-efficacy (Walker, 2018), and so forth. Key organizational factors are organizational attitude toward international operations, well-crafted international assignment policies, and HR policies (Furuya et al., 2009). Additionally, scholars have suggested several distinct learning mechanisms that facilitate learning from IE including the experiential learning cycle (Li et al., 2013; Pless, Maak, & Stahl, 2011; Woods & Peters, 2014); the transformative learning cycle (Oddou & Mendenhall, 2018); social learning mechanism (Caligiuri & Tarique, 2009, 2012); and the integrative learning ecosystem (Walker, 2018). However, these learning mechanisms have not been previously systematically analyzed and contrasted in the literature on global leader learning. The purpose of the present study is to synthesize the literature on individual and organizational enablers of learning and learning mechanisms of global leaders from IE in the light of recent GLD models (Mendenhall, Weber, Arnardottir, & Oddou, 2017; Osland & Bird, 2013, 2018).

Several earlier literature reviews have provided important groundwork for understanding how global leaders learn from their IE. For example, Suutari (2002) identified the need to understand the relationship between GL development and learning from international assignments. Cumberland, Herd, Alagaraja, and Kerrick (2016) indicated that global leaders learn differently from different developmental methods and classified IE as part of experiential and immersion approaches. Osland and Bird (2013, 2018) discussed three process models of GLD—the Chattanooga model, the Global Leadership Expertise Development model (GLED), and a Model for Developing Global Executives. The model for Developing Global Executives primarily focuses on the organizational role in developing global leaders, while the GLED model, an extension of Chattanooga model, suggested antecedents, moderators, and outcomes of the process of GL expertise development and classifies them into thematic categories. Both models identified elements of the transformational process, such as experiences, challenges, encounters, and decisions, and emphasize the role of CAIR factors (complexity, affect, intensity, relevance) in moderating expertise development in global leaders. Mendenhall et al. (2017) reviewed existing GLD models and highlighted the staged nature of these models which consisted of antecedents, transformational process, outcomes, and moderators. Furthermore, Mendenhall et al. (2017) were the first to specify the GLD process and to provide testable propositions in their Global Leadership Competency Development Process Model based on Transformational Learning Theory (TLT) (Mezirow, 1978). Additionally, in their review of developmental methods, Oddou and Mendenhall (2008, 2018) categorized IE as part of the experiential approach and delineated the transformational learning process of global leaders. They suggested three stages of the transformational learning process such as contract, confrontation, and remapping (earlier introduced by Black & Gregersen, 2000) and pointed out that global leaders' transformational learning is initiated by a trigger event.

However, no reviews known to the author have attempted to systematically map and synthesize the extant literature on either individual or organizational factors that enable global leader learning or the different learning mechanisms which can help facilitate global leaders' learning process. Therefore, following Osland, Li, Petrone, and Mendenhall's (2018) call to identify bridging mechanisms between individual-level dispositions and the development of GL capabilities and Osland, Li, and Mendenhall's (2017) call to specify the learning processes of global leaders, the key aim of this study is to integrate the extant literature on various factors enabling global leader learning from IE and on different learning mechanisms involved in learning process. The GLED model (Osland & Bird, 2018) was a helpful starting point to inform the author's effort to categorize individual and organizational factors enabling learning of global leaders, and the Process Model of Global Leadership Competency Development (Mendenhall et al., 2017) served as a beacon, guiding this study in its endeavor to identify and synthesize the variety of learning mechanisms global leaders use to learn from IE.

Thus, the present paper systematically synthesizes peer-reviewed studies on GL's development published between 1998 and 2019 and explores the following research question: *What are the key individual enablers, organizational enablers, and learning mechanisms for the method of IE in the domain of global leadership?*

The remainder of the paper is organized as follows: a methodology section, results section, and a discussion section that concludes with the study's contributions and implications, limitations, and suggestions for future study.

METHODOLOGY

This section explains how the studies for the literature review were selected and analyzed and presents the organizing framework used to report key findings. This study adopts Reiche, Bird, Mendenhall, and Osland's (2017, p. 556) definition of global leaders which suggests they are *"individuals who influence a range of internal and external constituents from multiple national cultures and jurisdictions in a context characterized by significant levels of task and relationship complexity."* They argue that the challenges facing global leaders differ in degree and in kind from the challenges leaders face in a domestic context (Bird & Osland, 2004; Osland, Bird, Mendenhall, & Osland, 2006).

Data Collection

To identify relevant articles, the author performed an article search in the databases SCOPUS, EBSCO, ProQuest, and Google Scholar using the keywords *"global leader"* or *"global manager"* or *"global executive"* or *"global leadership competencies"* in combination with at least one of the following words: *"IE"* or *"developmental method"* or *"learning process"* or *"learning mechanisms"* in the article titles, keywords, abstracts, or, in the absence of an abstract, in the introduction. Searching these databases is a common practice in contemporary literature reviews. Articles had to satisfy the following four criteria.

(1) The paper had to be peer-reviewed, written in English, and in the fields of HRM, management, leadership, international business, or psychology. Books, book chapters, PhD dissertations, and conferences papers were excluded to ensure a consistent high quality in the reviewed studies.
(2) The article had to describe the method of IE for developing global leaders. Studies describing IE among other methods for developing global leaders were included, but not studies with only brief mentions of IE for developing global leaders. Studies focused on multicultural teams were excluded as their leaders, and virtual teams warrant separate investigation.
(3) Articles on expatriates or host country managers working for foreign companies that were not explicitly defined as global leaders/managers were excluded because not all expatriates are global leaders (Bird & Osland, 2004) or are being developed as global leaders.
(4) Studies using MBA/EMBA students were included, but not studies based on bachelor and master students in non-MBA business master's programs or other disciplines. This was done in response to calls for studying managerial rather than student samples (Clapp-Smith & Wernsing, 2014; Ott & Michailova, 2018) and to ensure that the article's findings are relevant for

organizations trying to develop global leaders. For example, in studies of the effect of IE on expatriates and business travellers' CQ results, Gupta, Singh, Jandhyala, and Blatt (2013) and Tay, Westerman, and Chia (2008) reported results different from similar studies on student samples. Furthermore, global leaders are often senior leaders; using students with little work experience as proxies for global leaders in firms may introduce error. Therefore, in spite of a significant increase in recent studies exploring the development of GL capabilities through IE in business schools (e.g., Karla, Szymanski, & Olszewska, 2018; Lokkesmoe, Kuchinke, & Ardichvili, 2016; Mendenhall, Arnardottir, Oddou, & Burke, 2013; Osland et al., 2018; Quirk & Gustafson, 2018; Rowe et al., 2018), these studies were excluded to ensure studying of managerial samples.

Data Analysis

After applying the above-described criteria for the selection process, 42 studies remained and formed the basis of the final in-depth analysis. The author screened each article to extract information about the author(s), year of publication, journal, type of study, type of IE explored, type of GL competencies explored, conceptual framework used, and the study's findings. These 42 studies, published from 1998 to 2019, are broadly distributed across 20 journals. *Advances in Global Leadership*, which published 28.6% ($n = 12$) of these articles, is by far home to the largest number of these studies. Another five journals have at least two publications each: *Organizational Dynamics* ($n = 5$), *Human Resources Management* ($n = 4$), *Academy of Management Learning & Education* ($n = 3$), *Journal of World Business* ($n = 2$), and *Journal of Management Development* ($n = 2$). The remaining 14 studies have been published in 14 different journals.

Categorization of the 42 studies revealed that 21 studies are conceptual (see Table A1 in Appendix for a list of conceptual studies) and 21 studies are empirical (see Tables A2 and A3 in Appendix for lists of quantitative and mixed method and qualitative studies, respectively). Among the 21 empirical studies, 11 are qualitative (52.3%), 7 are quantitative (33.3%), and 3 use mixed methods (14.3%), confirming the primarily qualitative nature of the extant GLD literature. This could be attributed to the complexity of conducting research in a global business setting, the difficulty of accessing large and relevant samples of global leaders, and the fact that dynamic, emerging, and nonlinear GLD processes could be challenging to clearly specify and investigate quantitatively with a limited number of constructs.

The identified studies explored the development of different types of GL competencies and other outcomes of learning through different types of IE (from long-term international assignment to short-term business travel). The papers were categorized in Table 1 into one of the three types of IE: international assignments ($n = 26$); international corporate training programs ($n = 14$); and short-term business travel ($n = 2$).

Table 1. Categorization of the 26 Conceptual, 11 Qualitative, and 3 Mixed Method Studies for Method of International Experience.

	Types of International Experience (42)		
	Long-term International Assignment (26)	Global Leadership Development Program, International Service Learning Program, MBA study tour (14)	Short-term Business ravel (2)
Conceptual Studies (21)	Alon and Higgins (2005), Caligiuri (2006, 2013), Conger (2014), Gupta and Govindarajan (2002), Hall et al. (2001), Hollenbeck and McCall (2003), Javidan & Bowen (2013), Kets de Vries and Florent-Treacy (2002), Kohonen (2005), Li (2009), Lovvorn and Chen (2011), Mendenhall (2006), Mendenhall et al. (2017), Ng et al. (2009a, 2009b), Oliver et al. (2009), and Tung (2014)	Black and Gregersen (2000) and Caligiuri and Thoroughgood (2015)	Oddou, Mendenhall, and Ritchie (2000)
Empirical Studies (21)			
Quantitative (7)	Caligiuri and Tarique (2009, 2012), Furuya et al. (2009), Gerrard (2011), and Li et al. (2013)	Walker (2018) and Wood and Peters (2014)	—
Qualitative (11)	Terrell and Rosenbusch (2013)	Day and Barney (2012), Derven and Frappolli (2011), DiStefano and Maznevski (2003), Gundling, Grant, & Everhart (2014), Neary and O'Grady (2000), Pless and Borecká (2014), Pless et al. (2011), Sendelbach and McGrath (2005), and Tracy (2018)	Johnston (2014)
Mixed method (3)	Caligiuri and Di Santo (2001) and Gregersen et al. (1998)	Tuleja (2014)	—

The rationale for this categorization is the following: the GLD literature distinguishes several developmental approaches such as self-awareness, didactic, experiential, and immersion (Cumberland et al., 2016), which are the most suitable for development of particular capabilities. For example, the experiential approach enhances skills and abilities, while the immersion approach influences knowledge, skills, abilities, and, to some degree, personality characteristics (Caligiuri, 2006). Long-term international assignment represents the immersion approach, while short-term business trips and international corporate training programs reflect the experiential approach (Cumberland et al., 2016). Thus, synthesis and comparison of the enablers and learning mechanisms for three types of IE sheds light on whether/how learning processes within experiential and immersion approaches differ.

Out of 21 empirical studies, 18 studies (85.7%) use samples with global leaders and only 3 studies use samples with MBA students (see Tables A2 in Appendix for a description of the samples). Thus, it is fair to say that this literature review is based on managerial samples. Finally, all studies were categorized based on their use of one or more of the four different types of core GL competencies most frequently used in the extant literature—GL competencies, cultural intelligence (CQ), global mindset, and other specific cross-cultural competencies (Bird, 2018). Jokinen (2005) originally noted and Yari, Lankut, Alon, and Richter (2020) confirmed substantial overlaps among these competences. Due to space limitations, global leader learning in relation to each of the four types of identified GL competencies is not discussed in detail.

The qualitative nature of the studies led the author to employ content analysis of the data. The author closely read each paper, codifying all material relating to global leader learning from IE with special attention to diverse factors enabling the learning of global leaders and the mechanisms facilitating the learning process. Only seven quantitative studies and three mixed method studies explored global leader learning quantitatively (see Table A2 for a list of quantitative studies). The rest of the studies were qualitative and used words similar to "enable," "facilitate," and "enhance" to indicate that these factors were found to be important for global leader learning. Therefore, through performing a qualitative content analysis and categorizing all data to the themes and subthemes, the author identified two distinct groups enhancing global leader's learning: (1) *individual enablers of learning* and (2) *organizational enablers of learning*. Individual enablers of learning are defined as individual-level factors that enable global leader learning, while organizational enablers are organization-level factors performing the same function. Individual enablers were further categorized into five subcategories: (1) *personal traits*, (2) *individual capabilities*, (3) *learning ability*, (4) *learning behaviors*, and (5) *attitude to learning*. Organizational enablers of learning were further categorized into two subcategories: (1) *developmental qualities of the method* and (2) *organizational support* (see Fig. 1).

Additionally, content analysis of the reviewed studies revealed that individual and organizational enablers alone are not sufficient to guarantee learning outcomes. For high learning outcomes to occur, the correct *learning mechanisms*

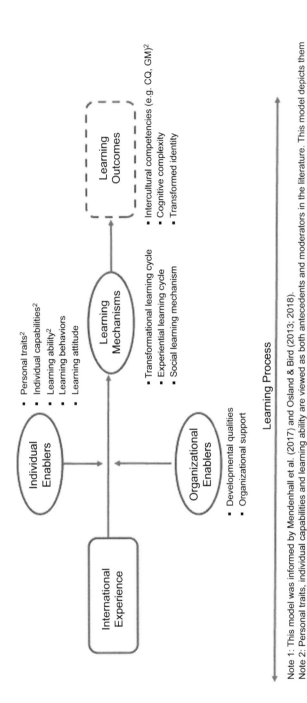

Note 1: This model was informed by Mendenhall et al. (2017) and Osland & Bird (2013; 2018).
Note 2: Personal traits, individual capabilities and learning ability are viewed as both antecedents and moderators in the literature. This model depicts them as moderators given the focus on global leader learning processes.
Note 3: Because learning outcomes were not included in this literature review, they are represented here with a dotted line.

Fig. 1. Key Elements of Global Leader Learning Process from International Experience (KEGLL model).

to produce learning also seem to be important. In this study *learning mechanism* is defined as a specific mechanism through which learning takes place during a developmental method (Pless et al., 2011). The next section presents the content analysis results of the reviewed articles. The key individual and organizational enablers and learning mechanisms are presented for three types of IE.

CONTENT ANALYSIS RESULTS

Overall, studies on the IE of global leaders are unequally spread across the three different types of IE. Twenty-six studies (62%; 16 conceptual and 10 empirical studies) explore how learning occurs during international assignments or how it occurs through a combination of methods where international assignment is one of the several key methods. Fourteen studies (33%; 2 conceptual and 12 empirical) explore how learning occurs during international corporate training programs, and only 2 studies (5%; 1 conceptual and 1 empirical) explore how learning occurs during short-term business travel. In addition, international assignments were more frequently explored in conceptual articles, while international corporate training programs were more frequently explored in articles mainly based on case studies.

International Assignment as a Learning Environment

Long-term international assignments are characterized by both the intensity and the length of the cultural experience. According to Mendenhall and Stahl (2000), an international assignment is the laboratory where global leaders learn, practice, develop, and master their capabilities. In particular, core GL competencies such as cognitive complexity, behavioral complexity, cross-cultural skills, business savvy, and the ability to manage uncertainty can be developed through international assignments (Osland, 2001). International assignments have created more scholarly interest than any other types of IE (see Table 1). This is not surprising because the investment for this type of IE is greater than other kinds of IE.

Individual Enablers of Learning from International Assignment

All five types of individual enablers and both types of organizational enablers play important roles in enhancing global leader learning from international assignments (see Table A4 in Appendix for the content analysis results).

Personal traits: Three conceptual studies (Caligiuri, 2006, 2013; Gupta & Govindarajan, 2002), four quantitative studies (Caligiuri & Tarique, 2009, 2012; Furuya et al., 2009; Gerrard, 2011), and two mixed method studies (Caligiuri & Di Santo, 2001; Gregersen, Morrison, & Black, 1998) explored the role of personal traits in global leader learning. The empirical evidence to date is mixed. For example, Caligiuri and Tarique (2009) reported that extroversion moderates global leader effectiveness as a result of receiving high-contact experience, but they (Caligiuri & Tarique, 2012) subsequently found that extroversion and openness are predictors of global leader's dynamic cross-cultural competencies (and, therefore, global leader effectiveness). Additionally, Furuya et al. (2009) reported that personal traits in the form of global competencies categorized as perception management, relationship management, and self-management and measured by the Global Competency Inventory (GCI) (Bird, Mendenhall, Stevens, & Oddou, 2010) predicted higher global management competencies learning, higher global management competencies transfer, and increased job performance after repatriation. Although Gerrard (2011) did not confirm that personal traits influence global leader performance, she indicated that emotional stability negatively correlates with withdrawal from international assignments. It would be helpful to further explore personal traits as antecedents or moderators in empirical studies.

Individual capabilities: In their conceptual studies, scholars have also highlighted the role of other individual capabilities for global leader learning and effectiveness, e.g., cognitive complexity (Hollenbeck & McCall, 2003); self-awareness, and foreign language skills (Alon & Higgins, 2005). In their quantitative study, Caligiuri and Tarique (2012) found that dynamic cross-cultural competencies (tolerance of ambiguity, cultural flexibility, and low ethnocentrism) predict global leader effectiveness. Interestingly, self-efficacy, explored in relation to international corporate training programs, has not been studied in relation to international assignments and presents a research opportunity (see Table A4).

Learning ability: In their quantitative study, Li et al. (2013) applied Experiential Learning Theory (ELT) (Kolb, 1984) to explain the link between IE and CQ of global leaders. They found that learning ability in the form of a divergent learning style moderates learning from IE and enhances CQ of global leaders. Other scholars have also applied ELT but proposed conceptually different relationships. Ng et al. (2009a, 2009b) suggested that CQ moderates experiential learning and that a higher level of CQ predicts higher learning from IE. Lovvorn and Chen (2011) suggested that CQ both mediates and moderates the development of global mindset of global leaders. Empirically clarifying the role of CQ in the global leader learning presents another research opportunity.

Learning behaviors: Only one qualitative study to date explored the learning behaviors of global leaders (Terrell & Rosenbusch, 2013) and found that intuitive and dynamic learning, learning in the moment and adapted to a particular situation, as well as engaging in self-reflection and generalization of the learnings to other situations, yields results for global leaders. Additionally, scholars argued conceptually that the following learning behaviors enhance global leader learning: learning how to learn (Hall, Zhu, & Yan, 2001); cultivating self-awareness (Gupta & Govindarajan, 2002); engaging in a sensemaking process and self-reflection (Kohonen, 2005); interacting with locals (Lovvorn & Chen, 2011); experimenting with new ideas (Tung, 2014); and applying learnings in real life (Oliver, Church, Lewis & Desrosiers, 2009). The field needs more conceptual and empirical studies devoted to this individual enabler.

Learning attitude: Last but not least in the group of individual enablers of global leader learning is learning attitude. Considering the decisive role of motivation in leader development (Guillen, Mayo, & Korotov, 2015), we still know surprisingly little about the role of motivation in global leader learning from international assignments. In their conceptual studies, Kohonen (2005) emphasized the importance of willingness to explore and reshape identity; Hollenbeck and McCall (2003) and Conger (2014) stressed the importance of motivation to work abroad and to lead in an international business environment. Additionally, in their qualitative study, Terrell and Rosenbusch (2013) high-lighted the role of positive attitude toward learning. Although their study was not included in this review, as it does not focus on global leader learning during an assignment, Björkman and Mäkela's (2013) quantitative study could inform future research on learning attitude of global leaders. They found that such factors as formal identification as talented, identification with corporate values, and perception of the effectiveness of international assignments positively affect the willingness of global leaders to take on challenging international assignments.

To sum up, current empirical evidence indicates that extroverted, open-minded, and emotionally stable global leaders (Caligiuri & Tarique, 2009, 2012) who possess the set of global competencies measured by the GCI (Furuya et al., 2009) and have a positive attitude toward learning (Terrell & Rosenbusch, 2013) and a divergent learning style (Li et al., 2013) benefit more from interna-tional assignments. However, as only a limited number of global leaders possess these particular traits, abilities, and attitudes, certainly the demand for such global leaders is greater than the supply. This is why the identification of five different groups of enablers—personal traits, individual capabilities, learning ability, learning behaviors, and learning attitude—could expand the pool of potential effective global leaders. When global leaders do not possess extrover-sion and openness, which are important for the success of global leaders but difficult to develop (Caligiuri & Tarique, 2012), they could potentially compen-sate for this lack by developing other capabilities; for example, by developing individual capabilities like self-awareness, self-efficacy, and cognitive complexity or by strengthening the motivation to be a global leader by identifying what truly motivates him/her to take on an assignment (Guillen et al., 2015). Investing efforts in developing a divergent learning style and practicing learning behaviors could potentially provide another way to compensate for the lack of requisite personal traits or other individual characteristics. Although, some scholars argue that, it is not so much possessing a specific set of competencies that is important, but rather the results a global leader can deliver, and that similar results could be achieved by global leaders with different sets of competencies (Hollenbeck & McCall, 2003), certain requisite competencies measured, e.g., by the GCI (Bird et al., 2010) and the GELI (Kets de Vries, Vrignaud, & Florent-Tracy, 2004) are important for any global leader. Thus, scholars in GLD now face the exciting task of clarifying the role of different individual enablers in global leader learning from IE.

Organizational Enablers of Learning from International Assignment
Interestingly, all 42 studies have suggested at least one organizational enabler. Content analysis revealed that two groups of organizational enablers have the

potential to influence global leader learning from international assignments: developmental qualities of international assignments and organizational support before, during, and after international assignments (see Table A5 in Appendix for the content analysis results).

Developmental qualities of international assignments: Several empirical studies emphasize the developmental qualities of IE. In their seminal quantitative studies, Caligiuri and Tarique (2009, 2012) reported the importance of high-contact/high-challenge work and non-work cross-cultural experiences for global leader learning and effectiveness. Furthermore, in their qualitative work, Terrell and Rosenbusch (2013) concluded that global leaders develop through first-hand cross-cultural experience enhanced by reflection. Additionally, many conceptual studies have articulated the importance of the developmental dimension of international assignment. For example, Hall et al. (2001) were among the first to propose an employee-centered perspective on international assignments, suggesting that international assignments be reconceptualized by including global leader learning as one of their performance indicators and rewarding them for developmental experience. Furthermore, Caligiuri (2013) emphasized the importance of the quality of an IE over the quantity of IE, and they suggested peer collaboration and immediate feedback as key factors that affected global leader learning (Caligiuri, 2013). Although important steps have been taken by scholars to decode the role of developmental qualities of assignments in global leader learning, much work in examining the role of different developmental qualities in global leader learning is still ahead of us.

Organizational support: Organizational support is another organizational enabler that has received much attention from scholars doing qualitative research. The empirical effort by Furuya et al. (2009), however, stands out as the first and only quantitative study to date on the role of organizational support. Furuya et al. (2009) reported the positive effect of organizational attitude toward its international operations, HR policies, and international assignment policies on global leader learning. In their conceptual studies, scholars suggested additional ways to ensure organizational support for global leaders such as ensuring the adaptability of a leader's family (Gregersen et al., 1998), developing an organizational environment that supports diversity, assigning a local mentor (Gupta & Govindarajan, 2002), demonstrating the link between the high CQ of global leaders and future career success (Alon & Higgins, 2005), creating a supportive organizational culture, involving senior leaders, direct supervisors, and colleagues (Caligiuri, 2013), talent monitoring, introducing performance scorecards, and repatriation policies (Conger, 2014). Additionally, the selection (Caligiuri & Di Santo, 2001; Caligiuri, 2013) and repatriation of global leaders (Conger, 2014; Furuya et al., 2009; Gregersen et al., 1998) have been repeatedly mentioned as factors facilitating global leaders' effectiveness.

Learning Mechanisms of Global Leaders from International Experience
While the majority of the reviewed studies focused on individual and organizational enablers of global leader learning from IE, fewer studies have

attempted to open the black box and theoretically explore the *learning mechanisms* that facilitate the learning process. However, it is essential to develop a better understanding of how the learning process of global leaders unfolds (Mendenhall et al., 2017). Although these studies are few in number, they use a variety of theoretical lenses to explain the learning processes of global leaders.

Three key learning mechanisms were identified in the reviewed literature: (1) the experiential learning cycle; (2) the transformational learning cycle; and (3) the social learning process (see Tables A6 and A7 in Appendix for details), which are briefly reviewed below.

The experiential learning cycle: The experiential learning cycle is explained through ELT, developed by Kolb (1984). It is a four-stage learning cycle in which a specific concrete experience is followed by a stage of observation and reflection, which can lead to the abstract conceptualization stage in which generalizations are formed, followed by hypotheses about future actions that are tested in the final active experimentation stage, resulting in knowledge. Several reviewed studies utilized ELT and the experiential learning cycle to explain how learning occurs in global leaders (e.g., Li, 2009; Li et al., 2013; Ng et al., 2009a, 2009b; Walker, 2018). They all used ELT to explain different relationships. As noted previously, Li and her colleagues (Li, 2009; Li et al., 2013) use ELT to explain how the application of a divergent learning style (which emphasizes both concrete experience and reflective observation) strengthens the positive relationship between the length of IE and global leader's CQ, while Ng et al. (2009a, 2009b) use ELT to explain how CQ moderates a global leader's experiential learning.

The social learning process: Based on Bandura's social learning theory (1975), social learning occurs by thoroughly observing others and interacting with peers, coaches, and mentors. Social learning occurs through the attention–retention–reproduction process in global leaders. Only three empirical studies by Caligiuri and Tarique (2009, 2012) and Walker (2018) applied this theoretical lens to examine social learning mechanisms. As global leaders spend more and more time in collaborative work (Huesing & Ludema, 2017), developing the ability to learn through observing others and interacting with others cannot be undermined. To date this theoretical lens (social learning theory) and social cognitive theory which evolved from it have not received the attention they have received in neighboring fields. We hope these useful theories will be discovered by more scholars in the future.

The transformational learning cycle: The transformational learning cycle is built on Mezirow's (1978) TLT and presents 10 phases of transformative learning triggered by a disorienting dilemma. These include some typical aspects of personal growth, such as self-examination, a critical assessment of one's assumptions, options of new behavior and perspectives, planning a course of action, and acquiring new skills, etc. This 10-stage cycle was later reduced to a 4-stage process (Mezirow, 1997) that resembles the experiential learning cycle on the surface. However, the differences among these learning mechanisms are substantial as the transformative learning cycle creates a foundation for transformational learning while the experiential learning cycle generates learning that is not necessarily transformational (Ensign, 2019b). Widely used in the education field and in the adult learning literature, TLT has been rarely applied in the global leadership literature, but it offers great potential for helping in revealing the learning processes of global leaders. For exceptions, see Mendenhall et al. (2017), Oddou & Mendenhall (2013, 2018), and Ensign (2019b). This theory has not yet been used in quantitative GL studies. The first attempt to examine it qualitatively was done by Ensign (2019a, 2019b) in her PhD dissertation. In addition to the above established theories, scholars have suggested multiple nontheoretical mechanisms for explaining how learning occurs in global leaders (see Table A6 in Appendix for other learning mechanisms). The research on learning mechanisms in GLD can be summarized as follows: Different learning mechanisms could occur during an international assignment. The experiential learning cycle has been more frequently examined in studies, with social learning mechanism being less frequently examined, and with transformational learning cycle being rarely examined. No study to date has explored if different learning mechanisms could occur in the same global leader over time and if these learning mechanisms could be examined quantitatively. The author will now overview how global leaders learn from two additional types of IE—international corporate training programs and short-term business travels.

International Corporate Training Program as a Learning Environment

Global Leadership Development Programs (GLDPs), International Service Learning Programs (ISLPs), and MBA study tour constitute another type of IE explored in this study. GLDPs are 12–18 month-long international corporate programs created either for high-potential future global leaders or for senior global leaders with IE embedded into the programs. ISLPs have the purpose of fostering responsible global leaders through involvement in nonprofitable projects in distant developing countries with the goal of solving socially meaningful and ethically challenging problems. They have recently gained popularity in corporations such as IBM, Glaxo Smith Klein, and Cigna (Raver & Dyne, 2018). MBA study tours are short-term immersive travel abroad experiences that take place within MBA programs. They are normally between 1 and 8 weeks in length. Participants of MBA study tours are adult students with at least several years of work experience which explains their inclusion in this review. Fourteen studies explored global leader learning from GLDPs ($n = 8$), ISLPs ($n = 3$), and MBA study tours ($n = 3$). Most of the extant studies on GLDPs are case studies of concrete developmental initiatives in organizations and are qualitative in nature. Specifically, nine studies are qualitative (64.4%), two studies are quantitative (14.3%), one study is a mixed method study (7%), and only two studies are conceptual (14.3%) (see Table A3 in Appendix for a list of qualitative studies).

Individual and Organizational Enablers and Learning Mechanisms
Scholars exploring global leader learning from international corporate training programs have mainly focused on the role of the developmental qualities. For example, they explored the importance of combining different developmental methods (DiStefano & Maznevski, 2003); aligning developmental talks with the personal developmental trajectories of global leaders (Day & Barney, 2012); embedding the tasks which arouse strong emotions (Pless et al., 2011; Walker, 2018); and ensuring peer-to-peer learning and networking (Tracy, 2018). Studies focused less on organizational support during a structured program. However, those that focused on it concluded that organizational support is essential for the program success. Scholars have also explored the role of learning behaviors, such as learning through creating paradoxical experiences, constructing a new life world (Pless et al., 2011), and mindfulness (Tuleja, 2014). To date, however, studies have not discussed learning ability or considered in depth the role of personal traits, individual capabilities, and leaders' motivation. Similar learning mechanisms such as the experiential learning cycle and the social learning process have been found to enhance learning from structured corporate programs; therefore, they are not specified again in this category (see Table A6 in Appendix for a description of learning mechanisms).

In summary, studies in this group are occupied with program design and delivery and with learning behaviors of global leaders. They pay less attention to participants' individual characteristics, capabilities, and to their learning attitude. Studies tend to emphasize the use of an experiential multi-method training approach in program design and either apply ELT or are atheoretical. Therefore, identifying additional individual and organizational enablers as well as learning mechanisms for global leader learning from international corporate training programs could be a fruitful research avenue.

Short-term Business Travel as a Learning Environment
Short-term business travel has been frequently proposed in recent years as a yet unexplored alternative to long-term international assignments. While long-term international assignments generate significant benefits, they also have many constraints for both organizations and their assignees (Conger, 2014; Johnston, 2014). For example, it is often difficult for an assignee's family to arrange to travel long term due to dual careers and schooling issues, and the home organization frequently finds it difficult to do without key employees for a long period of time. As a result, short-term business travel is a logical alternative even if the longer alternatives discussed above might produce somewhat better results in terms of developing global leaders. However, a dearth of research on short-term business travel exists. To date, the conceptual study by Oddou et al. (2000) and the qualitative study by Johnston (2014) are the only studies that address this type of IE in depth. Both studies recommend that short-term business travel has high potential for developing GL competencies and global mindset and that its developmental potential is not fully utilized by most companies.

Individual and Organizational Enablers and Learning Mechanisms

Oddou et al. (2000) suggested openness and curiosity to be important personal traits; cultural sensitivity to be an important individual capability for global leader; observing, asking questions, and writing a journal to be important learning behaviors; and willingness to stretch mental map to be an important learning attitude (Oddou et al., 2000). Additionally, Johnston (2014) stressed the importance of developing centralized corporate travel policies to establish the correct expectations and to ensure travel is designed in a way that has the highest chance of maximizing the developmental qualities of short-term IE. Although Oddou et al. (2000) emphasized that high-quality short-term business travel can become a source of transformational experience and, therefore, learning, they did not specify potential learning mechanisms and theoretical lenses to utilize. Furthermore, Johnston (2014) reveals that some global leaders perceive learning more as an event that occurs as a result of a critical incident, while other global leaders perceive it more as a process and evolution of their continuous sense-making process. She applied the concepts of cosmopolitanism and cognitive complexity (Levy, Beechler, Taylor, & Boyacigiller, 2007) and sensemaking behavior (Osland & Bird, 2000) to reveal five stages of global leader learning, namely, embark on travel, build relationships, seek deeper understanding, integrate and transfer experience to new context, and be open to additional learning. In sum, the short-term business travel as an IE has received very little attention. More research is needed in this stream to identify individual and organizational enablers and the learning processes that occur during short-term business travel and compare them to learning processes occurring during international assignments and corporate training programs.

SYNTHESIS AND DISCUSSION

Scholars have mainly focused on the role of international assignments and international corporate training programs in global leader learning and have mostly ignored the role of short-term business travel. They have started to decode how global leaders learn from international assignments and have successfully examined a number of individual and organizational enablers as well as learning mechanisms occurring in global leaders during international assignments. Additionally, scholars have actively addressed organizational enablers of global leader learning from international corporate training programs, but they mainly ignored personal enablers and learning mechanisms. Only few individual and organizational enablers of learning from short-term business travel were discussed with learning mechanisms not yet receiving scholarly attention. Due to the unequal attention payed to the three types of IE and little comparative research on the types of IE, useful comparison of individual and organizational enablers, as well as learning mechanisms, could only be partially done.

This comparison shows that potentially all five groups of individual enablers and two groups of organizational enablers could influence global leader learning from the three types of IE, but their effect should be further explored. However, findings show that the role of individual and organizational enablers could differ for different types of IE, with both individual and organizational enablers playing important role in global leader learning from international assignment and short-term business travel. Organizational enablers overweight the role of individual enablers in global leader learning from international corporate training programs. Whether it has more to do with researchers' choices than with the actual phenomena needs to be continued to be explored in future research.

The comparison of learning mechanisms reveals that the experiential learning cycle, the transformational learning cycle, and social learning mechanism could explain global leader learning from international assignments, whereas only experiential learning cycle to date explains global leader learning from international corporate training programs. As mentioned above, it is early to say whether it is due to the types of IE being predisposed to certain learning processes occurring or due to limitations of the studies in the field. Nevertheless, we suggest individual and organizational enablers as well as learning mechanisms to be critical elements of global leader learning process.

Thus, the author proposes a conceptual model of the Key Elements of Global Leader Learning process (KEGLL) for each of three types of IE building on the results of two extant models: Osland and Bird's (2018) GLED model and Mendenhall et al.'s (2017) Global Leadership Competency Development Process Model and insights gained from this literature review. The KEGLL model (Fig. 1) is based on TLT (Mezirow, 1978) and integrates individual and organizational factors and learning mechanisms relevant for the learning process of global leaders. It aims to increase our understanding of the nature of the relationship between IE and the outcomes of global leader learning.

First, the KEGLL model extends our understanding of the catalysts of experience (CAIR) in the GLED model (Osland & Bird, 2018). CAIR elements represent complexity (C)—the complexity of tasks, affect (A)—the potential to arise emotional response and evoke deep learnings in a global leader, intensity (I)—the intensity of interaction with locals, the degree of job challenge, and relevance (R)—the relevance of the developmental tasks and qualities of the international assignment. These four catalysts of the experience in the GLED model are represented by the following similar elements in the KEGLL model: developmental qualities of the international assignment (complexity), attitude toward learning (affect), individual capabilities (intensity), and organizational attitude (relevance). For example, the developmental qualities of IE are represented by high-contact experiences and by exposure to "stretching" assignments (Caligiuri & Tarique, 2009) and thus correspond to certain developmental potential or the level of complexity to be decoded by a leader; attitude to learning corresponds to a drive to learn (Conger, 2014) or an affect; the level of individual capabilities corresponds to a level of intensity of experience; and organizational attitude toward international operations (Furuya et al., 2009) corresponds to the relevance of the experience. In other words, by matching these four pairs of elements, the author suggests that the transformational power of experience and hence the outcomes of the learning from a challenging IE depend not only on developmental qualities of an IE but also on individual capabilities of global leaders in relation to this IE. Therefore, the same IE will result in different degree of transformation for leaders with different individual capabilities.

Second, the proposed KEGLL model extends Mendenhall et al.'s (2017) model by introducing a greater variety of potential learning mechanisms and suggests that individual and organizational enablers facilitate the learning process of global leaders and could play the role of antecedents or moderators of the learning process (Mendenhall et al., 2017). Furthermore, different learning mechanisms could be triggered as a result of individual and organizational enablers and their interaction. Importantly, involving multiple individual and organizational enablers could potentially trigger transformational experiences in global leaders and, therefore, lead to transformational learning. The KEGLL model identifies the variety of learning processes that could occur in a global leader and thus suggests increased possibilities for global leaders' successful learning from IE. Last, but not least, the KEGLL model empowers global leaders to take responsibility for their own learning. This could be done by encouraging global leaders to increase self-awareness about their learning ability, learning attitude, and learning behaviors through self-reflection and external feedback about their learning processes.

SUGGESTIONS FOR FUTURE STUDIES

The following topics for further study are suggested as being particularly useful for enhancing the understanding of the process of global leader learning from IE:

Individual and Organizational Enablers as Antecedents

- GL scholars have suggested more than 260 competencies of an effective global leader (Bird, 2018). However, exploratory research on GLD done to date examined only a limited number of competencies which positively effect global leader learning, e g., global competencies (perception management, relationship management, and self-management), openness and extroversion, a strong drive to learn, and a divergent learning style. Thus, there is a need to further explore the individual enablers of global leader learning from IE in order to develop a more detailed understanding of their role in global leader learning. Do they predict or moderate global leader learning from IE and under what conditions are they moderators and antecedents?
- Future research is needed to explicitly explore interaction of which individual and organizational enablers best predict the IE–global leader learning relationship. In their work Caligiuri and Tarique (2012) confirmed the direct effect of extroversion, openness, high-contact work, and non-work cultural

experiences. Future studies are encouraged to explore the relative importance of other developmental qualities or organizational support enablers.
- Extant research has focused on learning from long-term assignments, but short-term business travel is much more prevalent and cost/time-efficient. Therefore, more research is needed on how to facilitate learning from short-term business travel. A comparison of the learning enablers and learning outcomes from long-term and short-term IE would also be useful.
- There is a need to identify better scales to measure the developmental qualities of IE and potentially improved scales to measure organizational support. This would permit comparative research to define which types of organizational support are effective (Furuya et al., 2009).

Individual and Organizational Enablers as Moderators

- Future research is needed to expand the work begun by Caligiuri and Tarique (2009) to explicitly determine which individual and organizational enablers moderate the IE–learning relationship. However, they only explore the role of one individual enabler as a moderator and the potential moderating roles of many more individual and organizational enablers need to be explored. Future studies need to identify and rank all enablers in terms of effectiveness.

The Learning Mechanisms of Global Leaders from International Experience

- The identification of three learning mechanisms raises a myriad of interesting questions. For example, which learning mechanisms are most effective to facilitate global leader learning?
- It would be useful to explore if global leaders able to choose which learning mechanism they use or is it predetermined as a result of an interaction of individual and organizational enablers?
- Future research should explore how aware are global leaders of the learning mechanism they use? How important it is to be aware about this?
- If a certain learning mechanism is a result of an interaction of individual and organizational enablers, what is a correspondence between a global leader's particular set of individual and the organization enablers and a learning mechanism they activate?
- Are some individual or organizational enablers more essential than other individual or organizational enablers to activate a learning mechanism?
- Are individual enablers more influential than organizational enablers in "turning on" a learning mechanism?
- Do these learning mechanisms explain the same learning process through different theoretical lenses or are the learning processes suggested by Kolb, Bandura, and Mezirow differ in nature?

Explain Global Leader Learning through a New Theoretical Lenses

- Empirical testing of process models of GLD based on TLT would be useful.
- It would be beneficial to explore the relational approach to global leader learning from IE, e.g., how global leaders learn from diverse followers.
- Future research is encouraged to apply social cognitive and collaborative experiential theories.

Expand the Methodological Repertoire of Studies Exploring Global Leader Learning

- Much of the extant global leadership research is based on interviews with or questionnaires completed by global leaders. These are very useful methods, but the field would now benefit from also leveraging other research methods. For example, only one study (Huesing & Ludema, 2017) observed global leaders' behavior using a methodology similar to Mintzberg's (1973) seminal work. It would be useful for more future studies to follow organizational ethnography and observe what global leaders really do. Likewise, the global leadership field would benefit from more expert cognition studies (see Osland et al., 2012, Osland, Ehret, & Ruiz, 2017a; Osland, Li, & Mendenhall, 2017b), which used cognitive task analysis to frame and analyze critical incidents of expert global leaders to describe how they make sense of their work. Incorporating a narrative approach into GLD research can provide insight and a complementary view to extant research.
- Large-sample quantitative studies very limited to date have good potential to add value.

Executive Coaching and Peer Coaching

- Coaching has seldom been studied in the field of GLD, despite executive coaching's tremendous potential for ensuring immediate and effective feedback and self-reflection (Mendenhall, 2006; Rosinski, 2010; Salomaa, 2017). Exploring the moderating role of different types of coaching such as executive coaching and peer coaching in global leader learning from IE presents an interesting research possibility. For example, scholars could use ELT and TLT to explain the learning process of global leaders by examining the moderating role of executive coaching to facilitate reflection at the stages of reflective observation and abstract conceptualization or by investigating how executive coaching enhances each stage of the experiential learning cycle.
- Identifying under what circumstances and to what extent coaching enhances global leader learning from IE would advance the GLD field.

- A comparative study could demonstrate the effect of different types of coaching, e.g., executive coaching versus peer coaching, on global leader learning.
- The effect of the length, timing (before, during, and/or after the IE), and approach of coaching on global leader learning could improve GLD interventions.

Research Agenda Influenced by COVID-19

- Especially in times when people cannot travel not only due to COVID-19 but also due to the environmental impact, expense, and time requirements of international travel/assignments, it would be interesting to explore the extent to which IE for global leaders can be developed domestically through multicultural teams and global virtual teams. It would also be interesting to understand specifically what and how global leaders learn from domestic IE experience.

CONTRIBUTIONS, LIMITATIONS, AND IMPLICATIONS

This study has systematically reviewed and integrated research published between 1998 and 2019 on global leader learning from IE. My work is a response to Osland et al.'s (2018) call to identify bridging mechanisms between individual-level dispositions and the development of global leadership capabilities. Additionally, this study also addresses Osland et al.'s (2017a, 2017b) call to specify the learning processes of global leaders. It makes the following contributions.

First, this review systematically maps and integrates the extant literature on individual and organizational enablers of global leader learning from IE, laying a path for other scholars. Second, the study reveals that a variety of learning mechanisms facilitate global leader learning and proposes a dynamic understanding of learning processes for different learning domains. Current understanding in the field is that different developmental methods activate different learning processes in global leaders (Cumberland et al., 2016). For example, international assignments have a higher potential to activate the transformational learning process in global leaders (Oddou & Mendenhall, 2018), while short-term business travel and international corporate training programs could result in experiential learning. By contrast, this study suggests that the specific developmental qualities of IE, how leaders approach their assignments (individual enablers including attitude toward learning), and organizational enablers (like the provision of coaching, which helps leaders reflect on and thus learn more from their experience) could significantly influence what type of learning occurs. For example, a leader going on a long-term assignment, but living in an expatriate bubble with little significant interaction with locals, may gain very little learning. In turn, with careful design and proper motivation, short-term business travel could result in transformational learning. Such a result could be achieved, for example, by a leader/traveler who explicitly finds lodging in an area where many locals stay or with a family and makes great effort to interact with and get to know locals socially and at work (Johnston, 2014).

Third, this review suggests a variety of important future research directions for IE (detailed below). Fourth, the review is built on articles exploring only managerial samples (as opposed to student samples) and thus provides a useful perspective on the learning mechanisms of global leaders, which might be different from the learning mechanisms of undergraduate students who normally lack work experience.

This review is limited in part by its scope. Future reviews on global leader learning could extend beyond articles to include PhD dissertations, books, and book chapters on the topic in order to integrate the latest thinking in the field. Future reviews might also benefit from including research on global teams and virtual global teams, thereby strengthening the social learning perspective on global leader learning.

Global leaders may benefit from a more personalized approach to designing IE interventions adjusted to their personal traits, individual capabilities, and learning styles. This facilitate a higher degree of learning from IE. Additionally, structured corporate training programs are normally shorter than long-term international assignments, but their efficiency is still high (Pless et al., 2011) due to organizational support, attention to the program's design, and use of a multi-method approach. Thus, organizations could potentially add some elements of structured programs such as executive coaching, peer coaching, and networking to long-term international assignment and short-term business travel in order to create more learnings for participants.

Identification of five groups of individual enablers and two groups of organizational enablers could expand the pool of potential effective global leaders beyond the traits and capabilities empirically examined to date. For example, when global leaders do not possess extroversion and openness, which are important for the success of global leaders but difficult to develop, they could potentially compensate for this lack by developing other capabilities. For example, less extroverted leaders who have high self-efficacy and consistently employ learning behaviors to encourage reflection like journaling or who receive organizational support in form of executive coaching may also be successful global leaders. This suggestion has emerged in part from my current experience living in Finland and observing many somewhat introverted brilliant global leaders who, with high self-efficacy and extensive self-reflection, have been quite successful. Risto Siilasmaa, Nokia's former Chairman of the Board, is one example of such leaders.

ACKNOWLEDGEMENTS

The author would like to thank the Marcus Wallenberg Foundation for financial support, which made this research possible, and professor Mats Ehrnrooth, editor Joyce Osland, and anonymous reviewers for very helpful comments.

REFERENCES

Adler, N., & Bartholomew, S. (1992). Managing globally competent people. *Academy of Management Perspective*, *6*(3), 52–65.

Allport, G. (1954). *The nature of prejudice*. Boston, MA: Addison-Wesley.

Alon, I., & Higgins, J. M. (2005). Global leadership success through emotional and cultural intelligences. *Business Horizons*, *48*(6), 501–512.

Ang, S., van Dyne, L., Koh, C., Ng, K. Y., Templer, K. J., Tay, C., & Chandrasekar, N. A. (2007). Cultural intelligence: Its measurement and effects on cultural judgment and decision making, cultural adaptation and task performance. *Management and Organization Review*, *3*, 335–371.

Bandura, A. (1977). *Social learning theory*. Upper Saddle River, NJ: Prentice-Hall Inc.

Beckett, S. (2018). The role of Mezirow's ten phases of transformative learning in the development of global leaders (ProQuest dissertations publishing). Pepperdine University.

Bird, A. (2018). Mapping the content domain of global leadership competencies. In M. E. Mendenhall, J. S. Osland, A. Bird, G. Oddou, M. J. Stevens, M. L. Maznevski, & G. K. Stahl (Eds.), *Global leadership: Research, practice, and development* (3rd ed., pp. 119–142). New York, NY: Routledge.

Bird, A., & Mendenhall, M. (2016). From cross-cultural management to global leadership: Evolution and adaptation. *Journal of World Business*, *51*(1), 115–126.

Bird, A., Mendenhall, M., Stevens, M. J., & Oddou, G. (2010). Defining the content domain of intercultural competence for global leaders. *Journal of Managerial Psychology*, *25*(8), 810–828.

Bird, A., & Osland, J. (2004). Global competencies: An introduction. In H. Lane, M. L. Maznevski, M. E. Mendenhall, & J. McNett (Eds.), *Handbook of global management* (pp. 57–80). Oxford: Blackwell.

Björkman, I., & Mäkela, K. (2013). Are you willing to do what it takes to become a senior global leader? Exploring the willingness to undertake challenging leadership development activities. *European Journal of International Management*, *7*(5), 570–586.

Black, J., & Gregersen, H. (Summer/Fall 2000). High impact training: Forging leaders from the global frontier. *Human Resource Management*, *39*(2 & 3), 173–184.

Caligiuri, P. (2006). Developing global leaders. *Human Resource Management Review*, *16*(2), 219–228.

Caligiuri, P. (2013). Developing culturally agile global business leaders. *Organizational Dynamics*, *42*, 175–182.

Caligiuri, P., & Di Santo, V. (2001). Global competence: What is it, and can it be developed through global assignments?. *Human Resource Planning*, *24*(3), 27–35.

Caligiuri, P., & Tarique, I. (2009). Predicting effectiveness in global leadership activities. *Journal of World Business*, *44*, 336–346.

Caligiuri, P., & Tarique, I. (2012). Dynamic cross-cultural competencies and global leadership effectiveness. *Journal of World Business*, *47*, 612–622.

Caligiuri, P., & Thoroughgood, C. (2015). Developing responsible global leaders through corporate sponsored international volunteerism program. *Organizational Dynamics*, *44*, 138–145.

Clapp-Smith, R., & Wernsing, T. (2014). The transformational triggers of international experiences. *Journal of Management Development*, *33*(7), 662–679.

Conger, J. (2014). Addressing the organizational barriers to developing global leadership talent. *Organizational Dynamics*, *43*, 198–204.

Cumberland, D., Herd, A., Alagaraja, M., & Kerrick, S. (2016). Assessment and development of global leadership competencies in the workplace: A review of literature. *Advances in Developing Human Resources*, *18*(3), 301–317.

Day, D., & Barney, M. F. (2012). Personalizing global leader development @ Infosys. In W. H. Mobley, Y. Wang, & M. Li (Eds.), *Advances in global leadership* (Vol. 7, pp. 179–201). Bingley: Emerald Publishing Limited.

Derven, M., & Frappolli, K. (2011). Aligning leadership development for general managers with global strategy: The Bristol-Myers Squibb story. *Industrial & Commercial Training, 43*(1), 4–12.

DiStefano, J., & Maznevski, M. (2003). Developing global managers: Integrating theory, behavior, data and performance. In W. Mobley & P. Dorfman (Eds.), *Advances in global leadership* (Vol. 3, pp. 341–371). Bingley: Emerald Publishing Limited.

Ensign, T. (2019a). The seed of transformation: A disorientation index (Unpublished dissertation). Santa Monica, CA: Pepperdine University.

Ensign, T. (2019b). Triggers of transformative learning in global leadership development: The disorientation index. In J. S. Osland, B. S. Reiche, B. Szkudlarek, & M. E. Mendenhall (Eds.), *Advances in global leadership* (Vol. 12, pp. 125–150). Bingley: Emerald Publishing Limited.

Furuya, N., Stevens, M., Bird, A., Oddou, G., & Mendenhall, M. (2009). Managing the learning and transfer of global management competence: Antecedents and outcomes of Japanese repatriation effectiveness. *Journal of International Business Studies, 40*, 200–215.

Gerrard, M. (2011). Global assignment effectiveness and leader development. In J. S. Osland, M. Li, & Y. Wang (Eds.), *Advances in global leadership* (Vol. 6, pp. 243–266). Bingley: Emerald Publishing Limited.

Gregersen, J., Morrison, A., & Black, J. (1998). Developing leaders for the global frontiers. *Sloan Management Review, 40*(1), 21–33.

Guillen, L., Mayo, M., & Korotov, K. (2015). Is leadership part of me? A leader identity approach to understanding the motivation to lead. *The Leadership Quarterly, 26*, 802–820.

Gundling, E., Grant, T., & Everhart, D. (2014). Global leadership development at Ford. In J. S. Osland, M. Li, & Y. Wang (Eds.), *Advances in global leadership* (Vol. 8, pp. 317–338). Bingley: Emerald Publishing Limited.

Gupta, A., & Govindarajan, V. (2002). Cultivating a global mindset. *The Academy of Management Executive, 16*(1), 116–126.

Gupta, B., Singh, D., Jandhyala, K., & Bhatt, S. (2013). Self-monitoring, cultural training and prior international work experience as predictors of cultural intelligence – A study of Indian expatriates. *Organizations & Markets in Emerging Economies, 4*(1), 56–71.

Hall, D., Zhu, G., & Yan, A. (2001). Developing global leaders: To hold on them, let them go! In W. Mobley, & M. W. McCall Jr (Eds.), *Advances in global leadership* (Vol. 2, pp. 327–349). Bingley: Emerald Publishing Limited.

Hollenbeck, G., & McCall, M. (2003). Competence, not competencies: Making global executive development work. In W. Mobley, & P. Dorfman (Eds.), *Advances in global leadership* (Vol. 3, pp. 101–119). Bingley: Emerald Publishing Limited.

Huesing, T., & Ludema, D. (2017). The nature of global leaders' work, In J. S. Osland, M. Li, & M. E. Mendenhall (Eds.), *Advances in global leadership* (Vol. 10, pp. 3–39). Bingley: Emerald Publishing Limited.

Javidan, M., & Bowen, D. (2013). The 'global mindset' of managers: What is it, why it matters, and how to develop it. *Organizational Dynamics, 42*, 145–155.

Johnston, A. (2014). Short-term business travel and development of executive leader global mindset. In J. S. Osland, M. Li, & Y. Wang (Eds.), *Advances in global leadership* (Vol. 6, pp. 293–316). Bingley: Emerald Publishing Limited.

Jokinen, T. (2005). Global leadership competencies: A review and discussion. *Journal of European Industrial Training, 29*(3), 199–216.

Kalra, K., Szymanski, M., & Olszewska, A. (2018). Do all roads lead to global leadership? Three approaches to teaching global leadership in modern business schools. In J. S. Osland, M. E. Mendenhall, & M. Li (Eds.), *Advances in global leadership*, (Vol. 11, pp. 257–259). Bingley: Emerald Publishing Limited.

Kets de Vries, M., & Florent-Treacy, E. (2002). Global leadership from A to Z: Creating high commitment organizations. *Organizational Dynamics, 30*(4), 295–309.

Kets de Vries, M., Vrignaud, P., & Florent-Tracy, E. (2004). The global leadership life inventory: Development and psychometric properties of a 360-degree feedback instrument. *International Journal of Human Resource Management, 15*(3), 475–492.

Kohonen, E. (2005). Developing global leaders through international assignments. An identity construction perspective. *Personnel Review, 34*(1), 22–36.

Kolb, D. (1984). *Experiential learning: Experience as the source of learning and development*. Englewood Cliffs, NJ: Prentice-Hall.

Levy, O., Beechler, S., Taylor, S., & Boyacigiller, N. A. (2007). What do we talk about when we talk about 'global mindset'? Managerial cognition in multinational corporation. *Journal of International Business Studies*, *38*(2), 231–258.

Li, M. (2009). An examination of the role of experiential learning in the development of cultural intelligence in global leaders. In H. Mobley, Y. Wang, & M. Li (Eds.), *Advances in global leadership* (Vol. 5, pp. 251–271). Bingley: Emerald Publishing Limited.

Li, M., Mobley, W., & Kelly, A. (2013). When do global leaders learn best to develop cultural intelligence? An investigation of the moderating role of experiential learning style. *The Academy of Management Learning and Education*, *12*(1), 32–50.

Lokkesmoe, K., Kuchinke, K., & Ardichvili, A. (2016). Developing cross-cultural awareness through foreign immersion programs: Implications of university study abroad research for global competency development. *European Journal of Training and Development*, *40*(3), 155–170.

Lovvorn, A. S., & Chen, J. S. (2011). Developing a global mindset: The relationship between an international assignment and cultural intelligence. *International Journal of Business and Social Science*, *2*(9), 275–283.

Mendenhall, M. (2006). The elusive, yet critical challenge of developing global leaders. *European Management Journal*, *24*(6), 422–429.

Mendenhall, M. (2008). Leadership and the birth of global leadership. In M. E. Mendenhall, J. S. Osland, A. Bird, G. R. Oddou, M. J. Stevens, M. L. Maznevski, & G. K. Stahl (Eds.), *Global leadership: Research, practice, and development*. New York, NY: Routledge.

Mendenhall, M., Arnardottir, A., Oddou, G., & Burke, L. (2013). Developing cross-cultural competencies in management education via cognitive-behavior therapy. *The Academy of Management Learning and Education*, *2013*(3), 436–451.

Mendenhall, M., Weber, T., Arnardottir, A., & Oddou, G. (2017). Developing global leadership competencies: A process model. In J. S. Osland, M. E. Mendenhall, & M. Li (Eds.), *Advances in global leadership* (Vol. 10, pp. 117–146). Bingley: Emerald Publishing Limited.

Mendenhall, M. E., & Stahl, G. K. (2000). Expatriate training and development: Where do we go from here? *Human Resource Management*, *39*, 251–265.

Mezirow, J. (1978). Perspective transformation. *Adult Education*, *28*(2), 100–110.

Mezirow, J. (1997) Transformation theory out of context. *Adult Education Quarterly*, *48*(1), 60–62.

Mintzberg, H. (1973). *The nature of managerial work*. New York, NY: Harper & Row.

Neary, D., & O'Grady, D. (Summer/Fall 2000). The role of training in developing global leaders: A case study at TRW Inc. *Human Resource Management*, *39* (2 &3), 185–193.

Ng, K., Van Dyke, L., & Ang, S. (2009a). From experience to experiential learning: Cultural intelligence as a learning capability for global leader development. *The Academy of Management Learning and Education, 8*(4), 511–526.

Ng, K., Van Dyne, L., & Ang, S. (2009b). Developing global leaders: The role of international experience and cultural intelligence, In W. Mobley, M. Li, & Y. Wang (Eds.), *Advances in global leadership* (Vol. 5, pp. 225–250). Bingley: Emerald Publishing Limited.

Nonaka, I. (1994). A dynamic theory of organizational knowledge creation. *Organization Science*, *51*(1), 14–37.

Oddou, G., & Mendenhall, M. E. (2008). Global leadership development. In M. E. Mendenhall, A. Bird, M. Maznevski, J. Osland, & G. Oddou (Eds.), *Global leadership development: Research, practice and development* (pp. 160–174, 1st ed.). London: Taylor & Francis.

Oddou, G., & Mendenhall, M. E. (2013). Global leadership development. In M. E. Mendenhall, J. Osland, A. Bird, G. Oddou, M. Maznevski, M. J. Stevens, & G. K. Stahl (Eds.), *Global leadership development: Research, practice and development* (pp. 215–239, 2nd ed.). London: Routledge.

Oddou, G., & Mendenhall, M. (2018). Global leadership development: Processes and practices. In M. Mendenhall, J. Osland, A. Bird, G. Oddou, M. Maznevski, M. Stevens, & G. Stahl (Eds.), *Global leadership: Research, practice, and development* (3rd ed., pp. 229–269). New York, NY: Routledge.

Oddou, G., Mendenhall, M., & Ritchie, J. (2000, Summer/Fall). Leveraging travel as a tool for global leadership development. *Human Resource Management, 39*(2&3), 195–172.

Oliver, D., Church, A., Lewis, R., & Desrosiers, E. (2009). An integrated framework for assessing, coaching and developing global leaders. In W. Mobley, M. Li, & Y. Wang (Eds.), *Advances in global leadership* (Vol. 5, pp. 195–224). Bingley: Emerald Publishing Limited.

Osland, J. (2001). The quest for transformation: The process of global leadership development. In M. Mendenhall, T. Kuhlmann, & G. Stahl (Eds.), *Developing global business leaders: Policies, processes, and innovations* (pp. 137–156). Westport, CN: Quorum.

Osland, J., & Bird, A. (2000). Beyond sophisticated stereotyping: Cultural sensemaking in context. *Academy of Management Executive, 14*(1), 65–79.

Osland, J., & Bird, A. (2013). Process models of global leadership development. In M. E. Mendenhall, J. S. Osland, A. Bird, G. R. Oddou, M. L. Maznevski, M. J. Stevens, & G. K. Stahl (Eds.), *Global leadership: Research, practice and development* (2nd ed., pp. 97–112). New York, NY: Routledge.

Osland, J., & Bird, A. (2018). Process models of global leadership development. In M. E. Mendenhall, J. S. Osland, A. Bird, G. R. Oddou, M. J. Stevens, M. L. Maznevski, & G. K. Stahl (Eds.), *Global leadership: Research, practice and development* (3rd ed., pp. 179–199). New York, NY: Routledge.

Osland, J. S., Bird, A., Mendenhall, M. E., & Osland, A. (2006). Developing global leadership capabilities and global mindset: A review. In G. K. Stahl, & I. Björkman (Eds.), *Handbook of research in international human resource management* (pp. 197–222). Cheltenham: Edward Elgar.

Osland, J. S., Bird, A., & Oddou, G. (2012). The context of expert global leadership. In W. H. Mobley, Y. Wang, & M. Li (Eds.) *Advances in global leadership* (Vol. 7, pp. 107–124). Bingley: Emerald Publishing Limited.

Osland, J., Ehret, M., & Ruiz, L. (2017). Case studies of global leadership expert cognition in the domain of large-scale global change. In J. S. Osland, M. Li, & M. E. Mendenhall (Eds.), *Advances in global leadership* (Vol. 10, pp. 41–88). Bingley: Emerald Publishing Limited.

Osland, J., Li, M., & Mendenhall, M. (2017). Patterns, themes and future directions for advancing global leadership. In J. S. Osland, M. E. Mendenhall, & M. Li (Eds.), *Advances in global leadership* (Vol. 10, pp. 253–262). Bingley: Emerald Publishing Limited.

Osland, J., Li, M., Petrone, M., & Mendenhall, M. (2018). Global leadership development in the university settings and future directions for advancing global leadership research. In J. S. Osland, M. E. Mendenhall, & M. Li (Eds.), *Advances in global leadership* (Vol. 11, pp. 347–366). Bingley: Emerald Publishing Limited.

Osland, J., Li, M., & Wang, Y. (2014). Conclusion: Future directions for advancing global leadership research. In J. Osland, M. Li, & Y. Wang (Eds.), *Advances in global leadership* (Vol. 8, pp. 365–376). Bingley: Emerald Publishing Limited.

Ott, D., & Michailova, S. (2018). Cultural intelligence: A review and new research avenues. *International Journal of Management Reviews, 20*, 99–119.

Pless, N., & Borecka, M. (2014). Comparative analysis of international service learning programs. *Journal of Management Development, 33*(6), 526–550.

Pless, N., Maak, T., & Stahl, G. (2011). Developing responsible global leaders through international service learning programs: The Ulysses experience. *The Academy of Management Learning and Education, 10*(2), 237–260.

PwC. (2017). *CEO pulse survey.* London: PwC.

Quirk, S., & Gustafson, J. (2018). Developing the next generation of global leaders: Proposing an iterative framework for student global leadership development. In J. S. Osland, M. E. Mendenhall, & M. Li (Eds.), *Advances in global leadership* (Vol. 11, pp. 215–256). Bingley: Emerald Publishing Limited.

Raver, J., & Dyne, L. (2018). Developing cultural intelligence. In K. Brown (Ed.), *The Cambridge handbook of workplace training and employee development* (pp. 407–440). Cambridge: Cambridge University Press.

Reiche, B., Bird, A., Mendenhall, M., & Osland, J. (2017). Contextualizing leadership: A typology of global leadership roles. *Journal of International Business Studies, 48*, 552–572.

Rosinski, P. (2010). *Global coaching: An integrated approach for long-lasting results*. London: Nicholas Brealey Publishing.

Rowe, W., Krause, W., Hayes, G., Corak, L., Wilcox, S., Azam, G., … Varela, F. (2018). Canadian global leadership students engaged in strategic partnership in Ecuador. In J. S. Osland, B. S. Reiche, B. Szkudlarek, & M. E. Mendenhall (Eds.), *Advances in global leadership* (Vol. 11, pp. 281–311). Bingley: Emerald Publishing Limited.

Salomaa, R. (2017). *Coaching of international managers: Organizational and individual perspectives*. Vaasa: Library of the University of Vaasa. Retrieved May 20, 2020, from https://www.uni-vaasa.fi/materiaali/pdf/isbn_978-952-476-736-1.pdf

Sendelbach, N., & McGrath, M. (2005). Leadership development without borders. In W. Mobley, & E. Weldon (Eds.), *Advances in global leadership* (Vol. 4, pp. 229–254). Bingley: Emerald Publishing Limited.

Stroh, L., & Caligiuri, P. (1998). Increasing global competitiveness through effective people management. *Journal of World Business, 33*(1), 1–16.

Suutari, V. (2002). Global leader development: An emerging research agenda. *Career Development International, 7*, 218–233.

Tay, C., Westerman, M., & Chia, A. (2008). Antecedents and consequences of cultural intelligence among short-term business travelers. In S. Ang, & L. Van Dyne (Eds.), *Handbook of cultural intelligence: Theory, management, and applications* (pp. 56–70). Armonk, NY: M.E. Sharpe, Inc.

Terrell, R., & Rosenbusch, K. (2013). How global leaders develop. *Journal of Management Development, 32*(10), 1056–1079.

Tracy, M. (2018). Leadership development in a global chemical manufacturer. *Development and Learning in Organizations, 32*(4), 1–4.

Tuleja, E. (2014). Developing cultural intelligence for global leadership through mindfulness. *Journal of Teaching in International Business, 25*, 5–24.

Tung, R. (2014). Distinguished scholar invited essay. Requisites to and way of developing a global mind-set: Implications for research on leadership and organizations. *Journal of Leadership & Organizational Studies, 21*(4), 329–337.

Vijaiakumar, P., Morley, M., Heraty, N., Mendenhall, M., & Osland, J. (2018). Leadership in the global context: Bibliometric and thematic patterns of an evolving field. In J. S. Osland, M. E. Mendenhall, & M. Li (Eds.), *Advances in global leadership* (Vol. 11, pp. 31–72). Bingley: Emerald Publishing Limited.

Walker, J. (2018). Do methods matter in global leadership development? Testing the global leadership development ecosystem conceptual model. *Journal of Management Education, 42*(2), 239–264.

Wood, E., & Peters, H. (2014). Short-term cross-cultural study tours: Impact on cultural intelligence. *International Journal of Human Resource Management, 25*(4), 558–570.

Yari, N., Lankut, E., Alon, I., & Richter, N. F. (2020). Cultural intelligence, global mindset, and cross-cultural competencies: A systematic review using bibliometric methods. *European Journal of International Management, 14*(2), 210–250.

APPENDIX

Table A1. Conceptual Studies on Global Leader Learning from International Experience.

Author and Year	Type of IE	Type of Competencies	Conceptual Framework	Individual Enablers of Learning	Organizational Enablers of Learning	Learning Mechanisms
Black and Gregersen (2000)	GLDP	GL competencies	Contrast–confrontation– concept	Not specified	Ensure global leadership development training which can stretch mental maps	Contrast–confrontation–remapping
Oddou et al. (2000)	Short-term business travel	GL competencies	Quality of IE (high-quality short-term business travel can be a source of transformational experience)	Personal traits and abilities: openness, curiosity, willingness to stretch mental maps, sensitivity to differences, dealing with uncertainty; Learning behaviors: writing a journal, observing, and asking questions	Organizational support: corporate travel policies and rewarding for development	Not specified
Hall et al. (2001)	International assignment	GL competencies	ELT	Learning how to learn	Exposure to novelty and uncertainty, providing feedback	Define challenge—define experiences—develop mechanisms of getting leaders to these experiences
Gupta and Govindarajan (2002)	Formal education, cross-border teams, immersion, international travel, multicultural teams	Global mindset	Mindsets as knowledge structures with attributes of differentiation and integration	Personal traits: openness, curiosity, self-consciousness about own mindset	Exposure to novelty and diversity, providing local mentor, environment supporting diversity through set of core values, ownership rights, job rotation	Develop ability to integrate diverse knowledge bases

Kets de Vries and Florent-Treacy (2002)	4T (training, transfer, teamwork, travel)	GL competencies	Not specified	Not specified	Strong and supportive organizational culture and HR policies; multinational; mentors with global mindset; networking across borders; IE; family support	Not specified
Hollenbeck and McCall (2003)	IE	GL competencies	Not specified	Motivation to lead in international business context, openness to learning, cognitive complexity	Alignment of strategy and development; redefine top-management role in global leadership development	Identify job challenge—design experience—select global leaders
Alon and Higgins (2005)	Mix of methods	CQ	Multiple Intelligences, EQ, CQ	CQ—moderator of global leadership success; self-awareness, language fluency, motivation, learning from failure	Demonstrate connection between high CQ and successful career	Individuals go through the stages of motivation, awareness, and action to master CQ
Kohonen (2005)	International assignment	GL competencies	Identity construction	Exploring own identity; interaction with locals and self-reflection	Provide exposure to discontinuities, cultural novelty, duality of global versus local, critical incidents, providing feedback	Not specified
Caligiuri (2006)	Didactic, experiential (short-term business travel, GLDP, and IE (international assignments))	GL competencies	Tasks—KSAO—method; aptitude x treatment	Moderators: personal traits (extroversion, agreeableness, conscientiousness, emotional stability, openness)	Integrate IE into a broader management development program	Leaders benefit differently from experience—depending on their individual aptitude. Offer right experience to right leaders

Table A1. (*Continued*)

Author and Year	Type of IE	Type of Competencies	Conceptual Framework	Individual Enablers of Learning	Organizational Enablers of Learning	Learning Mechanisms
Mendenhall (2006)	Mix of methods	GL competencies	Pyramid model of global leadership competencies development	Higher level of development of leadership competencies, awareness of degree of possessing the competencies	Combination of the method and time	Combine other training methods with coaching
Li (2009)	International assignment	CQ	ELT, CQ, divergent learning style	Moderator of CQ: divergent learning style	Selection, cultural exposure, policies, and practices to enhance learning from experience	Learning as adaption in thinking, perceiving, feeling, and behaving
Ng et al. (2009a)	International assignment	CQ	ELT, CQ	CQ—moderator and experiential learning—mediator of global leader effectiveness;	Exposure to challenging tasks (to lead change, high level of responsibility, nonhierarchical relationships)	CQ moderate learning of global leaders from experience
Ng et al. (2009b)	International assignment	CQ	ELT, CQ	CQ—moderator and experiential learning—mediator of global leader effectiveness; learning behaviors: seeking experiences; reflecting on observations; interpreting conceptually; active experimenting	Selection, organizational policies, and practices to encourage experiential learning	Experiential learning cycle (select leader with high CQ, encourage all four stages of experiential learning)

Study	Methods	GL competencies	Framework		Developmental	Notes
Oliver (2009)	Combination of the methods of formal training, developmental experience, coaching	GL competencies	"Developmental framework 70-20-10"	Not specified	Developmental experience; learning behaviors (reflecting, looking for parallel situations where to apply learnings, seek new experiences), define critical experience	70-20-10 (70% of learning comes from on-job experience). IE should be combined with other methods
Lovvorn and Chen (2011)	International assignment	Global mindset, CQ	Global mindset, CQ	CQ as learning capability; CQ is moderator and mediator of global mindset	Exposure to novelty, encourage interaction with local people	CQ transforms experience into knowledge, as CQ develops it and reinforces learning from experience
Caligiuri (2013)	International assignment	Cultural agility	Developmental quality of cross-cultural experience	Personal traits: emotional stability, openness, and extroversion	Selection, developmental qualities of international assignment (peer collaboration, feedback), supportive organization culture	Selection, designing well-crafted cultural experiences, coaching in strong and supportive learning environment
Javidan and Bowen (2013)	Combination of IE, coaching, training, and networking	Global mindset	Global mindset	Antecedents: language fluency, previous IE, graduate degree, age	Antecedents: industry, organizational function, organizational level	Global Psy. Capital is most difficult to develop; it could be developed through coaching
Conger (2014)	International assignment, short-term business travel, training, coaching	GL capabilities	Not specified	Motivation to work abroad, drive to learning	Combining selection and organizational support (monitoring talent, developmental goals, repatriation policies)	Not specified
Tung (2014)	Area studies programs, sensitivity training, and	Global mindset	Not specified	Shed ethnocentric tendencies, experiment with new ideas, review one's own	Exposure to novelty and diversity	Not specified

Table A1. (*Continued*)

Author and Year	Type of IE	Type of Competencies	Conceptual Framework	Individual Enablers of Learning	Organizational Enablers of Learning	Learning Mechanisms
	international assignment			limitations, plan for change, learn about other cultures		
Caligiuri and Thoroughgood (2015)	ISLP	GL competencies	Responsible global leadership development, CSR values	Openness, extroversion, emotional stability	Collaboration with peers from diverse cultures, challenging assignments, projects fostering humility, altruism, and CSR values	Program should develop values and abilities
Mendenhall et al. (2017)	IE	Intercultural competencies	Global leadership development theory based on TLT, adult learning, and CBT	Moderator: developmental readiness (ability, motivation); aptitude, perceived difficulty, perceived magnitude	Learning context Company context	Trigger event > self-commitment > reflection > strategy > implementation > reflection
Number of studies with focus on individual enabler, organizational enabler, and learning mechanism				18	21	16

Note(s): *CBT*, cognitive-behavioral therapy; *CLT*, Cognitive Learning Theory; *CQ*, cultural intelligence; *EQ*, emotional intelligence; *ELT*, Experiential Learning Theory; *GL competencies*, global leadership competencies; *HLT*, Humanist Learning Theory; *IE*, international experience, *KSAO*, knowledge, skills, abilities, and other characteristics; *SLT*, Social Learning Theory; *GLDP*, Global Leadership Development Program; *ISLP*, International Service Learning Program.

Table A2. Quantitative and Mixed Method Studies on Global Leader Learning from International Experience.

Author and Year	Type of Study	Development Method	Conceptual Framework	Constructs Related to Learning	Sample	Results
Quantitative Studies (6) and Mixed Method Studies (3)						
Gregersen et al. (1998)	Mixed method	IA	Not specified	Not specified	108 Multinational corporation (MNCs) based in the United States (survey), 130 global leaders from 50 global MNCs	Study revealed key characteristics of global leaders: inquisitiveness, character, duality, and savvy. Key efforts to develop global leaders are selection, family's support, training, and repatriation
Caligiuri and Di Santo (2001)	Mixed method	IA	KSAO	IV: personality traits, knowledge, and abilities DV: global leader's effectiveness	50 Global leaders in 50 US-based MNCs 74 Global leaders from 3 US-based MNCs	Certain personality traits such as flexibility, openness, and ethnocentrism cannot be developed through IA, while knowledge and abilities can. Selection of global leaders with appropriate traits is essential
Furuya et al. (2009)	Quantitative longitudinal	IA	Theory of organizational knowledge creation	IV: intercultural personality characteristics (GCI) (+); self-adjustment experiences, organizational support (+); repatriation policies (+) Mediator: global management competency learning DV: global management competency transfer	305 Expatriate Japanese managers from 5 Japanese MNCs	Organizational support and intercultural personal characteristics (GCI) predict, and self-adjustment does not predict global management competency learning (GMCL). GMCL's mean $= 3.72$, $SD = 0.47$

Table A2. (*Continued*)

Author and Year	Type of Study	Development Method	Conceptual Framework	Constructs Related to Learning	Sample	Results
Quantitative Studies (6) and Mixed Method Studies (3)						
Caligiuri and Tarique (2009)	Quantitative	IE	SLT, contact hypothesis	IV: high and low contact experience (+) Moderator: extroversion (+), openness DV: global leader effectiveness (individual work performance)	256 Global leaders from the UK-based firm, representing 17 nationalities	High-contact experience predicts global leadership effectiveness when leaders have greater extroversion. Extroversion (personal trait) as a moderator. GLE's mean = 2.3, SD = 0.96
Gerrard (2011)	Quantitative	IE	Big five, job challenge profile, CQ	IV: role scope Mediator: dealing with diversity (+); creating change, responsibility level, managing boundaries DV: leader development, performance, withdrawal conditions	97 Global leaders and 30 global assignees from Australia, Brazil, Canada, and US	Dealing with diversity is different for the job with different scope. Dealing with diversity mediates relationships between role scope and leader development; leader's cognitive CQ predicts contextual performance. Emotional stability predicts tenure in international assignment
Caligiuri and Tarique (2012)	Quantitative	IA	SLT, contact hypothesis	IV: high contact non-work experiences (+), extroversion (+), openness (+) Mediator: dynamic cross-cultural competencies (cultural flexibility (+); tolerance of ambiguity (+); low ethnocentrism (+)) DV: global leader success	420 Global leaders and 221 supervisors	Extroversion, openness, and non-work experience predict dynamic cross-cultural competencies, which in turn predict global leader effectiveness. GLE's mean = 3.22, SD = 0.63

Li et al. (2013)	Quantitative	IA	ELT, CQ	IV: IE Moderator: divergent learning style (+) DV: CQ	294 Global leaders (China, Ireland, 18 more countries)	Divergent learning style moderates learning from IE and increases CQ of global leaders. CQ = 98 (out of 140), SD = 16
Tuleja (2014)	Mixed method	MBA study tour	CQ, mindfulness	Four stages of reflection state (nonreflection, understanding, reflection, critical reflection)	141 MBA students, USA, 2-week immersion tour to China	Mindfulness increases learning from immersion study tour and increases CQ of MBA students
Wood and Peters (2014)	Quantitative	MBA study tour	CQ	IV: IE DV: four CQ's facets	42 MBA students, 12-day trip	Study tour increases meta CQ, cognitive CQ, and motivational CQ. Meta CQ mean = 4.8, SD = 0.72; cognitive CQ = 4.24, SD = 1; motivational CQ mean = 5.61, SD = 0.9; behavioral CQ = 5.21, SD = 1.11
Walker (2018)	Quantitative	MBA	SLT, ELT, CLT, HLT	IV: formal and experiential learning, mentoring, peer learning Mediator: self-efficacy DV: Global Mindset	64 MBA students, Southwestern University, USA	Formal and experiential learning predicts self-efficacy; self-efficacy predicts GMI and its parts

Note(s) 1: IA, international assignment; *IE*, international experience; *GLDP*, Global Leadership Development Program; *ISLP*, International Service Learning Program; *STBT*, short-term business travel.

Note(s) 2: CLT, Cognitive Learning Theory; *CQ*, cultural intelligence; *ELT*, Experiential Learning Theory; *HLT*, Humanist Learning Theory; *KSAO*, knowledge, skills, abilities, and other characteristics; *SLT*, Social Learning Theory.

Note(s) 3: IV, independent variable; *DV*, dependent variable; (+) the hypothesis is confirmed.

Table A3. Qualitative Studies on Global Leader Learning from International Experience.

Author and Year	Data Collection	Developmental Method	Sample	Results
Qualitative Studies (12)				
Neary and O'Grady (2000)	Case study	GLDP	35 global leaders (12 non-US leaders)	Building on diversity, tolerating ambiguity—leader's key skills.
DiStefano and Maznevski (2003)	Case study	GLDP	MBA students in Europe	Combination of developmental methods yields the most optimal developmental results.
Sendelbach and McGrath (2005)	Case study	GLDP	Ford Motor and University of Michigan's MBA	Leaders need a framework for understanding global environment.
Derven and Frappolli (2011)	Case study	Global on-boarding	GLDP at Bristol-Myers Squibb	Peer coaching and networking provide learning and support.
Pless et al. (2011)	Case study	ISLP	70 global leaders from PwC	Effective ISLP provides deep learning in three learning domains: cognitive, affective, and behavioral.
Day and Barney (2012)	Case study	GLDP	4 groups of Infosys GLDP, India	Longitudinal design predicts when the development change occurs.
Terrell and Rosenbusch (2013)	Phenomenological study	IA	12 global leaders from 6 countries	Global leaders develop through first-hand experience learn intuitively and are open to learning and reflecting upon.
Gundling et al. (2014)	Case study	GLDP	Top 200 managers at FORD	Ability to influence without key authority—key global competence.
Johnston (2014)	Narrative interview	STBT	16 global leaders, USA	STBT is efficient in developing global mindset of leaders.
Pless and Borecká (2014)	Case study	ISLP	ISLP of six US-based leading MNCs	ISLP program has one of the three goals: leadership, organization, or community development.
Tracy (2018)	Case study	GLDP	Second largest chemical manufacturer	Peer-to-peer learning and networking is essential in GLDP.

Note(s): *IA*, international assignment; *IE*, international experience; *GLDP*, Global Leadership Development Program; *ISLP*, International Service Learning Program; *STBT*, short-term business travel.

Table A4. Content Analysis for Individual Enablers of Global Leader Learning from International Experience.

Type of Enabler	Results of Content Analysis	Summary for Each Type of an Enabler Key Evidence
Individual Enablers for International Assignment		
Personal traits	*Inquisitiveness (Gregersen et al., 1998)*; curiosity, openness (Gupta & Govindarajan, 2002); extroversion, agreeableness, conscientiousness, emotional stability, openness (Caligiuri, 2006); **intercultural personality characteristics as antecedents (Furuya et al., 2009);** extroversion as a moderator **(Caligiuri & Tarique, 2009); emotional stability as antecedent for staying in international assignment (Gerrard, 2011);** extroversion and openness as antecedents **(Caligiuri & Tarique, 2012)**; emotional stability, openness, extraversion (Caligiuri, 2013)	• **extroversion** (moderator for global leader effectiveness) • **extroversion and openness** (antecedents for global leader effectiveness) • **emotional stability** (predicts staying in international assignment) • inquisitiveness
Individual capabilities	Cognitive complexity (Hollenbeck & McCall, 2003); self-awareness, foreign language skills (Alon & Higgins, 2005); **dynamic cross-cultural competencies: tolerance of ambiguity, cultural flexibility, low ethnocentrism (Caligiuri & Tarique, 2012);** tolerance of ambiguity, cultural flexibility, low ethnocentrism (Caligiuri, 2013); foreign language fluency (Javidan & Bowen, 2013)	• **tolerance of ambiguity, cultural flexibility, low ethnocentrism** (antecedents of global leader effectiveness) • cognitive complexity • self-awareness • language fluency
Learning ability	Capacity to learn and adapt (Kets de Vries & Florent-Treacy, 2002); **divergent learning style as a learning ability (Li, 2009, Li et al., 2013);** CQ as a set of learning capabilities (Ng et al., 2009a, 2009b); CQ as a learning capability (Lovvorn & Chen, 2011)	• **divergent learning style** (moderator of CQ) • CQ (moderator of experiential learning) • capacity to learn
Learning behaviors	Learning how to learn (Hall et al., 2001); cultivating self-consciousness about own mindset (Gupta & Govindarajan, 2002); engaging into sensemaking process and self-reflection (Kohonen, 2005); reflecting; locking for parallel situations to apply these learnings; seeking new experiences; defining key critical experiences (Oliver, 2009); interaction with local people (Kohonen, 2005; Lovvorn & Chen, 2011); shed ethnocentric tendencies; experiment with new ideas; review one's own limitations; plan for change; understand other sociopolitical, cultural, economic systems (Tung, 2014); **using intuitive, situation-specific learning approach (Terrell & Rosenbusch, 2013)**	*use intuitive, situation-specific learning* • learn how to learn • increase self-awareness • engage in sensemaking process and self-reflection • interact with locals • experiment with new ideas • apply learnings in real life
Attitude to learning	Openess to learning; motivation to lead in international business context (Hollenbeck & McCall, 2003); willingness to explore and reshape identity (Kohonen, 2005); motivation to work abroad; drive for learning (Conger, 2014); *positive attitude toward learning (Terrell & Rosenbusch, 2013)*	*positive attitude to learning* • drive to learn • motivation to lead in global business environment • Motivation to explore and reshape identity

Table A4. (*Continued*)

Type of Enabler	Results of Content Analysis	Summary for Each Type of an Enabler Key Evidence
Individual Enablers for Short-term Business Travel		
Personal traits	Openness, curiosity (Oddou et al., 2000)	• openness, curiosity
Individual capabilities	Cultural sensitivity (Oddou et al., 2000); ***ability to demonstrate culturally responsive leadership and effective interpersonal communication (Johnston, 2014)***	• cultural sensitivity • ***culturally responsive leadership*** • ***effective interpersonal communication***
Learning behaviors	Observe, ask questions, write a journal, exercise behavioral flexibility (Oddou et al., 2000)	• observe, ask questions, write a journal, exercise behavioral flexibility
Attitude to learning	Willingness to stretch mental map (Oddou et al., 2000)	• willingness to stretch mental map
Individual Enablers for International Corporate Programs		
Personal traits	Openness, emotional stability, extraversion; intrinsic motivation	• openness, emotional stability, extraversion
Individual capabilities	***Self-awareness, tolerance of ambiguity (Neary & O'Grady, 2000)***; self-awareness; language fluency (Alon & Higgins, 2005); **self-efficacy (Walker, 2018)**	• *self-efficacy* • *self-awareness* • *tolerance of ambiguity* • language fluency
Learning behaviors	***Application of learning in a real world (DiStefano & Maznevski, 2003)***; learning from failure (Alon & Higgins, 2005); ***asking questions, being non-judgmental (Sendelbach & McGrath, 2005); ensuring mindfulness, journaling, and group discussions to enhance critical reflection (Tuleja, 2014)***; 10 learning behaviors: cultural self-awareness, invite the unexpected, results through relationships, frameshifting, expand ownership, develop leaders, add value, core values, and flexibility (Gundling et al., 2014)	• ***develop cultural self-awareness*** • ***invite unexpected*** • ***develop relationship*** • ***frameshifting*** • ***expand ownership*** • ***develop leaders*** • ***ask questions, journaling—to enhance critical reflection***
Attitude to learning	Motivation to lead in international business context (Alon & Higgins, 2005); intrinsic motivation (Caligiuri & Thoroughgood, 2015)	• learn from mistakes • motivation to lead in international business context • intrinsic motivation

Note(s): Findings highlighted in **bold** come from quantitative studies and are statistically significant; findings in ***bold italics*** come from qualitative and mixed method studies, and findings in standard black come from conceptual studies.

Table A5. Content Analysis for Organizational Enablers of Global Leader Learning from International Experience.

Type of Enabler	Content Analysis Results	Summary for Each Enabler
Organizational Enablers for International Assignment		
Developmental qualities of international assignment	Significant role transition; exposure to novelty and uncertainty; providing feedback (Hall et al., 2001); including developmental goals into performance measurements (*Caligiuri & Di Santo, 2001*); exposure to discontinuities, cultural novelty, duality of global versus local, critical incidents, providing feedback (Kohonen, 2005); cultural exposure (Li, 2009; Lovvorn & Chen, 2011; Tung, 2014); **providing leaders with high-contact cross-cultural leadership development experiences exposure (Caligiuri & Tarique, 2009)**; challenging tasks (to lead change; high level of responsibility; nonhierarchical relationship) (Ng et al., 2009a, 2009b); **ensuring non-work cross-cultural experiences (Caligiuri & Tarique, 2012)**; peer collaboration, providing feedback (Caligiuri, 2013)	• **ensure high-contact cultural experiences and non-work cultural experiences** • exposure to cultural novelty • "Stretching assignment" and developmental indicators • peer learning and networking • providing feedback
Organizational support	Ensuring adaptability of leader's family, providing training *(Gregersen et al.,1998)*; assigning local mentor; environment supporting diversity—through set of core values, ownership rights, meritocracy, job rotation (Gupta & Govindarajan, 2002); link development and business strategy, involvement of top management (Hollenbeck & McCall, 2003); geocentrically oriented organization; satisfying the needs of community, meaning, and pleasure; ensure internationally minded HR strategies exposure to foreign experience (Kets de Vries & Florent-Treacy, 2002); integrating IE as a part of a broader management development program (Caligiuri, 2006); **organizational attitude toward its international operations; well-crafted international assignment policies and HR policies (Furuya et al., 2009)**; organizational policies to encourage experiential learning (Ng et al., 2009a, 2009b); supportive organizational culture (Caligiuri, 2013); monitoring talent, introducing performance scorecard (Conger, 2014); facilitating repatriation (*Caligiuri & Di Santo, 2001*; Conger, 2014; *Gregersen et al.,1998*); teaching leaders how to learn from experience; seeing development as one of the outcomes of an international work (Javidan & Bowen, 2013); **selection of leaders with appropriate traits** (*Caligiuri & Di Santo, 2001*, Caligiuri, 2013; Conger, 2014; *Gregersen et al.,1998*; Kets de Vries & Florent -Treacy, 2002; Li, 2009; Ng et al.. 2009a, 2009b)	• **selection of global leaders with appropriate traits** • **organizational attitude toward international operations** • **international assignment policies** • **HR policies** • supportive organizational culture • top managers' involvement • assigning local mentor • ensuring family's adaptability • facilitating repatriation
Organizational Enablers for Short-term Business Travel		
Developmental qualities of STBT	*Ensure developmental qualities of short-term business travel (Johnston, 2014)*	• *developmental qualities of STBT*
Organizational support	Corporate travel policies (having a free time on a trip; interact with locals); rewarding for learning and using language (Oddou et al., 2000)	• corporate travel policies • rewarding for using language

Table A5. (*Continued*)

Type of Enabler	Content Analysis Results	Summary for Each Enabler
Organizational Enablers for International Corporate Programs		
Developmental qualities of international corporate programs	Consortium programs (Black & Gregersen, 2000); designing action learning projects and real global *business projects; arranging work in small teams; avoiding trouble-free experience (Neary & O'Grady, 2000); combining developmental methods; integrating technology into the program (DiStefano & Maznevski, 2003)*; incorporating blended approaches, robust needs analysis; adjusting the program to GM career cycle *(Derven & Frappolli, 2011), providing coaching (Day & Barney, 2012; DiStefano & Maznevski, 2003); ensuring first-hand experience; unstructured, complex in scope and in scale (Pless et al., 2011); providing knowledge, ensuring first-hand experience and critical self-reflection (Tuleja, 2014)*; define the purpose of a study tour, ensure interaction with locals, reflection; rewarding for use of foreign language skills **(Wood & Peters, 2014)**; qualities of the program: meaningful projects, collaboration with peers from other cultures, "stretch assignments," fostering humility and altruism, work with peers possessing CSR values: in-country coaching; encourage blogging about experience (Caligiuri & Thoroughgood, 2015); *peer-to-peer learning and networking (Tracy, 2018)*; dynamic and integrative approach to learning, where programs design is integrated, customized, and taps into cognitive, affective, and behavioral domains of learning **(Walker, 2018)**; *get leaders to the frontline, connect people, make it personal, teach influencing skills (Gundling et al, 2014)*; provide pre-assignment cross-cultural training and coaching, and post-program support: ensure application of acquired knowledge and skills (Caligiuri & Thoroughgood, 2015)	• *ensure effective design of the program which provides cognitive, affective, and behavioral outcomes* • provide coaching and ensure self-reflection • peer-to-peer learning and networking during and after the program • meaningful projects, get to frontline, connect with local people, use foreign language • ensure application of acquired knowledge and skills
Organizational support	*Engaging high ranking into the program (Neary & O'Grady, 2000)*; demonstrate connection between CQ and successful career (Alon & Higgins, 2005); *modeling personal development trajectories through assessment of leadership behaviors and matching it with a developmental challenge; consolidate organizational cross-cultural knowledge and business insights gained (Johnston, 2014)*; public display, support returning volunteers, future volunteer projects (Caligiuri & Thoroughgood, 2015)	• *ensure top-management involvement into the program design and implementation* • personalize global leader developmental plans • integrate diverse practical cultural knowledge within organization

Note(s): Findings highlighted in **bold** come from quantitative studies and are statistically significant; findings in *bold italics* come from qualitative and mixed method studies, and findings in standard black come from conceptual studies. When only the author's name is in **bold**, it means that this finding is not significant. When only the author's name is in *bold italics*, it means that this finding is not a central focus of the study.

Table A6. Content Analysis for Learning Mechanisms of Global Leader Learning from International Experience.

Learning Mechanisms (Explained Theoretically)	Content Analysis for Each Type of Learning Mechanism	Theoretical Lens	Key Learning Mechanism
Learning Mechanisms for International Assignment			
Experiential learning cycle	Experiential learning cycle (Hall et al., 2001); grasping experience and transforming experience; divergent learning style moderates learning from experience (Li, 2009); experiential learning is moderated by CQ (Ng et al., 2009a, 2009b); **experiential learning style moderates learning from IE (Li et al., 2013)**	**Experiential Learning Theory (ELT), Kolb (1984)**	**CE > RO > AC > AE**
Transformational learning cycle	*Trigger event–self-commitment–reflection–strategy–implementation–reflection* (based on adult learning, leadership development, TLT, CBT, and SLT) (Mendenhall et al., 2017; *Beckett, 2018*)*	Transformational Learning Theory (TLT), Mezirow (1978)	Trigger event > self-commitment > reflection > strategy > implementation > reflection
Social learning process	**Attention–retention–reproduction through participative modeling process (Caligiuri & Tarique, 2009); multiple intercultural experiences lead to positive attitude toward different cultures and lead to learning appropriate behaviors (Caligiuri & Tarique, 2012)**	Social Learning Theory (SLT), Bandura (1977)	Attention > retention > reproduction through participative modeling process
Learning Mechanisms for Short-term Business Travel			
—	*Not specified*	—	—
Learning Mechanisms for International Corporate Programs			
Experiential learning cycle	Contrast–confrontation–concept (Black & Gregersen, 2000); *learning methodology of the service learning program include assessment, challenge, and support. Individual and team coaching is an important part of all phases of the project (Pless et al., 2011); through a short-term business travel, participants engage into experiential learning cycle and enhance their metacognitive CQ, cognitive CQ, and motivational CQ (Wood & Peters, 2014); experiential learning through combination of individual learning, teambuilding, training, and coaching (Pless & Borecká, 2014)*	ELT, Kolb (1984)	**CE > RO > AC > AE**

Table A6. (*Continued*)

Learning Mechanisms (Explained Theoretically)	Content Analysis for Each Type of Learning Mechanism	Theoretical Lens	Key Learning Mechanism
Social learning process	"Attention–retention–reproduction" (Tung, 2014)	Social Learning Theory (SLT), Bandura (1977)	Attention > retention > reproduction through participative modeling process

Other Learning Mechanisms (Not Explained Theoretically)

- Job challenge—identify experience—select right person to this job challenge (Hollenbeck & McCall, 2003);
- Sensemaking process (Kohonen, 2005);
- Aptitude X treatment: Offer right developmental opportunities to right people (Caligiuri, 2006);
- International experience and CQ have a complex interrelationship; IE enhances CQ, in turn CQ transforms information from IE into knowledge, as CQ develops it and reinforces learning from IE (Lovvorn & Chen, 2011);
- *Assessment of leadership behaviors—matching it with developmental challenge—predicting personal development trajectory (Day & Barney, 2012)*;
- *Transformation through acquiring new behaviors. Key elements for transformation to happen: self-awareness, novelty, learning through relationships, frameshifting, own results, develop others, add value (Gundling et al, 2014)*;
- *Engaging in self-reflection and generalization to other situations (Terrell & Rosenbusch, 2013)*;
- *Mindfulness (reflective practice) is the link between knowledge and behaviors; it involves cultural sensemaking through framing, making attributes, and selecting scripts and enables transition from nonreflection to understanding to reflection to critical reflection through personal insights (Tuleja, 2014)*;
- *Learning process: (1) Embark on a travel; (2) build relationships; (3) seek deeper understanding; (4) integrate and transfer experiences to new context; (5) open to additional learning (Johnston, 2014)*;
- **Integrative adult learning mechanism through multiple types of learning; combination of ELT, SLT, CLT, humanist learning theory (Walker, 2018)**; **self-efficacy is developed through formal and experiential learning (Walker, 2018)**. IE is a pathway from self-efficacy into social capital, then to psychological capital; self-efficacy is developed through formal and experiential learning (Walker, 2018).

Note(s): Fingings highlighted in **bold** come from quantitative studies; findings in ***bold italics*** come from qualitative and mixed method studies, and findings in standard black come from conceptual studies.

*Transformative learning process in global leader development has been qualitatively examined in the doctoral dissertation "The role of Mezirow's 10 phases of transformative learning in the development of global leaders" by Beckett (2018).

Table A7. Conceptual Frameworks Explaining Learning Mechanisms of Global Leader Learning from International Experience.

Conceptual Framework	Author and Year	Development Method	Learning Mechanism	Conceptualization of Global Leadership Development
Empirical Evidence (Quantitative Studies)				
Theory of Organizational Knowledge Creation (Nonaka, 1994)	Furuya et al. (2009)	International assignment (IA)	Experience and feedback are central to learning process. Nature and framing of experience will shape the type of learning.	Global management competency learning is acquisition and enhancement of knowledge, skills, abilities across three domains: global business domain, global administrative skills, and intercultural employee management skills
Social Learning Theory (Bandura, 1977; Contact Hypothesis Theory (Allport, 1954)	Caligiuri and Tarique (2009, 2012)	IA	Attention > retention > reproduction through participative modeling process.	Global leadership development is viewed as a social learning process, in which global leadership competencies are developed through social interaction (through practicing and receiving feedback in a safe environment)
Experiential Learning Theory (ELT) (Kolb, 1984)	Li et al. (2013) and Wood & Peters (2014)	IA, MBA study tour	Concrete experience > reflective observation > abstract conceptualization > active experimentation.	Global leadership development is viewed as an experiential learning process which occurs through grasping and transformation of experience
ELT; Social Learning Theory; Cognitive Learning Theory; Humanist Learning Theory	Walker (2018)	MBA program	Formal and experiential learning predicts self-efficacy, self-efficacy predicts Global Mindset and its components (Global Intellectual Capital, Global Intellectual Capital, and Global Social Capital).	Global leadership development process is hypothesized to be sustained by multiple types of learning that build upon and reinforced each other. Global leadership development is viewed as an ecosystem where different learning methodologies interact with each other

Table A7. (*Continued*)

Conceptual Framework	Author and Year	Development Method	Learning Mechanism	Conceptualization of Global Leadership Development
Conceptual Studies				
ELT (Kolb, 1984), CQ (Ang et al., 2007)	Hall et al. (2001), Li (2009), and Ng et al. (2009a, 2009b)	IA	Concrete experience > reflective observation > abstract conceptualization > active experimentation.	Global leadership development is viewed as an experiential learning process which occurs through grasping and transformation of experience
Transformational Learning Theory (Mezirow, 1978)	Mendenhall et al. (2017)	IA	Trigger event > self-commitment > reflection > strategy > implementation > reflection.	Global leadership development is viewed as a nonlinear and organic transformational learning process of learning from experience which is characterized by dynamism and directionality

PART II

PRACTITIONER'S CORNER

GLOBAL COLLABORATION IN CRISES

Adriana Burgstaller, Bert Vercamer, Berta Ottiger-Arnold, Christian Mulle, Dominik Scherrer, Eyrún Eyþórsdóttir, Fabricia Manoel, Lisa Cohen, Matthias Müller, Monika Imhof, Myshelle Baeriswyl, Monwong Bhadharavit, Nozipho Tshabalala, Rachel Clark, Rorisang Tshabalala, Sherifa Fayez, Simone Inversini, Simon Papet, Susanne Reis, Takahiko Nomura and Tina Nielsen

ABSTRACT

Global collaboration, or the ability to collaborate with people different from ourselves or even across species, becomes increasingly important in our interconnected world to engage constructively with and across difference. As we face more complex challenges, both locally and globally, the need for the creativity and innovation made possible by diverse perspectives is only amplified. Through five stories from our work as consultants and practitioners helping organizations to collaborate, we explore the role of global leadership in collaboration during times of crisis in various sectors. We began by asking ourselves a series of questions about global collaboration that could also serve as future research directions for scholars. We argue that new forms of leadership are required in the global context where both tasks and relationship domains are characterized by high complexity. We conclude by providing insights and recommendations for global leaders to address those complexities

Advances in Global Leadership, Volume 13, 175–203
Copyright © 2020 Emerald Publishing Limited
All rights of reproduction in any form reserved
ISSN: 1535-1203/doi:10.1108/S1535-120320200000013011

through collaboration and help their organizations learn from their experiences in crises and beyond.

Keywords: Global collaboration; global leadership; trust; crisis; complexity; relationship-building; purpose; shared leadership; resilient organizations

INTRODUCTION

I am starting this introduction with *I*. We will end it with *we*.

When Joyce Osland contacted me (Dominik Scherrer) earlier this year to contribute to the *Advances in Global Leadership* book series, I said yes without hesitation, as the topic of global collaboration has been my passion for many years. At first, I thought I would write about some of my own experiences, but I soon realized I did not want to do that alone. I wanted to write about global leadership collaboration within a global collaborative context. So I started to get in touch with possible coauthors, and we formed a global team to tackle this subject.

A topic that was raised more than once in our early conversations was the meaning of "global" in global collaboration. Does it refer to geography? Is it meant to be the opposite of local? And if yes, is this a broad enough definition in a time when a neighbor next door can be more different than a person living on a different continent? Soon we realized that a more comprehensive approach would create a rich and inspiring new perspective as we tried to integrate as many dimensions of diversity as possible. We decided to define global collaboration in a very broad sense: working together across different contexts and through diverse identities. We explored the contours of the role of global collaboration in global leadership by sharing our past experiences of it in the workplace with each other. As we did so, we began to record our experiences into a series of stories in order to gather many different perspectives on global collaboration. The process of writing itself was a beautiful example of global collaboration in which we ended up with 21 authors around the globe, who together wrote 16 stories. This chapter features five of these stories, all of which relate to a timely issue: global leadership and collaboration in times of crisis (we plan to share the other stories in future papers). The objective of this chapter is to better understand global collaboration in relation to global leadership in times of crisis; in other words, to find answers to the question: **When crisis hits, what do global leaders need to pay attention to when collaborating with others?**

Global leadership research has a strong focus on the ability to handle both complex tasks and complex relationships. Reiche, Bird, Mendenhall, and Osland (2017, p. 556) define global leadership as "the process and actions through which an individual influences a range of internal and external constituents from multiple national cultures and jurisdictions in a context characterized by significant levels of task and relationship complexity." Similarly, global collaboration requires leaders to integrate different perspectives across various types of borders (organizational, national, functional, occupational, interspecies, etc.) while working on complex tasks (e.g., a global NGO fighting climate change, a cross-sector movement self-organizing to address issues in a city, a university hospital preparing for the COVID-19 pandemic, a large global company building trust with their staff before and during times of economic hardship, or a social movement overcoming apartheid).

Next, we identified a few topics and related questions that seemed relevant to explore in relation to global collaboration in a context of crisis. We hope that researchers will also benefit from these questions:

- What role does trust play in global collaboration in a crisis situation? And is trust a prerequisite or a result of successful collaboration—or both?
- Surely a shared vision and purpose are important, but are they always vital elements to begin a successful collaboration? Or can a deep connection between people sometimes be enough to engage in meaningful collaboration?
- What is the role of diversity in collaboration? How do we stay open to other ways of thinking and feeling, and how can we appreciate difference?
- Might the global competencies engaged when working with other cultures around the world also be useful in local contexts when other forms of diversity are at play? What skills and competencies are needed for global leaders to make global collaboration effective and meaningful in times of crisis?
- What forms of leadership are most effective at fostering global collaboration in times of crisis?
- What if collaboration were something more fluid, less tangible that cannot be reduced to simple recipes or an algorithm? What if collaboration were an organic process that cannot be controlled, but for which perhaps conditions can be developed? How do we deal with the ambiguity arising in this process of letting go?
- Sometimes, collaboration seems to improve in times of crisis: How can good collaboration not only be short term but survive beyond a crisis without people reverting to old routines?

What we found interesting from a global collaboration perspective, based on our experiences as practitioners and based on the five stories presented here, is that great things happen when 1) global leaders develop trusting relationships, when they let go of their need for control—even and maybe especially in times of crisis; and 2) they recognize the importance of having an action-oriented mindset when handling paradoxes that emerge from complex task and relationship challenges that the crisis produces (Reiche et al., 2017, p. 560).

As we wrote the stories, we realized how complex, fascinating, and even mysterious the topic of global collaboration is. And as we wrote, we learned that our own process of collaboration developed organically, was often unplanned, and yet unveiled surprising resonance among the stories. In this chapter, where we present five stories from different fields of work, we would like to show some of those complexities and our insights. We hope these will help global leaders enhance their positive impact on both tasks and relationships and on results and processes.

STORY 1: THE VALUE OF LEARNING THROUGH CRISIS IN TIMES OF COVID-19

Berta Ottiger-Arnold

The management of a university hospital in Zurich—as is the case in many university hospitals—is characterized by long, often highly complex decision-making webs, a substantial amount of political sensitivity, and incredibly complicated operational processes. The context of the rapidly developing pandemic of COVID-19 in 2020, with the early learnings and examples of hotspots such as Italy, created a high sense of urgency to prepare for its impact. The hospital's specialists, such as virologists and infectious disease experts, were being mobilized to find answers to this key question: How can we prepare a slow-moving tanker like our university hospital for a state of emergency, to treat as many patients as possible, while we define and implement protective measures for employees and patients as quickly as possible?

The sense of urgency and the drive to reach these common goals had incredible results:

(1) Within a few days, teams in previously disused buildings were equipped with everything that was necessary to start operating as COVID stations to test and treat patients. This involved procuring devices from units that were closed due to the shutdown of planned surgeries, searching for unexpectedly scarce medical material worldwide (e.g., disinfectants and masks), communicating with interrupted supply chains, and ordering large quantities of other medical equipment. The teams worked in shifts, almost around the clock.

(2) In one example, a project involving an oxygen tank had been repeatedly delayed for nearly two years. Having learned from other countries that COVID treatment with this specific equipment was key, the project was implemented over a weekend and an additional oxygen tank was installed.

(3) Internal communication, often vague or missing in the past, became transparent, and information and new knowledge were shared with staff on a frequent basis.

(4) The teams that were to maintain non-COVID-19–related services (e.g., medical engineering, building services, electrical power supply) self-organized into groups that functioned without physical contact so that a team would still be operational—and didn't have to go into quarantine—even if someone fell ill with the highly communicable COVID-19.

(5) An internal service was created by employees to support other employees who suffered from stress or anxiety. This allowed them to better perform their tasks.

(6) Some units were no longer busy, while others were overloaded. An internal job exchange market ensured that the overburdened units were given the necessary resources. Everyone was focused on the question: What else is needed to be ready for the "wave?"

The above examples were all managed in a great spirit of collective care: care for each other, the existing patients, and the future wave of patients. Teams and individuals went way beyond what was expected of them; they demonstrated great empathy and foresight. Everyone checked in with one other. People replaced the common salutation of "have a nice day" with "stay healthy." All of this tangible solidarity created positive energy. There was a lot of gratitude for the high level of commitment and the formation of ad hoc teams that managed all the necessary preparations. The extra work and extra effort that would normally have led to a great deal of discussion and negotiation evoked no complaints, and there was no evidence of interpersonal conflict.

All the while, important non-COVID-19–related projects had to continue. However, those departments that were burdened with a heavy COVID-19 work-load were spared whenever possible and allowed to postpone their contributions. Other departments were generally supportive and helpful.

What was remarkable was the focus people had, related to the shared goal of taking care of people's health: There was a great deal of cooperation and self-organization, and the courage to make decisions. Every instance, every idea, and every discussion was tested for its ability to add value to that larger goal. The resulting dynamics, speed, and simplicity are impressive. There are no more politics. All that counts is: Do our actions contribute to fulfilling our task of taking care of the population?

I am an in-house observer with some distance from operations, thanks to my cross-sectional function. I look with awe as I observe the shift in commitment and approach and the many changes and strengths, listed below, that this crisis and the sole focus on the common goal has brought to our hospital:

- a high degree of readiness and willingness to take responsibility, especially in middle and lower management
- a great deal of trust in the hospital's own specialists and people, as reflected in the internal communication from the top of the organization
- power and control took a back seat and made room for personal responsibility and a focus on the collective good
- new lines of hierarchy, such as the task force being taken seriously even when asked to clarify its decisions
- information given reliably and very frequently

It is clear that we all can learn to deal with extraordinary situations that will change our lives. The managers and important stakeholders are already critically discussing and reflecting on what has happened, so they can learn for the future. Drawing the right conclusions on lessons learned is important, as this won't be the last crisis. COVID-19 has not yet been overcome, and preparations are underway to set up a long-term crisis response strategy.

A larger question is what the impact will be on the hospital post-COVID-19, and not just in times of crisis. A key principle of change management is "having a sense of urgency." The COVID-19 pandemic clearly engenders that. While it will not be sustainable for staff and teams to overextend themselves, what of the current context can we keep and integrate into our "normal" way of working once this is over? What will the hospital look like when this immediate sense of urgency is removed?

Conclusions and Lessons Learned for Global Leadership

When reading this story, you might easily get the impression that this somehow just happened naturally as if an invisible hand moved the different organizational pieces. However, the conclusions and lessons learned below provide more insight into what took place behind the scenes:

- A classical and somewhat hierarchical approach to a problem was the formation of a task force involving the stakeholders who were directly affected by COVID-19. Approximately 16 people composed the task force, half from the executive committee and also staff from lower hierarchical levels with relevant expertise in virology, hygiene, or logistics. The nascent task force had extensive decision-making authority and clear goals; they met six times per week, made decisions quickly, and their decisions were implemented immediately.
- At the levels below the task force, something less directive and more organic evolved: People organized themselves based on the needs they perceived. In many instances, this informal organizing was opportunity-driven, or one might even say it was driven by chance or opportunity. For instance, a person in facility management, who in normal operations plays a low-key role, was highly involved in managing the crisis based on the time she had available and her talent.[1] Everyone was mindful of what could be helpful at any given moment during the crisis and felt empowered to act. Complexity could no longer be handled from the top, other than trusting and empowering the lower levels of the hierarchy to take meaningful action based on a deep inner purpose: averting the crisis and protecting the population. The role of leadership was to create the necessary space for collaboration to happen and, in some cases, to refrain from intervening.
- Never waste a good crisis: The next challenge for the University Hospital leadership will be to ask these questions: What can be learned from the crisis? When is the hierarchy helpful and when does it hinder the work? What will be done differently after the crisis?

The COVID-19 crisis remains a highly complex global challenge, while hospitals themselves are considered highly complex entities, high-reliability organizations with no room for error. For this double complexity to be addressed, it takes an integrative global leadership approach that carefully balances hierarchy with self-organization. Hierarchy alone could no longer handle the complexity and rapid change at play in the COVID-19 crisis. It takes leadership that fosters

---

[1]Similar to Project30 presented in the previous story and following Effectuation principles (Sarasvathy, 2008; Society for Effectual Action, 2018), the starting point of the process is available resources rather than predefined goals.

collaboration and the space to learn at all levels of the organization across hierarchies, functions, and roles, and the trust that people closest to the problem have the best insights and are able to decide and act decisively.

The university hospital's response to the pandemic proves that a typically slow-moving tanker can, if necessary, react as fast as a speedboat to accomplish a common mission: actively supporting the health of the population.

STORY 2: HOW CULTURE AFFECTS COLLABORATION IN GLOBAL BUSINESS

Rachel Clark

As business has become more global, the topic of culture and the discussions around it have become more intense. Quotes such as "Culture eats strategy for breakfast" are commonplace. But in my experience, even if companies recognize its importance, there is little understanding of how to define culture, how to address it or work with it; and what aspects of culture are supportive of this global, more complex reality. Culture is often seen as something that simply happens, good or bad. Instead, we must take a closer look at the impact culture has, at how it emerges and what values and practices it conveys, and at how to allow companies to be real enablers of a necessary global collaboration.

I started my career in the late 1980s in the military, working as a mechanical engineer. Reflecting on my 15 years' service, there clearly was a strong, specific, and consistent culture, regardless of where I moved. People who were outliers were easily identified and removed during basic training, which all service personnel attended. The result was a close-minded, team-oriented group that policed itself when someone stepped out of line—a good place to work unless you were different. The organization clearly lacked diversity, with only 1% female and 5% people of color. Homosexuality was still illegal, and if you were a woman and got pregnant, you had to leave. Creativity did not thrive, and it was not required. On a macro level, the organization seemed to collaborate effectively. On a micro level, unless you were with the "in crowd," you were ostracized until either you left or you complied and acted like the majority. Through a chance posting to a civilian unit, I was exposed to an alternative way of leading people, based on empowerment to improve practices. For the first time in 15 years, I felt I wasn't compromising my own values, and I requested to leave the military.

I joined a multinational engineering company based in Switzerland that had some characteristics of the military. However, it lacked the clear focus on what was precisely the culture it wanted to drive. Undefined, it shouted at you "command and control" arrogantly and aggressively. Leaders said they wanted teams to be more creative and empowered to improve things, but as I got to know the organization, it seemed unlikely that this would become a reality: Actions did not support that otherwise-inspiring incentive, and noncollaboration was a recurring, unaddressed problem. Edgar Schein (2004) refers to this phenomenon when he speaks of a culture where stated values are in contrast with the actual observed behavior, typically leading to unhealthy tensions.

When the economic crisis hit in 2008, the company expanded some of its production to "low-cost countries." Many people in the three original factories lost their jobs, and those who were left were upset about the way their colleagues were let go. There was significant resentment toward employees in the new factories.

Despite this resentment, there was a need for collaboration. Many people had to be upskilled in a short amount of time. Our department was set up for this purpose. I was managing a group of 40 experts that was taken from the three original factories and asked to create expert communities globally. We were responsible for training the future local experts and supporting them with local issues. However, many of the employees in our department had no management experience and had not met their new teams other than by phone. They had no authority over them, English language skills were highly variable, and the team members changed frequently. Needless to say, conditions for a fruitful collaboration were not present.

In those global teams' meetings, with original and new experts, the pattern was often the same. New experts remained mostly silent, while the original experts demanded responses and immediate decisions and grew louder and angrier as the meetings progressed. It resulted in nothing more than increasing the divide between us all. The arrogance of the original experts was palpable, exacerbated by their anger over the firing of their colleagues.

One unpleasant experience ended up creating an opportunity. Soon after our mission started, I went to visit our Chinese factories. As we arrived, my manager, who came from one of the original factories, refused to wear safety shoes despite the rule—an indication of what was to come. The local plant manager was highly experienced but very humble. She pointed out areas where capacity had been doubled in a few weeks, and others that still had problems, and what was being done to tackle them. As the visit went on, my manager became more critical and visibly angry, pointing out numerous issues, no matter how minor. At the end of the tour, he started shouting, telling our host that the place was a disaster though "she was supposed to be talented." Although she tried to reason with him, he became even more aggressive. After she started to cry in front of her whole team, he left us both there in the middle of the shop floor. Not knowing what to do other than putting my arms around her, I told her I would help her to solve all the issues.

I was concerned I may have made a cultural faux pas, but to my surprise, my approach won me a friend. This incident was the start of a great relationship with her and her team. Soon, they opened up about their difficulties, showing a form of trust and vulnerability that allowed collaboration with my team to kick in. To support it, I contacted our learning and development department, which proposed an intercultural team training. Its impact turned out to be profound. Many started to realize they needed to change their approach, even in small things: using video instead of voice-only calls, keeping time for small talk before the start of meetings, scheduling check-in one-on-one meetings with less vocal team members, etc. It helped to build relationships.

I used what I had learned to carry out similar trainings in our Chinese factories. In one of these sessions, I once asked, "What does it mean to you when people remain quiet after a lead expert asks, '*Does everyone agree?*'" Their answer came with a laugh: No, it didn't mean they agreed. But, how would the Western

European side interpret it? This led to further discussions on both "sides," which I concluded by asking both teams to discuss how to work together. Key aspects of collaboration, such as showing agreement or disagreement or managing feedback, were openly put on the table and commonly defined. This represented another small step toward each other.

Last year, I finally decided to change jobs, and I now work for a new company. In many ways, it is comparable to my previous one—an engineering firm, similar size, same male/female ratio—but with noticeable differences in terms of organizational culture and in how it is being actively steered. For one thing, I was recruited based not on my technical skills but on my experience of culture change and "soft skills," which fills me with hope. Ironically, I was first reminded of my military time when I was invited to a mandatory weeklong introduction to the company! The essence was the same: showing the company culture that you were expected to be a part of. However, some key aspects of that culture were actually supportive of global collaboration across branches, occupations, and hierarchy.

Humility is valued, which echoes throughout the organization, right up to the head of the family who owns the business. Employees' feedback is taken seriously, and the executive board adjusts their approach each year in response to suggested improvements. Innovation and creativity are highly regarded, creating a positive breeding ground for ideas. All employees can improve the environmental aspects of the business, via small work groups, questionnaires, and structured brainstorming sessions. Many ideas have already been implemented or discussed at the executive level. The message is clear: If you are not happy with something, you have the power to change it.

Each department has a coach, who takes every team through a development weekend every other year. This year's theme is self-care, addressing ways to improve sleep and avoid burnout with mindfulness. The appraisal system has recently shifted to a strength-building approach, and there is a process in place to match those strengths to roles within the business.

During the COVID-19 crisis of 2020, a video was shared with the whole business by our CEO and our business owner. The video explained that the head office was asked to volunteer a pay cut to provide money to our colleagues who are suffering financially from the virus. The owner will not take dividends this year, and he is making his own money available to ensure cash fluidity. His message is clear: Our people are the most valuable part of the business, and management's actions must demonstrate that. Redundancies will be the last resort. Ongoing communication from the company leaders is strong: Weekly updates are posted on our local sites and globally, and team leaders are advised to have weekly discussions with us individually to check if we and our families are OK. It is not perfect; not every team leader follows this rule, but most of them do. The message was the same in the 2008 economic crisis, and the company came through relatively unscathed. In this culture, espoused values resonate with observed behavior.

Investment in a company culture that promotes global collaboration across all branches, departments, occupations, and rank seems to pay off. The firm's global reputation is high and has remained so for many years. It is a consistent recipient of the "Top 100 places to work" awards.

Conclusions and Lessons Learned for Global Leadership

- An organizational culture based on humility, allowing vulnerability, and that puts people at the center is a solid base to create a respectful environment that is supportive of effective global collaboration—between different country cultures, occupational cultures, and beyond. It also creates the foundation to reflect on cultural differences and the opportunity for a "third culture" to emerge that integrates and leverages diversity.
- Building such an organizational culture, or "third culture," is based on asking questions, listening, observing, trying to understand difference, and then acting and openly sharing and communicating transparently. Highly empathetic, this culture as a whole is globally more "competent" and better prepared for global collaboration as it seeks, integrates, and promotes difference.
- An organizational culture where stated values and actual behavior are aligned lays the foundation for employee trust and global collaboration across diversity. Authenticity leads to credibility and, eventually, global engagement.
- Building respectful relationships, and therefore valuing individuals and their unique contributions, is a key lever for successful global collaboration. Prioritizing activities and practices that will encourage and strengthen relationships across difference, whether geographic, national cultural, or otherwise, allows for a stronger, more unified organizational fabric.

Developing such a culture of trust in a complex environment is highly dependent on effective global leaders who walk the talk, dare to be transparent, and are both authentic and credible in their day-to-day actions in line with the organization's espoused values.

STORY 3: PROJECT30: THE ART OF CROSS-SECTOR INNOVATION—IT TAKES 30 PEOPLE TO TRANSFORM OUR CITY

Takahiko Nomura with contributions from Dominik Scherrer

There are probably not many countries that need to be as prepared for natural disasters as Japan; earthquakes, tsunamis, typhoons, or volcano eruptions have always been a part of life on the islands. Accordingly, Japanese culture has found innovative ways of dealing with natural disasters, such as earthquake-proof architecture, alert systems for tsunamis and the preparation of its inhabitants from a very young age. Uncertainty avoidance has been identified by some interculturalists (Hofstede, 2020) as a value that has emerged in response to that environment and can be observed though different forms in what could be described as a more ritualized life based on a tightly-knit community that fosters a form of predictability in everyday life. In this context Takahiko Nomura has developed Project30, through which some of these communal elements are leveraged and developed further, by inviting people from government, business and civil society to collaborate across difference. Through Project30, he is helping to create a stronger social fabric based on trust forming a community with high resilience to respond to crises. Taka-san explains in his own words.

In 2011, we experienced the most powerful earthquake, called The Great East Japan Earthquake, ever recorded in Japan. The earthquake triggered strong tsunami waves that reached heights of up to 40 meters in the Tohoku region.

In the aftermath of the disaster, I visited Tohoku several times to support social entrepreneurs, having dialogue sessions among people living in the area. I was shocked to see the damage from the tsunami and, at the same time, pleasantly surprised to see the power of people who struggled to recreate the city beyond the boundary of sectors: private sector, public sector, and nonprofit sector.

One of the entrepreneurs in the area said that, among those coming from the outside to help, they only welcomed the people who were eager to recreate their society together with them. They needed collaboration and action, rather than sympathy. Through my visits and observing what was unfolding in front of me, I saw the future of society without boundary among the three sectors—business, government, and nonprofit organizations (NPOs[2]).

A new idea emerged, called Project30, which seeks to transform a city into a cross-sector platform. The most interesting part of this idea is that it takes only 30 people to transform a city. Can you imagine what your city might look like as a cross-sector platform? The question we pursue is: "What if corporations, governments, and nonprofit organizations (NPOs) could help each other to innovate to solve business, economic, social, and environmental problems in your city?"

In 2016, following the experience in the Tohoku region, I started the Shibuya30 project in the city of Shibuya and invited 30 people from three sectors: 20 from corporations, eight from NPO, and two from the local government. All of them lived in the same location, although they experienced it very differently and did not know each other. It was the first time we experienced the feeling of complete multistakeholder collaboration for Shibuya in one room.

We asked the group three things:

- Can you build a shared view of some of the problems inside your shared territory?
- What could be done to address them?
- What can we build with the diversity of the combined resources that we bring to the table?

With these questions as a framework, we launched an inspiring process where members of the project would meet, think, share, try out new things, ask for feedback, fail, and improve to come up with impactful solutions. Most importantly, they also created trust, by forging relationships across their differences.

The 30 project members tried to solve existing problems, but they also asked new and powerful questions from their diverse perspectives. A question may show new perspectives on the issue, or even a new issue, and through that inquiry invite

---

[2]Some countries refer to nonprofit organizations as NGOs, which stands for what they are not—nongovernmental organizations.

additional stakeholders to help collectively find solutions. Compared with other collective impact projects and innovation efforts, Project30 does not focus on goals, but on people and process. Our questions are not focused on "What is the best solution?" but on "Who should be invited into the dialogue?" or "Do the 30 people enjoy this process, and are they fulfilled?"

What makes the process unique is also the formation of the 30 individuals as a team of facilitators. They learn the skill of facilitating innovation processes, and they invite people from outside the group of 30. This expands the community to many hundreds of people, driving collaboration within the group while further enhancing its diversity. This multiplier effect through each member's communities allows for the diversity to be leveraged in a context of global collaboration.

The Shibuya30 has continued for four years; thus, we now have 120 people in this trust platform in Shibuya. Recently, the Shibuya30 network was activated when Shibuya needed to respond to COVID-19. One NPO in the Shibuya30 network launched an initiative to help restaurants to survive in the city, as well as to help mothers to prepare food for their families. The idea was to match restaurants and mothers and transform what would otherwise have been wasted food into a wonderful lunch box. The NPO asked Shibuya30 members to offer their space, as well as to spread the idea to others. After a while, the local government started to help residents get lunch boxes from restaurants in Shibuya. As such, the Shibuya30 platform led to the creation of new public systems via their network of trust, and via modeling the possible, rather than depending on governments alone to develop solutions.

Through cross-sector collaboration, corporations were able to create new business opportunities that were not visible before other sectors engaged with the issue and changed their own behavior. If a corporation believes that its resources and leverage could improve society, other sectors can provide complementary input to find a viable solution. A trusting relationship is the key to creative collaboration among the three sectors.

We found that a city is an organic container for three-sector innovation. A city naturally has three sectors, and we see this as a minimum unit for societal transformation. Through these three sectors, we can strengthen the social fabric in a city. Currently, there are four Shibuya30 spin-off projects in Japan as well as one planned in New Zealand and Switzerland, each named after their city, such as Zurich30.

I invite you to start a Project30 in your city. In Japan, we are leading Project30 in Shibuya, Kyoto, Nagoya, and Tohoku. We are also planning a first international Project30 gathering in New Zealand. Each Project30 platform is purely local, but the global network of Project30 could be a new platform of trust for idea sharing and global collaborations.

It is our dream to launch Project30 in most cities around the world. It would mean strong communities of trust covering the globe and connecting to each other, regardless of national borders or cultural boundaries. We are currently defining processes to launch Project30 for any city and plan to provide tools, trainings, and services to effectively share our knowledge and experiences.

Conclusions and Lessons Learned for Global Leadership

- At the beginning of a successful collaboration are people who build **relationships of trust.** Based on that trust, the community can more effectively respond to a crisis, which may be quite sudden and unpredictable, such as COVID-19. The community helped build an immediate solution for businesses by connecting restaurants, NPOs, and mothers. Although no one saw the pandemic coming, the trust in the community was strong enough to act quickly and collaboratively and to take innovative action. In Effectuation[3] terms (Sarasvathy, 2008; Society for Effectual Action, 2018), this can be called social capital and working with what you have as opposed to setting goals. It also involves leveraging the available resources to innovate or create something new in the world.
- Bringing together diverse perspectives and leveraging **diversity** are at the heart of this collaboration. Diverse perspectives bring additional resources and possibilities, leading to new, unexpected solutions.
- To bring that diversity together takes leadership. At the heart of that leadership is **facilitation,** not authoritarian command, even and especially in a complex crisis situation. Facilitation means above all **asking powerful and inspiring questions** that open up space for new perspectives and solutions to emerge and for people to take action.

Perhaps the leader who embodied this type of leadership the most was the mayor of Shibuya himself. He attended events without being intrusive, he asked humble questions and listened deeply, and he provided the space needed for people to interact, build trust, see new possibilities, and act.

The following two stories deal with ongoing crises.

STORY 4: CONVERSATION IS THE BIRTHPLACE OF ALL COLLABORATIVE ACTION

Nozipho Mbanjwa and Rorisang Tshabalala

In the spring of 2018, I was gripped by imposter syndrome as I embarked on my journey as a Desmond Tutu Fellow. We would be grappling with the question of what characteristics of African leadership were required to have a consequential effect on the many socioeconomic threats and opportunities that

---

[3]Effectuation is an approach to entrepreneurship that leverages existing resources. Sometimes it is compared to the process of cooking. A classical way of cooking is to decide on a meal and then buying the necessary ingredients. In Effectuation, the approach consists of opening the fridge, looking at what is inside to then deciding on a meal based on what is available. Similarly, in entrepreneurship, a person following the effectuation principles is looking at his or her resources—people he or she knows, competencies, experiences and financial means—to decide what business to launch.

confront the world in general and our continent in particular. Alongside the biographies of fellows who were doing everything from leading large investment corporations to occupying positions of influence in governments and multilateral organizations, my stock-in-trade asset of facilitating conversation across various roles as a corporate communications specialist, financial journalist, and conference moderator felt relatively inconsequential.

My paradigm-shifting moment occurred in one of the lectures when a guest speaker, Rachel Adams, stood in front of us and delved into what felt like the depths of my self-doubting soul with the words that forever changed my attitude and understanding of the significance of what I do: "Conversation is the birthplace of action," she said. At that moment, the penny dropped. What I, and others who work in my field, do is not to simply make sure that conversations happen. What I do ensures that whatever conversations are happening are conversations of consequence. Put simply, I help smart people to have simple conversations that actually make the world a better place. I am not just a moderator; I am a conversation strategist, tasked with not only bringing order to conversation but most importantly, generating consequence from conversation.

History bears testament to the consequential nature of conversation done right. From the domino effect of women gaining universal suffrage in the 1920s to and beyond the ending of apartheid in South Africa in the 1990s, these leaps in the progress of humankind have been the results of persistent and focused conversation toward those ends. It does not end there, however. The defining nature of conversations that have gone on to yield global impact is not just persistence and focus. In addition, they have been the result of thousands of people taking action beyond just geographical space and time but across generations too, in what I refer to as quantum collaboration.

The long, snaking queues of South Africans waiting to cast their first democratic votes in 1994 were the consequence of a conversation and struggle for liberation that had been taking place collaboratively across the world for generations, each generation making its own unique contributions to it before handing the baton over to future generations to make their own. Those queues were a consequence of the CODESA negotiations to end apartheid that began in 1991 between the apartheid government and the mass liberation movement. The CODESA conversations in turn were a consequence and continuation of conversations that had occurred between Nelson Mandela and President PW Botha in 1989, which in turn were a consequence and continuation of conversation initiated by Nelson Mandela with the apartheid government from his cell at Pollsmoor Prison toward the end of a 27-year incarceration. There, in 1985, he had concluded that, "The time had come when the struggle could be best pushed forward through negotiations. If we did not start a dialogue soon, both sides would soon be plunged into a dark night of oppression, violence, and war" (Mandela, 1994, pp. 625–626).

Those conversations were in turn a consequence and continuation of conversations that had led to Ghana being the first African nation to gain independence in 1957 under the leadership of Kwame Nkrumah, who, in acknowledging the quantum collaboration that had brought Africa her freedom said: "All the fair brave words about freedom that had been broadcast to the four corners of the earth took seed and grew where they had not been intended" (Nkrumah, 2020). Ghana's independence (and the subsequent independence of other African nations) was in turn a consequence and a continuation of conversations that had been led by the likes of Malcolm X, Rosa Parks, Elaine Brown, Martin Luther King Jr., and many other men and women, in their churches, in their community halls, and around their dinner tables.

Those conversations, still, were a consequence and a continuation of conversations that had been led by Abraham Lincoln toward the Emancipation Proclamation of 1863 that abolished slavery in the United States. Each of those were conversations that had occupied their own slice of history and yet collaboratively borrowed from and fed into one another to culminate in that moment that South Africa memorialized as its Freedom Day. After casting his first-ever vote on that day, Nelson Mandela went to the grave of the African National Congress's founding president, John Langalibalele Dube, and said: "Mr. President, I have come to report to you that South Africa is now free" (Ash, 2019, p. 22).

Such conversations that galvanize global mass action toward fundamental change begin and take place in separate spaces and continue across time and generations, driven by voices that realize that new action depends on finding the courage to connect with other voices in other spaces, concerned with the same issue—even if those voices carry dissenting views. What holds the conversation together is not shared space, shared time, or even shared beliefs. What holds it together across differences in political persuasions, world views, and generations is the mutual vestedness of all those involved in finding answers to the same fundamental questions along with a mutual courage, by all, to sort through the noise of prejudice and resentment and find the answers that represent the greatest good under the circumstances.

The question of how Africa can find more sustainable ways of funding its development and the consequent steps that have been taken toward meaningful action in that regard has been a case in point. It is a conversation that has been raging since Africa's independence; one that I have joined in lecture halls in my time at business school and one that I have participated in as moderator of conversations on the stages of the World Bank, International Labor Organization, and similar organizations around the world.

One such conversation that I had the pleasure of moderating was the International Finance Corporation's "Billions to Trillions" conference. The conference unlocked meaningful amounts of commercial capital for development and pushed for more funding for the 2030 sustainable development goals in this last decade of action. A foundation for this consequential outcome was not just the coming together of the various stakeholders around the issue of finding an answer to the question of innovative financing. It was the mutual vestedness of all participants in grappling with the question so as to arrive at the answers that represent the greatest good.

Of course, there is little chance that stakeholders with a very diverse and often competing set of priorities and constituencies—as is often the case in conversations with consequence at a global scale—arrive at meaningful decisions on action if they do not allow deep curiosity for different perspectives to supersede cynicism as the driver of their interactions. In the case of sustainably funding Africa's development, it is that curiosity-led approach to collaborative conversation that enabled institutional investors, portfolio managers, and policymakers to arrive at the type of breakthrough thinking that has reframed infrastructure gaps as asset classes whose risk can be managed through policy reform. Applying this idea to the energy infrastructure gap in South Africa has allowed clean energy to become a reality for many industries and South African homes.

Quantum collaboration then relies on a commitment by all involved to a better truth arrived at, through what Ray Dalio (2017) describes as "radical truthfulness." By this he means an openness to creating space for alternative truths to the ones that are known and understood, cultivating an openness to having existing truths debated, challenged, and, where necessary, abandoned in favor of better truths. This approach allows us to arrive at answers that represent the greatest good. Engaging in collaborative conversation of this nature is thus an extremely vulnerable act, born of a realization that our individual roles in those conversations are subservient to the broader, greater good, pursued by multitudes across space, time, and generations. And it is this quest for the greater good that ultimately leads from conversation to action.

Conclusions and Lessons Learned for Global Leadership

In summary, conversation, especially of the quantum sort, can be the birthplace of collaborative action, provided that:

- Time and space create the context for collaboration but should not limit the content of collaboration. Quite often new 5-year plans and 10-year goals are crafted with a "new broom sweeps clean" mindset that tends to ignore preceding bodies of work and voices on the issue. As the Ecclesiastical philosopher observed, there is nothing new under the sun, and we cannot arrive at the point of consequence, of making new mistakes if we are still determined to make the old mistakes first. Drawing from those preexisting wells of experience and wisdom can often help to focus collaborative efforts on those parts of the problem that would generate consequential outcomes.
- Collaborating at the level of resolving fundamental questions can foster alignment of end goals among divergent individuals and groups, who may still hold vastly different motivations and ideological underpinnings. Governments and private funders, for instance, have an alignment of interest in expanding access to clean energy, yet their motivations are not the same. The value and quality of collaboration can often get lost when what should be a debate of ideas on how to answer the fundamental questions in those collaborative settings becomes a distracting dispute of ideologies.
- Only a deep curiosity about and desire to find answers to the fundamental questions, coupled with humility, can allow us to rise above often intractable ideological differences and to realize the desired consequential outcomes.

This requires an open-minded approach to conversation along with a readiness to abandon every part of our beliefs that does not represent the essential truth of that moment and arrive at the types of actions that make change possible. Curiosity and humility cannot be assumed; instead they need to be institutionalized in the way we work, baked into the processes that underpin our work, and woven into the way we show up to engage. A useful way of doing this is by leading with questions and building the muscle of asking the right questions.

STORY 5: COLLABORATION WITH NATURE—WE ARE NOT ALONE

Christian Mulle and Dominik Scherrer

The World Wildlife Fund (WWF) Switzerland is a successful player in Swiss civil society and an influential partner in helping transform businesses to become more sustainable and reduce their environmental footprint. In 2017, WWF launched a strategy and reorganization process to address climate change and biodiversity more effectively. What was different from previous efforts was that the board of directors and the executive committee decided to take a less mechanical and more organic approach. Rather than following the classic route of defining a vision, goals, and key performance indicators (KPIs), they identified four questions that were to be explored with stakeholders inside and outside the organization.

The basic assumption was that questions rather than answers would inspire people to think, feel, and act in new ways. The leadership trusted their stakeholders to find answers to address the highly complex challenges of preserving climate and biodiversity. They had the humility and courage to ask questions and to show vulnerability by not having the answers. In a two-day workshop, the executive committee identified four key questions and over a period of nine months, a group of approximately 30 people were divided into teams that collaborated across functions, roles, hierarchies, and organizational and country boundaries to search for answers. The project was called "Colab for Nature."

One of the teams was inspired by one question in particular: "What does nature expect from us?" They started out sitting around a table: four WWF staff and an external, lateral thinker. They called themselves "NASA," after the US space exploration agency, because they did not want to be limited by "earthly," organizational constraints in their thinking and acting. Accordingly, they had no idea what they had to deliver. And it was certainly not about *must*: they *wanted* to deliver something. However, how, when, and what remained to be seen.

Open-ended, unconventional, and with an appetite to think deeply, differently, and beyond conventions, they listened to each other and were touched by the fresh thoughts and the personal stories they shared with each other. They decided on a norm for the team to adhere to: Crazy questions are welcome!

In line with the general question of what nature expects from us, Tom said, "I'd be curious to know what the fish would say about the fish ladders?" A radical change of perspectives was launched that unleashed the group's explorative and creative energies as the group realized that the human perspective was not the only one that mattered. Since humans are not alone on the planet, we must also learn from nature.

But first, let's back up a moment. Why was this so significant to the group? Man-made dams, locks, and waterfalls prevent fish migration up or down rivers. This prevents fish from completing their life cycle. One remedy is fish ladders—structures that allow migrating fish, like salmon and herring, to detour over or around artificial or natural barriers on a river. "The ladder contains a series of ascending pools that are reached by swimming against a stream of water. Fish leap through the cascade of rushing water, rest in a pool, and then repeat the process until they are out of the ladder" (National Ocean Service, 2020). This does sound harrowing from the fish's perspective, and in fact only a small percentage of fish survive due to the well-documented drawbacks of fish ladders, which are responsible for decreased fish stock (e.g., Brown et al., 2013; Goldfarb, 2018). Now back to the process that prompted Tom's question.

Step by Step: A Process-Based Approach

The team members did not want to pursue goals. They all agreed on that. It was impressive to see how that declaration of intent changed the perception and attitude toward collaboration. The quality of the conversations changed. They gave themselves the time to speak and listen. They let themselves be touched and inspired by coincidence and resonance. They were guided by what emerged from their exchanges and followed what was developing naturally.

In Harmony with Nature: Voices From Ancient Times

Collaboration with nature—what does the "co" actually mean? Their dialogues continuously led them to a world, to a time, and to places where they imagined an ideal relationship between humans and nature. Research in archaeogenetics, anthropology, and philosophy tell about possibilities, both past and future, of an intact, lively relationship between humans and nature, a life in harmony. This is evidence for humans to be part of the interdependent fabric of life on this planet in a respectful, creative, moderate interaction with the waters, the air, the plants, the animals. We are currently far from this harmony in our economic and social activities. The consequences are painfully visible. They all agreed on that.

The team's thinking was both shared and reinforced in the next stage of organization development and planning among WWF country programs.

Rethinking Our Narratives: A Shared International Spirit of Optimism

Staff at WWF Holland, England, and Sweden and in many other places were grappling with similar questions. In a joint initiative in the fall of 2019, an online event with the title "Whose Nature—Who Is Nature" was launched. It is an effort to challenge the perception of the relationship between humans and nature and to enrich the rationally shaped attitudes with the heart, emotions, and the mind.

What do philosophy, religions, and our personal experiences tell us? Over 60 participants from across Europe gathered in front of screens, listened to lectures, and shared. The communal launch demonstrated to participants that they were not in this effort alone.

The Project: Whose Nature at WWF Switzerland

In Switzerland, a different team, ranging from 12 to 20 members comprised of WWF staff and interested community members from all walks of life, wanted to leverage this international dynamic. Thus, a series of six afternoon workshops was designed for them. The workshops featured field trips to explore the question of the relationships between humans and nature. Clearly, an important part of the journey needed to be a concrete experience with nature. Thought-provoking Ignite talks[4] from science were complemented with work on their own mindsets via personal access to trees, creeks, the wind, and the landscape: their inner and outer natures.

Thus, they were on their way—a small, colorful group of sojourners who felt committed and challenged to allow for key inspirations and insights from these forays to flow back into WWF Switzerland and WWF International.

Dialogue with Nature: At Eye Level with the River and Its Fish

If we include nature and our living space in our thinking and actions, this will radically change our behavior in society, politics, and also in the economy. The separation of human beings and nature is a long, complex story. Exploring this story and remembering the natural state of connectedness has a healing effect. Concretely:

- Broadening our mindset, being open to a change in perspectives, and giving a voice to the fish and other wildlife will expand new possibilities.
- Opening our hearts and passionately engaging in a relationship with our essential, life-giving drinking water will secure life beyond us as humans.
- Letting go of a dominant and exploiting attitude with which we humans try to control life on earth will create new opportunities.[5]

The need for this change is urgent and the direction is clear:

- Move away from strongly hierarchical structures toward living, self-organized organisms and their natural habitats.
- Move away from resource-exploiting industries to circular, sustainable dynamics.
- Move away from ego systems to ecosystems.

---

[4]Ignite talks are limited to 5 minutes and 20 slides, which automatically advance every 15 seconds (see Buhr, 2015).
[5]See Scharmer's Theory U (Scharmer, 2009) and U Journaling (Presencing Institute, 2007-2020).

It is a long way to get there, but there are many initiatives, networks, concepts, tools, and living beings that support us—at eye level and in relation to everything alive. There is a lot to learn, but we are not alone.

Dialogue with Nature and Its Impact

Let's return to Tom and the impact of his question "I'd be curious to know what the fish would say about the fish ladders?" was like a pebble in the water:

- It led individuals to change perspectives and start asking themselves how wildlife sees the world. It invited them to imagine the perspectives of other species through empathy.
- It led individuals to rethink their relationship to nature: Am I part of nature? How am I in touch with nature? How do I communicate with nature? How can I be in dialogue with nature?
- It made people curious and wonder what it would be like if humans were able to communicate with other species. The question opened their minds and hearts to new possibilities of collaboration.
- It led to a dialogue in the organization about human relationship with nature and to recognize nature as an important stakeholder.
- It created space in the organization to think, act, and feel in new ways. At the same time, the presentations by the NASA group also raised some eyebrows: What exactly are they doing? How will that improve biodiversity? Still, the group created room to reflect deeply beyond immediate results, to value process in addition to goals, to recognize the importance of people telling the stories of their personal relationships with nature at the same level as goals and KPIs.
- It unleashed new energy which resulted in the creation of a community beyond borders that goes well beyond the original mandate of the "Colab for nature" project. Inspired by their deep purpose, the NASA group continues its dialogue and collaboration with nature in a self-organized way.

Finally, Tom's question also inspired the desire to find ways of communicating with other species that use different sensory organs than humans. If the "real" NASA invests heavily in communication with extraterrestrial life, would it not make sense to also invest in the ability to understand other species so that we can better live with them? And perhaps this understanding may eventually help us take more effective action that helps to solve challenges associated with climate change and biodiversity.

Conclusions and Lessons Learned for Global Leadership

- **Creating Trust by Relinquishing Control.** Leadership designs a process and identifies inspiring questions and allows people to work with their emotions and intuitions beyond command and control. Leadership recognizes that in an environment with complex problems to solve, control is not effective.

By trusting the process and by inspiring through questions, people are empowered to take action with tangible impact.

- **The Use of Inspiring Questions.** The CEO of WWF Switzerland used the metaphor of Terra Incognita to describe the journey of this strategic process: We are guided by questions that stimulate our curiosity and through our exploration, we find new ways of solving problems. Questions are at the heart of global leadership and collaboration in a highly complex environment, both in terms of relationships and tasks. To borrow the words of General Stanley McChrystal, who may appear to be an unlikely ally in this context: "In a complex world, it takes a humble leader more like a gardener than a heroic one like a chess player for global collaboration to be effective" (McChrystal, Collins, Silverman, & Fussel, 2015, pp. 220–232).
- **A Well-Defined Space and a Transparent Process.** In this example, leadership provided the space and the resources and designed a transparent process, even with other species, to co-create, for many voices to be heard, for resonance between ideas and inspirations to emerge, and for people to be touched through collaboration. At the heart of the process was not the outcome, but rather the journey itself. Maybe, paradoxically, this led to action with concrete outcomes and results.

A new type of leadership emerges from this story: global leaders who ask questions, listen deeply, are humble, and trust both life and people. These are leaders who can let go of the imperative to control and act bravely by walking toward the unknown.

CONCLUSIONS

As noted at the beginning of this chapter, we define global collaboration broadly: working together on a shared project across a multiplicity of different identities and contexts. The five stories in this chapter centered around the theme of crisis and ranged from collaborating with nature, cross-sector collaboration, working across professional roles in a university hospital, challenges in global business all the way to collaboration across generations leading to macro level transformations. National cultural differences figured in as well, as did the need to connect across differences to come to some action, ideally collaborative action. The process we experienced writing this chapter, with 21 people in nine countries, was its own form of global collaboration, illustrating the varied ways that humans can navigate across differences in service of a common goal.

In the process of writing together and through the five stories, we have experienced collaboration as working together toward a common vision based on a deep sense of purpose while being ready to give up individual interests. Behavior went beyond cooperation, which can be understood as a simple alignment of goals. In this sense, collaboration is transformative, whereas cooperation is more transactional (Ecloo, 2015). What sets global collaboration apart from other forms of collaboration is the increased diversity and complexity. Command and control are replaced with a shared purpose and the awareness of collaborating parties that predictability is low, ambiguity is high, and traditional planning often falls short. At the same time, global collaboration has the potential to harness diversity to innovate, to solve problems together in new and often unexpected ways due to different perspectives. What is true for diversity is also true for global collaboration: In order to lead to successful outcomes, it needs to be intentional and supported; it does not happen automatically. It is challenging, it sometimes hurts—and it brings about deep learning.

At the center of our explorative research through stories was the question: **When crisis hits, what do global leaders need to pay attention to when collaborating with others?**

Through the five stories, we have found valuable insights:

- Global leaders can prepare for a crisis on a task level by anticipating different outcomes and then plan for different scenarios. Yet in a world that is volatile, uncertain, complex, and ambiguous (VUCA World, 2020),[6] planning is a challenge as predictability is low. However, by **investing in relationships** that result in a stronger organizational or social fabric, global leaders can lay the foundations for crisis preparedness and resilience. Through the connections created in the cross-sector collaboration in Shibuya, novel and effective solutions for restaurant owners collaborating with mothers in times of COVID-19 rapidly emerged.
- The impact of investing in relationships is **trust.** Trust is built through the mindsets of humility, curiosity, and care which translate to respectful behavior: engaging in dialogue, asking questions, and listening deeply to other perspectives. Trust is also built through action when the actual behavior is aligned with stated values, such as when leadership of a global company takes a voluntary pay cut and checks in with their staff to ask how they are doing during COVID-19. Or on a macro level: When Nelson Mandela decided to engage in dialogue with the apartheid government while still in prison, this was the beginning of collaborative action that eventually led to the liberation of the people in South Africa.
- In an environment of trust, people develop their own deeper **purpose** that does not need to come from the top but that can be shared with others through collaboration. Laloux (2014) refers to the evolutionary purpose in organizations which is fostered by global leadership creating the necessary space and providing the support needed for people to collaborate effectively. The role of **leadership** in global collaboration is that of a **servant.** Leading is not a privilege or status but a service to the community to help set conditions that promote collaboration across difference, that value the divergent experiences and skills that everyone brings, and that provide the space for everyone to contribute in the way they can (Greenleaf, 2002). Servant leadership is crucial in addressing fears and skepticism in a nonthreatening way, by facilitating new forms of

---

[6]For consequences of VUCA for leadership, see, e.g., https://www.vuca-world.org/.

sincere dialogue to accomplish shared goals and **create the conditions for innovation.** In the case of WWF, leadership helped inspire the deeper purpose by asking relevant questions which led a small team to collaborate with nature, which resulted in repopulating a river with fish.

- When leaders ask questions and listen and empower people at all levels, a space for creativity and new possibilities emerges. That space, and a **relative lack of hierarchy,** empowers people to come up with collaborative solutions and take decisive action. People closest to the problem have the best insights into the complexity of both task and relationship domains. When global leaders show trust in their people, they set the ground for self-organizing, and the formation of diverse teams. The role of global leaders is to define transparent processes and inspiring questions. In the case of the university hospital preparing for the COVID-19 pandemic, some organizational structures were "unfrozen" (Schein, 2004, pp. 319–325) allowing for self-organizing teams to emerge and solve highly complex and challenging problems.
- Long-term crises, such as apartheid, self-rule, sustainable development, and the environmental crisis, also require conversation and perspective shifts to unfreeze entrenched positions and traditions.

Overall, we have learned that **global leaders who invest in relationships and value diverse perspectives set the foundation for a strong organizational and social fabric. The resulting trust is at the heart of these resilient organizations especially in times of crises as people closest to the complex problems are empowered to collaborate across hierarchies, roles, and other differences to co-create effective solutions.**

We have also learned that crisis situations help develop a deeper sense of purpose, which in turn enables new forms of collaboration to emerge if leadership provides the necessary space. The risk now is that once a crisis situation disappears, the sense of purpose may diminish, and everyone will revert to old routines. Leadership again plays a critical role now and beyond the crisis when global leaders are eager to learn from the crisis and ask relevant questions, specifically:

- What new forms of collaboration have led to better results?
- What new forms of leadership have led to better collaboration?
- What have we, as an organization, learned from the crisis? What have we been able to do that we did not manage to do before, and why?
- What are the changes, both formal and more superficial, that we want to implement beyond the crisis?

In our stories, we see global leadership that starts asking those questions, demonstrating humility and curiosity. It is that type of leadership that has made the shift from telling to asking and listening and from directing to facilitating that we believe has the greatest chances of transforming their organizations to foster global collaboration and building a resilient organizational fabric that is prepared when the next crisis hits.

Myshelle Baeriswyl, Ph.D., dissident psychologist and sex educator, is a scientific speaker and publicist on gender diversity, an expert on sexual health, addiction prevention, as well as gender diversity and inclusion. She was the director of an addiction prevention and an AIDS center. She also initiated consultation services for gender variant people in Eastern Switzerland. Currently, she works as a consultant for transgender persons at Checkpoint Bern. She is a member of the transgender network Switzerland TGNS, the association Zurich Pride, the association QueerAltern (*aging as queer*) Zurich and transgender expert groups in Zurich and Bern. Notable publications include "Trans & Sexualität" (2018) (*Trans and Sexuality*), "Belastung statt Betreuung" (2017) (*Burden rather than Care*) and "Queering Psychotherapie" (2016) (*Queering Psychotherapy*).

Monwong Bhadharavit is the Managing Director of M.B. System Automation Company Limited (MBSA), an IT consulting and development house in Bangkok, Thailand. Before setting up his own company, Monwong worked as a Systems Engineer with IBM Thailand. Following his mantra of "Technology cannot surpass the power of the human spirit," Monwong supports companies and organizations to define an inspiring vision and clear goals before implementing technical solutions. In the context of an outsourcing project for AFS Intercultural Programs, he successfully integrated global IT operations into his company. Introducing a collaborative mindset, agile work methods, and principles of organizational development into IT has made Monwong not only a successful entrepreneur but also an inspiring lecturer at Mahidol University in Bangkok.

Adriana Burgstaller is a neuropsychologist, organizational development consultant, mediator, and coach. She has been working as an independent coach and consultant for over 10 years (adrianaburgstaller.ch). She works with leaders and organizations in all work sectors with a main (but not exclusive) focus on healthcare, nonprofits, and the social area. Her main interests are collaboration across difference and systemic interdependencies that form the social fabric of every organization. She is a member of the Swiss Association of Mediators, the Swiss Professional Association of Coaching, Supervision and Organizational Development and the OD Forum Switzerland.

Rachel Clark is a Lean and continuous improvement specialist working in Liechtenstein and living in Switzerland. She spent 15 years as a military engineering officer before being introduced to self-directed teams and Lean manufacturing. She specializes in change management and coaching predominantly in global manufacturing and service organizations where she strives to build a working environment that is fun, engaging, and productive and where everyone has a voice.

Lisa Cohen is a coach, consultant, and educator who has spent over 25 years working in international education and intercultural exchange. As head of training for AFS Intercultural Programs based in New York (2007–12) and US Peace Corps Headquarters in Washington, DC (2012–2017), Lisa had the opportunity to support organizational and leadership development, curriculum design, and navigating difference. At Peace Corps she cofounded the Intercultural Competence, Diversity & Inclusion initiative. Currently, she is a board member for Cultural Vistas, the cohost of a monthly race and belonging roundtable, and, together with her husband, is launching a small family foundation, Open Horizon.

Eyrún Eyþórsdóttir is an assistant professor in police studies at the University of Akureyri, Iceland. Eyrún is currently finishing her Ph.D. in Social Anthropology at the University of Iceland. Eyrún was educated as a police officer in 2003 and has mostly worked within the police. Her main areas of interest and knowledge, both within police and academia, are policing and diversity, human rights aspects of policing and hate crime. Eyrún is currently working on a research project on hate crime in the Icelandic context. She also works with the social enterprise Mundialis in an Erasmus funded project on diversity training within tourism.

Sherifa Fayez has been National Director of AFS Egypt Intercultural Educational Programs since 2004. Fayez spearheaded restructuring the developmental plans of the organization to focus on intercultural communication through training and impactful intercultural projects for youth and communities. She holds a Master's degree in Intercultural Relations from University of the Pacific in California, and an Economics degree from American University in Cairo. Fayez lives in Egypt and specializes in trainings that focus on intercultural competency, targeting different age groups and professionals in Egypt, the Middle East, Africa, and the United States. She is passionate about spreading this learning, particularly in school curriculum and professional workplaces. Fayez coauthored *Communication Across Cultures With People From the Middle East* in the Encyclopedia of Intercultural Competence and teaches courses related to her region: *The Arab World: Meaning, Identity, and Discovery* at the Summer Institute for Intercultural Communication in Portland and in multiple cross-cultural organizations in Europe.

Simone Inversini, Ph.D., is a work psychologist and works as an independent organizational consultant and coach (wülserinversini.ch). She supports leaders and organizations in strategic processes, personal, organizational, and leadership development as well as collaboration. She is a lecturer in coaching and organizational consulting education and a co-organizer of conferences centering around the future of work, as well as relevant and current topics in the field of organizational development. She was an innovation researcher at the University of Bern and completed her Ph.D. at the University of Potsdam on change management. During many years, she was an active member of the Board of the OD Forum Switzerland and helped build a strong community of OD practitioners. She is also the cofounder of SAO, an NGO supporting women refugees in Greece.

Monika Imhof is a human resource and organizational development specialist: Among other things, she has set up the respective department in Switzerland's largest trade union. After studying German and Italian linguistics as well as history, she joined the Unia trade union unemployment fund, where she was responsible for education and training. During several years, she was the program manager for tobacco prevention in one of the Swiss cantons. Her work focuses on participatory projects and is President of the participatory initiative "Historical Museum of Winterthur" located in her home town. Monika is in the process of building up a community for participatory methods to foster collaboration across borders. For the last two years, she has worked independently and has led the project "Paradise Töss," a project with and for migrants. She is convinced that collaboration and participatory methods are crucial to solve the problems of the future.

Fabricia Manoel is the Program Development and Innovation Senior Consultant of AFS Intercultural Programs. She helps organizations develop and implement projects at local, national, and international levels in the areas of organization and product development to improve efficiency, embrace change and innovation across cultural differences. Fabricia has worked for more than two decades helping AFS Network Organizations to achieve realistic, evidence-based solutions. Fabricia's practical approach combined with her experience working with AFS staff and volunteers from 60 different countries has shaped numerous AFS training programs.

Christian Mulle's work has focused on the relationship between humans and nature for many years. As a former career officer in the Swiss Army, he started out in the area of management and leadership development until he discovered his passion centering around dialogue with nature. In 2009, he founded his own company walkout (www.walkout.ch). He supports people in organizations in the context of organizational and team development and coaching. He also accompanies individuals in life transitions. He is a cofounder of the movement *dialogue with nature* (www.natur-dialog.org). In 2017, he published his book called "*Wilde heile Welt*" (wild whole world).

Matthias Müeller, MSc, works as a consultant for sustainable development and digitization. He published studies about sustainable development in business as well as fictional and nonfictional books. He was president of The Natural Step Switzerland and is recognized as one of the mentors of human-centered design in Switzerland.

Tina Nielsen holds a Master's degree in Political Science from the University of Zurich and is a certified coach. She worked in a Swiss bank in various senior HR functions. Today, she works in the Municipality of Winterthur, Switzerland, where she and her team are responsible for HR for the Construction Department with its 300 employees. In this role, she reports directly to the Councilor and is part of the Executive Management team.

Takahiko Nomura, Ph.D., is the CEO of Slow Innovation, Inc. He is a Business School Professor at the Kanazawa Institute of Technology and an Executive Research Fellow of the Global Communication Center at the International University. He has been researching in the fields of innovation and collaboration for 20 years and has consulted to over 100 organizations. His current focus is cross-sector innovation among business, government, and nonprofit organizations in various cities to help them transform to become more resilient and innovative.

Berta Ottiger-Arnold has been the head of staff of Facility Management at the University Hospital of Zurich, Switzerland, since April 2019. She is responsible for the unit's project, change and transformation management. She has a medical background with broad experience in supporting different surgery clinics and hospital hygiene. Quality management (business excellence coach), a master's degree in organizational development and a diploma of advanced studies in Facility Management complement her knowledge in the medical field. She has successfully completed various digitization projects in the hospital environment centering around medical documentations and reorganizations of telephony and alarm systems. As a member of a regional hospital executive board for seven years, she also led the planning of various construction projects in the context of modernization of hospital infrastructures.

Simon Papet is a consultant in Organizational Development and HR based in Paris. He specializes in the fields of Collaboration, Recruitment, and Governance development, mainly in the nonprofit sector. He has regularly worked on the topics of intercultural learning, engagement management, and network development, through his experience at AFS Intercultural Programs—France, as an associate of ecloo, a collaborator of Recruitment Office Orientation Durable and as an independent practitioner. He studied Intercultural Communication and Sinology at the National Institute of Oriental Languages and Cultures in Paris and lived in China, the United States, and Italy.

Susanne Reis comes from a business background and has worked for more than a decade in various small, mid-size, and global organizations. Having gained experience in different roles (leader, project manager, expert) and teams, she developed a strong interest in wanting to understand the "secrets" of good leadership and collaboration in a business context, which led her to change careers and study Organizational Psychology and later Gestalt Psychotherapy. She has worked as an independent consultant and coach for more than 20 years. Supporting leaders and teams in their development and transformation processes remains the most interesting and satisfying mission imaginable for her. She is part of the ecloo network and helped build the OD Forum Switzerland as an active member of the board for many years.

Dominik Scherrer has worked in the field of global and intercultural collaboration for over 20 years. He was a member of AFS Intercultural Programs' executive board responsible for global IT, Organizational Development and Training. In 2015, he founded his own coaching and organizational consulting company ecloo (ecloo.ch) which specializes in collaboration across difference. He has created a developmental model of collaboration for organizations across all sectors and around the globe. He studied history and literature in France, Switzerland, and the United States as well as Organizational Development, Consulting, and Coaching in Switzerland.

Nozipho Tshabalala is a conversation strategist moderating global conversations that are designed to have measurable outcomes. As an internationally acclaimed conference moderator and Human Capital Advocate for The World Bank and Global Citizen, she has moderated conversations at the World Economic Forum, United Nations agencies including UN Women, the World Bank, and the International Monetary Fund among other global bodies. She has also facilitated dialogues with targeted outcomes for a number of African institutions including leading listed and unlisted multinational corporations, business schools, and civil society organizations that seek to leverage conversations for change. She holds two master's degrees in Development Finance (Stellenbosch) and International Studies

(London). In October 2019, Nozipho was listed among 2019's 100 Most Influential Young Africans and most recently 2019's 100 Most Influential Young South Africans.

Rorisang Tshabalala is the Chief Executive and Founder of Chapter One Innovation. He leads the firm in its mission to be the platform that launches market winners, industry leaders, and world changers, including both the organizational systems and the people who work on them. Rorisang is a classical corporate strategist specializing in business model and innovation strategy. He holds an MBA (specializing in social innovation and entrepreneurship) from the University of Cape Town Graduate School of Business and a Bachelor of Commerce majoring in Financial Accounting, Auditing and Taxation from the University of Pretoria. Rorisang is also an adjunct member of faculty at Duke University CE, delivering a portfolio of corporate education programs. He is an African Leadership Institute/Oxford University Desmond Tutu Fellow, an Africa Leadership Initiative/Aspen Global Leadership Network (YALI) Fellow, and a Bertha Foundation Social Innovation and Entrepreneurship Fellow. Among Rorisang's hidden talents is that he is both a retired politician and a retired radio show host.

Bert Vercamer is a differencist, consultant, and strategist. He is a former CEO who worked in 45 countries, and lived in 6, with extensive experience in organizational development ("something's up in my organization or team"), global skill development, diversity—equity—inclusion—belonging, cultural integration, innovation (design thinking), startup, change management, and strategy. His work revolves around the questions: How do we collaborate with those who don't think like we do, and how do we bridge effectively to perform, bring change, and impact? He has worked with startups (founding CEO of one), established corporations, nonprofit organizations, and educational institutions. He has a Master's in economics from Belgium and a Master's in Intercultural Relations from the United States. He led the team that created the Global Competence Certificate (afs.org/certificate).

REFERENCES

Ash, P. (2019, July 14). Mandela magic. *Sunday Times.*

Brown, J. J., Limburg, K. E., Waldman, J. R., Stephenson, K., Glenn, E. P., Juanes, F., & Jordaan, A. (2013). Fish and hydropower on the U.S. Atlantic coast: Failed fisheries policies from half-way technologies. *Conservation Letters, 6*, 280–286. doi:10.1111/conl.12000

Buhr, S. (2015). Community speaker series ignite gets a reboot. November 16, 2015. Retrieved from https://techcrunch.com/2015/11/16/letsbecyborganthropologists/. Accessed on 21 May, 2020.

Dalio, R. (2017). *Principles.* New York, NY: Simon & Schuster.

Ecloo. (2015). Collaboration methodology. Retrieved from https://www.ecloo.ch/methodology. Accessed on 18 May, 2020.

Goldfarb, B. (2018). What's the future of fishways? *Hakai Magazine*, January 29, 2018. Retrieved from https://www.hakaimagazine.com/news/whats-the-future-of-fishways/. Accessed on 18 May, 2020.

Greenleaf, R. K. (2002). *Servant leadership: A journey into the nature of legitimate power and greatness.* Mahwah, NJ: Paulist Press.

Hofstede. (2020). *Hofstede insights.* Retrieved from https://www.hofstede-insights.com/country-comparison/japan. Accessed on 18 May, 2020.

Laloux, F. (2014). *Reinventing organizations: A guide to creating organizations inspired by the next stage of human consciousness.* Brussels: Nelson Parker.

Mandela, N. (1994). *Long walk to freedom.* London: Abacus.

McChrystal, S., Collins, T., Silverman, D., & Fussel, C. (2015). *Team of teams. New rules of engagement for a complex world.* St Ives: Clays.

National Ocean Service. (2020, May 18). *What is a fish ladder?* Retrieved from https://oceanservice.noaa. gov/facts/fish-ladder.html. Accessed on 18 May, 2020.

Nkruma, K. (2020). Goodreads. Retrieved from https://www.goodreads.com/author/quotes/414621.Kwame_ Nkrumah. Accessed on 18 May, 2020.

Presencing Institute. (2007-2020). Presencing Institute Toolkit. Retrieved from https://www.presencing. org/files/tools/PI_Tool_UJournaling.pdf. Accessed on 18 May, 2020.

Reiche, B. S., Bird, A., Mendenhall, M. E., & Osland, J. S. (2017). Contextualizing leadership: A typology of global leadership roles. *Journal of International Business Studies, 48,* 552–572.

Sarasvathy, D. S. (2008). *Effectuation: Elements of entrepreneurial expertise.* Cheltenham: Edward Elgar.

Scharmer, C. O. (2009). *Theory U: Leading from the future as it emerges.* San Francisco, CA: Berrett-Koehler.

Schein, E. (2004). *Organizational culture and leadership.* Hoboken, NJ: John Wiley & Sons.

Society for Effectual Action. (2018). Effectuation. Retrieved from https://www.effectuation.org/. Accessed on 18 May, 2020.

VUCA World. (2020). Leadership skills and strategies. Retrieved from https://www.vuca-world.org/. Accessed on 18 May, 2020.

AN INTERVIEW WITH HAL GREGERSEN: THE ART OF QUESTIONING IN GLOBAL LEADERSHIP

Mark E. Mendenhall

ABSTRACT

Hal Gregersen is one of the pioneers of the field of global leadership. Along with J. Stewart Black and Allen Morrison he created one of the early foundational competency models in the field that was published in their book, Global Explorers: The Next Generation of Leaders *(1999). Since that time, Hal has studied the skills associated with innovative leadership with Clayton Christensen and Jeff Dyer. A good introduction to this research is their award-winning book,* The Innovator's DNA: Mastering the Five Skills of Disruptive Innovators *(2011). His most recent book,* Questions are the Answer: A Breakthrough Approach to Your Most Vexing Problems at Work and in Life *(2018), explores the art of questioning – a skill he argues is critical to leadership productivity. We were curious about Hal's research journey from the study of global leaders to his current research focus – the power of questions – and he graciously agreed to be interviewed for this volume of* Advances in Global Leadership. *Hal is a Senior Lecturer in Leadership and Innovation at the MIT Sloan School of Management. Before joining MIT, he taught at INSEAD, London Business School, Tuck School of Business at Dartmouth College, Brigham Young University, and in Finland as a Fulbright Fellow.*

Keywords: Global leadership; questions; questioning; problem-solving; global leaders; curiosity

Advances in Global Leadership, Volume 13, 205–218
Copyright © 2020 Emerald Publishing Limited
All rights of reproduction in any form reserved
ISSN: 1535-1203/doi:10.1108/S1535-120320200000013006

Mark: Hal, you are one of the pioneers of the field of global leadership. I'm interested in learning more about your intellectual journey in moving from global leadership to studying the competencies of innovators with Clayton Christiansen and Jeff Dyer and your more recent research on the power of asking questions to help people live, lead, and work in more powerful ways. I think people would find your journey interesting.

Hal: Sure. The initial focus of my research was around global leaders and globalization. After that, it focused on leading change and transformation and then it turned to leading innovation, and now is increasingly centered on leading digital transformation and digitization. If I go back and look at the leaders that others and I have had the chance to interview as part of either paper or book projects – going global, transforming, innovating, digitizing – every one of those leaders were operating on the edge of uncertainty where they face an enormous number of "unknown unknowns." At that edge of uncertainty, questions really are the answer because the answers aren't there to be found.

The model that Stewart, Allen, and I built had as its foundation the skill of inquisitiveness – it was the core of six or seven skills that we found necessary for global leadership based on interviews and research work. Then, in the initial version of the book, *Leading Strategic Change* (co-authored with Stewart Black), we had a section focused on inquisitiveness as the fuel that drives change. Then, with Clay and Jeff we studied the world's most innovative leaders, folks like Jeff Bezos, Pierre Omidyar, and Diane Greene, guiding firms that investors believed were the world's most innovative companies. We found five primary skills of innovative leaders and one of them was the ability to ask questions that challenge the status quo. Indeed, questioning was at the core of the ability to innovate. So, in retrospect, it started out with inquisitiveness being critical for global leadership and it stayed that way as I studied leading change and transformation.

I think the cognitive aspect that applied to all three of those research streams, at that point, leading up to our work that we published in the *Innovators DNA* book was Openness to Experience, one of the Big Five personality factors. Openness to Experience was also an assessment element for global leaders and it was part of how Stewart and I approached our research on leading change. Later, Clay, Jeff, and I wound up splitting Openness to Experience down into more specific elements, which was questioning and observing, networking for new ideas, and experimenting based on our research interviews with over 100 innovative leaders and our self and 360 survey assessment database that now includes over 20,000 respondents.

Mark: That's fascinating. If you could go back in time to the late 1990s, but bring with you your framework of questioning, how would that change the model you developed with Stewart Black and Allen Morrison? How would the model look different? Or would there even be a model? Knowing what you know now, and if you were to transport yourself back in time…

Hal: No doubt, there are probably lots of criticisms of my work and how I have approached things over the years. Whether it's the global leadership model or the leading change model or the Innovators DNA model, or my current model on questioning, all of which were driven by reasonably legitimate academic work, either interview or survey-based data collection. I have always had a deep desire to translate research findings in ways that are useful and practical for managers. Thus, I always had a drive to simplify – simplify to the point that leaders could actually get their arms around the constructs and do something practical with them.

If I could go back in time knowing what I know now, where might the models have been radically different? Maybe they would have differed in terms of causality and been a bit more circular, a little less linear. I think a lot of the key constructs would have stayed the same. Would I change the design a whole lot? In terms of the inquiry-centered focus of the research over the years, no. I remember interviewing AG Lafley, who was not the CEO of Proctor & Gamble when we interviewed him for our *Global Explorers* book. He was, I think, a regional president. I think he was running the Asia region at that point. AG asked me more questions than I asked him in that research interview. It's no surprise that a decade or so later, Proctor & Gamble tapped AG to take over leading change and innovation. I think it was an 11% innovation premium boost over his decade long tenure as CEO, which is a huge financial impact on the positive side that others and he created. AG was an exceptional global leader. He was just absolutely off the chart. His ability to ask questions and then shut up and listen really well to other people helped him figure out "what-he-didn't-know-that-he-didn't-know" before it was too late. This was a skill he possessed way before he ever became a CEO.

Mark: That leads into my next question. As I was reading *Questions are the Answer* (2018), I found myself thinking about curiosity. It struck me that curiosity might be a foundational pre-requisite to be able to ask the right type of questions as a leader. Could you reflect on the role curiosity plays inherently in people's ability to ask powerful questions or if they're low in curiosity, does that hinder their ability to do that?

Hal: An enormous amount of research has been done over the years on curiosity, as you well know. Before my current work on questioning, Spencer Harrison, now faculty at INSEAD, worked with me as a research assistant on *The Innovators DNA* (2011). We spent an enormous amount of energy diving into the curiosity literature. One of the intriguing things we discovered was the varied components of curiosity. One variation is a very specific kind of curiosity where someone is trying to figure something out here and now – for example, "why is that bird flying out the window at this moment?" Another variation of curiosity is manifested in a more generic, generalized way. For example, some people seem to be simply interested in everything.

I do think curiosity in all of its manifestations makes a deep difference in our human ability to articulate questions. In thinking about the people I interviewed for these last couple of research projects and books – I didn't collect data on this, so I'm just going off on a limb here – my instinctual response is that the best leaders at questioning excelled at both dimensions of curiosity – the specific and the general. They had a wide-ranging sense of curiosity about all sorts of things. When they were latched onto a challenge, opportunity, or problem. they were trying to figure out, you know, they couldn't be pried away from the challenge no matter how hard you tried.

Mark: If what you have said about curiosity is true, which I think it is, both from your model and from your research, then it may be that that's one of the most fundamental competencies, traits, or orientations global leaders would need in the global context.

Hal: Yes. I agree with you fully. In conversations a few years back I had with Clay Christensen, we were trying to figure out how one goes about learning "what you don't know you don't know" – the "unknown unknowns." Clay raised the phrase, "you must actively seek passive data." That's what curious people do, and it's a great way to frame a global leader's work – actively seeking the passive data that's not actively coming at you. If you fail to do that, it's at your own peril because it's the undiscovered passive data that ends up – at some point – becoming your or your team's, or your organization's, or even your country's demise. Every blind spot is an "unknown unknown," and the only way we can figure out that crucial blind spot is by actively seeking passive data. For me, asking a question and engaging in the conversation around whatever that question provokes is the essence of actively seeking passive data. That's the magical means by which global leaders, I think, figure things out.

Mark: In the acknowledgement section of *Questions are the Answer* (2018), you observed that it takes a community to build a questioning capacity in leaders. Would you reflect on how global leaders, and really any

Hal: I think it's both. When working with C-suite leaders who care about trying to become more innovative – and often on a big global scale – my first direct question to them is, "How do you find and solve problems? Just describe what you do behaviorally." If their problem finding and solving approach is largely reactive in nature, meaning it's a status quo analysis based on secondary data that's discussed and debated at headquarters, you know that they're pretty ripe for getting blindsided and setting themselves up for some sort of disaster.

Contrast that with that leader or team of leaders who take a very systematic, intentional and purposeful mode of actively seeking out passive data, day in and day out. In my most recent research project interviewing over 200 creative leaders like Elon Musk and Orit Gadiesh, these folks created conditions or situations for themselves and for their people to be uncomfortable instead of comfortable and reflectively quiet instead of constantly filling the room with noise. Those behaviors are not the kinds of things that we normally do when performance pressures are on. Innovative leaders and global leaders are masters at going out of their way, being in many places and talking to a variety of people that force them – in one sense, cause them – to realize that, "Oh no, part of my mental model is dead wrong!" And further, "Ouch! That data point just cut to the core of an assumption I thought was true but isn't. This hurts, but I am not going to run from it – I'm going to slow down, reflect a bit, and see where it goes."

When we put ourselves and others in situations where we're wrong, uncomfortable and reflectively quiet, that's when catalytic questions emerge that otherwise wouldn't. They may emerge in our own mind, or because we have created a safe enough space for others to ask us fearless questions.

Mark: So, in addition to possessing inherent curiosity or the desire to ask questions, additionally leaders have to possess both the desire and the ability to form a team around them and create a questioning culture within the team. That seems like it would be a very difficult thing to pull off.

Hal: It's super difficult to pull off, and it takes a very deep commitment from a founder or from senior leaders to be willing to put themselves in such situations over and over and over again. Jeff Wilke, who is the CEO of consumer products worldwide for Amazon which covers a

leader for that matter, can go about cultivating a questioning community around themselves? Have you seen that happen with some of the CEOs and others who you have interviewed? Or do most of them tend to drive questioning themselves?

huge swath of that organization, operates this way. He knows that his mental model has errors in it, that it's flawed. When he wakes up in the morning, he tries to figure out what is he wrong about not what he is right about. He actively puts himself in situations with people or in places where his model gets provoked and challenged. If he realizes something is off kilter with his model, he relishes the chance to change it. In the Amazon world, they have built in practices and approaches where the people know, in particular settings, that they are obligated to ask the toughest questions, and everyone needs to be ready to engage with them, because that's what the particular meeting is all about. They call it a "working backwards process" and everyone from the top to the bottom is expected to engage with it.

So, for example, "I've got an idea. I write up a six-page document. Here's what the idea would look like if we did it in five years. Here's the press release when we deliver on the idea. Here are six pages of questions and answers that are important to address if we actually try to make this idea happen in five years." Then, people sit down in a room and read that document for 15–20 minutes, knowing that at the end of that 20 minutes, they're obligated to ask tough questions of the person and their team who created that working backwards document. The creators are obligated to engage with the questions, and it's a very intense, truth seeking, back and forth experience. But people know that's the space where it happens – that's where, in a very specific way, they are expected to ask and answer the toughest questions they could ever imagine about the issue.

Pixar is totally different. You've got a whole range of questioning, ranging from brain trusts to dailies to Notes Day to peer pirates, to reverse mentoring, to fill in the blank. But so much of that creative work is Ed Catmull's construction because of his deep, undeviating commitment to building an organization that's full of candor and truth seeking. The prime directive there is to define and solve problems that make great movies. For example, if you're a director and you're unwilling to sit in a three hour meeting multiple times during the course of the creation of a movie where 15 other directors and senior people literally rip apart your ideas at whatever stage they are in with questions and responses in a brain trust process that absolutely takes all of the emotional energy out of you – if you're not willing to go into that kind of space and live in that kind of world, it's not going to work. If you don't buy into that truth-seeking logic behind making something great, then you don't belong there.

Mark: Is it your finding or your conclusion from your research that the ability to ask robust profound questions that can lead to amazing outcomes is transcultural? Does it manifest itself in CEOs or other leaders all around the world? Or are there situations where either national or traditional organizational cultural norms dampen it more so than other regions?

Hal: I'm old enough, Mark, and distant enough from the current literature on culture that using Hofstede might date me as an ancient. But I'm going to because I think it's relevant. The point is: questions flourish where power distance is low. If you've got high power distance and people pay attention to hierarchy, you're not going to have the kind of inquiry that you would otherwise. So you take some of those dimensions and yes, there are undoubtedly cultural differences about adults asking catalytic questions that challenge false assumptions and give energy to change the system, absolutely.

Mark: I noticed there were examples of leaders with questioning skills from Asia and all around the world in your book.

Hal: And that's where, again, it's a distribution thing for me. In the Innovators DNA work, we collaborated with Credit Suisse to create an innovation premium index that evaluates companies on investors' beliefs about whether or not the companies were going to do something different in the future. The simple way of putting it is to start with "what's the net present value of the income stream of your existing businesses?" For some companies that's the entire share price and for others, there is a "premium" above and beyond that income stream from the existing businesses because investors believe the company will do things differently in the future. Well, you look at the companies with the highest innovation premiums, they hail from all over the world. They're the top 10%–15% of the best of the best. So whether it's Rose Marcario at Patagonia or Pony Ma at Tencent, it's the same story as Richard Branson at Virgin or fill in the blank.

Mark: It's similar to what Kenichi Ohmae found back in the 1980s that the best strategists are all over the world, that excellent strategizing is not related to nationality but to the mindset they're operating from.

Hal: For me, the more dominant factor on the question of a leader's ability to ask better questions is related to the home and educational environment of the leader than it is culture. In the Innovators DNA work, we realized that close to half of the people we interviewed had very nontraditional educational experiences. Many of them were in Montessori or international baccalaureate schools when growing up. Those places are project centered – you show up in the morning and they ask, "What are you interested in? Okay, let's use all your knowledge to figure it out." Even if they weren't in that kind of school setting, innovative leaders often had parents or neighbors or grandparents who created projects for them to do in the summers or on the weekends or evenings to teach them that the world revolves around finding something you care deeply enough about to do something about it, to create a project about it. That's the absolute opposite of a lock step educational system where most teachers are teaching to subject content in order for students to get moved from one grade to the next. In such settings it's all about answers and it's all about getting them right and getting them fast. It kills kids capacity to ask questions.

Mark: So given that most people probably aren't raised in those kinds of environments, what kinds of things have you seen that act as catalysts for people to wake up to the power of asking questions when it wasn't natural to them before? I'm curious if you spent much time looking at people who were not initially oriented that way but became that way.

Hal: People can and do change in their ability to ask increasingly better questions. Some of that can be fueled by working with somebody who demands that kind of inquisitive, truth seeking, candor-driven, problem-focused approach to the work they're doing. A leader who has the orientation of, "This is not about you. This is not about your advancement. This is about finding and solving something here and now that matters. If that's not why you're working on this team, then you don't belong here."

Mark: It's kind of a crucible experience where they either leave or-

Hal: Or step up.

Hal: Those are pretty unusual leaders to work with and for. I'd say at best they're two out of 10. Wherever I am in the world, and I've taught at a lot of universities because I'm incapable of keeping a job, it's the same story. Whether it's in an EMBA or an MBA class of people trying to become better leaders, more than half of those people – even in the best B-Schools – work for organizations that excel at crushing questions. In the seminars they look a little bit like deer in the headlights, and they feel like "I agree, questions are important, but I can't do that at my company. I'd get my head cut off or fired or demoted!" So my response to them is to ask them a question: "Fast forward 15 or 20 years from where you are now in your career. What kind of leader do you want to be?" If they want to be the kind of leader that currently leads them, I suggest they stay in the organization they're in since that's how they will turn out. If they envision themselves being a different type of leader than the type their organizational culture sustains, my suggestion to them is frankly to start asking fearless, focused questions in super small, super local, and super stealthy ways. You personally figure out some opportunity or challenge that you care about, that you don't have an answer to, and then the invitation is to us a variety of questioning tools and other innovation skills to solve that problem in a way you normally wouldn't.

Mark: I'd just like to say in your book you have some great practical ways that anybody can use to do that. We won't go over them now. We'll just put the plug in to read the book. That's one of the things I took away from the book, that there really are practical ways and tools that people can use to engage in more powerful questioning, if they desire to go down that path.

Hal: There absolutely are. So part of that path is, yes, you can find lists of questions, more in others' books than mine, but to me it's a sequential logic of relying on a series of recursive questions to figure out what is going on, like "what's working, what's not, and why?" Sometimes we forget those simple foundational kinds of questions and potential sequencing. The other part though is to consider ramping up the sheer frequency of questions asked, because doing that can help people build questioning skills. One surprisingly powerful way to do this is the question burst method that you noticed in *Questions are the Answer* (2018). Based on several thousand data points collected on this method, I've discovered that it consistently helps people make progress in whatever challenge they're stuck on.

For example, I had 50 CEOs yesterday in a seminar at the Porsche Experience Center in Atlanta and after running them through the question burst process, they saw first-hand how well it worked. Eighty-five percent at least slightly reframed their challenge and generated at least one valuable new idea to help move the challenge forward. They instantly moved beyond an intellectual comprehension of question burst dynamics described in Chapter 3 of *Questions are the Answer* (2018) to experience them real-time. However, I know from past experience that at least half of these senior leaders will be scared to death to use the question burst method one more time with another set of people back at their firms.

Mark: What strikes me as I'm listening to you is that one of Kenichi Ohmae's competencies he found in excellent strategists was the courage to challenge constraints. What I'm hearing from you is that people can easily learn to be better questioners, but do they have the courage to take it back to their companies? It's a scary thing for them to, I guess, take back.

Hal: Yes, and for someone who works in an organization that does not value innovation and inquiry, taking it back to the company is just utterly daunting, and that's where once again, my advice to them is to start small, start on a specific challenge, consider the question burst method as one way of asking some different questions about it and make some progress. The core challenge for more than most CEOs is that they are isolated – people tell them things that they think the CEOs want to hear and stop telling them things that they think the

CEOs don't want to hear, and that's the classic global leader/expat challenge when global leaders land in a new country as well. So the issue once again becomes, "Am I actively seeking passive data in my everyday work to discover what I don't know I don't know before it's too late?"

For me the classic counter example is Travis Kalanick, co-founder of Uber and former CEO, getting in the back of an UBER car, being recorded, having a driver complain about Uber's policies and practices for drivers, and Kalanick just chewing him up like "you're the problem, not us!" This viral video led in part to Kalanick getting fired because I suspect that's how he behaved in general and this incident was not an anomaly. Fadi Ghandour, founder and former CEO of Aramex, is exactly the opposite, inviting Aramex delivery truck drivers to take him from airports to hotels when traveling from logistics hub to logistics hub around the world so he could actively seek passive data to learn the subtle but significant nuances of the delivery process at his own company.

Mark: In your book you talked about a variety of conditions that can suppress or enhance the potential for people to tend to ask questions. If we consider working in a global context as a condition, would you reflect on the degree the global context is a facilitator or inhibitor to the generation of powerful questioning for global leaders?

Hal: If I'm a leader who is regularly operating in a multicultural environment, then every moment holds the potential for me to get surprised. Surprise is a key condition for asking powerful questions. So, when people are coming into our space with starkly different world views, there's a good possibility that if we let them enter our space fully, we're going to get surprised with something that causes us to be wrong, instead of right, and to be uncomfortable, instead of comfortable. And, if we're quiet enough and reflective enough to let the surprise sink in, we will ask or be asked questions we wouldn't otherwise ask. So for me, global leaders – of all people on planet Earth – are most likely to ask the better question. Global leaders are regularly primed with the right conditions for fearless questions to flourish. They travel into spaces and live in places that are physically and culturally different and engage with people day in and day out who often have highly divergent worldviews. In fact, everyday routines hold a huge probability that global leaders are going to engage with folks who on one or more dimensions will differ wildly from them. The whole issue distills down to, "Am I behaving in ways that would invite those differences to become a part of my life?" The same dynamic is true for someone who shows up in a non-global work environment, but global work uniquely holds the potential to develop especially strong questioning skills.

Mark: And yet we see people in a global context trying to shut down, so maybe it gets back possibly to the issue of degree of inherent curiosity. If people find themselves working globally, do they have enough inherent curiosity to respond with questions as opposed to erecting barriers and retreating to comfort zones?

Hal: I think part of it relates to inherent curiosity. I'm a deep, long term fan of Carolyn Dweck's work around performance versus growth mindsets. The quickest way to shut down inquiry is to wake up with a performance mindset. "I've got to keep proving to the world that I'm worth something by performing at a certain level" and when I'm in that mindset, if that's all that matters to me, there's a very high probability that I'm not going to be an inquisitive, questioning leader. Or, they may well ask a lot of questions, but in the end, they're all the wrong ones.

Mark: A final question: In your book you talk about keystone questions. As I understand it, they are core questions that are often mostly unconscious, but that guide us through life. It would seem that it might be possible that until a person understands their keystone questions, and assesses them, and maybe formulates more edifying keystone questions after assessment, that it might be difficult to engage in powerful questioning about all other kinds of things.

Hal: The idea of keystone questions was sparked years ago when exploring the intersection of Edward Deci's work in, *Why We Do What We Do*, and Raina Maria Rilke's famous quote from *Letters to a Young Poet*: "Be patient toward all that is unresolved in your heart. Try to love the questions themselves. Do not now seek the answers, which cannot be given because you would not be able to live them." And then we get his crucial conclusion: "And the point is to live everything. Live the question now. Perhaps you will then gradually without noticing it, live along some distant day into the answers." Somehow, I sensed back then that certain questions held more power over our everyday habits than others. More recently, I interviewed Tony Robbins who observed that when people run into problems, it's usually because they're asking the wrong question and by default, living the wrong question. That's the core dimension of a keystone question; it's one that we live productively by choice. I've come to also grasp the idea of a shadow question and am now exploring with a friend and colleague, Roger Lehman, the yin-yang dynamic between keystone and shadow questions at work and in life. We're seeing shadow questions as quite related to Kegan's work on hidden competing commitments. Kegan's written several books, but I will summarize his process.

         First you ask, "How do I want to be a radically different or better leader?" After thinking about it, you might decide that "I want to say 'no' more often." Then, the question becomes, "What do you do and not do every day that keeps you from saying 'no' more often?" The next question is a powerful follow-up to the previous one: "What are you fundamentally committed to that's causing you to do those things that keep you from doing what you want to do differently?" Your answer reflects the hidden commitments that hinder you from doing what you really want to do differently. And hidden even deeper behind those competing commitments are usually big, bad ugly assumptions, such as, "If I stop saying yes, people are going to hate me, and I'll be ostracized." Or, "if I stop saying yes, I'm going to lose my job and end up on the streets homeless." We're trying to take Kegan's work a little bit further by translating these big assumptions into shadow questions. So, one question that might flow out of these big, bad assumptions is, "How can I be nice to people? That's the shadow question.

What I love about Kegan's path-breaking work is that it can help people in literally one hour surface a shadow question that is influencing their thoughts and behaviors. It's one practical and systematic way to surface shadow questions. Another way, at least for me, was having a heart attack 5 years ago and 2 weeks later having a marriage counselor tell me, "Hal if you don't stop being nice to people, you are going to gift yourself another heart attack and probably die."

You know, that caused me to think twice about why am I being nice to people. It goes back to all kinds of family role theory, in my situation, where a father was emotionally abusive and at times physically. When you're a little kid growing up in that kind of unpredictable world, all you care about is protecting yourself, and when you get old enough there's maybe some spillover protection going on toward your siblings and mother. All you're trying to do in that fearful space is avoid the big blow up, which caused my siblings and me to ask, "What can I do that is nice right now that will keep this authority figure in my life from being mean or whacking me on the side of the head?" So, beginning about 15–20 years ago, through a variety of experiences, I started to get the sense that I may well be living the wrong question. Then, a heart attack 5 years ago made the shadow question so crystal clear. Now I wonder "What's the positive catalytic, keystone productive question that could take its place, or better yet, complement it?" Truth be told, trying to construct a more positive keystone question is still a work-in-progress. I have some good alternatives, for example, "How can I honor and magnify your light here and now?" and I try to live them better now I've found that keystone questions anchor the way in which we move and operate through the world of this thing we call leadership – as well as in life.

Mark: One of the things I took away from reading your most recent work is that the competencies that cause good global leadership also cause a person to be a good parent, a good friend, a good spouse, a good human being. It may be that when we carve up competencies and categorize them it is an artificial process. In other words, if we have the foundational competencies set, all the others may flow from them more naturally, and then there is a higher probability we will get a lot of things right, whether we're working in a global context or trying to be a parent or trying to lead a company.

Hal: I would agree. There were exceptions, but often the leaders whom I've interviewed in the last 15–20 years had significant adults in their lives when they were growing up who modeled the power of inquiry, the power of questioning, the power of curiosity, the power of caring about challenges and opportunities in the world, the strength of ruthless truth seeking, and the courage to engage with the world in ways that you truly figure out what really is going on before trying to do something about it.

So you've got Sara Blakely who founded Spanx, whose father asked her every week, "What did you fail at this week?" If by the end of the week she hadn't made a good big mistake, he told her that she wasn't trying hard enough. Similarly, Tiffany Shlain, who founded the Webby Awards and now does amazing work trying to change the world with technology use and nonuse, had a father who told her one day, "You know, Tiffany, if you're not living on the edge, you're taking up too much space." And – and this is a crucial "and" – he gave her the tools to live on the edge, and to do it exceptionally well. These are some of the huge gifts that we can give to people around us, especially younger people.

Last year I had the chance to visit Pixar and be a fly on the wall when Ed Catmull gave two of his almost 30 speeches when retiring from Pixar and Disney Animation Studios. He spoke to small groups of people at Pixar and Disney where he shared with them the key things about leadership that mattered most to him and more importantly, he framed a few key questions that he thought folks should wrestle with to create the future of Pixar and Disney Animation Studios.

Ed, at the core, is a truth seeker. At the core, he's a problem solver. To him, creativity and innovation are problem finding and problem solving, period. It is just a way of life for him, but he worked very hard at Pixar to try to create and sustain a culture where candor rules and where people really are given license to find and solve the big problems, to make really brilliant Pixar movies. As I watched people interact with Ed in his final farewell talks, I sensed love in the room. There was affection. It was genuine, and I think it comes from somebody who created a psychologically safe enough space in a wisely chosen web of systems, processes, and personal leadership approaches, that signaled to everyone around him, "We are here to make the world better, and we're going to do that by making great movies that push the edge of technology and engage the viewer in profound ways. To do that, we're going to do things in our everyday work that we've never done before, which means you're going to be living on the edge all the time if you work here. We are going to go out of our way to make sure over time that somehow we don't become a big ossified bureaucracy that's going to shut down your fearless questions and your problem-solving capabilities." It was utterly inspiring.

Mark: Hal, on behalf of the editors and readership of Advances in Global Leadership I cannot thank you enough for sharing your journey from the early period of the global leadership field to the present. Thank you for sharing with authenticity your passion for asking powerful questions as a way to help us all become better global and domestic leaders and better human beings.

REFERENCES

Black, J. S., & Gregersen, H. (2002). *Leading strategic change: Breaking through the brain barrier.* Upper Saddle River, NJ: Financial Times/Prentice Hall.

Dyer, J., Gregersen, H., & Christensen, C. M. (2011). *The innovator's DNA: Mastering the five skills of disruptive innovators.* Boston: Harvard Business Review Press.

Gregersen, H. (2018). *Questions are the answer: A breakthrough approach to your most vexing problems at work and in life.* New York, NY: HarperColllins Publishers.

HOW DOES AN ANTHROPOLOGIST TEACH GLOBAL LEADERSHIP TO ENGINEERS? AN INTERVIEW WITH JULIA GLUESING

Joyce S. Osland

ABSTRACT

In this interview, Dr. Julia Gluesing describes her career trajectory and the successful approach to teaching global leadership that evolved from her anthropology and communication background, coupled with deep knowledge of the auto industry and the engineering context. Her lessons are applicable and invaluable for anyone teaching global leadership – or engineers.

Keywords: Global leadership; global leadership development; teaching; engineers; business anthropology; pedagogy

INTRODUCTION

Julia Gluesing is a business and organizational anthropologist with more than 40 years of experience in industry and academia as a consultant, researcher, and trainer in global business development focusing on global leadership development, managing global teams, managing change, and innovating across cultures and cross-cultural communication and training. She teaches graduate seminars in Anthropology at Wayne State University, where she is also a part-time faculty member in their Industrial and Systems Engineering Department. Julia teaches engineers the Management of Technology Change course and serves as a leadership project advisor in the Engineering Management Master's Program (EMMP). This program grew out of a university–industry partnership begun in 1990 that included Wayne State

Advances in Global Leadership, Volume 13, 219–234
Copyright © 2020 Emerald Publishing Limited
All rights of reproduction in any form reserved
ISSN: 1535-1203/doi:10.1108/S1535-120320200000013007

University, Ford Motor Company, and later Visteon Corporation. Julia was instrumental in creating and maintaining this partnership, which established the EMMP to meet the educational needs of the automotive companies' technical managers in southeast Michigan. She also teaches courses in qualitative methods, global leadership, and global perspectives in the Global Executive Track Ph.D. Program for engineers, which she co-founded and co-directs. Julia has a Ph.D. in Business Anthropology from Wayne State University and a master's degree in Organizational & Intercultural Communication from Michigan State University.

Joyce: Julia, every year *AGL* issues a special call for papers. For Volume 13, we encouraged submissions from other disciplines to better understand, conceptualize and develop global leadership. When it came to doing a practitioner/teaching interview, you were our first choice. I've been fascinated by what you bring to the classroom as an anthropologist and by your approach to teaching engineers ever since I saw your *Insights from Master Teachers* presentation in 1999. The book that resulted, *Crossing Cultures: Insights from Master Teachers* (2004) edited by Dick Goodman, Nakiye Boyacigillar and Maggi Phillips is still one of my favorite teaching reference books. Thanks for taking the time to be interviewed.

Julia: I've been looking forward to it.

Joyce: Me too. When did you start teaching Global Leadership?

Julia: I think it was around 2006 because I have a former student who graduated from the Master's in Engineering Program in 2008 who is a Global Director of Engineering at Bridgestone-Firestone now. He called me up and said, "I want you to teach about culture and global teams and global leadership for me online during this pandemic." I have about 50 engineers around the world that I'm teaching online.

Joyce: That's a wonderful testament! How would you describe your basic approach to educating others?

Julia: I think of my students as learning partners, and we built this terminology into our global executive track program in Industrial and Systems Engineering. This orientation came from my participation in the design of that program and thinking about engineers, particularly in that program, as knowing a lot and bringing a lot to the table. As one of the admission criteria, they have to be in a global engineering position for at least five years and preferably 10. So, it's an acknowledgement that they know a lot already from their practical experience. I'm always learning from them, and that's one of the things that makes teaching so much fun for me. I learn from them and they learn from me, and, together, we make it happen. It's a shared learning experience.

Joyce: David Kolb, "Mr. Experiential Learning," always showed students at the beginning of every class a list of ways that adults learn. One point was that, unlike children, adults already have all this knowledge in their brain. And it's our job as teachers to help them organize it better, so they can more easily access it and explain it to others.

Julia: Exactly! Give them frames and ways to think about it – words and labels that they can put on things that they have experienced, but don't know what to do with. They don't even have a way to talk about it. So you bring out their learning, and you label it and frame it for them, and give them a way to make sense out of what they are experiencing, and then they run with it. They love it!

I taught a required course in business anthropology 2–3 times to undergraduate juniors from all disciplines (150 students with six sections and teaching assistants). And I did fine in it, but it was so frustrating for me sometimes. There were a lot of people in the class that didn't really want to learn – they were just there to check off a requirement. This is not anything new to anybody who's taught, but I got really frustrated and said, "I can't do this anymore." I found I like teaching working engineers and older anthropology graduate students, while a lot of my colleagues much prefer to teach undergraduate than graduate students. It depends on your personality, I guess.

Joyce: We all have to figure out what gives us joy in the classroom and what we're best suited for.

Julia: Yes!

Joyce: What about your background in anthropology? Does that influence what you teach or how you do it?

Julia: Absolutely – completely and totally! I think it's one of the success factors in my teaching, because I have been quite successful in teaching in industrial and systems engineering. I bring in my anthropology background and my master's work in organizational communication and intercultural communication, which dovetails with cultural anthropology.

Most of the students entering my classes know something about me in advance, based on what they've heard from other students. They hear good things, but they also hear, "Oh my god, she makes you read so much, and you really have to work hard!" It's less than 100 pages a week, but they think that is so much. In graduate school, for anthropology, we read 400–500 pages a week, which was just taken for granted. These guys would fall over! I don't think they could do it (*smiling*). One of the things I had to learn about engineers is that they don't read much, and they're not used to reading the kinds of material I assign. So I've had to tailor things accordingly.

Joyce: How exactly does anthropology impact your teaching methods?

Julia: Anthropological practice has honed my skills of observation and adjusting on the spot to the environment in which I find myself. As an anthropologist, I learned to adjust my communication style to whomever I was interviewing, which required perceptual acuity. I bring these heightened observation skills and reactions to my teaching. I'm always adjusting to what's going on in the class and to different students. I have an idea at the start of every class how I'm going to approach it, but then I adapt every class session, depending upon where they are at that particular point in time and the particular mix of students. You have to adjust, and I think my anthropological skills have helped immensely in that. So it's not just the way I teach, it's also what I teach.

Joyce: This makes sense to me. I also go to class with a plan that I am willing to throw out the window, depending on the students. What teaching methodologies do you use and why?

Julia: I have them do reading and then I have them write about what they've read and make sense of it in terms of their own work. So I make them think about their work and give me examples from their own work experience that illustrate the principles that that they're learning about in their readings. So, every single thing they read, they have to tie to their work lives. I teach in a seminar format. I don't think I've ever had more than about 14 students in a seminar, and most of the time it's around eight. We sit around a conference table, and it's very casual, and we talk a lot. We have conversations. I do have slides, but for a 5-hour class, I probably have no more than 30 slides that I use as prompts. A lot of times the slides will have questions or statements on them, and we spend a lot of time talking about them.

I always make sure I hear from everyone in the class. And one of the ways that I do that is to have them read news articles that they choose from reputable news sources like *The Financial Times, The Wall Street Journal, The Economist* or *Fortune,* or some other widely respected news publication. I ask them to go to these news sources and find an example of global leadership and analyze it, based upon whatever principles we're discussing or learning at the time. They love this assignment and get a lot out of it.

I'm also trying to teach them to be observant by having them look for examples of leadership and critique what they see based on what they are learning about leadership. I ask them to critique leaders in their own organizations. In a final project, I make them actually go out and talk to people in their organizations about leadership. They have to select a crucial leadership problem that's facing them and others in the organization and interview people about it, analyze their findings, and make recommendations about what can be done to solve the problem.

One of my main objectives is to make theory and research practical and useful and teach them how to do that. Many of our doctoral students have extensive work experience, and for class they have to read scientific articles – and they have real difficulty making their way through these articles! So, I use your book, *Global Leadership: Research, Practices, and Development* (Mendenhall et al., 2018), which I think is fantastic. One of the reasons I like it is that it covers some history of leadership and what we know about leadership, and then addresses what makes global leadership different, with many ways to approach that particular topic. Before using this book, I used whatever journal articles I could find that would be less scholarly in tone so that they would not fall asleep on the first page.

The global executive track students have to learn a new scholarly language, and that's hard for them. One of the things that I intro-duced into the program is a literature review course that they take early on. They have to do a literature review, which they don't know how to do for the most part when they enter the program. They don't know how to search for the articles, navigate the library, read the articles, and then critique the literature and write up a review. By the time they get to me in the global leadership course, they are better at these skills.

It was clear to me very early on with the first cohort of students that people needed lots of help and learning how to do this, which is completely understandable because their master's degrees are in engineering. We are bringing in more international business and management and soft skills that they have never really learned before.

Joyce: And then there's so much more uncertainty.

Julia: Oh, yes! They have to understand the uncertainty. When I taught undergraduate engineering students, in the very first class I would hold up my hand, palm out, fingers spread, and ask them to describe it: "What is this?" They would tell me, "Oh, it's five fingers." Or they would describe the joints, the blood vessels, etc. After all the explanations that they could give me, I then held my hand up again and would ask, "Well, what if I do this (opening and closing my hand)? Does that tell you anything more?" They'd say, "It's a useful tool for grasping" and share all the physical, tangible descriptions they could find. And then I would tell them, "This class is about all the spaces in between the fingers and all the things that you cannot see. This hand works because there are relationships. There are relationships between these five digits, with the palm, the way the hand is attached to the body. It's all about the relationships that you cannot see that make it work." And then they would moan, "Oh no!" (*laughing*)

Joyce: Time to transfer to another section! (*laughing*)

Julia: Yes, then they would freak out, right? But they knew what they were
            getting into, which is what I wanted them to know. And then I would
            tell them I was going to make it easy for them.

            I also teach, if you can believe this, a qualitative research design and
            methods class to engineers – and they are really scared at the
            beginning because they don't know how to do any of that kind of
            research. But by the end of the class they love it or at least can
            understand and appreciate it. And many of them go on to do
            qualitative dissertations. These are engineers! When they experience
            it and apply it, they see what value it brings to their own decision
            making and to their ability to deal with work problems.

            I still have students who come back to me who are now in CEO
            positions who tell me their classes with me that included a large
            cultural component changed their thinking forever about what was
            going on around them. It gave them tools that a lot of other leaders
            do not have that helped to advance their careers in ways that others
            just couldn't compete against. So, there's the anthropology, for sure,
            giving them observation skills that they didn't have before. I try to
            bring that not just to the methods classes, but to all my classes.

Joyce: Well, my next question was going to be: "What always works for you
            in the classroom?" But it sounds as if you've figured out over the
            years how to make everything you do in the classroom "always
            work."

Julia: True, these methods always work, along with giving them practical
            real-world problem-solving exercises. I have also used cases in my
            teaching, but I find that it works a lot better if they bring in cases
            from their own work environment and then we all talk about them.
            When students discuss issues with their fellow learning partners in
            the class it becomes a shared sense-making experience, and they're all
            bringing their personal experience with similar problems from their
            different contexts. It's just a whole series of sense making exercises
            that by the end of the course, they get it and can do it on their own
            without my help. They don't even need me anymore.

Joyce: Tell me more about their personal cases. What form are they in?

Julia: While talking about their homework assignments or the writing
            assignments, somebody will say, "I've got this thing going on at my
            work, and this engineer or leader is doing X, Y, and Z and it's
            throwing a wrench into the works. I don't why the leader is behaving
            this way." And then we will sit there and discuss it. A lot of times, I
            will initially encourage them just to describe the issue, which again is
            an anthropological practice.

They have a tendency to make judgments right away. When I have them interview people at work about the situation, they invariably come back and say, "I thought I already knew the answer to this, and I didn't need to go out and talk to anyone, but, "Whoa, there's a whole different perspective that I never thought of – I learned so much that is new." It opens their eyes!

Joyce:　　Will you give me an example of a student research question in their own organization? How did they arrive at the topic and do the research?

Julia:　　One of my students in the global executive track just finished her doctoral dissertation; she mainly did a qualitative study, but she also did a survey. The dissertation topic was essentially: "What is the relationship between innovation and quality?" She was focusing on the product development process. Many of my students come from a variety of organizations – supplier companies for the automotive industry, healthcare, the military, defense contractors – but this particular student happened to be at Ford. Quality in an organization like Ford or any automotive company is something that has been looked at in an after-the-fact kind of way by looking at consumer surveys, like JD Power, to see what consumer research says about the quality of your vehicles. And the automotive companies these days have taken a very different approach because they think, "We can't wait until we get reports saying things have gone wrong to assess the quality of our vehicles. We need to have quality at the table early in product design, and we have to integrate quality with innovation. When the people doing concept design hear that, they have tended to think, "Oh my God, here comes Quality! They're going to make us jump through 80 million hoops, and they're going to slow us way, way down, and we don't want these guys at the table. So let's just not invite them. We're not going to put them on the meeting invitation." But Quality has had to redefine itself as an organization, or as a discipline in these companies so that they are not – quote–unquote, "the instructors" but instead, the facilitators of innovation. And because innovation has to be fast and you can't have bureaucracy slowing it down, you have to figure out how to make quality a whole mindset and philosophy and introduce that into advanced engineering.

Her research question was: How do we do this? There's no research out there that says how you do it. So, she had to figure out what we even mean by this – what is the meaning of quality? What is the meaning of innovation? The question lent itself beautifully to qualitative research. Anytime you get this kind of question dealing with meaning and culture and people's beliefs and values, it's perfect for qualitative research.

Joyce: I hope her study can make a difference.

Julia: She is already doing that in her job, and her first publication is in the *Journal of Business Anthropology*. It's a special issue on the future of transportation. But it's very much an anthropological kind of study.

Joyce: Wonderful! Let's go back before you started teaching global leadership. Where else have you taught or trained people and what was your career trajectory?

Julia: I was doing training, way back in the 1970s in the hotel industry. When I was in management, I would be one of those that would be tasked with training new hires – cashiers and room clerks, etc. I just always like it, and I guess I was good at it. By the early 1980s, I was writing training workbooks for the Sales and Marketing Association for the hotel administration sector on topics like situation analysis, which is basically research. I also gave seminars at the Hotel Sales and Marketing Association conferences. When I started graduate school at Michigan State University in communication, I was teaching in the Hotel School (Michigan State has a very good hotel school like Cornell's), which was housed in the business school. I taught undergraduate and graduate classes in the Hotel School, because the hospitality industry was my background.

          My first job in the hospitality industry was working in 1971 for the San Francisco Convention Visitors Bureau. So I was able to learn every aspect of the hospitality industry – restaurants, hotels, tour companies, etc. And then I had my own tour company in San Francisco, "Native Sons Tours," because the partners were all born in California. I enjoyed informing tourists about San Francisco. You could call that teaching, too – giving tours. Two other guys and I started our own company doing ground services for big conventions. We had our own fleet of minibuses, and I was in charge of the tours for international visitors. I used to give tours in French and Russian. So you can picture me driving a 14-person mini-bus with a microphone on doing tours of San Francisco, the wine country, whatever.

Joyce: That's amazing! What happened to the company?

Julia: Eventually we ended up selling the company, and I started working for Westin Hotels and was employed at the St. Francis Hotel on Union Square in San Francisco. I helped to open a hotel in Hawaii on Maui, and I helped open up the Bonaventure in Los Angeles. So again, I was really teaching even then. I was one of the crew that got sent down to teach others how to do things right. So it was kind of a natural progression. And then I worked on Mackinac Island as a hotel manager. I also used to teach hotel management for a travel school in Boston when I was working and living there. So I moved around a lot and did a lot of different things before I ever went back to graduate school.

Joyce: But it's always so interesting to see how many threads in a person's life remain the same.

Julia: Oh yes, the teaching, the education, the international stuff – that's been there my entire life. What else could I do, given the way I grew up? I went to a local high school in San Francisco that was 70% Chinese, and I lived in a very multicultural neighborhood. I grew up in a Greek-American household, and my mother worked at San Francisco State University as a librarian where she had coworkers who were Swedes, Iranians, Japanese and African Americans. We used to have these international Christmases and celebrations where everybody would come and bring food. We lived on Guam for quite a while, and I went to a local Guamanian school with lots of Filipinos and Koreans. We used to go to the little village celebrations on Guam with all the locals. I was exposed to multiple languages. My mother threw me in a Russian class when I was 13 at San Francisco State when they were testing out the audiolingual method – they needed "guinea pig" child learners. And I also studied French from age 11 until I graduated from college.

Joyce: That's quite the intercultural history! How did you end up teaching engineers?

Julia: Well, being in Southeast Michigan, you are always around engineers. Even when I was at Michigan State working in communication, we did a lot of our studies on participative decision making in automotive supply companies, and I got introduced to engineers and engineering in the early 1980s. After I earned my master's degree, I went to work for a communication consulting company in the Detroit area. Almost all of the clients were engineering-type technical organizations. The biggest client was General Motors.

          I was assigned to a project in 1985 to help with communication at General Motors where engineering and operations were coming together in a big push to fix a car that was a disaster from a quality point of view. The engineers fascinated me, because it was such a different way to reason and look at problems and a different approach to problem solving. My mouth was open on the job, jaw dragging on the ground for weeks, because I could not believe how they even got one car out the door to sell! It was like, "How do they even begin to do it? They don't know how to talk to each other!" There were so many errors, and I learned how complex an automobile is and how complex it is to even think about making just one of them, much less mass-produce them. It just blew my mind! I was fascinated by it and found myself learning another language.

The first couple of meetings I was sent to, I simply observed to see how they communicated with each other. I had the Director of Engineering and the Director of Operations, two areas that are always at loggerheads, plus various respected people from these organizations in the room. I was writing everything down, but I had no clue what they were talking about! It was like another language, and they used acronyms constantly. When I asked about them, they gave me a binder that was inches thick filled with acronyms and their definitions! But the same acronym used in different functional areas had different meanings, so you had to first understand who was saying it! The opportunities for misunderstanding were gigantic, and nobody in the room understood each other. It was clear to me that they were talking past each other and had no clue what each other was saying. It was an opportunity to apply what I knew and help people internal to General Motors to design a communication strategy so that they could make progress on the solving their problems. It was a huge learning experience for me, and I learned a lot about different types of engineers and engineering.

When I was a graduate student, I worked on National Science Foundation projects in various automotive companies and suppliers. I roamed the companies observing early product design where they make clay models all the way to final production processes in manufacturing plants. It was fascinating work learning about the process of car-making from beginning to end. There are not many people inside those companies who have that breadth of experience because they generally go deep into a functional role and do not work broadly across the organization. I lucked out because this was a real gift. I think one of the major reasons I've been successful in doing what I do and in teaching engineers is that I know how to talk to them. I know what they're saying. I know about their organizations. I can relate what I'm teaching to everything that they do. I've also done a lot of consulting – some that involved training engineers, which also provides fodder for the classroom.

Joyce: Previously, you said that when you were first exposed to engineers, you were fascinated by the way they think and how they approached and solved problems. How are they different, and what does that mean for people who teach engineers?

Julia: For the most part, they were completely oblivious to a whole lot of cues and clues around them that could give them insight into the problem because they had such a narrow focus. I fault their education for that. One of the things we've tried to do in the College of Engineering at Wayne State is to change that early on in undergraduate education, so that they don't take 40 bazillion engineering courses and never learn anything about people.

Joyce: Right!

Julia: They have to know something about people, and they have to learn how to use different sources of data besides the numbers that the machines on the manufacturing lines spew out. I learned that they don't think broadly. Instead, the thinking is very, very narrow, and they're really focused on the concrete. But to interpret the numbers correctly, they have to understand that there are people in those numbers – people who have some influence on how those numbers turn out that to whom they'd better pay attention. It was a real challenge. But I've learned a lot from the engineers about problem solving and ways to attack problems that I never would have known if I hadn't been exposed to them.

Joyce: What exactly did they teach you about problem solving?

Julia: They taught me how to appreciate really practical and concrete data about something as simple as tire pressure, as an example. Most of us don't think that tires are all that complex, right? They're just kind of an afterthought when it comes to designing a car, right? I used to think that. But engineers taught me to ask the question, "What is so important about a simple number like tire pressure?" and start peeling it apart and understanding that there is a whole lot more to it than a simple number. So they taught me a lot about complexity, and they taught me not to take anything for granted and not to make assumptions. And I know from year-long projects that I've worked on with teams of engineers that something as simple as designing a tire is a very complex process, and you have to consider many, many factors and their impact on the larger technical systems in an automobile.

Joyce: In a way, it sounds like you're returning the favor by trying to teach them about human systems and complexity.

Julia: I am! I'm trying to teach them about people systems to go along with their technical systems. I try to show them that they already understand systems, so they just need to take that thinking they are already used to and apply it to people.

Joyce: So that leads into my next question, which is, "Does the training and background of engineers require educators to approach pedagogical design and delivery somewhat differently compared to business executives and managers?"

Julia: Totally. You can't do it in the same way. I teach the anthropology students in a completely different way than I teach engineers.

Joyce: And can you explain how you do that?

Julia: With anthropology students, I don't have to tell them people are important. They know that. I don't have to spend a lot of time giving them basic observation skills or focusing on the idea that culture impacts everything we do – that culture is not a variable or that in an organization, culture *is* the organization or that an organization is a culture. I can start farther down this road and hit the ground running with anthropology students.

I <u>do</u> have to teach anthropology students about engineers if they're going to do applied work. And sometimes these students have taken courses in which corporations and business are painted as evil oppressors, so they have an anti-power, anti-business attitude, which has been a real uphill battle for those of us in business anthropology. It's certainly much more accepted now than when I first started back in the 1980s. I brought one anthropology student into my teaching and my work on the leadership projects I was advising at Ford, and she came to class every week as a teaching assistant. I gave her lots of tips and told her what she could and couldn't do, so she was very closely supervised by me in these settings. I couldn't have been more pleased when she went back from a meeting in the Anthropology Department attended by a large group of graduate students and professors and told me that the graduate students went off on their usual diatribe of bad-mouthing business, talking about "How can they make these products?" and "They're out there to kill us all, right?" She jumped right in to defend engineers, telling the anthropologists that they were all wrong. And that the engineers were actually nice, genuine people who were really and truly concerned about the safety of the people who drove the cars, and they all had kids and families just like real people, and their own families and loved ones rode around in the cars they designed and built. (*laughing*)

Joyce: So, what specific advice do you have for other professors about teaching engineers as a group?

Julia: I would say that that they absolutely have to make whatever it is they're teaching as concrete as they possibly can and give lots of examples. You have to draw out what the engineers already know and have already talked about and relate that to the material you're trying to teach them. You have to relate it to what they know. You can't just teach them in the abstract, which means that the instructors need to know something about the people they're teaching. For example, in the virtual seminar with 50 engineers that I'm teaching for Bridgestone-Firestone right now, I have them fill out an expectation form before I begin teaching them. I ask what they want to get out of the class, and I always ask them about their jobs and their experiences and to give me two or three different examples of something, like problem solving, or how culture has or has not affected their work. I have to know at least something about them before I even get started.

Joyce: In a virtual experience, how does that knowledge about them as individuals help you? What do you do with it?

Julia: It helps me come up with examples that they can relate to. When I'm talking about an abstract concept, I will draw on two or three examples that I learned from them and relate what I'm saying to those examples. In the very first class right after introductions, I put up a slide that says "Expectations" followed by my content analysis of their course expectations. And I say, "This is what I heard from all of you. This is what you want, right? Is there anything else?" So, they know right from the very beginning that I am listening to them and trying to address their needs. If they have specific needs or questions, I want to make sure I cover them in my lectures. I try to answer the questions or address the issues that they want to know about. I do that in my assignments. I also try to be concrete and relate it to their work in my assignments. When they bring in examples of leadership in the news, we debrief it in light of the readings they've done and the concepts they're learning. And I ask them for related examples from their own company: "Can you give me an example of where this occurs in your workplace?"

Joyce: You mentioned earlier that engineers tend to pay less attention to people. How do you help them be more tuned into people?

Julia: I give them an assignment where they have to actually go observe a meeting, for example. I'm trying to teach them to be more observant and to pick up on cues that maybe they don't pick up on ordinarily. I usually give them some sort of an observation sheet, because they need something concrete. You can't tell them, "Just go observe." You have to give them some kind of tool. I give them something basic, where they're jotting down something like turn-taking[1] – who's taking turns in the conversation? I have them observe other communication patterns too. For example, how many times women talk versus men? How many women are there in the room versus men? This is useful because they often pay no attention to anything like that. And then I ask them, how many times do people ask questions versus just give information and give opinions? There's a great turn-taking app on an iPhone, or you can use paper and pencil guidelines and questionnaires – all of them are useful tools.

Joyce: Some of my engineering students work on skills related to emotional intelligence (EQ). The personal development plan for a recent graduate was observing people in meetings and trying to read their emotions. Do you do anything related to EQ?

Julia: Mostly I have used things they can watch, like movie clips or clips from the news where there's actually something cross-cultural going on, and I ask them to take a look at it and analyze the incident. What do you see in there? Is there misunderstanding or not? And if so, where does it come from?

One thing I do teach them does not come from anthropology, but from my communication background – I teach them how to get to know people.

Joyce: That's always important. How do you teach culture?

Julia: I teach them the theory without them knowing it's the theory. You know, tying it to what they do on a day-to-day basis. That's the most important thing because they aren't going to internalize it any other way if it's too abstract. They don't think that way. It doesn't mean they can't understand theory, or that they can't understand academic vocabulary, because they do. But if you make it concrete, they remember it and they can apply it.

I start with cultural generalizations and the difference between generalizations and stereotypes. And that's a very important thing because they think that if they make any kind of generalization, it's a stereotype. Well, it's not necessarily a stereotype. People and cultures are patterned, and it's okay to find those patterns and talk about them. It doesn't mean that there isn't intracultural variation. I teach them about people who are in the mainstream culture, under the bell curve, and those that are marginal. There's a lot of variation under there, but there are still patterns, and that's where you are when you're dealing at the cultural level.

You have to give them tools that they can hang onto. You can give them the concepts and everything behind it, but you've got to accompany it with something that they can take and use right away. The HELP model and my one-page core cultural axioms, because engineers don't want to read much, are very useful for this purpose (Gluesing, 2004). They like any kind of formula. The whole point of the core cultural axioms is that they inform the system of logic. If you can understand them and how they originated, they inform everything you need to know about a culture. And those basic things don't change that much over time.

The HELP model (Habits, Expectations, Language, and Perspectives) is a simple way to break down culture. Habits refer to patterns of thinking and behavior. Expectations are the expectations for ourselves and others in any given situation. Language is verbal, nonverbal, and contextual communication, and perspectives on the world are your beliefs, your values – what's important and what's not.

In addition to the culture level, at the societal level, you also have all these different HELP systems that have to do with the groups that you belong to – your organization, church group, etc.

Whatever the groups are that you are part of shapes your behavior, thinking, vocabulary and perspectives. The HELP systems at the cultural and sociological levels are about how people are alike, how they are similar to all the others in the group. And then when you get to the psychological level, that's when you find out how people are different from all others in their cultural and sociological groups.

If you really want to communicate well with others, and I teach this in global teaming, you have to learn something about them. And that's at the psychological level. You have to learn about them as individual people even in a group-oriented culture.

Julia: You have a HELP system that is part of your culture of origin, however you grew up, that is a combination of your family upbringing, and your experiences. And then you have all the other HELP systems that you learn every time you join a new group. So, you can add HELP systems to your repertoire without ever giving up your culture of origin. You just keep adding; and there's nothing wrong with that. Your culture of origin does not have to go away. You're just adding to your repertoire.

Joyce: I think some people struggle with that. When they're called upon to code switch and behave in a way that's more acceptable to another culture, they feel like they're not being authentic.

Julia: Yes, but that's not true at all. It's just another HELP system that you draw on that helps you get along in the world and in the situation in which you find yourself. It doesn't mean that you're giving up your authentic self. If you did give up your identity, you'd have a lot of psychological problems. I think in all the discussions about biculturalism, the people who have the most problems are those that think they have to deny one or the other.

Joyce: And now, the last question: If I were to interview former students about you and your courses, what do you think would be the general consensus?

Julia: Oh, I think they would have a lot of praise and that I give them a lot of reading!

Joyce: Julia, thank you for all the contributions you bring to global leadership from anthropology, communication, and your industry knowledge. The *AGL* editors really appreciate your willingness to share your wisdom and experiences to improve how global leadership is taught. We are also grateful for the teaching resources you provided below.

---

[1]In conversation analysis, turn-taking is the manner in which orderly conversation normally takes place (Sacks, Schegloff, & Jefferson, 1974). Competitive versus cooperative overlap in conversations can affect rapport and the balance of power.

REFERENCES

Mendenhall, M. E., Osland, J. S., Bird, A., Oddou, G. R., Stevens, M. J., Maznevski, M. L., & Stahl, G. K. (2018). *Global leadership: Research, practices, and development* (3rd ed.). London: Routledge.

Sacks, H., Schegloff, E. A., & Jefferson, G. (1974). A simplest systematics for the organization of turn-taking for conversation. *Language, 50*(4), 696–735.

TEACHING-RELATED RESOURCES

Baba, M., Gluesing, J. C., Ratner, H., & Wagner, K. (2004). The contexts of knowing: Natural history of a globally distributed team. *Journal of Organizational Behavior, 25*, 547–587. For a teaching case excerpted from this article, see "Celestial's Global Customer Teams" in Osland, J. S., Kolb, D. A., Rubin, I., & Turner, M. E. (2007). *Organizational Behavior: An Experiential Approach* (8th Ed., pp. 685–699). Upper Saddle River, NJ: Prentice Hall.

Gluesing, J. C. (2004). Teaching culture "on the fly" and "learning in working" with global teams. In R. Goodman, N. Boyacigiller, & M. Phillips (Eds.), *Crossing cultures: Insights from master teachers* (pp. 235–252). New York, NY: Routledge.

Gluesing, J. C. (2017). Ethical challenges and considerations in global networked organizations. In T. De Waal Malefyt & R. J. Morais (Eds.), *Ethics in the anthropology of business: Explorations in theory, practice, and pedagogy* (pp. 70–86). New York, NY: Routledge.

Gluesing, J. C. (2018). Using boundary objects to facilitate culture change and integrate a global top management team. *Journal of Business Anthropology, 7*(1), 32–50. http://dx.doi.org/10.22439/jba.v7i1.5491

Gluesing, J. (2020). Global teams. Oxford Research Encyclopedia of Anthropology. Retrieved from https://oxfordre.com/anthropology/view/10.1093/acrefore/9780190854584.001.0001/acrefore-9780190854584-e-11. Accessed on August 21, 2020.

Gluesing, J. C., Alcordo, T., Baba, M., Britt, D., Wagner, K., McKether, W., ... Riopelle, K. (2003). The development of global virtual teams. In C. Gibson & S. Cohen (Eds.), *Virtual teams that work: Creating conditions for virtual team effectiveness* (pp. 353–380). San Francisco, CA: Jossey-Bass.

Gluesing, J. C., & Gibson, C. (2003). Designing and forming effective global teams. In H. W. Lane, M. L. Maznevski, M. E. Mendenhall, & J. McNett (Eds.), *Handbook of global management: A guide to managing complexity* (pp. 199–226). Malden, MA: Blackwell.

Gluesing, J. C., Riopelle, K., Chelst, K., Woodliff, A., & Miller, L. (2008). An educational partnership for immediate impact. In E. Briody & R. Trotter (Eds.), *Partnering for performance: Inside culture and collaboration* (pp. 125–142). Lanham, MD: Rowman & Littlefield Publishers, Inc.

Gluesing, J. C., Riopelle, K. R., & Danowski, J. A. (2014). Mixing ethnography and information technology data mining to visualize innovation networks in global networked organizations. In S. Dominguez & B. Hollstein (Eds.), *Mixed methods social networks research: Design and applications* (pp. 203–236). New York, NY: Cambridge University Press.

Itabashi-Campbell, R., & Gluesing, J. C. (2014). Engineering problem-solving in social contexts: 'Collective wisdom' and 'ba.' In B. Williams, J. Figueiredo, & J. Trevelyan (Eds.), *Engineering practice in a global context: Understanding the technical and the social* (pp. 129–158). London: Taylor & Francis.

Itabashi-Campbell, R., Gluesing, J. C., & Perelli, S. (2011). Engineering problem solving and operational sustainability: An epistemological perspective. Decision Science Institute (DSI) Annual Meeting 2011, Boston, MA.

Philippart, N., & Gluesing, J. C. (2012). Global E-mentoring: Overcoming virtual distance for an effective partnership. 4th ACM International Conference of Intercultural Collaboration, March 21–23, 2012, Bengaluru: ACM Digital Library.

PRACTITIONER INSIGHTS FROM 25 YEARS OF DEVELOPING GLOBAL LEADERSHIP

Mark Frederick

ABSTRACT

This reflection on the trajectory of the field of Global Leadership Development identifies shifts from in-person training to virtual coaching leveraging assessment tools. Practitioners can now choose from a wide variety of assessments and learning systems, identified herein, to structure coaching over time in an online environment. Based on decades of experience, the author explains how to select an assessment and incorporate it into one's developmental approach. This chapter also clarifies how to structure coaching and effectively deliver virtual sessions. Several examples from leading companies illustrate how these best practice approaches can be built into global leadership development initiatives.

Keywords: Global leadership development; virtual coaching; assessment tools; best practices; training designs; global leaders; evolution of global leadership development; global competencies; VUCA

This reflection is based on my experiences and client work over the past 25 years in the area of Global Leadership Development. A little background on that before engaging the topic more directly: I started in this field in 1996 working for one of the initial North American companies providing support services to professional expatriates working in the private sector—International Orientation Resources (IOR) in Chicago. At the time, IOR was considered an industry leader in intercultural leadership training and had a model where executives would fly into Chicago for several days, at least two, for training that often involved a host of external advisors/experts in four focus areas: Area studies of the host country (mostly historical, political, economic, and societal

Advances in Global Leadership, Volume 13, 235–242
Copyright © 2020 Emerald Publishing Limited
ISSN: 1535-1203/doi:10.1108/S1535-120320200000013008

background provided by an academic expert); Values and norms of the host country (often a discussion with a host national who has lived and worked outside of their country to have a deeper comparative perspective); Business Practices of the host country (could be either a host national or another expatriate with significant work experience in the host country); and finally Daily Living in the host country (oftentimes an expatriate who could discuss practical adjustment such as finding a house or apartment, setting up utilities, identifying a school if children were accompanying, etc.). The IOR model was widely used by competitors in the industry and was significantly influenced by training models used in the Peace Corps. It is remarkable to reflect on how much the intercultural training industry has changed from 25 years ago with major events like 9/11 and the Dot-Com crash as primary disrupters.[1] COVID-19 will no doubt drive further industry transformation.

After several years working in global leadership training and development, I began my first independent practice and was one of the initial few who were putting their cards out as "intercultural consultants."[2] It's interesting to note there are now hundreds, if not thousands, working professionally in the inter-cultural global leadership development area with the advent of the "golden age" of freelance work that has more recently emerged. Working independently, I was partnering with a wider variety of service providers and increasing my levels of experience across industry sectors and levels of leadership. I returned to IOR in 2006 to grow consultative and coaching services for global leaders with a talent management focus, which involved a more systemic view of leadership development to include how talent is identified, onboarded into the organiza-tion, developed, engaged, retained, and promoted.[3] After 10 years in that leadership role, I returned again to private practice, which has been my primary focus the past four years. All told, I have had the opportunity to work with thousands of global leaders from over 60 countries across four continents, from C level leaders and SVPs (senior vice presidents) to directors and project managers. It's important to note that my reflections and observations come

---

[1] After 9/11, the private sector heavily reduced air travel for training and development and many business leaders were reluctant to fly unless absolutely necessary. The centralized training model never recovered and leaders started insisting that the training come to them at their company locations or even at their private residences, which started emerging as a trend later in the 2000s. The Dot-Com crash greatly reduced budgets for this kind of global leadership development which disrupted the "4 expert" model described above and placed more emphasis on the expertise of the trainer/consultant working with the business leader.
[2] This can still seem like an elusive brand to many professionals today, but it has become far more common with the advent of professional social media networks like LinkedIn, especially when compared with the late 1990s.
[3] It's important to mention that talent management advanced as a business concept around 2000, largely driven by McKinsey, a global management consultancy. The IOR training model previously described was nearly exclusively focused around development of global leaders without any greater organizational talent management context.

mostly from the private sector, although I have worked with some nonprofit leaders as well as academic leaders.

I find one of the most important developments in the field is the increased use and availability of assessment tools. Twenty-five years ago, there was some incorporation, but there was a distinctive lack of assessments focused on intercultural dynamics of global leadership. Now there are far more choices and availability, and clients can choose from a range based not only on method but also pricing, reporting, and accessibility online. In fact, there are so many choices that it becomes quite challenging as a consultant to keep track of them all and develop an adequate level of professional capability with them. That said, practitioners can really benefit from increased familiarity with the variety of assessments and how they can be used to determine the best level of fit with the client, which ultimately creates more value for organizations. There are many aspects for fit consideration ranging from the practical, i.e., cost and length of time required to complete the assessment, to what the instrument actually measures and how that aligns with the leadership development goals and ideals of the organization. This aspect is particularly important when adopting a talent management approach in global leadership development, as the essence of that derives from the organization's culture and how well integrated that might be on a global level.[4] I feel it's critical to align the use of intercultural assessments with the organizational culture and be able to provide some degree of choice to clients for customization. I have seen companies choose assessments based on either their simplicity (e.g., they measure one component of global leadership) or their complexity (they measure a range of qualities/competencies). In some cases, I have observed companies choosing an assessment based on the accessibility of the language of the report results and dismissing others for overly theoretical language and concepts.

Access and incorporation of these assessment tools drive another major movement in the field, which is greater use of coaching methodology. I would argue that some limited form of coaching was happening in the intercultural training previously described where global leaders would prepare for an expatriate assignment. For example, at the end of the Business Practice discussion, a trainer would often ask the leader how they might apply what they have learned and what sort of goals they would set for themselves. Those training engagements, however, had a fixed time span, usually several days in length, and had a sense of finality to them as there was no opportunity for developmental follow-up. Leveraging assessment tools allows for extended coaching engagements over time with multiple touch points and the opportunity to discuss and evaluate ongoing experiences. One can also use an assessment as a pre and post global experience measurement as another way to capture and discuss how attitudes and

---

[4]It is amazing to me how much tension there still is between an organization's headquarters culture and regional offices. This has been a topic since I started in the field, and while some companies like GE and IBM have made significant progress shaping a globally integrated culture, just this week alone I worked with two Fortune 500 clients facing major challenges as a result of friction between headquarters and regional centers.

behaviors may have changed. This form of coaching approach creates far more value for clients than 2-day training programs and also shapes the opportunity to improve performance and drive a degree of behavior change, which is in my view the ultimate goal of global leadership development.

The length and nature of coaching assignments can vary greatly and are oftentimes largely driven by budget. For high-level leaders like C-suite officers and SVPs, I have often seen year-long engagements with a cadence of monthly sessions, although those can ebb and flow depending on challenges encountered and the emergence of important changes and decisions. This is another distinct advantage that coaching has over formal training, as its informality and accessibility aligns nicely with the VUCA[5] business climate we find ourselves in, where change and ambiguity are constants. It's highly effective to be able to process challenging situations with a coach in real time and also have a follow-up discussion as to how things went. And there are also coaching engagements built around developmental assignments and goals that are shorter in duration, oftentimes three to five sessions in which leaders can also take advantage of a continuous development focus over time. These types of engagements are ideal for organizations with limited budgets as well as younger generation emerging global leaders that are building skills as they prepare for higher levels of strategic leadership.

I often design a global leadership coaching engagement starting with a competency-based assessment like the GCI (Global Competencies Inventory). This assessment is very rich with material and can be focused on the three areas of Perception Management, Relationship Management, and Self-Management. However, one of the strengths of this instrument is how the individual competencies from the different areas interrelate. For example, I have found that leaders who are able to adjust their style and approach effectively in different cultural environments frequently have higher norm scores in both the Social Flexibility and Emotional Resilience competencies. This is logical because Social Flexibility involves trying different behaviors and Emotional Resilience helps people bounce back and try again when those attempts don't quite work. It took some time to develop this appreciation and understanding for the interrelated aspects of these competencies, and I found it has been important to reflect on how they show up in individual leaders and seek practical examples of how they experience them in their positions. When developing coaching expertise, it's critical to build reflection time after each session to analyze what the leader shared and capture key points and examples for reference in future sessions. This is particularly helpful for identifying behavioral patterns and trends in leadership behavior.

One can build coaching conversations around each section of the GCI assessment and then weave the three sections together so that the leader has a more synthetic understanding of how the competencies interrelate. From that, a coach can work with the leader to design a development plan over time, ideally

---

[5]VUCA – volatility; uncertainty; complexity; ambiguity.

six months to a year. I find it's effective to align a competency assessment with an intercultural online learning system such as GlobeSmart, Country Navigator, or CultureWizard when framing a development plan. These types of learning systems have cultural work style assessments built within them that are connected to a variety of self-guided learning paths which provide deeper insight into self-awareness and behavioral considerations for adaptation and adjustment. The learning paths can be incorporated into a leader's development plan based on their specific global work context. In discussions about these plans, I've observed that various cultures emphasize the GCI competencies as well as communication styles in different ways. For example, in the US business environment, many leaders highlight the importance of projecting optimism,[6] both in terms of attitude and displays of nonverbal communication like facial gestures and smiles. In German business environments, there is usually a more channeled and low context approach to communication and excessive optimism can be perceived as naiveté or lack of seriousness and focus. Chinese business contexts also tend to have far more neutral nonverbal expressions and smiles can possess very different meanings than in the United States, such as embarrassment or discomfort. When coaching global leaders, it's important to contextualize the use of a competency-based assessment with an intercultural work style profile to create finely tuned conversations that capture the nuances and complexity of different cultures.

In addition to the use of various assessments in coaching for global leaders, one should incorporate a variety of questions so that the leader reflects on their experiences with depth rather than on a shallow level. This often means working in more of an inquiry mode as opposed to advocacy. The Coaching Mindset Index assessment defines inquiry as the process of using open-ended questions in conjunction with active listening so that the questions build on the coachee's responses. Advocacy is when the coach focuses on sharing experiences, stories, and providing guidance and advice. In many ways, advocacy relates more to training and consulting skills. While useful at times, it's important to focus attention on the leader's experiences and help them examine their own responses and reactions to situations. I have found over the years that I have started to consciously place far more energy and emphasis on inquiry so that the ratio feels like 70/30. I devote more time to deep and reflective listening and will hold back on experience sharing so that I am mindful of when best to impart guidance or explain concepts. Every global leadership development professional will find her or his own balance on this scale, but it's critical to reflect on the activity and energy level between these two dimensions and ensure there is a healthy variety of open-ended questions to allow for depth of introspection on attitude and behavioral change.

The increase of coaching in global leadership development also correlates with the rise of virtual video platforms such as Skype, WebEx, and Zoom.[7] These

---

[6]Optimism is a Self-Management competency in the GCI.

[7]As referenced on the first page, COVID-19 is propelling the usage of virtual video platforms across all industries. This type of communication will likely become a "new normal" moving forward and global leadership development professionals will need to adapt to that.

platforms make coaching for global leaders far more convenient and accessible, creating greater opportunity to interact with leaders no matter their location. I have noticed a marked increase in video-based leadership coaching in my own practice and find that the video technology has become more stable and produces high quality audiovisual experiences. It can take some time for a participant to develop comfort with the camera, but in my experience, most leaders move quickly away from phone-based conversations in favor of the higher degree of connection and engagement that comes from a visual interface. That said, a coach needs to be mindful of their visual environment and how they show up on camera. This involves the background surroundings so that they appear professional along with adequate lighting to avoid what I call "facial shadows." This can be particularly tricky to manage when scheduling calls in distant time zones when it's either late at night or before dawn. There have been numerous occasions when I'm adjusting lamps given lack of natural light so that I don't appear to be hovering in a black hole. It's also essential to accept and manage the level of ambiguity that comes with virtual platform use in different global regions. Several of the Indian and Brazilian leaders I work with can experience power disruption and have connectivity issues due to infrastructure challenges, especially if there is high user volume or an extreme weather event like monsoonal rains. One needs to be agile and have a backup technology platform as well as equipment, but rescheduling due to unforeseen technical challenges is a reality. Despite this, the flexibility and convenience of video coaching will continue to drive its usage and popularity in the field.

One client example, from a Global 100 medical devices and pharmaceutical company, illustrates many of the dynamics I've been discussing and could be considered a leading practice. The company provides a developmental assignment opportunity ranging from a year to two years in order to develop greater global leadership capability. Given this company has a strong headquarters-centric culture, many leaders who participate are chosen from regions important to the business to gain experience at the US headquarters. US leaders are also sent to key emerging markets on expatriate assignments. Once leaders accept the assignment, they are fitted with a coach. The process of assessing fit is particularly important for the coaching relationship as so much of the success of coaching is driven by the quality of the relationship between coach and coachee. Fit is usually assessed based on the coachee's preferences, i.e., degree of coaching structure, communication style, professional background of the coach, and their experience in the assignment target culture. The coach then administers two assessments – one competency based and the other focused on intercultural work styles. There are three coaching sessions to discuss the results, culminating in an intercultural development plan. The program also involves two stakeholder leaders identified by the coachees; these are often their leaders in the host and home countries. These stakeholders assess the development plan and provide feedback. Once aligned, the coaching commences over time, usually once a month, with check-ins on what is working and what is challenging along with various learning components based on the plan. After six months, there is a mid-point stakeholder meeting wherein the coach interviews the stakeholder leaders to obtain their feedback. The coaching nears its end as the international assignment concludes. At this stage, a continuing action plan is developed in concert with the coach to reflect on the overall assignment experience and map out the future path to better leverage the new skills and knowledge in the home office location upon repatriation.

Another strong example of an organization effectively developing global leaders is a US-based privately held consumer goods company in the Midwest. This company is particularly dedicated to identifying leadership talent for the future, so the majority of participants are from the Millennial generation. This generation is particularly motivated by international travel experiences, so the program also serves as a talent engagement and retention initiative. Candidates for the program are nominated by managers in the various business units, resulting in a class of approximately 30 young emerging leaders. They initially gather for a day of formal training at the company headquarters and complete an online cultural work style assessment. The assessment enables them to learn about their own styles, the styles of their peers, and how various cultural regions important to their business prefer to work and communicate. Having facilitated this program over seven years, I've been able to identify and customize various internal company business cases for the participants based on actual complex intercultural challenges others have faced as global leaders. Using authentic business case scenarios really increases the level of participant engagement and better prepares them for what they may likely face in the company at a global level.

After the training session, participants are assigned an internal mentor in a different cultural region where they do a project-based rotation. It's crucial that the mentors have an in-depth onboarding to the program and receive some coaching about their work style preferences along with the preferences of the mentee. These rotations can be three months to a year, depending on the needs of the business since the emerging leader is assigned to current projects. This increases the motivation and engagement of the regions in hosting these participants because they are active contributors to projects that either increase operational efficiencies or develop new commercial opportunities. During the rotation, the company leverages an internal website where the participants are required to share their experiences on a regular basis. Oftentimes, this involves recording and uploading video narrations. This serves as an effective reflection exercise that contributes to greater self-awareness as well as shared learnings for the participants. Sometimes a featured experience is chosen and highlighted on the company intranet to promote global thinking and learning among the regions. This program is a particularly apt example of how one can develop a global leadership development approach that weaves together talent management strategy, company and country cultures, business needs, technology, and learning systems.

Technology drives so much of the direction of global leadership development these days, whether it's providing access to online assessment instruments, offering platforms for virtual coaching or forums for shared learnings within company programs. It will be interesting to see how the rise of AI and robotics will further shape the global leadership landscape. There are already many self-directed online learning paths available for participants within a variety of virtual learning systems. But given the VUCA nature of global business, it is hard to imagine impactful developmental scenarios without the benefit of regular human interaction with a coach and/or mentor. I feel it is ultimately the coaching process over time that truly helps global leaders manage and contextualize the challenging and complex experiences they encounter when living and working in different cultural environments and leading highly diverse multicultural teams.

REFLECTIONS ON DEVELOPING A GLOBAL LEADERSHIP COURSE

Davina Vora

ABSTRACT

This article provides some reflections on developing a global leadership course at a public, regional, US university. Considerations for developing such a course are provided. Specifically, issues such as level and format of the class, course philosophy, and assignments and exercises are discussed—along with suggestions, recommendations, and lessons learned. This article may be helpful for individuals who are considering developing a course or module on global leadership.

Keywords: Teaching global leadership; global leadership skill development; global leadership course development; course design; teaching methods; pedagogy; global leadership exercises

INTRODUCTION

The need for global leadership skills is well known. For example, the 2013 World Economic Forum's "Global Agenda Outlook" stated that global leadership was one of the 10 biggest challenges in the world, and a study by McKinsey noted the importance of cultural proficiency among leaders for global success (Maznevski, Stahl, & Mendenhall, 2013; McKinsey, 2012; World Economic Forum, 2013). Related, there is a talent shortage of global leaders, which is impacting firms' global initiatives (DDI, 2015; PWC, 2012). About 44% of surveyed CEOs mentioned lack of availability of key skills as a reason they were unable to pursue market opportunities (PWC, 2019). Furthermore, global leadership skills are relevant for any leader—not just those working in an international context. For example, research on leadership has highlighted the importance of influencing others, making ethical decisions, and leading change (e.g., Bass & Steidlmeier, 1999; Canterino, Cirella, Piccoli, & Shani, 2020;

Advances in Global Leadership, Volume 13, 243–259
ISSN: 1535-1203/doi:10.1108/S1535-120320200000013009

Fischer, Dietz, & Antonakis, 2017), which are three global leadership competencies (Bird, 2018; Bird & Osland, 2004). Similarly, the global leadership competencies of spanning organizational boundaries (e.g., across different functional areas or departments) and having strong interpersonal, team building, and cross-cultural skills (Bird, 2018; Bird & Osland, 2004) are vital for leading in today's business environment characterized by high levels of diversity (Dahlin, Weingart, & Hinds, 2005; Milliken & Martins, 1996; Pieterse, van Knippenberg, & Dierendonck, 2013).

Considering the importance of global leadership, we might expect a plethora of classes and programs at a wide range of universities. However, simply glancing at business school curricula at various universities reveals this is not the case. There may be several reasons for limited global leadership courses, such as lack of familiarity with global leadership, lack of awareness of the need for global leaders, lack of institutional support, or concern for how to develop such a course. The purpose of this article is to share my experience and considerations in developing a global leadership course. While some points may seem basic to any course, my hope is that sharing my experience may spur others to develop courses or modules related to global leadership.

Context

It may be helpful to provide some background on my institution and general environment. The State University of New York at New Paltz (SUNY New Paltz) is a public, regional, and comprehensive university located in a small town about 90 miles from New York City. There are about 6,500 undergraduate students and 1,000 graduate students (New Paltz at a glance, n.d.), mostly from New York state, primarily from nearby towns and the New York City metropolitan region. The School of Business has about 700 undergraduate and 100 MBA students. Roughly half the undergraduate students are transfer students. MBAs are a mix of full-time students continuing directly from our undergraduate programs and part-time students with full-time employment. The School of Business faculty is relatively small, with about 30 full-time faculty, 2 of whom are in the field of international business. International business is among the smaller majors, and it is challenging to find international-oriented internships for our students. Most companies in the area are small, local businesses focused on the New York region. In terms of resources, as a public university in the United States, SUNY New Paltz is facing declining state support and it can be challenging to find financial resources for new endeavors.

Some of these factors may make you wonder why I decided to develop a global leadership course. There were several reasons. First, I have been interested in global leadership for several years and had previously attended several conference sessions about global leadership. I believe the development of global leadership skills is important. This is not simply a personal opinion, but it is supported by research suggesting its value for companies (e.g., DDI, 2015; Maznevski et al., 2013; McKinsey, 2012; PWC, 2012; World Economic Forum, 2013) as well as links to characteristics of leaders in the traditional leadership literature (e.g., Bass & Steidlmeier, 1999; House & Aditya, 1997). Second, I had included aspects of global leadership development in other courses and thought a full-blown course would be interesting to and benefit our students. It would not only help those hoping to work internationally, but also those working in a highly diverse workforce. Third, the Dean of the School of Business was enthusiastic about adding such a course. She recognized that developing our students' global leadership skills could improve their effectiveness in the workplace and provided me with the resources needed to do so. She supported my attendance at a GLLab session at San Jose State University to learn more about teaching global leadership and was flexible in reallocating faculty to enable this course to occur. So, the timing seemed right to try to develop a global leadership course. That led to several considerations in developing the course, which may be relevant to those working at regional, teaching-oriented universities with limited resources whose students tend to work domestically, yet still can benefit from global leadership development.

CONSIDERATIONS

Level and Format

One of the first questions that arose was whether to offer a global leadership course at the undergraduate or graduate level. The main advantage of teaching such a course at the undergraduate level was a larger pool of students and the potential to add this as a "track" to our management and/or international business majors, which could in turn attract more students. On the other hand, global leadership skills are high level in nature, and associated exercises and assignments as well as the textbook seemed better suited for graduate students. In addition, our graduate classes are limited to 25 (vs. 50 for undergraduate students) and thus are better suited to individual-level feedback important for global leadership development. Furthermore, the course could potentially spur interest and thus enrollment in our graduate programs. In the end, I decided to offer the course at the graduate level. This was the right decision for me because I believe our undergraduate students would have found some components of the course overly challenging.

With regard to format, many of our graduate courses are offered online. However, I wanted students to benefit from in-class exercises and build camaraderie with each other, as well as to get a sense of their reaction to different aspects of the course in person. Therefore, I offered the course as a seated, in-person class that met once a week for the duration of the 15-week semester. Students did indeed develop friendships with one another, and I found it easy to ask them directly about their views (positive and negative) of aspects of the course. In addition, about half of the class had international experience, and they organically brought up points that added greatly to the discussion.

Course Philosophy and Design

The entire philosophy of the course was built around global leadership development. The primary goal of the course was to develop global leadership skills, with the additional goal of increasing students' knowledge of culture, cross-cultural effectiveness, methods to lead effectively in diverse contexts, and processes helpful for developing innovative solutions to global issues. These goals were used as the basis of developing course components. Furthermore, backward design principles (Wiggins & McTighe, 2005) were used in designing the course. Specific skills and content areas for proficiency were identified; then considerations for ways to assess them were considered; and finally topics, assignments, and exercises were selected to develop global leadership knowledge and skills, ordered in a logical way for scaffolding, with learning goals and the rationale for activities being shared with students (Childre, Sands, & Pope, 2009; Jones, Vermette, & Jones, 2009; Wiggins & McTighe, 2005).

In striving to follow best practices for developing global leadership skills, I used a combination of didactic and experiential methods (e.g., Birnbaum, 1984; Warkentin, 2017). Lectures, readings, and group discussions were the main didactic components to emphasize theory and content knowledge, while experiential exercises along with reflection and discussion were used to try to develop skills per common practice (e.g., Birnbaum, 1984; Dennison, 2005; Warkentin, 2017). As most educators are familiar with didactic learning experiences and experiential learning is vital for global leadership development (Herd, Cumberland, Lovely III, & Bird, 2019; Oddou & Mendenhall, 2018), I focus on the latter in this article.

Given the importance of experiential learning for developing global leadership skills (Herd et al., 2019; Oddou & Mendenhall, 2018), I designed class assignments and activities to provide concrete experiences for students to become aware of global leadership competencies in general and in themselves, reflect on these experiences, and grow. Drawing upon the global leadership expertise development (GLED) model (Osland & Bird, 2018), I planned to include assessments of individual characteristics, provide cultural exposure and global education, and include assignments in multicultural teams that worked on a global problem. My hope was that these activities would develop students' global leadership expertise in terms of cognitive processes like expert decision-making, global knowledge, intercultural competence, and global organizing expertise per the GLED model (Osland & Bird, 2018).

I also used the pyramid model of global leadership (Bird & Osland, 2004) in designing the course. Per the model, I wished for students to gain global knowledge, assess their threshold traits and attitudes and orientation, and develop interpersonal and system skills. Indeed, I explained to students how our semester-long activities were designed to assess and improve these skills and abilities.

In addition, I designed major assignments to tap into the main content domains of global leadership as outlined by Bird (2018): business and organizational acumen, managing people and relationships, and managing self. While there are several frameworks and lists of global leader competencies (e.g., Bird, Mendenhall, Stevens, & Oddou, 2010; Jokinen, 2005), in my view Bird's (2018) captured major components across frameworks in a clear and concise way. This made it easier for me to consider what types of assignments to include, as well as to explain to students how our assignments were designed to develop these global leadership competencies.

Assignments

The first assignment was designed to help students better understand themselves, how they relate to others, and ways they could better interact with others. It drew upon cognitive-behavioral therapy principles of increasing self-awareness and trying to enact changes in thoughts and behaviors, applying these principles to management education in terms of global leadership development per Mendenhall and colleagues' suggestion (Mendenhall, Arnardottir, Oddou, & Burke, 2013). Consistent with the first step in cognitive-behavioral therapy, students took a variety of assessments to better understand their strengths and weaknesses (Mendenhall et al., 2013; Osland, Dunn-Jensen, Nam, & Wells, 2017). While a number of universities have the resources for a global leadership assessment center, enabling staff to provide students with personalized feedback to several assessments (e.g., see Herd et al., 2019; Lane, Bird, & Athanassiou, 2017; Osland et al., 2017), this was not the case at my institution. I would be the point-person for all assessments. In addition, students generally have limited financial resources, so it was important to keep costs down. Therefore, I selected a few low cost or free assessments that were available online. These included the Big Five personality test, a work styles test similar to the Myers-Briggs Type Indicator®, a cultural values assessment with Globe-Smart® (Aperian), and the Kozai Group's Intercultural Effectiveness Survey (IES) bundled by Aperian. When deciding which assessments to use, faculty may wish to consider the financial resources of students, goals of the course, and differences among global leadership assessments (see Bird & Stevens, 2018 for a summary of several assessments).

After students completed these assessments, we briefly reviewed the aspects of the different assessments in class. In addition, students discussed their results in their social innovation project groups (discussed later in this article), developing and submitting an action plan for managing differences among group members. The group-level action plan was designed to help students reflect on themselves, group member differences, and ways to manage people and relationships. On the positive side, these assessments and the group action plan assignment seemed to help students reflect and provide a basis for changing behaviors to benefit the group. However, on the negative side, several groups were fairly superficial in their analysis and only included a few differences (e.g., personality, but not culture). It may be helpful to emphasize that all major differences among group members should be addressed. To ensure a high level of diversity in personalities, work styles, and cultures, it also might be worthwhile to assign groups (rather than allowing students to select their teammates).

The first major assignment was a personal development plan project that was completed throughout the semester. First, students selected one or two of the low-scoring intercultural effectiveness competencies (from their IES assessment results) that they wished to work on. Next, they created a personal development plan that involved specific activities being completed at least once every two weeks to develop these competencies, and they submitted periodic progress reports in class on their activities. I provided individual feedback to students regarding their plans to ensure their activities tapped into the targeted competency and were measurable, as well as feedback on their periodic progress reports and their final report (see also Osland et al., 2017 for a more detailed description of components of this project). For the final report, students included key learnings, reflections about fulfilling their plan, and takeaways from the project, as well as post-test IES scores to show whether or not their competencies improved and how they could improve their competencies in the future. Thus, consistent with the four-phased approach for developing students' cross-cultural competencies using the principles of cognitive-behavioral therapy whereby (1) cross-cultural competencies are assessed and (2) methods to develop these competencies in a domestic setting were used (3) within an academic period and (4) were individuated for self-directed competency development (Mendenhall et al., 2013), students spent an entire semester developing intercultural skills within their home country using self-directed methods that also included individualized feedback. This assignment also fit into the "managing self" and "managing people and relationships" competencies (Bird, 2018), as students developed their own character and resilience, along with skills associated with cross-cultural communication and interpersonal skills through fulfilling this plan. Taking the same IES assessment at the end of the semester also provided useful information on their potential growth. Although I made clear that score changes were not necessary and students were not graded on improvements, the reflection on why or why not their scores changed—as well as on the experience itself—can improve self-learning.

Personal development plan projects are vital for global leadership development and the basis of any global leadership course (e.g., see Lane et al., 2017; Mendenhall et al., 2013; Osland et al., 2017). In addition, such plans can be fulfilled even in homogeneous, domestic environments, so they can benefit students wherever they are located. Therefore, I encourage anyone developing a global leadership course to have such a project. That being said, resources can influence how to provide feedback on the assessments and personal development plans. As we do not have a global leadership assessment center, I was responsible for providing all student feedback. When I have done this personal development plan project as part of fairly large (30–40 student) undergraduate international management classes, it took several hours to review and individually meet with students individually to develop their plans. At times it required two to three meetings before their plans were actionable, with most meetings lasting 15–30 minutes. This leads to a few suggestions for efficiently and effectively providing individualized feedback.

To reduce repetition and work for both students and faculty, I recommend students develop a preliminary draft of their personal development plan for class discussion purposes and then a "final" version of their personal development plan to be graded in the class period after class discussion. To review the competencies and methods to develop them, for large classes, I would encourage faculty to spend class time reviewing students' preliminary plans for each competency. For example, faculty could spend 30 minutes of class discussing and critiquing students' plans for improving the "world orientation" competency. During these 30 minutes, students who do not plan to develop this competency could discuss their plans for developing other competencies with each other in pairs or small groups. After 30 minutes on the "world orientation" competency, faculty could spend the next 30 minutes on the next competency, eventually covering all competencies to help students have a stronger final plan by listening to each other's ideas and hearing faculty feedback. For smaller classes, all students' plans could be discussed in class. For my MBA global leadership class, students preferred to stay together as a full class to hear everyone's plans. So, we went through each competency in class, having all students hear each other's ideas for improving each competency and providing feedback to one other about the plan (as well as hearing my perspective). This way, students received personalized feedback from both me and their peers. This feedback was then used to develop a "final" personal development plan, which was graded and then acted upon (after being approved) for the rest of the semester. Note that, similar to Lane et al. (2017), students could change their plans during the semester if they believed a different activity would better suit them for developing a competency. Students simply needed to get my approval before changing their plan. This has rarely happened, but it is helpful to mention because the goal is for students to develop these competencies, not to fulfill certain tactics per se.

The second major assignment was a social innovation project. This was modeled after Joyce Osland's project at San Jose State University (see Osland et al., 2017 and Osland & Lester, 2020 for more details) and was designed to tap into the "business and organizational acumen" as well as "managing people and relationships" global leadership competencies (Bird, 2018). For this assignment, students developed a solution to a global problem. Students were given free rein to select an issue and consider solutions, which led to a variety of projects. For instance, in my class, one group addressed the issue of poverty in a nearby town through developing a voucher system for various services in collaboration with a number of local businesses. Another group developed an online app to encourage individuals to reduce pollution by providing information on where to recycle as well as a profile to track their progress in reducing their carbon footprint and share this on social media.

There were several steps to the social innovation project. First, students worked with their teams to develop group processes, completing a team charter that concerned their goals, processes, and plan for completing the assignment. Second, students wrote a report regarding how culture, personality, and work styles influenced the team as well as an action plan for resolving such differences (discussed earlier in the paragraph on assessments). Third, students determined the global issue they wanted to focus on and developed solutions for it. About a month into the semester, students submitted a preliminary proposal report in which they discussed a global issue that needs to be resolved, providing general information about issues surrounding the problem along with preliminary ideas for solutions. These reports were shared with everyone in the class, and every student had a week to complete a feedback form about other groups' proposals stating one to two positive aspects, two to three critical comments about what could be improved, two to three actionable suggestions to improve the project, one to two questions, and any other comments or questions. A week after the proposals were submitted, groups gave a 5–7 minute proposal presentation, followed by a question–answer period regarding both the presentation and groups' written proposals. The completed student feedback forms were given to every group after the proposal presentations so the feedback could be used to improve upon groups' social innovation projects. On the last day of class, groups submitted their final social innovation project report that outlined the global issue, issues surrounding the problem, and the group's solution to the problem. The solution needed to include information on potential users, market size, potential benefit to the users, uniqueness and competitiveness of the idea, and its feasibility. Groups also gave a final presentation to the class on their social innovation project.

The social innovation project worked well, both as a project where students needed to work together and as a way to consider global issues from a business perspective. In addition, students appreciated the detailed feedback they received from other students (and me) in their preliminary reports and presentations. Several students mentioned that this feedback was helpful in thinking about other issues in their reports. On the other hand, there were some ways in which this assignment could be improved. Perhaps easiest, I had mentioned that they should use the design thinking approach and methods we used in class to consider the issue and develop solutions. Few groups adopted this approach, perhaps not realizing how it might help them innovate. In the future, I plan to be more explicit about the relevance of design thinking principles to their social innovation projects, requiring them to report what design thinking methods they used and why. Related, several students seemed to be hesitant to approach people they were targeting—either to learn about their needs or to obtain feedback about their proposed solutions. While some of this relates to the global issue being addressed, it might be beneficial to spend class time discussing ways to safely and appropriately approach people for this purpose. Students could also be encouraged to spend "a day in the life" of the target group, following and observing the group to learn more about needs, desires, and ideal solutions (Think Design Collaborative, 2020).

Students also mentioned they found the social innovation project's open-ended nature daunting and were not convinced their innovations could help to solve a global problem. In the future, I might have a theme for their social innovation project (instead of asking them to select a topic of interest). We could review the UN sustainable development goals (Sustainable Development Goals, n.d.) and have the class select an issue for the semester. Alternatively, it might be helpful to collaborate with a local nonprofit organization, having the organization provide a presentation on issues it tries to solve as well as work with students to facilitate conversations about users' needs and potential solutions. In addition, similar to Osland and Lester (2020), it might be helpful to have students present their projects to organizations who are working on these issues and/or other entrepreneurial ventures instead of only their classmates. Feedback from these organizations may help to improve students' business and organizational acumen.

The third major assignment was a cultural immersion experience. This was based on a similar assignment (e.g., Lane et al., 2017; Maznevski, 2019; Osland et al., 2017) to try to improve both the "managing self" and the "managing people and relationships" competencies (Bird, 2018). For this assignment, students selected an unfamiliar cultural setting, which did not necessarily mean national or ethnic culture. Culture was interpreted broadly and included any group with which the student was unfamiliar. This could be cultural, ethnic, or religious groups, the blind or deaf community, a nursing home, homeless or women's shelters, a commune, or any subculture. Students were expected to directly interact with the culture, being a participant-observer for 2–5 hours while being engaged in a typical activity associated with the culture. The purpose of the assignment was for them to experience entering and interacting with a different culture directly, as well as to reflect on this experience. As such, it was designed to try to culturally "displace" students, putting them in a situation where their own values, attitudes, beliefs, and behavioral norms likely misaligned with others. This assignment had two parts. The first was a pre-entry report where students stated the culture they chose and why, what they expected to see and experience, and their plan for observing and participating in the culture. I provided feedback on their plan, ensuring that it was feasible, safe, and fit the goals of the assignment. The second was a post-entry report where students described the experience and reflected on their feelings, lessons learned, confirmed expectations or surprising aspects, and how the experience related to course material.

The cultural immersion experience is ideal in several ways. It provides students with a cross-cultural experience without leaving the country (Mendenhall et al., 2013) and requires preparation and reflection, which can help to build cross-cultural competence. Students reported learning and growing from this experience, and some seemed to truly change their perspective on the group they visited. However, the quality of the experience seemed to vary based on the length of time and type of experience. For example, one student attended a religious ceremony, but did not know much about the ceremony in advance and only asked a few questions of other participants. In contrast, another student visited a homeless shelter and spent the entire day there as a volunteer, providing food, talking with other volunteers, and interacting with the homeless. The second student had a much richer and stronger experience. In the future, I may require a longer time period (e.g., 5–10 hours), perhaps also including some kind of direct interaction with others (instead of simply "participating" as in a religious ceremony) to ensure greater learning. It may also be helpful to provide some training in ethnography, so students are more prepared for their role as participant-observers. Similarly, I may consider asking students to interview people familiar with the culture (either during their visit or at another time) and provide them with guidelines (e.g., per Osland et al., 2017). In addition, because some students had issues gaining entry within the timeframe, I may require an intermediary assignment where students provide documentation of permission to enter or verification that they may come on certain dates.

The final assignment was for students to give a presentation about a global leader. I developed this assignment based on mid-semester feedback where some students recommended including examples and case studies about global leaders. To get different perspectives on global leadership and reinforce learning about the topic, students were asked to think about people they consider global leaders, including current or recent historical (i.e., post-1950s) politicians, businesspeople, or others. Students then developed a short presentation about a global leader that stated who the person was, why they considered the person a global leader, how the person's characteristics fit class discussion about global leadership (e.g., application of framework, competencies shown), and two to three main "takeaways" about effective global leadership based on the individual. Students could either work individually or in pairs—but if they worked in pairs, they needed to select one political and one nonpolitical leader.

Honestly, I was surprised by the level of positive responses I received for this assignment. It was an additional assignment, so a few students initially expressed their frustration at having another assignment at the end of the semester. However, after the presentations, the consensus was that this was an excellent assignment. They appreciated doing research on actual global leaders, seemed to recognize how their view of global leaders fit our class discussion throughout the semester, and enjoyed hearing about different global leaders from other students. While this assignment seems better suited to understanding the content domain of global leadership rather than developing global leadership skills, I think it is helpful for students to recognize role models as well as reinforce learning of the material. Furthermore, considering that role models have been found to influence individual behavior per social learning theory (e.g., Brown & Treviño, 2014), such an assignment could also serve to facilitate global leadership behaviors.

In the future, I may ask students to give me 2–3 names of people they are considering presenting about to ensure that no leaders are presented more than once and to try to have more gender or other diversity in leader selections. I also may be a bit more specific in requesting a certain number of links to class concepts, terms, and frameworks because some students focused only on the definition of global leadership, while others delved more deeply into different frameworks. Another twist on the assignment would be to ask students to consider a global leader at the beginning of the semester to spur their thinking about global leadership skills. They might present or write about this person initially. Then, at the end of the semester they could reflect more deeply on this person's global leadership skills, applying course material as relevant.

Exercises

Given that experiential learning provides the greatest potential for global leadership competency development (Oddou & Mendenhall, 2018), I used several experiential exercises in my global leadership class. Although it was beyond the scope of the class to provide international assignments and travel, both formal (e.g., lecture) and developmental learning activities were used (Oddou & Mendenhall, 2018). Specifically, the class engaged in several role-playing exercises. For example, students participated in the Bafa Bafa cultural role-playing simulation, alpha-beta negotiation, Tip of the Iceberg online global collaboration simulation (Neeley, 2017), and Aracruz multi-stakeholder exercise (Reade, Todd, Osland, & Osland, 2008). These activities mimic intercultural experiences, providing insight into how it feels to enter another culture, challenges of negotiating with other cultures, language and coordination issues in global teams, and developing consensus through mutual understanding and compromise with diverse stakeholders in an international context. Apart from students enjoying a nontraditional teaching format, they recognized the challenges associated with global leadership and could work on trying to develop global leadership skills, albeit in a classroom setting.

While I plan to continue using all these exercises in the future, there were some challenges. First, for several of these exercises I needed extra rooms and at least one assistant. Faculty considering using these exercises should consider the resources available at their institution. There happened to be open classrooms during my class time, I had a graduate assistant who could help facilitate when needed, and I was able to recruit another student to help when needed. Second, some exercises required a certain number of participants. For example, the Tip of the Iceberg online simulation (Neeley, 2017) requires a minimum of 4, but not 6, 7, or 11 participants for the simulation to work (Neeley, 2018). Faculty may need to find additional students to volunteer to participate (and pay their simulation fee) if class size or attendance on the day of the simulation is an issue.

LESSONS LEARNED AND NEXT STEPS

Overall, the course was a success. The students said they recognized the real-world application of the course and believed their experiences would help them in the future. However, there are some modifications I plan to make the next time I teach this course. Table 1 summarizes the different components of the class, along with recommendations.

In addition to previously discussed suggestions, I plan to make a few other changes. First, I would advertise this course. As it is an elective and this was the first time the course was offered at my institution, most students did not know what the course entailed. Putting flyers in the School of Business, using online media to advertise the course, and reaching out to local businesses that may have some international connections could be useful. Faculty working in smaller universities with limited enrollments and/or awareness of global leadership may find this beneficial as well.

Table 1. Summary of Global Leadership Course Components, Outcomes, and Recommendations.

Parameter	Initial Choice	Outcome	Recommendations for Future	Considerations for Others
Teaching mode	Weekly in-class sessions over a 15-week semester	Pros: • Effective in developing a cohesive class • Mix of in-class exercises, lecture, and discussion maintained engagement throughout the semester Cons: • Relevant exercises spread over weeks delayed the start of some assignments • Limited registration of full-time employees	Hybrid • Two weekends of intense in-person exercises toward the beginning of the course to enable quicker start on major assignments while building class cohesiveness early on • Online, asynchronous lectures, student presentations, and discussions to allow flexibility and minimize in-class lecture	• Nature of student body (e.g., full-time employees vs. full-time students) • Internet connectivity of students • Ability to offer hybrid courses (e.g., technology, space, university expectations)
Assessments	Personality test, work styles test, GlobeSmart®, IES	Pros: • Mix of assessments led to broad-based awareness of different facets of self • Overall inexpensive choices Cons: • IES is not as comprehensive as GCI • No cultural knowledge assessment	• Use GCI instead of IES if not cost-prohibitive • Include a cultural knowledge assessment	• Course goals (e.g., focus on one area like culture vs. several aspects) • Student level (e.g., IES is simpler and well-suited to undergraduate students) • Cost
Assignments	Personal development plan, social innovation project, cultural immersion experience, global leader presentation	Pros: • Variety (e.g., individual and group, experiential and research-oriented) • Tapped into different leadership competencies	• Adapt personal development plan feedback session based on class size • For social innovation project, be clear on the need to use design thinking principles, develop a	• Course goals • Course length (e.g., personal development plans may be less effective for skill development in a 4-week module than in a longer 15-week course)

		Pros/Cons	Recommendations	Considerations
		Cons: • Students desired more structure at times (e.g., social innovation project) • Requirements not specific enough to consistently fulfill learning objectives (e.g., cultural immersion experience)	theme for projects with contacts, and have them present their ideas to businesspeople • Require the cultural immersion experience to include direct interaction for a longer period of time. Provide ethnography training and guidelines • Request in advance the names of global leaders to be presented and specify the number of links to class concepts	• Class size • Student initiative (e.g., desire for guidance on ideas for social innovation project vs. develop on their own) • Student experience (e.g., level of need for ethnographic training)
In-class exercises	Bafa Bafa, alpha-beta negotiation, Tip of the Iceberg, The Owl, Aracruz multi-stakeholder exercise	Pros: • Interactive, engaging, and experiential in nature • Designed to misalign one's own values and norms with others and to develop cross-cultural competence Cons: • Several are resource-intensive in terms of time and need for facilitators	• Continue to use these exercises, planning in advance for resource needs	• Course goals and topics • Resources (e.g., space, facilitator availability) • Class length (e.g., 1 hour vs. 3 hours) • Class size (e.g., Tip of Iceberg has participant number requirements)
Readings	Mainly book chapters, some practitioner journal articles	Pros: • Relevant information • Fairly comprehensive reviews of topics Cons: • Some chapters were difficult for students to follow due to their length and academic writing style • Some topics not directly relevant to students	• Include more practitioner journal articles • Omit book chapters and topics that are not vital to fulfilling course objectives	• Course goals (e.g., full overview of content vs. focus on a few key content areas and skill development) • Reading level of students • Norms for amount of reading by students • Practical orientation versus theoretical orientation of students

Second, I would change the format of the course to be hybrid. I would organize it such that students would watch a series of short lectures about the material in the first two weeks of class. Then, they would attend two weekends in person at the start of the semester. These in-person sessions, similar to GLLab at San Jose State University, would be devoted to highly interactive simulations and other in-class exercises. Students would have the foundation of knowledge and experience to build upon, as well as personal relationships with one another to share their experiences online in an open way for rest of the semester. By focusing content and experiential exercises in the first few weeks of the semester, students would be on track to work on all their projects for the rest of the semester. They could have an earlier start on their social innovation project, have more time to work on their personal development plans, and plan better for their cultural immersion experience. In addition, the flexibility of having only two weekends in class rather than weekly meetings throughout the semester may attract more full-time employees who may or may not already be enrolled in our MBA program.

Third, I would consider a few other modifications to better suit our student population. Mid-semester, students suggested more articles about topics rather than the textbook, which they found difficult to follow at times. While I believe the Mendenhall et al. (2018) text provides an excellent basis for studying global leadership, I would try to find more practitioner-oriented readings and supplement these with select chapters from the book. In addition, while I believe the assessments were appropriate, I may change some in the future. For example, the longer Global Competencies Inventory (GCI) provides a more fine-tuned assessment of intercultural competence than the IES and may be better suited for MBA students (Osland et al., 2017); depending on price and overall cost of course-related materials for students, I may adopt the GCI instead of the IES. It also would be beneficial to include a general assessment of global knowledge, perhaps similar to the Global Knowledge Quiz or Test (Lane et al., 2017; Osland et al., 2017) to enable students to recognize their level of global knowledge, which is the base of the pyramid of global leadership competencies (Bird & Osland, 2004).

Finally, I might somewhat adjust the conversation in class based on the students' background. Some of my students had international work and travel experience but did not always raise points related to their experience. In the future, I might try to facilitate more sharing of their experiences with the class. The class also included a few short-term international students who were unaware of some sensitivities of Americans (e.g., their social innovation issue was obesity; in their presentation they said, "Americans are obese," citing data, but without realizing that many students would be offended by this statement). While in the end both sides seemed to recognize each other's perspective, in the future I will be more prepared to have an impromptu reflection session.

CONCLUSION

Global leadership competencies are relevant to all leaders, particularly in today's diverse global business environment, yet developing such courses in a public, regional university setting holds not only several challenges, but also opportunities. There is a wealth of resources available, and the global leadership community is extremely supportive and open to sharing their ideas. Students also appreciate the clear real-world application to what they are learning and experiencing. When developing a course, I recommend using backward design principles (Wiggins & McTighe, 2005) along with a combination of didactic and experiential methods (Birnbaum, 1984). It may also be helpful to develop assignments in line with the GLED model (Osland & Bird, 2018) and Bird's (2018) major categories of global leadership competencies: business and organizational acumen, managing people and relationships, and managing self. There are several types of assignments that can develop global leadership competencies, but I found that assessment of several attributes and skills, a personal development plan project, a social innovation project, and a cultural immersion experience were beneficial for such skill development. The experiential learning basis of these assignments is the likely reason for this (Herd et al., 2019). Role-playing and other interactive exercises and activities are also helpful to facilitate global leadership development (Oddou & Mendenhall, 2018), while presentations on global leaders may help students find role models, reinforce knowledge about global leadership, and potentially spur global leader behaviors. Faculty naturally should consider their own goals, institutional context, and resource availability when designing a course, but should recognize that students can develop global leadership skills even in a domestic, regional environment where few students have international business experience.

REFERENCES

Bass, B., & Steidlmeier, P. (1999). Ethics, character, and authentic transformational leadership behavior. *The Leadership Quarterly*, *10*(2), 181–218. doi:10.1016/S1048-9843(99)00016-8.

Bird, A. (2018). Mapping the content domain of global leadership competencies. In M. Mendenhall, J. Osland, A. Bird, G. Oddou, M. Stevens, M. Maznevski, & G. Stahl (Eds.), *Global leadership: Research, practice, and development* (3rd Ed., pp. 119–142). New York, NY: Routledge Publishing.

Bird, A., Mendenhall, M., Stevens, M., & Oddou, G. (2010). Defining the content domain of intercultural competence for global leaders. *Journal of Managerial Psychology*, *25*(8), 810–828. doi: 10.1108/02683941011089107.

Bird, A., & Osland, J. (2004). Global competencies: An introduction. In H. Lane, M. Maznevski, M. Mendenhall, & J. McNett (Eds.), *Handbook of global management* (pp. 57–80). Oxford: Blackwell Publishing.

Bird, A., & Stevens, M. (2018). Assessing global leadership competencies. In M. Mendenhall, J. Osland, A. Bird, G. Oddou, M. Stevens, M. Maznevski, & G. Stahl (Eds.), *Global leadership: Research, practice, and development* (3rd Ed., pp. 143–175). New York, NY: Routledge Publishing.

Birnbaum, M. (1984). The integration of didactic and experiential learning in the teaching of group work. *Journal of Education for Social Work*, *20*, 50–58.

Brown, M., & Treviño, L. (2014). Do role models matter? An investigation of role modeling as an antecedent of perceived ethical leadership. *Journal of Business Ethics*, *122*(4), 587–598. doi: 10.1007/s10551-013-1769-0

Canterino, F., Cirella, S., Piccoli, B., & Shani, A. (2020). Leadership and change mobilization: The mediating role of distributed leadership. *Journal of Business Research*, *108*, 42–51. doi:10.1016/j.jbusres.2019.09.052.

Childre, A., Sands, J., & Pope, S. (2009). Backward design. *Teaching Exceptional Children, 41*(5), 6–14.

Dahlin, K., Weingart, L., & Hinds, P. (2005). Team diversity and information use. *Academy of Management Journal, 48*(6), 1107–1123. doi:10.5465/AMJ.2005.19573112.

DDI. (2015). *Global leadership forecast 2014-2015*. Development Dimension International. Retrieved from https://media.ddiworld.com/research/global-leadership-forecast-2014-2015_tr_ddi.pdf. Accessed on 15 August, 2020.

Dennison, S. (2005). Enhancing the integration of group theory with practice: A five-part teaching strategy. *Journal of Baccalaureate Social Work, 10*(2), 53–68.

Fischer, D., Dietz, J., & Antonakis, J. (2017). Leadership process models: A review and synthesis. *Journal of Management, 43*(6), 1726–1753. doi:10.1177/0149206316682830.

Herd, A., Cumberland, D., Lovely III, W., & Bird, A. (2019). The use of assessment center methodology to develop students' global leadership competencies: A conceptual framework and applied example. In J. Osland, M. Mendenhall, & M. Li (Eds.), *Advances in global leadership* (Vol. 11, pp. 175–196). Bingley: Emerald Publishing Limited. doi: 10.1108/S1535-120320180000011006

House, R., & Aditya, R. (1997). The social scientific study of leadership: Quo vadis?. *Journal of Management, 23*(3), 409–473. doi:10.1177/014920639702300306.

Jokinen, T. (2005). Global leadership competencies: A review and discussion. *Journal of European Industrial Training, 29*(3), 199–216. doi:10.1108/03090590510591085.

Jones, K., Vermette, P., & Jones, J. (2009). An integration of "backwards planning" unit design with the "two-step" lesson planning framework. *Education, 130*(2, Winter), 357–360.

Lane, H., Bird, A., & Athanassiou, N. (2017). Translating theory into practice: Developing global leaders through undergraduate experiential education. In J. Osland, M. Li, & M. Mendenhall (Eds.), *Advances in global leadership* (Vol. 10, pp. 193–220). Bingley: Emerald Publishing Limited. doi:10.1108/S1535-120320170000010011

Maznevski, M. (2019). Cross-cultural immersion fieldwork project. In R. Nielsen & J. Osland (Organizers), *Best practices for teaching global leadership*. Panel conducted at the Academy of International Business annual conference, Copenhagen.

Maznevski, M., Stahl, G., & Mendenhall, M. (2013). Thematic issue: Towards an integration of global leadership practice and scholarship: Repairing disconnects and heightening mutual under-standing – Introduction. *European Journal of International Management, 7*(5), 493–500.

McKinsey. (2012). McKinsey global survey results: Managing at a global scale. Retrieved from https://www.mckinsey.com/business-functions/organization/our-insights/managing-at-global-scale-mckinsey-global-survey-results. Accessed on 25 January, 2020.

Mendenhall, M., Arnardottir, A., Oddou, G., & Burke, L. (2013). Developing cross-cultural competencies in management education via cognitive-behavior therapy. *The Academy of Management Learning and Education, 12*(3), 436–451. doi: 10.5465/amle.2012.0237

Mendenhall, M., Osland, J., Bird, A., Oddou, G., Stevens, M., Maznevski, M., & Stahl, G. (2018). *Global leadership: Research, practice, and development* (3rd Ed.). New York, NY: Routledge.

Milliken, F., & Martins, L. (1996). Searching for common threads: Understanding the multiple effects of diversity in organizational groups. *Academy of Management Journal, 21*(2), 402–433. doi: 10.5465/AMR.1996.9605060217.

Neeley, T. (2017). *Global collaboration simulation: Tip of the iceberg*. Boston, MA: Harvard Business Publishing.

Neeley, T. (2018). *Teaching note. Global collaboration simulation: Tip of the iceberg*. Boston, MA: Harvard Business Publishing.

New Paltz at a glance. (n.d.). Retrieved from https://www.newpaltz.edu/about/glance.html. Accessed on 25 January, 2020.

Oddou, G., & Mendenhall, M. (2018). Global leadership development: Processes and practices. In M. Mendenhall, J. Osland, A. Bird, G. Oddou, M. Stevens, M. Maznevski, & G. Stahl (Eds.), *Global leadership: Research, practice, and development* (3rd Ed., pp. 229–269). New York, NY: Routledge Publishing.

Osland, J., & Bird, A. (2018). Process models of global leadership development. In M. Mendenhall, J. Osland, A. Bird, G. Oddou, M. Stevens, M. Maznevski, & G. Stahl (Eds.), *Global leadership: Research, practice, and development* (3rd Ed., pp. 179–199). New York, NY: Routledge Publishing.

Osland, J., Dunn-Jensen, L., Nam, K.-A., & Wells, P. (2017). The global leadership advancement center: Developing global leadership expertise in a university setting. In J. Osland, M. Li, & M. Mendenhall (Eds.), *Advances in global leadership* (Vol. 10, pp. 221–249). Bingley: Emerald Publishing Limited. doi: 10.1108/S1535-120320170000010012

Osland, J., & Lester, G. (2020). Developing socially responsible global leaders and making a difference: Global leadership lab social innovation projects. In L. Zander (Ed.), *Research handbook of global leadership: Making a difference* (pp. 250–363). Cheltenham: Edward Elgar.

Pieterse, A., van Knippenberg, D., & Dierendonck, D. (2013). Cultural diversity and team performance: The role of team member goal orientation. *Academy of Management Journal, 56*(3), 782–804. doi:10.5465/amj.2010.0992.

PWC. (2012). Annual Global CEO Survey. Retrieved from https://www.pwc.com/gx/en/ceo-survey/pdf/15th-global-pwc-ceo-survey.pdf. Accessed on 25 January, 2020.

PWC. (2019). 22nd Annual Global CEO Survey. Retrieved from https://www.pwc.com/mu/pwc-22nd-annual-global-ceo-survey-mu.pdf. Accessed on 24 April, 2020.

Reade, C., Todd, A., Osland, A., & Osland, J. (2008). Poverty and the multiple stakeholder challenge for global leaders. *Journal of Management Education, 32*(6), 820–840. doi:10.1177/1052562908317445.

Sustainable Development Goals. (n.d.). Retrieved from https://sustainabledevelopment.un.org/?menu=1300. Accessed on 27 January, 2020.

Think Design Collaborative. (2020). A day in the life. Retrieved from https://think.design/user-design-research/a-day-in-the-life/. Accessed on 24 April, 2020.

Warkentin, B. (2017). Teaching social work with groups: Integrating didactic, experiential, and reflective learning. *Social Work with Groups, 40*(3), 233–243. doi:10.1080/01609513.2015.1124034.

Wiggins, G., & McTighe, J. (2005). *Understanding by design* (2nd Ed.). Alexandria, VA: Association for Supervision and Curriculum Development.

World Economic Forum. (2013). *Global Agenda Outlook, 2013.* Geneva: World Economic Forum. Retrieved from http://www3.weforum.org/docs/AM13/WEF_AM13_Report.pdf. Accessed on 25 January, 2020.

AT THE HEART AND BEYOND: WHAT CAN GLOBAL LEADERSHIP RESEARCHERS LEARN FROM PERSPECTIVES ON THE COVID-19 PANDEMIC?

B. Sebastian Reiche, Mark E. Mendenhall, Betina Szkudlarek and Joyce S. Osland

ABSTRACT

In this concluding chapter, we discuss insights and reflections from our invited contributions on the COVID-19 pandemic and derive areas of meaningful future research to advance the global leadership domain. Specifically, we call for (1) strengthening the link of the global leadership domain with related research fields, (2) expanding our view on what are necessary global leadership competencies, (3) moving beyond individual global leadership toward a more collective and collaborative understanding of the phenomenon, (4) further enhancing the growing field of responsible global leadership, (5) examining the various competing tensions that global leaders need to balance, and (6) engaging in greater reflexivity among global leadership scholars ourselves.

Keywords: Global leadership; pandemic; COVID-19; crisis; future research; global leadership and effectiveness

In our Call for Papers for Volume 13 of *AGL*, we specifically encouraged submissions that would shed light on what other disciplines can contribute to better understand, conceptualize, and develop global leadership. In other words, we

Advances in Global Leadership, Volume 13, 261–282
ISSN: 1535-1203/doi:10.1108/S1535-120320200000013010

aimed to expand from what has been the heart of global leadership research thus far and identify other areas that can help advance our understanding of the phenomenon. Spanning the boundaries of a given field of research, we argued, not only serves to mature a domain further but also situates it within the nomological network of related fields. Importantly, interdisciplinary insights from fields such as anthropology, (intercultural) communication, leadership, linguistics, neuroscience, psychology, political science, international relations and diplomacy, international development, social work, or public health all have the potential to expand the ways scholars operationalize and make sense of such a complex phenomenon as global leadership.

Little did we know that our collective experiences in the first half of 2020 would make this endeavor ever more salient. As COVID-19 spread around the globe in unprecedented pace and severity, leaders in all countries and organizations were put to a test of how to address and cope with a globally interconnected health crisis and its grave social, political, and economic repercussions. As the many essays in this volume demonstrate, global leaders greatly varied in their attitudes, interpretations, and responses to the COVID-19 crisis. Yet, we believe the essays also push the boundaries of our understanding of what global leadership is; collectively, they highlight the very nature of global leadership as an interdisciplinary and transdisciplinary phenomenon that needs to be studied and understood as such, especially during times of crisis.

Thus, what can we glean from the various reflections on global leadership during the COVID-19 pandemic? How do the reflections about, the expectations toward, and the experienced actions of global leaders around the globe inform global leadership research? In this article, we aim to integrate the various essays in order to derive meaningful directions of future research, moving beyond the heart of the global leadership domain. Table 1 summarizes our suggestions for future research that originate from our integrative review.

GLOBAL LEADERSHIP DURING A PANDEMIC: IMPLICATIONS FOR FUTURE RESEARCH

In the following sections, we outline six areas of future research that we believe are particularly promising to advance the global leadership domain. As echoed across our various invited essays, these areas of research demonstrate how as global leadership scholars we can work together to expand our research domain beyond what has become an increasingly maturing core. Specifically, the proposed future research directions involve (1) strengthening the interlinkage of the global leadership domain with related research fields; (2) expanding our view on what might be necessary for global leadership competencies given increased levels of volatility, uncertainty, complexity, and ambiguity (VUCA); (3) moving beyond individual global leadership toward a more collective understanding of how global leadership is enacted; (4) further enhancing the growing field of responsible global leadership (RGL); (5) examining the various competing tensions that global leaders need to balance; and (6) encouraging

Table 1. Future Global Leadership Research Directions Based on COVID-19 Essays.

Area of Research	Specific Suggestions for Future Research
Intersections between global leadership and related research fields	• What attributes does humility in global leaders reflect? How does humility emerge in global leaders and how is it developed? Can it be purposefully trained in prospective global leaders or should it be a selection criterion? • Does humility in global leaders spread via social contagion to decision-makers and wider society and if so, under what conditions? • How do self-effacement and self-aggrandizement communication styles interact with the acceptance and perception of humility in global leaders? • In times of great uncertainty, what messages should global leaders communicate and what communication channels are most effective? • What is the linkage between servant leadership and global leadership? • To what extent does effective global leadership involve creating value for the community and helping subordinates grow and succeed? Are these servant leadership dimensions more important in times of a setting characterized by complex and interconnected problems and uncertainty? • As a result of the COVID-19 pandemic, how did the degree and type of complexity faced by global and domestic leaders change and with what consequences? • In the context of a pandemic, to which extent is complexity the primary differentiator between domestic and global leadership? • To which extent does an environmental jolt like the pandemic foster more collective behavior to address the complexity of the challenge, leading to the understanding of how global leadership is enacted by organizations, communities, and societies? • How can we measure the degree of environmental complexity and the task and relationship complexity faced by global leaders in comparison with domestic leaders? • What insights from related fields could advance our theorizing of complexity in the domain of global leadership?
Global leadership competencies revisited	• What global leadership competencies are needed under extreme conditions, such as those represented by the COVID-19 pandemic? • Which of the competencies identified thus far are more salient in times of crisis, and which are missing altogether from existing conceptualizations? • What can scholars and practitioners do to hone global leadership competencies vital in times of crisis?

Table 1. (*Continued*)

Area of Research	Specific Suggestions for Future Research
	• How can global leadership research and practice help in overcoming collective blindness of global leadership competency? • To what extent is the coexistence of skills and attributes of global leadership lived and developed in corporate practice?
Collective and collaborative global leadership	• What does collective leadership look like in the context of global leadership? How can it be operationalized and assessed? • What would a typology of global leadership roles look like for collective global leadership? • Under which conditions is it preferable to have leaders with similar versus complementary sets of competencies, expertise, and self-concepts? • How can diverse global leaders collaborate most effectively toward inspiring and influencing all constituents? • What are the various facets of global collaboration at the individual global leader level, and what are the most effective ways to develop them? • What defines effective collective global leadership and what are its antecedents? • What does systemic trust look like? Is it an aggregate of interpersonal skills or a subset of what we already call "community building"? And how do we measure and develop systemic trust?
Balancing competing tensions	• How can global leaders balance the various competing tensions during crisis situations such as COVID-19 pandemic and beyond? • What does this mean for global leaders' communicative repertoire? Importantly, what does this mean for how global leaders ought to adapt their message in the face of (cultural) diversity? • How can global leaders quickly and accurately perceive and adapt their understanding of the thoughts and feelings of diverse followers in rapidly changing, high-stakes environment? • What is the role of global leaders' identities in executing the global leadership role that unites rather than divides? • What personal and situational factors facilitate global leaders' dynamic balancing of competing demands and multiple logics simultaneously?
Responsible global leadership	• What are the behaviors that distinguish responsible global leaders from other leaders, and what are the causal variables that underlie those behaviors? • What is the nature and constitution of ethical dilemmas, paradoxes, trade-offs, and opportunities that are inherent in the global context of leading? How can leaders responsibly and ethically deal with those?

Table 1. *(Continued)*

Area of Research	Specific Suggestions for Future Research
	• With both opportunities and challenges created by globalization, how do leaders balance the advantages of globalization with its inevitable costs?
	• Is the concept of responsible global leadership redundant as all effective global leadership needs to be responsible and ethical at its core?
Toward greater reflexivity among global leadership scholars	• To which extent is current global leadership research too focused on global leaders from the largest, most powerful countries?
	• To which extent is global leadership scholarship unwittingly biased toward knowledge originating in the contexts of developed economies and multinational enterprises?
	• How can global leadership scholarship expand the scope of its research focus beyond those contexts to remain relevant for a diverse set of stakeholders and communities?
	• How can our theorizing of global leadership be advanced through examination of extreme cases such as the COVID-19 pandemics?
	• How can historic analyses of leadership action improve our sensemaking of leadership effectiveness?

greater self-reflection among ourselves as global leadership scholars in terms of the questions we ask, the lenses we take, and the conclusions we draw to advance the field.

Intersections between Global Leadership and Related Research Fields

Over the past few years, global leadership scholars have started to invoke other disciplines to advance the field, such as examining global leadership development programs through a critical identity theory lens (Gagnon & Collinson, 2014), studying cosmopolitan capital in British higher education (Friedman, 2018), or bringing insights from related applied fields of work such as diplomacy (Leki, 2019). A particularly relevant and related domain for global leadership is the traditional leadership literature. So far, however, there have been few theoretical and empirical links between both fields despite recent calls for cross-fertilization (e.g., Herman & Zaccaro, 2014).

To this end, the essays submitted to *AGL* 13 hint at interesting insights that can enrich global leadership theorizing. Humility, for example, is an important but underresearched concept in the global leadership studies. Bird and Osland (2004) argued that humility is a passive counterpart to inquisitiveness (Black, Morrison, & Gregersen, 1999) that, unlike arrogance and ethnocentrism, allows oneself to be taught by others. Bird (2018) further conceptualized humility as a facet of inquisitiveness that "does not let pride or self-consciousness interfere with learning." Humility was also identified as a threshold trait in the Pyramid Model of Global Leadership (Osland, 2008) due to the significant amount of learning demanded of global leaders. Thus, the importance of humility surfaces in interview data (e.g., Cseh, Davis, & Khilji, 2013; Holt & Seki, 2012) and is assumed by global leadership scholars, but it has not been studied directly.

In their submissions, Terrell (Chapter 1) emphasized the learning mindset as a necessary precondition for growth and development in responding to crisis, while Adler (Chapter 1) and Taylor (Chapter 1) highlighted the need for honesty and humility and the courage to say, "We don't know." They called for global leaders to deploy competencies similar to those found in the emerging field of humble leadership. This field defines humility as an interpersonal attribute that emerges in social settings and reflects (1) a motivation to view oneself accurately, (2) an appreciation of others' strengths and contributions, and (3) an openness to new ideas and feedback (Owens, Johnson, & Mitchell, 2013). Importantly, evidence suggests that leader humility follows a process of social contagion and can generate humility at the level of the team (Owens & Hekman, 2016), which has important implications for spreading positive leader behaviors at times of great uncertainty and upheaval, when subordinates are looking for specific guidance from their superiors. Drawing from the literature on humble leadership and placing its theory and findings in a global context might reveal interesting and robust theoretical insights for the field of global leadership.

The COVID-19 pandemic also underscores the related concept of servant leaders, who are characterized as "those who focus least on satisfying their own personal needs and most on prioritizing the fulfillment of followers' needs" (Liden, Wayne, Liao, & Meuser, 2014, p. 1434). In particular, some dimensions of servant leadership, such as "creating value for the community" and "helping subordinates grow and succeed," appear highly relevant at a time when, as Girola (Chapter 1) writes from his location at the United Nations, solutions to seemingly intractable problems lie in the community and require a "whole-of-society approach." The very nature of solving complex and interconnected problems is integral to global leadership in all sectors, and we encourage scholars to further develop the linkage between servant leadership and global leadership.

Extreme complexity is frequently cited in both conceptual (e.g., Lane, Maznevski, & Mendenhall, 2004; Reiche, Bird, Mendenhall, & Osland, 2017) and empirical (Gitsham, 2008; Osland, Bird, & Oddou, 2012; Osland, Ehret, & Ruiz, 2017) research on global leaders. Many scholars take for granted that a complex global environment triggers a corresponding need for both cognitive complexity and behavioral flexibility in global leaders. And some argue that the key difference between domestic and global leaders is the degree of task and relationship complexity that delineates their roles (Reiche et al., 2017). The concept of complexity also figures prominently in the COVID-19 essays. For example, Bird (Chapter 1) acknowledges the increased levels of task and relationship complexity on simultaneous fronts for global leaders as a result of the crisis. Yet, the pandemic has also heightened the complexity confronting domestic leaders with more locally bounded roles and responsibilities. What does the increased complexity for the leadership function in general mean? Is the relative difference in complexity maintained between the two types of leaders or has the relative difference decreased? Should we question the assumption that complexity is the sole or the most salient defining attribute of global leadership (see Reiche et al., 2017)? In this regard, Bird, borrowing from strategy and organizational theory, cites Meyer's (1982) compelling research on environmental jolts. This concept could help global leadership scholars better refine the idea of global complexity and its dynamics, which in turn may allow scholars to deliver more nuanced theories and research studies on global leadership dynamics, processes, and best practices.

We also see the COVID-19 crisis as an opportunity to develop novel theory about the global leadership phenomenon itself, an endeavor that we believe holds great promise to advance global leadership research (Reiche, Mendenhall, Szudlarek, & Osland, 2019). Extreme cases often serve as a fertile ground for testing the boundary conditions of our current understanding of a given phenomenon (Eisenhardt, 1989), while also allowing scholars a chance to make sense of potentially ambiguous findings from past research. As such, we would encourage scholars to draw on the context of the pandemic to examine, contrast, and expand our current conceptions and operationalizations of global leadership.

Last but not least, the COVID-19 crisis calls for research that will advance timely and relevant solutions to grand challenges such as pandemics. The field of global leadership, as any other domain of management research, has an opportunity to contribute to this important ambition (George, Howard-Grenville, Joshi, & Tihanyi, 2016). Through careful examination of various leadership styles, approaches, and actions, our contributors raise the importance of advancing global leadership research that will inform practice and translate into strong and effective responses to crisis and beyond. Thus, we encourage global leadership scholars to address not only interesting but also, first and foremost, important research questions (Tihanyi, 2020).

Global Leadership Competencies Revisited

The various essays also point to critical competencies necessary for global leaders to address the health crisis, collaborate globally, overcome the ensuing social and economic difficulties, and help their constituents navigate through uncertain terrain. For example, our essayists highlighted the need for integrity (Bird, Chapter 1), resilience (Shi, Chapter 1), humility and courage (Adler, Chapter 1), self-reflection (Miska and Zilinskaite, Chapter 1), anticipation (Neeley, Chapter 1), empathy (Stahl, Chapter 1), a shared purpose (Bolden, Chapter 1), and the ability to balance dualities and paradoxes (Lee, Chapter 1). At the same time, the reflections also expose a seeming lack of relevant competencies among global leaders. To borrow Levy's (Chapter 1) terminology, rather than possessing a global mindset, why do some global elites apparently suffer from collective blindness, and how can scholars alleviate this problem?

Although social scientists have identified more than 200 global leadership competencies (Bird, 2018), not all of them are as crucial as others in the

COVID-19 crisis. Does the pandemic's heightened volatility, uncertainty, complexity, and ambiguity, the VUCA environment multiplied many times over, require specific competencies? Bolden (Chapter 1) highlights the need for systems thinking, another topic in global leadership that has received limited attention (Cseh et al., 2013; Osland et al., 2017).[1] Moreover, some essential competencies may be missing from current conceptualizations of global leadership. As suggested by Huesing (Chapter 1), there could well be a tension between the traditional skills expected of global leaders and those skills that are more appropriate in times of crisis. However, it is also possible that global leaders implicitly focus too much on *skills*, such as problem solving, to fulfill their roles and make sound decisions. Perhaps, in order to make the right choices, especially during times of turbulence and crisis, leaders first and foremost need the right *values and attitudes*. While global leadership competency models typically comprise both skills and attributes (Bird, 2018; Jokinen, 2005; Lobel, 1990), it would be worthwhile to study in greater depth to what extent the coexistence of skills and attributes is indeed lived and developed in corporate practice. Therefore, how can leaders balance conflicting skills and attributes, such as decisiveness and caution or humility and confidence?

The implications and advice for global leaders that the contributors offered seem, at their core, to require the competency of creativity. As argued by Shi (Chapter 1), creativity for problem solving should be a well-funded priority in global leadership development. Early in the field, Black et al. (1999) identified curiosity as the most important global leadership competency. Similarly, Weick (1993, p. 641) noted that curiosity is what "organizations most need" in times of turbulence and instability because curiosity serves as the raw material to adapt creatively to changing conditions. What then is the relationship between curiosity and creativity? Recent research, for example, suggests that specific curiosity is a state that fuels creativity through idea linking, defined as a cognitive process that involves using elements of early ideas as input for subsequent ideas in a sequential manner, such that one idea is a stepping stone to the next (Hagtvedt, Dossinger, Harrison, & Huang, 2019). But what predicts curiosity in the first place? Is this akin to being wired somewhat like Disney's "Imagineers," employees who work in the company's famous R&D area (Prosperi, 2018), in terms of cognitive complexity and high proclivity to create new structures, ideas, processes, and realities? What constitutes this proclivity to create? We encourage global leadership scholars to look to the creativity literature to draw new insights in terms of relevant competencies and theoretical insights. This is a particularly promising endeavor as the broader literature has mostly studied outcomes of curiosity, including creativity, rather than curiosity itself (Harrison, 2016).

A closely related competency to creativity is what we may call strategic defiance. On the one hand, the contributors and the community at large called for a

---

[1]The concept of VUCA (volatility, uncertainty, complexity, and ambiguity) was introduced by the US Army War College to describe war conditions.

united response to the COVID-19 pandemic. The advice was to follow experts and authorities such as the World Health Organization (WHO). At the same time, some leaders made bold decisions that defied global authorities—decisions that, we now know, saved lives. For example, Australia's Prime Minister defied the WHO's advice and introduced a travel ban for all travelers from China much earlier than any other country did. This travel ban remained in place despite numerous calls by the international community to keep borders open. It remained in place despite huge negative consequences for the Australian economy. This act of defiance has resulted, as of May 17, 2020, in a relatively small number of COVID-19 infections and less than 100 deaths. Experts say that Australia reacted quickly and had good leadership (Megalokonomos, 2020), but their strategic defiance also played a role, whether it was due to luck or other reasons unknown to the public. Yet, the question remains how such acts of defiance relate to the call for unity, the primacy of science, and the general advice to follow experts and authorities. How can global leaders navigate the complex web of stakeholder interests, types of authorities, and sources of information, and what enables them to do so more effectively?

Collective and Collaborative Global Leadership

Another theme that featured prominently among the reflections is the shift in attention from an individual "hero" toward global leadership as a collective and collaborative effort. For example, authors referred to the need "to collectively chart a course toward the future we want" (Courtice, Chapter 1), involve civil society (Girola, Chapter 1), build a shared purpose (Bolden, Chapter 1), foster global collaboration (Lee, Vaiman, & Vaiman, Chapter 1), develop a coordinated response (Boyacigiller, Levy, & Oddou, Chapter 1), develop partnerships (Stahl, Chapter 1), and engage in boundary spanning (Bird, Chapter 1). This shift toward collective and collaborative leadership arises from a number of critical factors. First, leaders have been compelled to access and draw from expertise and insights from a great range of different stakeholders, whether they are medical experts, scientists, politicians, educators, the wider community, and even supranational actors, and bring them together. Second, given the global scale and interconnectedness of the crisis, any suitable solution and strategic course of action proposed by experts, policy makers, and leaders necessarily calls for the engagement, input, and buy-in across all segments of society and needs to provide the psychological safety that one's unique circumstances are understood and accounted for in proposed solutions. Without collective and collaborative leadership, credible and sustainable solutions and courses of actions are unlikely to be achieved and implemented.

Third, a collaborative approach also facilitates a shared sensemaking of the situation, which is an important antecedent to action. Indeed, research has shown that organizational decision-makers' shared sensemaking of an external shock, such as a radical change or a crisis, shapes the various local responses to that shock and determines the extent to which they are aligned with each other (Balogun, Bartunek, & Do, 2015). The lack of broad coordination in the United States to the COVID-19 crisis reflects the lack of shared sensemaking among decision-makers as well as the politicization of the crisis. However, the latter is also true in many countries, including Australia and Germany, where country-wide recommendations are different from those proclaimed by local authorities. In countries like Poland, health representatives were silenced from making public statements. At the global level, collaboration seems to be a bimodal phenomenon. On one end, many scientists are collaborating around the clock to find treatment solutions, tests, and vaccines (Apuzzo & Kirkpatrick, 2020) with no thought of national boundaries. At the other end, many countries have reverted to nationalism and national solutions (Soutphommasane, Chapter 1). Obtaining needed medicine and supplies is framed as a zero-sum game; countries with fewer resources fear that any vaccine that is developed will go to the countries who can pay the most (Kurmanaev, Andreoni, Casado, & Taj, 2020).

Holt and Seki (2012) argued that global leaders are under pressure to both achieve results and collaborate with multiple global stakeholders. International service learning programs were shown to develop collaboration skills in global leadership development (Pless, Maak, & Stahl, 2011). However, in all its forms related to global leadership, global collaboration has surprisingly not received much attention. What are the various facets of global collaboration at the individual global leader level, and what are the most effective ways to develop them? Is global collaboration also a systemic variable, like trust, and if so, how is it created and maintained? What are the antecedents to global collaboration among both global leaders and organizations?

The call for more collective and collaborative leadership highlights the need for more distributed forms of leadership. The sheer enormity of the challenge compels leaders to empower others to take actions, while also giving appropriate credit and recognition for the work that is done. For example, in their reflections, both Nielsen (Chapter 1) and Soutphommasane (Chapter 1) address the need for local responses despite the global interconnectedness of the crisis. Nitin Nohria (2020), quoted in Stahl's (Chapter 1) essay, similarly talks about alternative forms of organizational design and the need to delegate decision authority to lower levels, especially during crises. Trust is a necessary component for such delegation to take place.

Moving beyond global leadership as an individual role involving specific competencies, the pandemic encourages a more collective enactment of global leadership itself. Two examples of collective action related to COVID-19 are the heartwarming actions taken by large groups, such as the night-time singing of quarantined Italians and New York City's (and other cities') daily evening claps and cheers to thank first responders and health care workers as they change shifts.[2] We don't know how these actions began, but they clearly evoke an emotional reaction and a sense of unity. In the global leadership literature, the closest

---

[2]First responders are Emergency Medical Technicians, paramedics, firefighters, and police officers.

approximations to collective enactment may be organizational efforts to create a global mindset (French, 2019; Levy, Beechler, Taylor, & Boyacigiller, 2007) or a global identity (Erez & Gati, 2004) in employees. Trust is usually conceptualized as an interpersonal skill in global leaders (e.g., Hitt, Keats, & Yucel, 2003; Morrison, 2001). Instead, Maznevski (Chapter 1) argues that the COVID-19 response of some global organizations exhibited systemic trust. Modeled by global leaders at the top, trust was collectively enacted throughout their organizations as opposed to asking employees to put their trust in a centralized war room or an individual leader.

A shift toward more collective and collaborative forms of global leadership has a range of implications for future research. For example, research on complex, virtual teams (e.g., Hill & Bartol, 2016; Toegel & Jonsen, 2016) has pointed to the importance of distributing leadership responsibilities to achieve effective collaboration. Global teams, despite their complexity and dispersion, are a fairly bounded context, but how can leadership be effectively distributed when a greater number of relevant stakeholders are involved? We know from the literature on self-managed forms of organizing that autonomy and local, decentralized decision-making only work when paired with alignment, accountability, and cohesion (Lee & Edmondson, 2017). As such, how can cohesion and alignment be achieved when organizational and societal incentives and preferred solutions differ greatly?

Global leadership scholars have primarily focused their conceptualizations on individual global leaders, including their competencies (Bird, 2018), their role requirements (Reiche et al., 2017), their expertise (Osland et al., 2012), or their self-concepts (Herman & Zaccaro, 2014). Taking the global leadership phenomenon to a meso level of analysis has important implications for both theoretical and empirical research in the domain. For example, what would a typology of global leadership roles look like for collectives of global leaders? Under which conditions is it preferable to have leaders with similar versus complementary sets of competencies, expertise, and self-concepts? And how can diverse global leaders collaborate most effectively toward inspiring and influencing all constituents?

Balancing Competing Tensions

The reflections also point to a number of competing tensions that global leaders have experienced and had to balance. A first concerns the tension for unity and distinctiveness. In a way, the COVID-19 pandemic has affected all individuals in terms of their physical and mental well-being, their proclivity for infection, and the resultant economic, political, and social repercussions. For example, Bolden (Chapter 1) notes that at "times like this it is our similarities rather than our differences that define us," while Courtice (Chapter 1) observes that

...if there is any solace to be had, it is that we are facing this unique moment in history together, 7.8 billion of us, going through the same experience at the same time, creating an unprecedented bond between us.

Invoking a sense of belonging and perceived similarity fulfills an important human need irrespective of the context (Baumeister & Leary, 1995), but it is a particularly important ingredient for overcoming situations of stress and turbulence.

And yet, we are not all in the same boat—far from it. In his essay, Girola (Chapter 1) warns that COVID-19 may undermine social cohesion. Indeed, as mentioned earlier, we have witnessed significantly different responses to the virus at the country level—and even within countries. This may be due to leaders' defiance, the significant time lag between actions and their effects, the sheer complexity of the challenge, or a general uncertainty as to what actions are effective given our still insufficient understanding of both the virus and the broader subsequent social and economic implications. The crisis has also exposed a grave risk of greater social inequality in numerous ways. Joblessness and economic hardship have increased, and some groups are more vulnerable to infection due to health conditions or the type of work they perform. Stark differences in the availability of resources and expertise have been laid bare between healthcare systems—both between developed and developing countries as well as between developed nations. Children have vastly different access to the necessary infrastructure for home schooling, and individuals, families, organizations, sectors, and societies greatly differ in terms of how long they can weather the crisis. Thus, as global leaders navigate COVID-19, they are compelled to accept and deal with huge differences that divide rather than unite followers.

The tension between achieving unity or belonging on the one hand and accepting or fostering distinctiveness on the other hand lies at the core of how individuals construct and maintain their identities. In his seminal work, Brewer (1991) highlighted that individuals seek an optimal balance between achieving belongingness to a group and also retaining their own unique defining attributes. As such, identity not only reflects the subjective concept of oneself as a person (Ramarajan, 2014) but also comprises individuals' social identities, including their cultural identities (Schwartz, Montgomery, & Briones, 2006). COVID-19 has not only uncovered glaring differences but also arguably increased people's national cultural identity, as hinted at in Soutphommasane's (Chapter 1) essay, thereby further separating responses and attitudes toward what is a global crisis. How then can global leaders foster unity during COVID-19—and more generally?

One set of implications concerns how global leaders frame and build narratives around a given issue or situation—with communication being another very salient competency during times of crisis (Coombs, 2011). Global leaders need to be both conscious and considerate in how they frame their messages. But, as Ruiz (Chapter 1) stressed, they must also open up channels and encourage communication from their subordinates. At the same time, attempts to unite and create belongingness can be easily mistaken as ignorance or hypocrite. For example, global leaders whose prior words and actions have not emphasized unity cannot readily convince followers that they now believe in pulling together to confront the crisis. Similarly, global leaders speaking from a position of privilege cannot easily claim a deep understanding of the needs of the least fortunate members of their organizations or societies.

Attempts to create positive distinctiveness, by contrast, may similarly be interpreted as a lack of concern for collaboration and cooperation. For instance, followers who believe a global crisis warrants global collaboration have lost respect for national leaders focused solely on their country or their own supporters. What does this mean for global leaders' communicative repertoire? Importantly, what does this mean for how global leaders ought to adapt their message in the face of (cultural) diversity? For example, recent research has demonstrated that the meaning of communicative practices is not only influenced by the cultural context but also by how leaders adapt specific communicative content (Cole, 2015; Outila, Mihailova, Reiche, & Piekkari, 2018). Therefore, global leaders may need to make use of rich and redundant communication to effectively transmit their message, and it would be worthwhile for future research in the global leadership domain to examine this in greater depth. Moreover, global leaders also need to take into consideration the need for shared cognitive sensemaking, authenticity, and the heightened emotional state of recipients in times of crisis. Maak and Pless (Chapter 1) stressed the importance of communication characterized by compassion and care, while Shi (Chapter 1) argued for empathy in building partnerships. Effective communication always involves an understanding of the thoughts and feelings of the recipients (Szkudlarek, Osland, Nardon, & Zander, 2020). It would be helpful if researchers understood how global leaders can quickly perceive and adapt this understanding with diverse followers in rapidly changing, high-stakes environments.

There are also implications for how leaders can foster more superordinate identities in the face of people's tendency toward differentiation. Identity scholars have highlighted how members of different social groups can be induced to view themselves as a single, more inclusive superordinate group rather than as two separate groups, thereby reducing intergroup bias (Dovidio, Gaertner, & Saguy, 2009). One salient superordinate identity in the context of global work is global identity, which is defined as a sense of belongingness to mankind in a global community that transcends national boundaries and cultural divisions (Arnett, 2002; Erez & Gati, 2004). Recent inductive research, indeed, suggests that individuals maintain different configurations of culture-specific and culture-general identities and that a superordinate global identity holds important benefits (Lee, Masuda, Fu, & Reiche, 2018). This suggests that global leaders may play an important role in nurturing inclusive, superordinate identities, and we would encourage future research to examine other forms that such identities may take.

The tension for unity versus distinctiveness—or between a global crisis and its local responses—is, however, not the only countervailing issues that surfaced in the pandemic. Maak and Pless (Chapter 1) listed several other dualities:

> Leadership in crisis must be decisive, cautious but compassionate, self-transcendent and geared toward helping others, with a clear set of priorities and a good sense of the systemic risks involved—based on evidence and science, not on hunches, gut feelings, and self-serving ideologies.

The battle between science and ideology in some countries and the duality between science and emotion are noteworthy. Orly Levy (Chapter 1) listed the rejection of science, evidenced in positions on climate change and anti-vaccination, as a factor in the "global blindness" in leader responses to COVID-19. Global leaders need evidence-based responses to design strategies and make decisions, but they also need to address the overwhelming emotional response, including fear, that drives people's behavior.

Another duality that is sometimes aligned with ideology and an anti-science stance is the tension between the common good and individual rights. As Miska and Zilinskaite (Chapter 1) argue, the COVID-19 pandemic

> ...redefines VUCA and poses unprecedented challenges for global leaders: national protectionism becoming legitimized, unemployment numbers raising to record-highs, and fundamental personal rights being curbed—all in the name of health protection.

Requests for social distancing and mask usage are perceived as an infringement on individual rights rather than a protective measure for the common good. There are several related ethical issues as people debate whether to prioritize the economy and economic survival over health and where the bounds of personal freedom extend in a pandemic with life and death consequences.

Lee (Chapter 1) discussed three other pairs of dualities, beginning with *global collaboration versus local protection*. The nature of this crisis has prompted most national governments to pull up the drawbridge and focus on safe-guarding their own people. However, the sheer size and intricacy of the COVID-19 pandemic seems to indicate that long-term eradication, or at least wrestling the virus into some form of submission, and reviving our economies calls for global collaboration on several fronts.

Lee's second duality is *long-term versus short-term perspective*. As he noted, a crisis like this involves "pressing demands and imperatives of urgency on many fronts" and "working against the clock." We heard some of this in the essays by practitioners who were scrambling to put safety and virtual work measures into place (Ruiz & Lyndgaard, Chapter 1). However, this short-term perspective is counterbalanced by the need for a long-term focus on what the future should look like once the crisis abates, a question addressed by many of our essayists. One could argue that academics, particularly those holed up at home with ongoing employment, have the luxury of focusing on the long view. However, global leaders in healthcare, business, nonprofits, and many government agencies are tasked with balancing these two perspectives simultaneously.

Positive versus negative emotions is Lee's third duality. Successful global leaders in the crisis have been able to generate positive emotions and instill hope while frankly conveying the situation's negative realities. Positive emotions make hardship more tolerable, but knowing how bad things could get also decreases uncertainty and allows for both physical and mental preparation. "Global leaders who understand that honesty and facts are valued more than optimism will enable their followers to draw the right conclusions instead of feeling gaslighted" (Huesing, Chapter 1). Conversely, at the other end of the spectrum, messages that trigger only negative emotions, such as unhealthy fear and xenophobia, can lead to negative consequences.

How can global leaders handle these tensions or dualities? Lee (Chapter 1) proposes dynamic balancing, an ongoing process of paying attention to competing demands and multiple logics simultaneously, and balancing one's response, depending on exogenous and endogenous factors as the situation evolves. Thus, this appears to be a combination of a global mindset that is constantly scanning and monitoring both poles and making situationally contingent responses. Taylor (Chapter 1) recommends that global leadership development and coaching focus on what Kegan and Lahey (2009) call the self-transforming mind.

> With a self-transforming mind we can step back from and reflect on the limits of our own ideology or personal authority; see that any one system or self-organization is in some way partial or incomplete; be friendlier toward contradiction and opposites; seek to hold on to multiple systems rather than projecting all but one onto the other. Our self coheres through its ability not to confuse internal consistency with wholeness or completeness, and through its alignment with the dialectic, rather than either pole. (Kegan & Lahey, 2009, p. 17)

Responsible Global Leadership

Many contributors highlighted the need for responsible leadership and implicitly or explicitly posed the question whether the current crisis is a fertile ground for *less* responsible leadership or an opportunity for *more* responsible leadership, as witnessed by the responses of a few political leaders and several business leaders that our contributors described. Responsible leadership is a relatively nascent field in the management domain, having emerged out of an intersection of the fields of corporate social responsibility, sustainability, leadership, and ethics (Miska & Mendenhall, 2018). Responsible leadership is generally characterized as a "social-relational and ethical phenomenon, which occurs in social processes of interaction" (Maak & Pless, 2006, p. 99) and involves a focus on "balancing external pressures of conflicting stakeholder interests with leaders' internal tensions of having to lead coherently and consistently with integrity across multiple contexts" (Miska & Mendenhall, 2018, p. 118). Recently, scholars have increasingly theorized about and investigated the construct of responsible leadership in the global context, giving rise to an ancillary subfield, RGL (Mendenhall, Žilinskaite, Stahl, & Clapp-Smith, 2020).

The RGL literature developed over the past decade from an intersection between the literatures related to globalization, global leadership, and responsible leadership (Mendenhall, Miska, & Stahl, 2020). The integration of these research fields was fueled, in part, by global corporate scandals, rapid change in national and international political value systems, the increase in nationalism across the word, turbulent cross-border migrations, and terrorism (Mendenhall, Miska, & Stahl, 2020; for an introduction to the field of RGL, please see Bird, 2020; Caligiuri & Thoroughgood, 2015; Daellenbach, Seyour, & Webster, 2020; Osland & Lester, 2020; Puffer, Wesley, Dau, & Moore, 2020; Stahl, Miska, Noval, & Patock, 2020; Stahl, Pless, Maak, & Miska, 2018; Stahl & Sully de Luque, 2014).

Many of our contributors observed a paucity of RGL competencies in the global leaders they observed during the pandemic. Perhaps drawing from competency research in both the responsible leadership and RGL literatures (c.f., Miska, Stahl, & Mendenhall, 2013) and applying it to crisis contexts would be a fruitful endeavor for scholars working in the global leadership field. The importance of some of the recent calls for research to extend the scope of understanding of the RGL phenomena (Mendenhall, Miska, & Stahl, 2020) reverberated with us as being applicable to the context of the COVID-19 pandemic. For example, what are the behaviors that distinguish responsible global leaders from other leaders, and what are the causal variables that underlie those behaviors? What is the nature and constitution of ethical dilemmas, paradoxes, trade-offs, and opportunities that are inherent in the global context of leading? And how can/should leaders make sense of paradoxes in global contexts and mediate seeming paradoxes and reconcile trade-offs? What are the anticipated or realized outcomes of RGL, and how can they be assessed and measured? With both opportunities and challenges created by globalization, how do leaders balance the advantages of globalization with its inevitable costs?

Finally, it may be time to consider the possibility that constitutionally there is no difference between the constructs of global leadership and RGL—that separating them is a false conceptual distinction. Perhaps all global leadership is RGL, and that the subconstruct of "responsible" should simply be theoretically embedded within the construct of global leadership. Why is it necessary to distinguish the two? Is there a way for both of these fields to be merged into a single stream of scholarship where "responsibility" is simply viewed as a primary aspect of global leadership?

Toward Greater Reflexivity among Global Leadership Scholars

Finally, we believe that, collectively, the essays about leading through the COVID-19 crisis also encourage us toward greater self-reflection in our role as global leadership scholars. Reflexivity is relevant for the design, conceptualization, and operationalization of any research study, but it is a particularly critical attribute for conducting research that spans different cultural contexts. For example, Easterby-Smith and Malina (1999) pointed to the importance that power differences and contrasting views about research can have on the conduction of cross-cultural studies. Miska and Žilinskaite (Chapter 1), in their essay, make a similar point. However, we would contend that, as a field of research, we are perhaps not always fully conscious of the type of questions we ask, the lenses we take, and the conclusions we draw.

Our esteemed contributors hail from a large diversity of cultural backgrounds. And yet, despite some notable exceptions, it was intriguing to see that the perspective taken was markedly Western. In particular, while a variety of countries were mentioned as examples for handling the crisis better or worse, the level of specificity and granularity of the examples and contextual background provided was clearly higher for Western countries. Similarly, there was little discussion of the differences in strategies and effectiveness of the global leaders of New Zealand, Iceland, Sweden, Taiwan, or South Korea compared to those of China, the US, the UK, or Germany. What does this tell us about the breadth and depth of our current thinking in the global leadership domain? Is our research domain too focused on global leaders from the largest and most powerful countries? Do global leadership scholars need to expand the scope of their awareness? Are we unwittingly biasing our thinking and theorizing from the countries in which we are based, or from our tradition—situated in the International Business field—of focusing on economic power as is the case with multinational enterprises as a primary unit of analysis? Does this mean we are missing insights from other parts of the world regarding what global leaders are doing? While it is of course understandable to selectively focus on a particular lens given the page and time constraints our contributors were under, it does suggest how difficult it is, especially during times of crisis, to fully open our cognitive (and emotional) blinders.

Our somewhat selective focus on certain global leaders relative to others also raises the question of the role models that we support or even *create* through our research. For instance, at present, the two most revered political leaders for their handling of the pandemic seem to be Jacinda Ardern, Prime Minister of New Zealand, and Angela Merkel, Chancellor of Germany (Taub, 2020). How much do we know about the effectiveness of role models like them and others and their effectiveness as understood from within their respective contexts and systems? Some of our essays as well as the press also focus on other political leaders for perceived mishandling of COVID-19 as evidenced by a high death rate. History may well validate this criticism, but we don't fully know what the outcomes of political leaders' respective strategies will be. Are we too quick to judge leaders and assume that leaders' actions and temperaments that we philosophically disagree with are ineffective, and therefore that these leaders are ineffective? For example, Singapore's and South Korea's leadership was initially praised but later criticized for failing to prevent pockets of transmissions after the initial success in suppressing the virus. Are we falling prey to taking "snapshot" pictures of global leaders instead of accepting that time is needed before a careful evaluation is possible? As the comparative number of cases and deaths increases and decreases over the course of the pandemic, will history view political leaders as irresponsible or simply lacking information provided by hindsight? There is a broader risk of mistakenly linking actual outcomes to global leadership expertise when, especially in times of crisis, global leaders, and even epidemiologists, cannot be expected to provide all the answers.

Our previous reflections and the questions we pose also have implications for how we understand global leadership effectiveness more broadly. In the context of the COVID-19 pandemic, effectiveness cannot be measured in health-related statistics alone, given the inherent difficulty of collecting and comparing them, as well as the many potential confounding variables that are at play. Instead, political leaders also show effectiveness by providing hope, determination, and faith in the people they lead. This is particularly critical as the crisis will engender—and already has engendered—social class resentment from citizens who are without work, live in crowded neighborhoods, and who are at greater risk of contracting the virus. Leaders will need to address the social inequality—which is further compounded by political divisiveness—irrespective of their countries' particular health care systems and policies. In countries where health care workers are attacked and abused in public, how have their national leaders failed? Taking a more inclusive view toward what constitutes effective—and ineffective—global leadership not only promises to advance the global leadership domain, which has thus far paid little attention to how effectiveness should be conceptualized and measured, but also to the leadership literature in general, which is similarly fragmented in its understanding of leader effectiveness (Hiller, DeChurch, Murase, & Doty, 2011).

Of course, academic research is always, at least partially, a means for exploring issues that are close to our heart as scholars. As such, we believe that the reward for engaging in greater reflexivity regarding the questions we ask, the lenses we take and the conclusions we draw as global leadership scholars is also an opportunity to learn more about ourselves as a person!

CONCLUSION

During the early weeks of the COVID-19 lockdown, Northern Irish artist, illustrator, and writer Oliver Jeffers offered free live readings of his various children's books. In one of his famous books "*The Heart and the Bottle*," Jeffers tells the story of a little girl whose head was filled with "all the curiosities of the world," which she explored together with her paternal figure—until one day he was not there anymore. To cope with her sadness, she decides to put her heart in a bottle to keep it safe. This seems to help at first. And yet, by doing so she loses her curiosity and meaning in life. Only when one day—as a grown-up—she meets another curious little girl, she decides to pull her heart out of the bottle and puts it back where it belongs.

Similarly, if there can be a positive aspect in the turbulence we are living, then maybe the pandemic serves as a curiosity trigger to further advance meaningful research on global leadership. Collectively, the six areas of future research outlined in the preceding sections and summarized in Table 1 point to the very heart of the global leadership domain. And yet, we believe that—informed by the invited reflections about global leadership during the COVID-19 pandemic—they also encourage us to unbottle ourselves and move beyond the current heart of global leadership research in order to provide improved guidance for how leaders around the globe can effectively influence and serve their constituents and lead through times of turbulence and crisis. For the *Advances in Global Leadership* co-editors, the way forward involves focusing more on global leadership effectiveness, the special focus for next year's Volume 14 of *AGL*, and incorporating the many lessons throughout the book into our teaching of future global leaders.

REFERENCES

Apuzzo, M., & Kirkpatrick, D. K. (2020). Covid-19 changed how the world does science, together. *New York Times*, April 14. Retrieved from www.nytimes.com/2020/04/01/world/europe/coronavirus-science-research-cooperation.html. Accessed on May 15, 2020.

Arnett, J. J. (2002). The psychology of globalization. *American Psychologist, 57*, 774–783.

Balogun, J., Bartunek, J. M., & Do, B. (2015). Senior managers' sensemaking and responses to strategic change. *Organization Science, 26*, 960–979.

Baumeister, R. F., & Leary, M. R. (1995). The need to belong: Desire for interpersonal attachments as a fundamental human motivation. *Psychological Bulletin, 117*, 497–529.

Bird, A. (2018). Mapping the content domain of global leadership competencies. In M. E. Mendenhall, J. S. Osland, A. Bird, G. Oddou, M. J. Stevens, M. Maznevski, & G. Stahl (Eds.), *Global leadership: Research, practice and development* (3rd ed., pp. 119–142). New York, NY: Routledge.

Bird, A. (2020). In search of responsible global leadership that makes a difference. In L. Zander (Ed.), *Handbook of global leadership: Making a difference* (pp. 383–392). Cheltenham: Edward Elgar.

Bird, A., & Osland, J. (2004). Developing global competencies. In H. Lane, M. Mendenhall, M. Maznevski, & J. McNett (Eds.) *Handbook of global management: A guide to managing complexity* (pp. 57–80). Oxford: Blackwell.

Black, J. S., Morrison, A. J., & Gregersen, H. B. (1999). *Global explorers: The next generation of leaders*. London: Routledge.

Brewer, M. B. (1991). The social self: On being the same and different at the same time. *Personality and Social Psychology Bulletin, 17*, 475–482.

Caligiuri, P., & Thoroughgood, C. (2015). Developing responsible global leaders through corporate-sponsored international volunteerism programs. *Organizational Dynamics, 44*, 138–145.

Cole, B. M. (2015). Lessons from a martial arts dojo: A prolonged process model of high-context communication. *Academy of Management Journal, 58*(2), 567–591.

Coombs, W. T. (2011). *Ongoing crisis communication: Planning, managing, and responding* (3rd ed.). Thousand Oaks, CA: SAGE.

Cseh, M., Davis, E., & Khilji, S. E. (2013). Developing a global mindset: Learning of global leaders. *European Journal of Training and Development, 37*, 489–499.

Daellenbach, K., Seymour, R. G., & Webster, C. M. (2020). Exploring responsible global leadership in corporate-community transactions. In L. Zander (Ed.), *Handbook of global leadership: Making a difference* (pp. 202–221). Cheltenham: Edward Elgar.

Dovidio, J. F., Gaertner, S. L., & Saguy, T. (2009). Commonality and the complexity of "we": Social attitudes and social change. *Personality and Social Psychology Review, 13*, 3–20.

Easterby-Smith, M., & Malina, D. (1999). Cross-cultural collaborative research: Toward reflexivity. *Academy of Management Review, 42*, 76–86.

Eisenhardt, K. M. (1989). Building theories from case study research. *Academy of Management Review, 14*, 532–550.

Erez, M., & Gati, E. (2004). A dynamic, multi-level model of culture: From the micro level of the individual to the macro level of a global culture. *Applied Psychology: International Review, 53*, 583–598.

French, R. P. (2019). *Cultivating global mindset in multinational organizations*. Newcastle upon Tyne: Cambridge Scholars Publishing.

Friedman, J. Z. (2018). The global citizenship agenda and the generation of cosmopolitan capital in British higher education. *British Journal of Sociology of Education, 39*, 436–450.

Gagnon, S., & Collinson, D. L. (2014). Rethinking global leadership development programmes: The interrelated significance of power, context and identity. *Organization Studies, 35*, 645–670.

George, G., Howard-Grenville, J., Joshi, A., & Tihanyi, L. (2016). Understanding and tackling societal grand challenges through management research. *Academy of Management Journal, 59*, 1880–1895.

Gitsham, M. (2008). Developing the global leader of tomorrow. Report of 1st Global Forum for Responsible Management Education, Ashridge Business School and the European Academy of Business in Society, Ashridge Faculty Publications, New York, NY.

Hagtvedt, L. P., Dossinger, K., Harrison, S. H., & Huang, L. (2019). Curiosity made the cat more creative: Specific curiosity as a driver of creativity. *Organizational Behavior and Human Decision Processes, 150*, 1–13.

Harrison, S. H. (2016). *Fueling, curating, connecting and fascinating: Why and how creativity provokes curiosity*. In M. Škerlavaj, M. Černe, & A. Dysvik (Eds.), *Capitalizing on creativity at work: Fostering the implementation of creative ideas in organizations* (pp. 76–85). Cheltenham: Edward Elgar.

Herman, J., & Zaccaro, S. (2014). The complex self-concept of the global leader. In J. Osland, M. Li, & Y. Wang (Eds.), *Advances in global leadership* (Vol. 8, pp. 93–111). Bingley: Emerald Publishing Limited.

Hill, N. S., & Bartol, K. M. (2016). Empowering leadership and effective collaboration in geographically dispersed teams. *Personnel Psychology, 69*, 159–198.

Hiller, N. J., DeChurch, L. A., Murase, T., & Doty, D. (2011). Searching for outcomes of leadership: A 25-year review. *Journal of Management, 37*, 1137–1177.

Hitt, M., Keats, B. W., & Yucel, E. (2003). Strategic leadership in global business organizations: Building trust and social capital. In W. Mobley & P. Dorfman (Eds.), *Advances in Global Leadership* (Vol. 3, pp. 9–35). Bingley: Emerald Publishing Limited.

Holt, K., & Seki, K. (2012). Global leadership: A developmental shift for everyone. *Industrial Organizational Psychologist: Perspectives on Research and Practice, 5*, 196–215.

Jokinen, T. (2005). Global leadership competencies: A review and discussion. *Journal of European Industrial Training, 29*, 199–216.

Kegan, R., & Lahey, L. (2009). *Immunity to change: How to overcome it and unlock the potential in yourself and your organization*. Boston, MA: Harvard University Press.

Kurmanaev, A., Andreoni, M. Casado, L., & Taj, M. (2020). Latin America's outbreaks now rival Europe's. But its options are much worse. *New York Times*, May 12. Retrieved from https://www.nytimes.com/2020/05/12/world/americas/latin-america-virus-death.html. Accessed on May 15, 2020.

Lane, H. W., Maznevski, M. L., & Mendenhall, M. E. (2004). Globalization: Hercules meets Buddha. In H. W. Lane, M. L. Maznevski, M. E. Mendenhall, & J. McNett (Eds.), *The Blackwell handbook of global management: A guide to managing complexity* (pp. 3–25). Oxford: Blackwell.

Lee, M. Y., & Edmondson, A. C. (2017). Self-managing organizations: Exploring the limits of less-hierarchical organizing. *Research in Organizational Behavior, 37*, 35–58.

Lee, Y.-T., Masuda, A., Fu, X., & Reiche, B. S. (2018). Navigating between home, host, and global: Consequences of multicultural team members' identity configurations. *Academy of Management Discoveries, 4*, 180–201.

Leki, R. S. (2019). Growing global resilience leadership: Working with diplomats. In J. S. Osland, B. S. Reiche, B. Szkudlarek, & M. E. Mendenhall (Eds.), *Advances in global leadership* (Vol. 12, pp. 191–206). Bingley: Emerald Publishing Limited.

Levy, O., Beechler, S., Taylor, S., & Boyacigiller, N. (2007). What we talk about when we talk about 'global mindset': Managerial cognition in multinational corporations. *Journal of International Business Studies, 38*, 231–258.

Liden, R. C., Wayne, S. J., Liao, C., & Meuser, J. D. (2014). Servant leadership and serving culture: Influence on individual and unit performance. *Academy of Management Journal, 57*, 1434–1452.

Lobel, S. A. (1990). Global leadership competencies: Managing to a different drumbeat. *Human Resource Management, 29*, 39–47.

Maak, T., & Pless, N. M. (2006). Responsible leadership in a stakeholder society—a relational perspective. *Journal of Business Ethics, 66*, 99–115.

Megalokonomos, M. (2020). Australia has recorded fewer than 100 coronavirus deaths - why do other countries differ so much? *SBS News,* May 12. Retrieved from www.sbs.com.au/news/australia-has-recorded-fewer-than-100-coronavirus-deaths-why-do-other-countries-differ-so-much. Accessed on May 15, 2020.

Mendenhall, M. E., Miska, C., & Stahl, G. K. (2020). Responsible global leadership: The anatomy and promise of an emerging field. In M. E. Mendenhall, M. Žilinskaite, G. K. Stahl, & R. Clapp-Smith (Eds.), *Responsible global leadership: Dilemmas, paradoxes, and opportunities* (221–232). New York, NY: Routledge.

Mendenhall, M. E., Žilinskaitė, M., Stahl, G. K., & Clapp-Smith, R. (Eds.) (2020). *Responsible global leadership: Dilemmas, paradoxes, and opportunities.* New York, NY: Routledge.

Meyer, A. D. (1982). Adapting to environmental jolts. *Administrative Science Quarterly, 27*, 515–537.

Miska, C., & Mendenhall, M. E. (2018). Responsible leadership: A mapping of extant research and future directions. *Journal of Business Ethics, 148*, 117–134.

Miska, C., Stahl, G. K., & Mendenhall, M. E. (2013). Intercultural competencies as antecedents of responsible global leadership. *European Journal of International Management, 7*, 550–569.

Morrison, A. (2001). Integrity and global leadership. *Journal of Business Ethics, 31*, 65–76.

Nohria, N. (2020). What organizations need to survive a pandemic. *Harvard Business Review*, January 30. Retrieved from https://hbr.org/2020/01/what-organizations-need-to-survive-a-pandemic, Accessed on April 27, 2020.

Osland, J. S. (2008). An overview of the global leadership literature. In M. Mendenhall, J. Osland, A. Bird, G. Oddou, & M. Maznevski, (Eds.), *Global leadership: Research, practice, and development* (pp. 34–63). London: Routledge.

Osland, J. S., Bird, A., & Oddou, G. (2012). The context of expert global leadership. In W. H. Mobley, M. Li & Y. Wang (Eds.), *Advances in global leadership* (Vol. 7, pp. 107–124). Oxford: Elsevier.

Osland, J. S., Ehret, M. & Ruiz, L. (2017). Case studies of global leadership expert cognition in the domain of large-scale global change. In J. Osland, M. Li, & M. E. Mendenhall (Eds.), *Advances in global leadership* (Vol. 10, pp. 41–88). Bingley: Emerald Publishing Limited.

Osland, J. S., & Lester, G. V. (2020). Developing socially responsible global leaders and making a difference: Global Leadership Lab social innovation projects. In L. Zander (Ed.), *Handbook of global leadership: Making a difference* (pp. 350–363). Cheltenham: Edward Elgar.

Outila, V., Mihailova, I., Reiche, B. S., & Piekkari, R. (2018). A communicative perspective on the trust-control link in Russia. *Journal of World Business*, 100971. https://doi.org/10.1016/j.jwb.2018.11.001

Owens, B. P., & Hekman, D. R. (2016). How does leader humility influence team performance? Exploring the mechanisms of contagion and collective promotion focus. *Academy of Management Journal, 59*, 1088–1111.

Owens, B. P., Johnson, M. J., & Mitchell, T. R. (2013). Expressed humility in organizations: Implications for performance, teams, and leadership. *Organization Science, 24*, 1517–1538.

Pless, N. M., Maak, T., & Stahl, G. (2011). Developing responsible global leaders through international service-learning programs: The Ulysses experience. *The Academy of Management Learning and Education, 10*, 237–260.

Prosperi, L. (2018). *The imagineering process: Using the Disney theme park design process to bring your creative ideas to life.* New York, NY: Theme Park Press. Retrieved from http://themeparkpress.com/

Puffer, S. M., Wesley, D., Dau, L., & Moore, E. (2020). The 4 Cs of MNE strategic responses to global governance. In J. A. Osland, B. Szkudlarek, M. E. Mendenhall, & B. S. Reiche (Eds.), *Advances in global leadership* (Vol. 13, pp. XXX). Bingley: Emerald Publishing Limited.

Ramarajan, L. (2014). Past, present and future research on multiple identities: Toward an intrapersonal network approach. *The Academy of Management Annals, 8*, 589–659.

Reiche, B. S., Bird, A., Mendenhall, M. E., & Osland, J. S. (2017). Contextualizing leadership: A typology of global leadership roles. *Journal of International Business Studies, 48*, 552–572.

Reiche, B. S., Mendenhall, M. E., Szkudlarek, B., & Osland, J. S. (2019). Global leadership research: Where do we go from here? In J. S. Osland, B. S. Reiche, B. Szkudlarek, & M. E. Mendenhall (Eds.), *Advances in global leadership* (Vol. 12, pp. 213–234). Bingley: Emerald Publishing Limited.

Schwartz, S. J., Montgomery, M. J., & Briones, E. (2006). The role of identity in acculturation among immigrant people: Theoretical propositions, empirical questions, and applied recommendations. *Human Development, 49*, 1–30.

Stahl, G. K., Miska, C., Noval, L. J., & Patock, V. J. (2020). Responsible global leadership: A multi-level framework. In L. Zander (Ed.), *Handbook of global leadership: Making a difference* (pp. 178–201). Cheltenham: Edward Elgar.

Stahl, G. K., Pless, N. M., Maak, T., & Miska, C. (2018). Responsible global leadership. In M. Mendenhall, J. Osland, A. Bird, G. R. Oddou, M. J. Stevens, M. L. Maznevski, & G. K. Stahl (Eds.), *Global leadership: Research, practice, and development* (3rd ed., pp. 363–388). London: Routledge.

Stahl, G. K., & Sully de Luque, M. F. (2014). Antecedents of responsible leader behavior: A research synthesis, conceptual framework, and agenda for future research. *Academy of Management Perspectives, 28*, 235–254.

Szkudlarek, B., Osland, J. S., Nardon, L., & Zander, L. (2020). Communication and culture in international business – moving the field forward. *Journal of World Business.* https://www.sciencedirect.com/science/article/abs/pii/S1090951620300547.

Taub, A. (2020). Why are women-led nations doing better with Covid-19? *New York Times*, May 15. Retrieved from www.nytimes.com/2020/05/15/world/coronavirus-women-leaders.html?smid=em-share. Accessed on May 17, 2020.

Tihanyi, L. (2020). From "That's Interesting" to "That's Important". *Academy of Management Journal, 63*, 329–331.

Toegel, G., & Jonsen, K. (2016). Shared leadership in a global context: Challenges of transferring control to team members. In J. Osland, M. Li, & M. E. Mendenhall (Eds.), *Advances in global leadership* (Vol. 9, pp. 151–185). Bingley: Emerald Publishing Limited.

Weick, K. E. (1993). The collapse of sensemaking in organizations: The Mann Gulch disaster. *Administrative Science Quarterly, 38*, 628–652.

INDEX